OUR LONG NATIONAL DAYDREAM

By the same author

THE RISE OF THE COUNTER-ESTABLISHMENT
THE PERMANENT CAMPAIGN

OUR LONG
NATIONAL DAYDREAM

A Political Pageant of the Reagan Era

Sidney Blumenthal

1817

HARPER & ROW, PUBLISHERS, New York
Cambridge, Philadelphia, San Francisco
London, Mexico City, São Paulo, Singapore, Sydney

Grateful acknowledgment is made to the following for permission to reprint previously published material:

The Washington Post: Copyright © 1985, 1986, 1987, 1988 by The Washington Post Company. Reprinted by permission; *The Washington Monthly; The New Republic:* © The New Republic, Inc. Reprinted by permission of The New Republic; *Foreign Policy:* Copyright 1987 by the Carnegie Endowment for International Peace. Reprinted with permission from *Foreign Policy* 69 (Winter 1987–88).

FIRST EDITION

Designed by: Erich Hobbing

Library of Congress Cataloging-in-Publication Data

Blumenthal, Sidney, 1948–
  Our long national daydream.

  1. United States—Politics and government—1981–
2. Reagan, Ronald.   I. Title.
E876.B575   1988   973.927   88-45015
ISBN 0-06-015973-1

88 89 90 91 92 CC/HC 10 9 8 7 6 5 4 3 2 1

For Hendrik Hertzberg, who was my editor at the *New Republic*. Without Rick, I do not believe I would have accomplished anything that is in this book.

Contents

Acknowledgments

From late 1983 to early 1985, I was the national political correspondent for the *New Republic*, for which I covered the presidential campaign. I joined *The Washington Post* as a staff writer in the spring of 1985, during the heyday of Reaganism. Most of the pieces in *Our Long National Daydream* first appeared in these publications. Other pieces appeared in *Foreign Policy* and the *Washington Monthly*. I am grateful to all of them for permission to reprint my work. Many of the pieces have been slightly re-edited for inclusion here. References that seemed dated have been cut. I have also expanded a few pieces.

At the *Post*, I am indebted to the editorial assistance of Robert Kaiser, Mary Hadar, David Ignatius, and particularly Jeffrey Frank. At the *New Republic*, my reviews were improved by the insights of Leon Wieseltier. My agent, Kathy Robbins, is really responsible for making this book happen, and she deserves much of the credit for my literary career. Ted Solotaroff, my editor at Harper & Row, helped shape the conception of the book as one about the Reagan era and ably edited it. Once again, I express my indebtedness to my wife, Jackie, who shared in the passions of the time and is my best critic.

Introduction

The pieces in *Our Long National Daydream* were written as events occurred, often on the run, some in hotel rooms, almost all on deadline. But this is not a reporter's notebook. Piece by piece, event by event, it is an effort to cut to the heart of an era. Immediacy, of course, can lead to superficiality and loss of perspective, but being present at many of the key scenes of the period may have been necessary to grasp its essence. The Reagan era has been a period of political fantasy, and considering it in conventional categories would drain it of its special character. During the 1984 Republican convention at Dallas, I sat in the Anatole Hotel for hours with members of Reagan's political directorate. At the apex of Reagan's popularity, in the penthouse of power, Reagan's men were entranced with the movie *Ghostbusters* and its relevance to the upcoming election. They fully shared my belief that fantasy and myth lay at the center of this presidency, though none of us were aware then of the astrological influence in the White House.

The Reagan era will present unique challenges to the historian, precisely because of its heavy element of fantasy. Fantasies easily evaporate into the ether of time, and it is difficult to recapture them. Through hindsight they may be seen as rational concepts and thus distorted. Or they may be dismissed as curiosities, peripheral to the big issues. By analyzing the Reagan era as it happened—not retrospectively—one can get closer to its core.

When Ronald Reagan was president all things seemed possible, as they do in daydreams. We would be rich, powerful, and sleep well. No effort, besides wholeheartedly giving ourselves over to Reagan's cineramic projections, would be required; no side effects would be experienced. Tax revenues would rise when taxes were cut. The Russians would be stopped in their tracks by the conquest of

Grenada. The terrifying paradoxes of deterrence would be abolished by building an astrodome in outer space. And so on. It was a form of mind cure, oddly reminiscent of one of the faddish doctrines of the 1920s promulgated by the renowned positive thinker Émile Coué: "Every day, in every way, I am getting better and better." Millions in the age of Harding and Coolidge nodded their heads in the effort to uplift their brain waves. Their minds could conquer matter; optimism could foster the conditions that give rise to it.

Reagan's mission, as he repeatedly stated, was therapeutic: to make us feel good again. Nothing earned his contempt more than "gloom and doom," a psychological condition at the source of our misery, which he charged to his predecessor. At his jauntiest, Reagan likened himself to his youthful hero, Franklin D. Roosevelt, even as he was attempting to dismantle FDR's legacy of affirmative government. Some of Reagan's admirers preferred to cast him as Dwight Eisenhower, the last president to serve two terms, an older, steady president—and a Republican. Some of Reagan's detractors regarded him as a latter-day Warren G. Harding. The 1980s, like the 1920s, was indeed a time of contradictions: a return to traditional values and sybaritic self-indulgence. Nowhere were these extremes more obvious than in the executive branch, led by a president daily extolling a return to basics and staffed by more corrupt individuals than any previous administration, including Grant's and Harding's.

Reagan's presidency, in many ways, was the culmination of another's, whom he never chose to employ as a reference: Richard Nixon. Nixon was the first president to gain political energy from the reaction to the social movements of the 1960s. It was Nixon who consciously attempted to foster a Republican realignment of the electorate on the scale of the New Deal. And it was Nixon who sought to cloak himself in a Gaullist mystique by means of public relations. Nixon, however, lacked the self-confidence to manage his role. He was undone perhaps more by his insecurity than by his cynicism, which may have been merely a symptom.

The most obvious fact about Reagan was often dismissed as too banal to possess serious significance: he was an actor. To recall his prepolitical career was somehow to commit the offense of "persistent underestimation." Yet those who wanted to remark upon his talent for political leadership and slight his theatrical past denied Reagan credit where credit was due. The essential quality for any actor is to induce in his audience a willing suspension of disbelief. Without it, the play cannot go on. The audience would simply feel the absurd sensation of sitting in the dark: Why are the lights off? For an actor to transport theatergoers into the world of imagination he must also suspend disbelief within himself, giving himself over to the role and the scene. Reagan's grip over the nation partly lay in his ability to maintain his grip over himself. Above all, he was a true believer in his role. He used that role to persuade that wishing was doing, that saying something made it so.

Nixon's efforts to attain a monarchical status were, at best, completely transparent: for example, dressing the White House guard in mock Ruritanian uniforms as though they were extras in *Duck Soup*. The strip of sweat on his upper lip, the telltale sign of his anxiety, always made it difficult to think of him as regal. His aspiration to grandeur, at worst, led to tyrannical excesses, summed up in the word "Watergate," or as his successor, Gerald Ford, put it, "our long national nightmare." Ford, for his part, could not provide the illusion of a new beginning because of his pardon of unindicted co-conspirator Nixon. Ford was a parenthesis. In short order, he was followed by Jimmy Carter, who pledged technocratic competence and purity of heart. On his inauguration day, he entered the White House after taking a democratic stroll down Pennsylvania Avenue. He would banish disgrace by banishing the imperial style.

Nixon and Carter were post-war presidents, determined to put the Vietnam conflict behind the country. "Bring us together" was Nixon's campaign slogan in 1968—an earlier therapeutic promise. Carter's first act as president was to grant an amnesty to Vietnam-era draft evaders—a stroke to put the war in the past. But his presidency was overwhelmed by uncontrollable events, a theme expounded every night on an ABC news program entitled *America Held Hostage*—the forerunner to *Nightline*. Reagan defeated Carter with the promise to make America number one again. This was, of course, Nixon's theme; America, he had said, would not be "a pitiful, helpless giant." Reagan was the beneficiary of both Nixon's and Carter's failures.

Unlike Nixon, Reagan performed the monarchical function without straining. Where Nixon was abrasive, he was soothing and as expert with ceremony as he had been with a script. Nixon was never above the fray, and when he made the claim that he was, nobody believed him. Reagan was said to be teflon-coated because criticism did not stick to him. Lowly facts did not perturb him, especially when they got in the way of his royal principles. He was monarchical in his public image of strength, while his subordinates remarked upon his private passivity, which complemented his simple certitude. Thus the Iran-contra scandal did not drag Reagan down, as Watergate did Nixon. In the end, Nixon was responsible, Reagan irresponsible. Nixon forgot nothing and ensured that he wouldn't with a

White House taping system. Reagan couldn't remember anything. His forgetfulness was his defense. He had had no trouble acting as a monarch; it was only in the actual details of being president that difficulties arose.

In the beginning, with Reagan, was the daydream. He embraced a normalcy that was not normalcy but a new approach entirely. In any play some roles are dictated by the nature of the play. Other roles are invited by the central character. Still others are excluded. The self-deluded Willy Loman, for example, cannot walk into the cynical world of David Mamet's *Glengarry Glen Ross.* The Reagan era was organized around a daydream president with a tenuous grasp of the possible consequences of his actions. When the Iran-contra scandal was exposed, Reagan defended trading arms for hostages with the Iranians by claiming they were "moderates" and that, in any case, he wasn't trading arms for hostages.

In the White House, the main standard of judgment on most matters was Reagan's favorability rating in the polls, which became an end in itself. After the Reykjavik summit, for example, the press in Washington was roiled by a frenzy of administration officials attempting to "spin" the story as Reagan standing tall. The president's ill-preparation, his astonishing on-the-spot proposals for massive ICBM reductions, which collapsed upon his "dream" of a theoretical Star Wars defense system, were to be instantly forgotten.

The abuse of history was one of the era's defining features. According to Reagan, the Nicaraguan contras were the "moral equals of the Founding Fathers"; the Nazi SS soldiers buried in the Bitburg military cemetery were "victims, just as surely" as the Jewish victims of the Holocaust; and the apartheid regime in South Africa "eliminated the segregation that we once had in our own country." All arms control agreements, according to the neoconservatives, were no different from the appeasement of Hitler at Munich. And so on.

Certain subordinates flourished under such conditions. The most successful were self-propelled and often self-sustaining. Many had spent years developing a network of contacts in the Congress, the press, and the neoconservative movement. Richard Perle, the assistant secretary of defense, the most important administration figure on arms control, was a consummate example of the type. He used Reagan's dreams as the basis for advancing his own agenda, which he ultimately justified by the Munich analogy. His elaborate bureaucratic game-playing was made possible by the strength of the presidential figurehead and the weakness of presidential policy-making.

Certain intellectuals also flourished. Reagan had a few broad beliefs that were a license for ideologues, eager to fill in with axioms and corollaries of their own. From the law to the budget, they laid down their principles, almost invariably asserted as absolute truths. They never claimed responsibility for what their ideas ultimately meant in action, say, the relationship between "original intention" in constitutional law and the conduct of Attorney General Edwin Meese's Justice Department, or the Reagan Doctrine and the Iran-contra affair. Much of the neoconservative intellectual energy was invested in proving that those with whom they disagreed were dishonest or unpatriotic. "Who lost Nicaragua?" was a jibe leveled at the Democrats who questioned the wisdom of the contra policy, just as "Who lost China?" was hurled at Democrats in the early 1950s. The queen of the neoconservatives was Jeane Kirkpatrick, the United Nations ambassador in the early Reagan years. She wrote long articles justifying kleptomaniacal dictators in the name of national security, and from the 1984 GOP convention platform called the Democratic Party the "Blame America First" party. On the night the Argentine military junta decided to launch a war against Britain by invading the Falkland Islands, Kirkpatrick was happily supping at the Argentine embassy. When Filipino dictator Ferdinand Marcos was on the verge of being toppled by a democratic upsurge, her instinct was to rush to his defense in her syndicated column.

The neoconservative intellectuals had an enormous effect on the tone of public discussion during the Reagan era. Through a host of publications, from the Moonie-owned *Washington Times* to *Commentary* magazine, they attempted to dominate the political discourse. Reagan's electoral victories filled them with the belief that their ideas were shared by a majority of the country. This inflated their already considerable sense of certitude; the self-importance of a Michael Ledeen or a David Horowitz was part of the fantasy of the age. George Will, the most widely read conservative columnist, presented himself as a high-Tory, the First Lady's social escort and the president's intellectual escort.

Few neoconservatives, however, assumed the Tory identity. Instead, they refurbished the Old Left, importing the reductive style of their earlier sectarianism into the political debate: extreme accusations and ad hominem attacks were their stock-in-trade. Norman Podhoretz, the *Commentary* magazine editor, who helped Kirkpatrick gain her initial prominence, and his wife, Midge Decter, were at the forefront of a concerted effort to reduce intellectual life to vulgar ideological combat. Decter's main contribution was a newsletter, *Contentions,* entirely consisting of personal denunciations written in an unintentional parody of the Stalinist mode. Their son-in-law, Elliott Abrams, became the assistant secretary of state in charge of the contra war. He was their idea of an intellectual in power. In time, he was barred from testifying before the Senate Foreign Relations Committee because of his repeated and self-confessed lying.

There is little in this volume about the opposition to Reagan, another sign of the time. One could hardly write about Nixon without writing about those on his enemies list. But Reagan's success at striking the monarchical stance confounded those who wished to mobilize against him. With Nixon, the battle was against the all-too-real. Reagan, however, made reality seem as if it were an abstraction. And his regressive version of Keynesian economics—mixing tax cuts with massive military rearmament—softened the edges, even as the problems deepened.

The Democrats learned from their polling the paradoxical lesson that Reagan's policies might be unpopular, but he was not. Much timidity and confusion followed. Reagan was rarely attacked directly. In 1984, Walter Mondale believed the Reagan presidency to be so fantastic as to be unreal. According to his strategy, he had only to assemble the components of the Democratic coalition to create a triumphant majority. His method opened him to an insurgency within his own party as the stalwart of the old regime, organized by Gary Hart, who offered himself as the tribune of the future. All this was of a piece within the period. Reagan shaped the Mondale campaign which, in turn, shaped the Hart campaign. Finally, with Reagan's reelection, the daydream continued.

Much has already been written about Reagan's legacy. His effect on public policy has been scrutinized; the degree of political realignment has been gauged. Numbers on government spending and partisan identification show the trends. But there is an aspect of his legacy that is more difficult to chart because it does not have a material basis. It is, writes Daniel Patrick Moynihan in *Came the Revolution,* the problem of "the leakage of reality in American life: our seeming weakness at grasping the probable consequences of what we do or fail to do." This is the main theme of *Our Long National Daydream.*

PART I

The Spirit of the Age

Reagan the Unassailable

Journalists assigned to the White House lock Ronald Reagan in their sights, fire, and believe they've made direct hits. Yet he walks away unscathed. He has survived the assaults of the press better than any president in decades. "I don't know why it doesn't add up," says Curtis Wilkie of the *Boston Globe,* who covered the president for two years. "Everyone is talking about what a free ride Reagan's getting, but if you look at the body of work coming out, there have been very tough stories written. People are writing up all the ludicrous foolishness he says, his errors in press conferences, his 'cave man' jokes, and 'evil empire' speeches. These stories fall off the face of the earth."

Lou Cannon of *The Washington Post,* the dean of Reaganology, who has spent most of his adult life covering Reagan, said recently, "Reagan is getting a fairer press than he deserves." But for the most part the press has not been derelict in holding the president to strict standards. Every statement he makes is closely scrutinized for accuracy. And every error is publicized, at least by the leading reporters of the leading newspapers. But the techniques reporters employed with such devastating effect on previous presidents seem to have little impact on Reagan. His egregious misstatements have not become a public issue; his popularity has not waned. Why Reagan escapes when other politicians might be in retreat or even destroyed appears to be a mystery. The clues to that mystery lie in his philosophy—and that of the press. The canons of reporting, which enabled journalists to penetrate the enigmas of recent presidencies, are inadequate in the face of Reagan. The president and his pursuers operate on very different planes, as evidenced by their wildly divergent use of facts.

Reporting is a bastion of empiricism. In its ideal form, events are depicted as separate occurrences, unrelated except in the sequence of time. Only those things which can be proved by facts are considered true; there can be no truths before investigation. Empiricists disdain the contrary method—the method that assumes that an analysis can be performed before the gathering of all data, that reason itself possesses a logical validity apart from the amassing of all evidence, that truth can be discovered prior to facts. To empiricists, this is too metaphysical, too philosophical. Empiricism is a philosophy of which reporting is a particularly radical expression; and empiricism is definitely not the philosophical bent of the current president.

Presidents of the recent past were well suited to classical coverage. Deep Throat, the ultimate source in his investigation of Watergate, instructed Bob Woodward of *The Washington Post:* "Follow the money." And thus Richard Nixon's clandestine methods were uncovered. The true story was exposed, the "smoking gun" found. Nixon himself believed in facts; he was, after all, a lawyer. But he was a frequent and unconvincing liar. When it was proved that he wasn't telling the truth, by his own words immortalized on the White House tapes, his tenure abruptly came to an end.

Jimmy Carter's faith in facts was one of his major political themes. During the 1976 campaign, he promised never to lie—a post-Watergate promise. In a curiously ironic way, his thought paralleled that of reporters. Carter tried to accumulate as many facts as he could. He had no coherent world view and acted on an ad hoc basis. He wanted the mass of facts to determine each case. His essence was his parts. He was neatly constructed for dissection because journalists deal in particulars. Catching Carter in isolated errors established his general incompetence.

Ronald Reagan, however, deals in universals—the free market and the Soviet Union's "evil empire." His ideology is not just another event, another particular: it is the continuing source of events. The way he thinks is obviously crucial to his presidency, and it presents journalists with an unfamiliar difficulty. Follow the ideology?

Reagan's ideas may be simple, but the pattern of his thought is complex. He has a comprehensive world view that can coherently explain the cosmos. From his ideology, Reagan infers the truth of facts and the need for policies. When facts prove mistaken or policies have unexpected consequences, he can shift ground without making any fundamental change in his beliefs. Perhaps the facts or the policies were the wrong inferences, perhaps they were compromised by his opponents: he can always explain what goes wrong. Criticism of his statements or policies never touches his central beliefs. These attacks may actually confirm for him the duplicitous character of his opposition, since he *knows* his critics have a distinct point of view. They are not open about their premises; he is.

With Reagan, facts don't determine the case. Facts don't make his beliefs true. His beliefs give life to the facts, which are parables tailored to have a moral. If one fact doesn't serve, another will. Time and again, presidential assistants have told White House reporters that even if the president missed a fact, his general point was still correct: what's an extra zero or two when we're talking about real waste and abuse in social programs?

The artillery of the press has been aimed mainly at Reagan's factual misstatements. By correcting the president's profuse errors, the press tries to create a context. But it's the press's context, not Reagan's. For Reagan, facts are means. For journalists, facts are ends, the alpha and omega. An implicit tenet of the orthodoxy is that collections of facts add up to the truth, particularly if the facts are balanced. "The rules of Establishment journalism are constraining in making a judgment," says Steven R. Weisman, who covers the White House for the *New York Times*. "The boundaries are narrow, especially compared to European standards. The thing we seize on the most is these inaccuracies. It's one of the things we can write about that's permissible. And it tells you something fundamental about Reagan. His misstatements get right to the fundamental misunderstanding he may have of the issues."

To prepare for a Reagan speech, Weisman routinely arms himself with the facts in anticipation of mistakes. "We have to be vigilant of his misrepresentations," he explains. (On July 22 the headline on Weisman's story for the *Times* was: REAGAN SEES GOOD JOB NEWS; LABOR STATISTICIAN DISAGREES.) Other reporters perform similar labors. "Talk about frustrated!" says Curtis Wilkie. "After every press conference, Tom Oliphant (another *Globe* reporter) and I go over the transcript and come out with a story the next day pointing out the six or eight errors he made." Lou Cannon, who writes a weekly column in the *Post* entitled "Reagan & Co.," has gone so far as to introduce a regular feature called "Reaganism of the Week." The "Reaganisms" are humorous presidential quotes, usually fantastical inaccuracies. "I've written stories about Reagan's funnyisms going back to 1967," says Cannon. "I think more people should be writing about whether he knows what he's talking about."

The principal question the press is asking is this: what didn't the president know and when didn't he know it? A substantial literature on the subject is piling up. Curtis Wilkie's article in the June issue of *Playboy*, "The President As ComicKaze," cites numerous gaffes, misstatements, and absurd incidents. Here's Reagan at a state dinner in Brazil toasting "the people of Bolivia." There he is welcoming the boxer Sugar Ray Leonard and his wife to the White House as "Sugar

Ray and Mrs. Ray." He calls Samuel Doe, the leader of Liberia, "Chairman Moe." "If ignorance is bliss," Wilkie writes, "the Reagan Administration is the embodiment of the politics of joy. . . . Sometimes it seems we are covering the Single Stooge Show." According to Steven Weisman, the article "was the favorite of the White House press corps."

Columns on Reagan's mistakes, a ready-made topic, are seemingly innumerable. On July 29 in the *Post,* for example, Judy Mann reviews Reagan's record on women and finds his facts lack credibility. Reagan says housewives can now get Individual Retirement Accounts because of administration action. Wrong. Reagan says we have almost doubled the tax credit for child care. Wrong. Reagan says he has appointed "over a thousand women in executive positions." Wrong. And so on.

Reagan's misstatements could fill a book, and they have. The book is *There He Goes Again: Ronald Reagan's Reign of Error,* edited by Mark Green and Gail MacColl. It is a treasure trove of misstatements on almost every conceivable subject, from taxes (Reagan says, "Justice Oliver Wendell Holmes once said, 'Keep the government poor and remain free.'" Wrong, Holmes never said it, though he did say that taxes are the price of civilization) to foreign policy (Reagan says, "Incidentally, the first man who proposed the nuclear freeze was in February 21, 1981, in Moscow—Leonid Brezhnev." Wrong, it was Senator Mark Hatfield). The editors of this volume of tragicomedy have such faith in Reagan's incorrigibility that they end the book with blank pages labeled, "Add Your Own."

The misstatements mount, but the impact on Reagan's standing with the public appears negligible. "I have the feeling it has no important impact whatsoever," says Wilkie. "When I did it with Carter I had the feeling it reinforced feelings that he was an incompetent boob. That's the frustrating thing." Lou Cannon believes that Reagan's errors "help him or don't have any impact. The kinds of mistakes Reagan makes are the kinds we all make—the wrong name, the wrong date. People identify with it. It's a function of his humanity. We could double the number of Reaganisms a week and it wouldn't change anything."

Nobody believes Reagan is lying. He doesn't willfully distort the facts; his mistakes are unintentional and spontaneous. So even if the press catches Reagan in inaccuracies, he's not caught. For reporters, getting the facts wrong is a cardinal sin; they can get fired for a series of lapses. But there's no unity in reporting except in the method. The parts are the whole. However, all the events and facts swirling around Reagan are seen by him as expressions of a greater unity which exists in his head. Examining fragments can never fatally undermine the unifying vision.

Jimmy Carter discovered this about Ronald Reagan during the 1980 campaign. Carter believed, according to his aides, that if Reagan got his facts wrong in their debate, Carter would win the election. Indeed, in the debate Reagan got some significant facts wrong. He said, for example, that he'd never been against Social Security. Carter awaited Reagan's demise, but nothing happened.

Appropriately, the principal victim of the so-called Debategate affair, in which Reagan campaigners were charged with purloining Carter's confidential campaign memos, is a member of the press, George Will. Will's offense was coaching Reagan for the debate and then declaring his player the winner after the event on ABC. (Imagine if Howard Cosell were also Billy Martin, but nobody knew it.) Will failed to uphold excruciatingly correct behavior. He was the perfect victim for the moment, having failed the rules of reporting, the very grounds on which the press tests Reagan.

The orthodox doctrine of reporting makes an absolute claim: that all events can be covered, and that their sum equals reality. This orthodoxy is a closed system of logic that doesn't admit a priori reasoning. Yet a priori reasoning is Reagan's mode of discourse. His subjectivity is an objective fact. But according to the empirical dogma, the causation between idea and act that exists in Reagan's case can't be reported; without documents, it is pure speculation. The metaphysics of the press prevents it from fully covering the metaphysics of the president.

The fact-obsessed press rarely addresses the kinds of questions that most concern the president: can public belief in a policy make the policy work? Does budget cutting forge moral character? Does a negative press inhibit economic recovery? Most important: will recreation of a free market in this society engender a new sense of community? Such questions are seen not only as false but also as meaningless because they can't be verified empirically.

The central story about Reagan is not that he misses facts. It is that he has a world view in which facts are not important. Facts are pawns of his vision. There are great flaws and inconsistencies in Reagan's vision, but questions about them—like the ones above—can't be asked in the hurly-burly of a press conference. Reagan could easily deflect them with a joke and a grin, and those who asked the questions would lose face with their peers. Reporters feel obligated by their own competitive pressures to ask fact-oriented questions. This is hardly something they're unaware of. "If you have an interview with the president," says Steven Weisman, "reporters are always interested in finding out news. Nobody has sat down with him and had a philosophical discussion of the underpinnings of his beliefs. Certainly, he's been asked how he got this conservative philosophy. He'd respond that his philosophy is based on his experience and historical truth. He's not stimulated by counterarguments. His answer would be predictable and not very rewarding. You couldn't formulate a question that would get at the core of the fallacy of his views. I'm not hopeful it would produce results. He's a very frustrating quarry."

The best journalists may adhere to the orthodoxy of their craft verbally, but they always have an animating idea they apply to the events they're covering. In fact, what are called significant facts are always based on rational analysis. Cannon says he often acts on his "intuition" about Reagan, a process that provides him with scoop after scoop. By starting with a premise in advance of doing the story, reporters are closer to the way Reagan thinks than they are when operating by the rigid empirical method. Weisman says, "Carter figured that if you learn a lot about a situation you'll be able to find the best solution. Reagan would say what he wants to accomplish; it would begin with a philosophical premise. Reagan's philosophy is ultimately irrefutable, even if you have all the facts."

To the extent that reporters depart from the exacting and metaphysical doctrine that collections of isolated facts equal the truth, they have broken with the conventional wisdom of their profession. They do so in order to get the story. Thus, the actual practice of journalism often contradicts the orthodoxy of journalism. Empiricism is undermined paradoxically by experience.

In the orthodox version of journalism, discerning the pattern in the facts is left to the reader (an abstract person)—even though the facts themselves have inevitably been arranged by human selection. An implicit assumption of the orthodoxy is that reporting isn't guided by analysis. Hence the category "news analysis," which is viewed as being something distinct from "news"—even though "news analysis" is in fact often the reporting of patterns or of possibilities. These pieces of news may be as true, even as "factual," as the news of an appointment or the arrival of a foreign dignitary; yet the split is decreed between analysis, which is regarded as subjective, and reporting, which is regarded as objective. A side effect of this split is the blurring of the distinction between interpretation (which is the ordering of facts, connected by the tissue of reason) and opinion (which praises or blames, drawing a conclusion for action). In the orthodoxy, interpretation is conflated with opinion; they're both considered subjective expressions. This logic completes the empiricist's partition between analysis and reporting. It renders analysis marginal, a separate and lower order of reality. For Reagan, however, "analysis" is the only reality.

Reporters feel most keenly the clash between their theory and their work when faced with the fact of Reagan. "The conventions of journalism don't allow you to get close to Reagan," says Cannon. "All the appalling and appealing things about him are outside the realm of what we do well. They require people to make judgments of what he means, what he understands. All of these are difficult judgment calls. The misstatements get you away from the problem. He has this dimension that is beyond facts—it's extraterrestrial. You have to deal in essences, convictions. You have to go outside the conventions because Reagan is unconventional."

Among other things, Reagan has demonstrated more conclusively than any president in recent memory the limits of press power. And he's done it by ideas. "This president," says Weisman, "really knows how to control an agenda."

The issues that really draw Reagan's blood are ideological—"fairness," for example. But that action is not mainly in the court of the press. It is in the court of the president's ideological adversaries. Only an opposing political vision can be a true alternative to Reagan. In the meantime, using "the facts," the press painstakingly draws precise pictures of Reagan's shadows.

(September 1983)

PART II

Ghosts

Richard Nixon's Ambition

The night of John F. Kennedy's inauguration, after the oratory about the torch being passed, the loser toured the mostly deserted Washington streets. Until the bewitching hour of midnight, Richard Nixon still commanded his official vice presidential car. He ordered his chauffeur at last to take him to the Capitol. He marched alone past the Senate chamber, down a corridor to the vast and empty Rotunda, and on to a balcony, where he gazed at the darkened horizon. Nixon had virtually willed himself to within a few thousand votes of the presidency. And in this portentous scene of departure, his will was almost palpable. Yet the story did not end here; his lonely leave-taking became the prelude to a return—and worse.

Stephen E. Ambrose's *Nixon: The Education of a Politician* (Simon & Schuster) is an old-fashioned sort of biography. The author, a historian at the University of New Orleans who has written the definitive two-volume biography of Eisenhower, seeks balance, not irony. Ambrose's facts are lined up in rows and made to march to a very measured judgment. His prudent interpretations do not stray from the accumulated details. There are no great themes, no theories of history, no analytical leaps. In short, Ambrose has written the standard, a middle point of reference, around which all Nixonia may be organized.

Ambrose's extension of the historian's empathy to his subject seems at first to make Nixon's motivation understandable. But the more we know, the more unknowable Nixon becomes. There is no searching point of view; and finally the professionally "balanced" approach to an unbalanced subject does not penetrate deep enough. Still, this sheer massing of material on Nixon cannot help but evoke a certain reaction. Ambrose's affectless prose is not without effect; this vanilla has an aftertaste.

The first of two volumes, the opening of an American tragedy, *Nixon* is utterly chilling in its inexorability. Even as we begin the first page, the last terrible one is known. Nixon does not exactly drift toward his fate. Instead, his ambition builds into a juggernaut, driving him toward rule and ruin. Each of his passages was final, sealing him off from possibility. The more tightly Nixon coiled his ambition, the more he became entangled in forces outside himself. The biographer's piling up of facts seems almost heartless, because they are ultimately crushing; yet Ambrose's naturalistic style implicitly fits the amoral rise and fall of his subject. Richard Nixon's story belongs in Theodore Dreiser's world.

Nixon's trajectory has been described conventionally (and unconventionally in Garry Wills's *Nixon Agonistes*) as a parable of the Protestant ethic, according to which work and ambition produce virtue and success. Perversely, the worldly-wise Nixon twisted his success into failure: the self-made man unmade. *Nixon*, however, is at least as much about environment as it is about character, about a mechanical politician in a mechanistic universe, who was found by forces he eagerly rode.

Nixon, for his part, projected the impersonal as the enemy. Always he faced a faceless conspiracy that had to be brought under control. He was the individual against the crowd below and the elite above; the choice was always between order and chaos. Though his ascent to power was amazingly rapid—elected vice president at age 39—he believed he was constantly being thwarted. He sought to conquer a society with which he was radically at odds. And he never felt that he had arrived, that he could loosen his grip on himself. Thus his spirit was stunted by a fierce obsession with survival. "I had to win," he said, justifying his sordid first campaign. The situation was always desperate; he was always cornered by circumstance.

Nixon's most enduring piece of writing, *Six Crises*, about his struggle, is Benjamin Franklin's *Autobiography* with a paranoid subtext: half-banal, half-mad. Any self-revelation on Nixon's part was unintentional. He was certain that he risked destruction if he displayed authenticity; against his enemies, he carried insincerity as a shield. The political obliterated the personal. "In my job," he said in 1959 to columnist Joseph Alsop, "you can't enjoy the luxury of intimate personal friendships. You can't confide absolutely in anyone. You can't talk too much about your personal plans, your personal feelings."

Nixon grew up, surrounded by a loving family, in a religious, Quaker community. Like many Quakers, he was bred to be reserved in private but confident in public. The great mystery is his inability as an adult to trust. There is "nothing" to explain it, according to Ambrose. The death of his little brother, Arthur, made him strive harder to please his parents. He recited poetry, played the piano, debated like a champion, and rose every morning at 4 to pick up vegetables at a farmers' market for the family store. In high school, he ran for class president, losing to an "athlete and personality boy." He had no close friends; but he was widely respected and he had no enemies.

When he won a scholarship to Harvard, necessity demanded that he choose the hometown Whittier College. His family could not afford his living expenses elsewhere because his older brother, Harold, had contracted tuberculosis. Nixon, however, showed no discernible bitterness. Harold's death two-and-a-half years later apparently intensified his will to succeed. Nixon was the Big Man on Campus—class president, founder of a fraternity, rotten football player but good sport, and winner of the Reader's Digest Southern California Extemporaneous Speaking Contest of 1933. He was also the lead actor in the school play, so skilled that he could cry on cue. "Buckets of tears. I was amazed at his perfection," said the drama coach. The school yearbook recorded:

> After one of the most successful years the college has ever witnessed we stop to reminisce, and come to the realization that much of the success was due to the efforts of this very gentleman. Always progressive, and with a liberal attitude, he has led us through the year with flying colors.

Then on to Duke Law School, where he closed the library every night, including weekends, and lived in a small shed lined with cardboard, without heat. He graduated with honors, third in his class. "His life to date," says Ambrose, "had been an unbroken record of achievement and success."

Nixon's political career had its origins during the war, on a remote Pacific island, where the navy man ran a small store, just like at home, and was an expert poker player, known for his disciplined bluffing. He carefully guarded his winnings, exhibiting the virtue of frugality, and saved the money for his first campaign. He came rushing out of the war, and almost immediately a goal for his energy materialized.

In his congressional district, a group of small businessmen called the Committee of 100 had formed, searching for a bright young man to support against the long-time incumbent, a New Dealer, Jerry Voorhis. "Like their counterparts throughout Southern California, and indeed through the nation," writes Ambrose, "these middle-class Old Guard Republicans were in a mood close to desperation." They believed they were true-blue Americans, but they had lost their rightful place in the world because of the unnatural Depression for which they had no explanation. Roosevelt's presidency was a warp in time. Yet again and again they had been frustrated. Liberalism was leading to socialism, which led to communism. What kept this un-Americanism in power was an unholy alliance of labor unions and minorities, Hollywood celebrities and federal bureaucrats. (This enemies list—cast as special interests, radical chic, and big government—has lasted for decades.) Two systems were in conflict, according to Nixon: "One advocated by the New Deal is government control in regulating our lives. The other calls for individual freedom and all that initiative can produce." With this formulation, Nixon convinced the Committee of 100 that he was the man to slate.

"Had enough?" was the Republican slogan of 1946. (These magic words were manufactured for the GOP by the Harry M. Frost advertising company.) Like the late 1970s, the late 1940s was a period of economic and foreign-policy turmoil. And the right had ready answers. Communists and fellow travelers were "gaining positions of importance in virtually every federal department and bureau," Nixon told an American Legion crowd. "They are boring from within, striving to force private enterprise into bankruptcy, and thus bring about the socialization of America's basic institutions and industries." What's more, he elaborated at another campaign stop, "There are those walking in high official places . . . who would lead us into a disastrous foreign policy whereby we will be guilty of . . . depriving the people of smaller nations of their freedoms." Here was an anticipation of McCarthyism, and the prehistory of rollback and the Reagan Doctrine.

The symmetry between the right's frustration on the domestic scene and its frustration with the international scene was striking. At the war's end, communism, or more precisely the Red Army, was on the march. To conservatives, no explanation made so much sense as that President Roosevelt had betrayed Eastern Europe at Yalta. For the right, the acceptance of the cold war, and of containment, and later of deterrence, meant reconciling itself to permanent frustration. The incumbent Democratic stewardship of this policy provided the opportunity to taint the Democrats as unpatriotic. By contrast, the right began to move away from the old isolationism toward an eschatological anticommunism—a program of simple vengeance that would result in an America once again untroubled by foreign problems. Nixon, in time, supported the Marshall Plan, the pillar of containment. Yet he cultivated the right's anxieties about a tense world; they were useful as a political instrument.

Nixon's campaign for Congress consisted of unalloyed lies, innuendos, and distortions. The words the judicious Ambrose uses to describe it are "vicious . . . snarling . . . dirty." Many of the neighbors and friends who had known Nixon since he was a boy were shocked by the apparent transformation of character. "To them, this was a 'new Nixon.' " Later, a group of them prevented the Whittier City Council from naming a street after their most famous son, then vice president. "I had to win," was Nixon's rationale—the Protestant ethic without ethics. *This* Nixon was the only "new Nixon" that ever really mattered.

But the emergence of the first "new Nixon" involved more than a question of character. From the beginning, Nixon's lack of principles was in the service of the principle of partisanship. He was very much a member of the resurgent Republican class of '46, and within that a creature of the embittered right wing. *U.S. News,* a purveyor of mostly uncritical Republicanism, immediately proclaimed 1946 as Year 1 in "a new cycle in American political history." This was wishful thinking, but it contained some truth, as Nixon's progress would bear out.

The realignment theory that emerged in the wake of Ronald Reagan's election has tended to overlook that realignment's true origin in the old Republican minority and in its reaction against the New Deal, which brought it little but sorrow until the midterm elections of 1946. For the GOP, no greater gains have been recorded since: 56 House and 13 Senate seats. This shift was traumatic enough to inspire Senator J. William Fulbright to call for President Truman's acceptance of the electoral returns as a vote of no confidence and, in the British way, to step down. Despite the shock, though, the general features of the old party system seemed stable, as the Truman victory two years later confirmed. Beneath the surface, however, there were deep cracks.

The 1946 results were a tremor, a premonition of the coming Republican strength in the Sunbelt and the mountain states. In Congress, the conservative southern Democrats and the right-wing Republicans made an alliance of convenience that was not defeated until Lyndon Johnson assumed the civil rights cause as his own in 1964. The Democratic setback in 1946 also exposed the party's ideological confusion about the post-New Deal era, a confusion that is still to be resolved. But the right wing demonstrated its willingness to engage in a single-minded politics of desperation. This sentiment was later made into a complex formula by Kevin Phillips, an aide to Nixon's 1968 campaign manager, John Mitchell. In *The New Republican Majority,* Phillips proposed a polarization of the electorate along racial, ethnic, and regional lines. It was Nixon's historic mission to exploit these tensions to create a lasting GOP advantage.

Nixon's entrance onto the political scene was a sign to the old right of both hope and vengeance. He was loved for his enemies. His early Washington years illustrated the evil of the conspiracy that the old guard believed had been in power since 1933. "I was elected to smash the labor bosses," he declared upon arriving in the capital. He was tutored by Father John Cronin, one of the communism experts who attached themselves to the right, to expose Communists "in the State Department." So Nixon chose an assignment on the House Un-American Activities Committee.

That Alger Hiss turned out to have been almost certainly guilty was Nixon's great luck. He did not enter his first "crisis" as a disinterested party, but out of sheer partisan impulse. At a crucial juncture in the case, Nixon secretly met in a New York hotel room with the "senior brain trust of the Republican Party, and had this group decided to withhold its approval, Nixon would have had to drop the case." These men (John Foster Dulles, who was Thomas Dewey's chief foreign-policy adviser; Allen Dulles; C. Douglas Dillon; Christian Herter) were the personifications of the GOP eastern establishment, held in contempt by the old guard. Yet Nixon's determination had made the case such a partisan cause that they were drawn into it. And Nixon convinced them to bless his continuing struggle.

Nixon had hit upon a theme that Republican candidates used with tremendous effect in the 1950 midterm elections. It was a theme that the GOP had been marketing at the lower frequencies for years, without much result. Now it worked: "Fear. Nixon knew that fear was the way to get to the public. Fear of Alger Hiss and his kind; fear of Stalin and his bombs and rockets; fear of change; fear of someone getting ahead in the arms race; fear."

When Hiss was convicted, Nixon immediately intensified his partisanship. "This conspiracy," he said, "would have come to light long since had there not been a definite . . . effort on the part of certain high officials in two administrations [Roosevelt's and Truman's] to keep the public from knowing the facts." Among the congratulatory notes he received was one he "cherished most," from the old guard icon-in-exile, Herbert Hoover: "At last the stream of treason that existed in our government has been exposed in a fashion that all may believe."

By now, Nixon was running for the Senate, attacking the Democrats as the blame-America-first party, a party that "has been captured and is completely controlled by a group of ruthless, cynical seekers after power—committed to policies and principles completely foreign to those of its founders." His senatorial campaign against Democrat Helen Gahagan Douglas was as noteworthy for its scurrilousness as his congressional effort against Voorhis had been. Ambrose notes that Douglas herself was not entirely innocent of mudslinging. But once the campaign turned to mud, she was vastly outdone by the master.

Senator Nixon became Vice President Nixon in a thoroughly characteristic way: by becoming indispensable to the aspirations of a force larger than himself—those seeking the nomination of Dwight Eisenhower at the 1952 Republican convention. His role required nothing less than the betrayal of the old guard that had previously sustained him. Nixon had already been handpicked for the position by talent scout Dewey, who escorted him into a meeting with the Eisenhower political directorate months before the convention. Thus Nixon allied his ambition publicly with the force he had initially and privately encountered in the Hiss case.

The nomination turned on the outcome of a credentials fight between competing southern delegations—one group pledged to Ike, the other to Senator Robert Taft, the old guard standard-bearer. And the key to the outcome of this issue was the vote of the big California delegation. Within the delegation, the central figure was Nixon, who, with great aplomb, fostered the notion that Taft was unelectable. Nixon then gave an eloquent speech on the convention floor, swaying delegates to vote for the Eisenhower southerners, who were thereby seated. Years later, in 1969, while swearing in Nixon as president, Chief Justice Earl Warren, who, as governor, had been the nominal leader of that California delegation, confided to Nixon aide Herb Klein "that but for Nixon he might have won a compromise nomination for president himself in 1952."

Two months after the convention, Nixon was revealed to have maintained an $18,000 "slush fund," set up by friendly businessmen, for his personal use. His famous defense in the televised "Checkers speech" commingled themes from Horatio Alger with themes from Alger Hiss. There was the paean to hard work—"every dime we've got is honestly ours"—and the resolve to root out the all-encompassing conspiracy—"I am going to campaign up and down America until we drive the crooks and communists and those that defend them out of Washington." Quickly, Eisenhower embraced him: "You're my boy!" Back home, his old drama coach at Whittier College, Professor Upton, watched his former student on television, put his head on Senator William Knowland's shoulder and weep tears of joy. "That's my boy?" Upton shouted. "That's my actor!"

For Eisenhower, Nixon served as the partisan id. He spoke the unspeakable, earning him Adlai Stevenson's sobriquet as "McCarthy in a white collar." Ike kept his distance, while gaining the benefit. Nixon was his bridge to the old guard, his conduit to McCarthy, and generally a source of political information. The vice president's many suggestions for foreign intervention, including dropping atom bombs on Vietnam in 1954 when the French were besieged at Dien Bien Phu, were uniformly rejected by the commander in chief. But he learned a great deal, traveled widely, and ran for the White House in 1960 on his superior experience.

Within a year of his honorable defeat by Kennedy, he was thinking of running for governor of California, a base from which he could again venture forth to win the GOP presidential nomination. The party establishment, "from Eisenhower on down," feared that the California right would seize control of the state party. Since 1946 the southern California right had grown more confident and virulent. Its motor, in the early 1960s, was a forerunner of the new right, founded in the bitter aftermath of Taft's 1952 convention defeat: the John Birch Society. The shift from the time of Representative Nixon was apparent in the election as congressman of John Rousselot, the Birch regional director for southern California and five Sunbelt states. Rousselot's 1962 fund-raising dinner featured the renowned toastmaster Ronald Reagan.

The suggestion that Reagan might be a candidate for governor quickened the pressure on Nixon. After he announced, his fund-raising lunch at the Bohemian Club was attended by the massed corporate titans of California—"quite a contrast to the Committee of 100 from the 1946 campaign," writes Ambrose. But Nixon was not anointed. Instead he endured a primary against a right-wing candidate, Joe Shell, a former college football star turned oilman. Nixon attempted to denounce the Birch Society while giving credence to its anticommunist passion; he also did not want to alienate its activists and the many Republican officeholders who were Birch members. In the meantime, liberal Republicans deserted him to support the incumbent Democrat, Edmund "Pat" Brown. Soon Nixon was giving his most memorable performance since the Checkers speech: "You won't have Nixon to kick around anymore, because, gentlemen, this is my last press conference." But he was wrong. There would be new Nixons; for them we must await Ambrose's concluding volume.

The Reagan years, filled with rhetoric about "a new cycle in American political history," have curiously obscured Nixon. After all, it was Nixon, the native Californian, who began what Reagan hopped aboard. Unlike Reagan, he was painfully self-conscious about what he was doing, and about the price that was being exacted from him and others. Nixon actually lived and bore the scars of the social Darwinism that to Reagan has always been romance.

Moreover, the achievements of what is called the "Reagan revolution" pale next to the transformations that Nixon accomplished at all levels. Nixon in China is still breathtaking. By contrast, the most celebrated Reagan accomplishment—the change in the national brain waves from worried to happy, partly intended to induce amnesia about Nixon—has been the most ephemeral. Reagan's current bouts of cheerfulness, while the special prosecutor prepares his briefs, are more detached from reality than ever. In retrospect, Reagan may be seen as the end of the era that Nixon inaugurated.

As Reagan's benumbing optimism wears off, many of those who had faith in its powers are returning to a primordial resentment. Conservative activists and placemen, columnists and policy makers are getting themselves in the mood for a young Nixon. If he cannot be found in 1988, a reconstituted Committee of 100 undoubtedly will begin the search.

He's back.

(July 1987)

The Progressive Tradition
and George McGovern

When George McGovern announced that he was running again for president, the derision was widespread. Even his wife said she hadn't encouraged him and wouldn't campaign for him. Because everyone knew he didn't stand a chance of winning, he was in danger of being tainted not only as a loser but as a fool: the Democratic counterpart of Harold Stassen, the perennial Republican contender. In becoming a candidate for President in 1984, McGovern risked what was left of his dignity. Yet it is precisely his dignity that his campaign has enhanced.

McGovern's influence is greater than his poll numbers suggest. He evokes spontaneous warmth in many younger voters, for whom he is a nostalgic figure, part of the *Big Chill* syndrome. Certainly more people support him emotionally than electorally. He's been to the far side of failure, and even his direct pleas for votes seem relaxed. He's utterly serene and candid, making some of the other candidates look anxious and evasive by contrast. He doesn't have the desperate longing of someone who can't let go. "I don't feel that I personally have to be in charge of this country, that I personally have to be president," he told me. "Life will go on. I've never been more at peace with myself than I am right now. But I still feel strongly." McGovern appears freed from ordinary ambition. "It's quite incredible," said a top aide to Walter Mondale. "He's running as a sage."

His immediate goals are to present his ideas and to act as a party healer. He has a ten-point program that combines classic New Deal economics (Point Four: "Put unemployed Americans back to work *now*, cleaning up the environment and rebuilding the infrastructure of our country") with a dovish foreign policy (the nuclear freeze, a 25 percent reduction in military spending, the end of U.S. military operations in Central America). He still believes in détente with the

Soviet Union, and when he praised Richard Nixon in a lecture for his Soviet policy, the former president sent his former nemesis an autographed copy of his latest book. After an exchange of letters, they finally met. "I was trying to see if my perception about him was right," says McGovern. "Did he still believe in détente? And he does." It's the ultimate bipartisan coalition. But the shared view of the two men who once epitomized their parties is out of favor in Reagan's Washington. Ironically, McGovern's meeting with Nixon has been a highlight of his 1984 campaign, along with his spirited defense of civility in the New Hampshire debate and his peroration ("Don't throw away your conscience") in Iowa.

McGovern's manner, more than his policies, has commanded attention. He recalls all too well how cutting words spoken by Democrats during a primary can be used by Republicans in a general election. Thus, when John Glenn heatedly attacked Mondale in the New Hampshire debate, McGovern intervened. He assumed the role of party protector, reminding his colleagues that "front-runners sometimes get nominated." Later he told me: "We were delivering swords to Reagan that he would turn on Mondale." As the arbiter of campaign discourse, McGovern elevates himself above the fray. He becomes the elder statesman he wants the party to recognize. This is his unspoken goal in 1984: admittance into the pantheon of the Democratic Party, the party of Roosevelt, Stevenson, Kennedy, Humphrey—and McGovern.

His place in the party's history will mostly depend upon whether he offers it a usable past. Because he was the standard-bearer at the moment of maximum internal turmoil, he now represents continuity. He is a bridge between the older and new generations, a healer of contending factions. Most important, he has what all politicians need: the charisma of purpose. McGovern understands that values animate the party and that the party shelters the values. His contribution to the campaign, therefore, will be not his proposals but his perspective. Against Reaganism, McGovern poses a deeply rooted political philosophy—one that could give Mondale's message intensity and connect Gary Hart's with a tradition.

McGovern is a minister's son whose faith has been Progressivism, practiced first as a history professor and then as a politician. He still admires the works of Charles A. Beard and Vernon L. Parrington, quintessential Progressive historians. The Progressive historians, who were typically midwesterners, tended to see American history as the unfolding progress of the democratic spirit in a perpetual contest with vested interests. They saw a pattern of fundamental dichotomies: western rebels against eastern bankers, working people against the privileged, progressives against reactionaries. By the 1950s, the Progressive historians were regarded as hopelessly old-fashioned, insufficiently ironical, and overly simplistic. Their central tenet, that America has been molded by great conflicts, was considered plain wrong by the new breed of historians, who argued that our history was always marked by an underlying "consensus." In the history profession as elsewhere, the "end of ideology" was proclaimed. George McGovern, in a sense, is the last Progressive historian.

He grew up in a strictly religious, and Republican, family. But by the time he arrived as a graduate student at Northwestern University, after a stint in World War II as a bomber pilot, he was a liberal, inspired by the "social gospel." His doctoral thesis was about violent miners' strikes in Colorado early in the century; his doctoral adviser was Arthur Link, Woodrow Wilson's biographer. In 1948, almost everyone in Northwestern's history department supported Henry Wallace of the Progressive Party for president. McGovern was a delegate to the Progressive Party convention, an association that was a significant cause of the AFL-CIO's refusal to endorse his 1972 candidacy. But McGovern didn't vote for Wallace after all. At the Progressive convention he experienced what his biographer Robert Sam Anson called a "great disillusionment" over the "fanaticism" of Wallace's entourage, some of whom were communists. Although McGovern continued to agree with many of Wallace's criticisms of cold war policy, the experience helped make him a staunch Democrat. In any case, his politics had its true source in South Dakota populism, with its unique mixture of self-reliance and cooperative banks.

In the early 1950s, there was virtually no Democratic Party in the state. McGovern took on the task of organizing it, leaving his teaching post at Dakota Wesleyan College to become the party's executive secretary. He recruited the entire party apparatus, from the precincts to the candidates. "I lived on the road literally for two-and-a-half years," he says. What he was doing was part of a larger transformation. Throughout the upper Midwest, in the post-New Deal era, the Democratic Party coalesced with populist groups—a fusion of values and party, power and purpose. The trick was to put the populist flame into the iron lantern of the Democratic Party without extinguishing it. In Minnesota, Hubert Humphrey was the founding father; in neighboring South Dakota, it was McGovern.

In 1960, McGovern lost a race for the U.S. Senate. The consolation prize was his appointment by President Kennedy as director of Food for Peace—a plum, especially for one who viewed the Midwest as the garden of the world. McGovern explained his new mission in the language of the cold war, and Arthur Schlesinger Jr. would call it "the greatest unseen weapon of Kennedy's Third World policy." But the program had ideological value because it fed millions; the propaganda was truthful.

In 1962, McGovern was at last elected to the Senate. He was an exemplary Democrat, standing tall with President Johnson in 1964 by voting for the Tonkin Gulf resolution, the justification for the escalation of the Vietnam War. A year later, McGovern publicly came out against the war; he was a dissenter, but never a party renegade. He maintained his close ties to the Kennedy faction, supporting Robert F. Kennedy when he ran for president in 1968. After Kennedy's assassination, McGovern announced for the presidency himself in order to hold together the Kennedy forces at the cataclysmic Chicago convention. When Humphrey was nominated, McGovern, unlike many doves, did not stalk out. "No one," he says, "opposed the war more than I did, and no one reached the podium faster than I did to hold up Hubert's hand." He believed he was not compromising his principles but upholding the principle of loyalty. He didn't see how liberals would be served by Nixon's election. But Nixon beat Humphrey, and in 1972 he beat McGovern too.

The day after Nixon delivered his inaugural address, McGovern gave a foreboding speech at Oxford University on the state of the Democratic Party. He knew he had lost badly, but he worried about what would happen to the party if it lost its ideals. "The Democratic Party," he warned, "is in peril of becoming a party of incumbency out of power, much like the Whigs of the nineteenth century—a party with no principles, no programs, living only from day to day, caring only for the perquisites of office. . . . Without principles, there is no party."

The party, in fact, was riven between factions whose titular heads were the past two losing nominees. Yet the issue that had precipitated the rupture, the Vietnam War, was receding. In 1974, Humphrey privately apologized to McGovern for the unkind things he had said about him in 1972. In the late summer of 1975, McGovern put a proposition to his old friend. "I thought the party was defeated in 1968 and 1972 because we were divided," he recalls. "We had a majority of voters. But Humphrey went down in 1968 because the doves sat on their hands. I went down to defeat partly because the Humphrey wing of the party sat on their hands. What I had in mind for 1976 was that Hubert would announce for president and also announce that I'd be his running mate. I thought it would bring the

Democratic Party together. We'd beat any contenders and Gerald Ford." McGovern says that when he finished talking, he "noticed that Hubert had tears in his eyes. He was deeply moved." Humphrey wanted to think the idea over. About a month later, he told McGovern he couldn't do it. He didn't give a reason. "Possibly he was worried about his health," says McGovern. "I'll always think it was a good idea. It would have been duck soup."

The collapse of his scheme, McGovern is convinced, cleared the way for an interloper. The Humphrey and McGovern factions, represented in 1976 by Henry Jackson and Morris Udall, were both defeated by Jimmy Carter. McGovern regards Carter as "a mistake. In a way, he won by default. It was something that couldn't have happened at any other time." To McGovern, none of the main currents of the party coursed through Carter's politics. He was, according to McGovern, "the first neoliberal. He campaigned against the government. It was more or less an effort to marry old-fashioned Republicanism to the Democratic Party." Carter's record ended up giving credence to Reagan's assertion that government is inherently incompetent. His legacy within the party is the absence of a legacy.

The McGovern legacy, however, lives on, in spite of the neoconservative effort to read him out of the party. When the neoconservatives saw McGovern, they saw "acid, amnesty, and abortion"—a horde of student radicals, black militants, and feminist banshees who had kicked out labor and the faithful party regulars. They felt displaced, and in their search for order and stability they tried to paint McGovern as an outsider: a cultural radical, a purist, a party-wrecker. But McGovern never fit this image of "McGovernism." While they tried banishing him and his influence, most neoconservatives themselves wound up abandoning the party when Reagan was elected President. "People like [former U.N. Ambassador] Jeane Kirkpatrick, someone working for a right-wing ideologue, who claims to be a lifelong Democrat—I never could understand that," says McGovern. "They've deserted the party. The neoconservatives were more interested in their own ideology than in the party. I haven't agreed with a lot of Democratic foreign policy, but I have never had any doubt about supporting the party. I'm not an outsider. What do you have to do to be considered a solid Democrat?"

In the Democratic pantheon, McGovern can't be put in the hall of losing presidential candidates who set no directions for the party—Alton B. Parker, James M. Cox, and John W. Davis. He belongs in the same gallery as Stevenson, Humphrey, and William Jennings Bryan. The comparison with Bryan is particularly suggestive: old-stock midwestern Protestants, they both sounded the chords of Progressivism, echoing with scriptural references. Bryan, however, was the champion of the declining agrarian yeomanry, and McGovern has been the mentor of the new class of college-trained professionals. McGovern, then, is no throwback; he's an early modern who helped bring a new generation and a new class into politics. He lost, but millions of people who entered politics in his 1972 campaign are still active in the party—including, of course, his campaign manager, Gary Hart, and (McGovern claims) about a hundred more members of Congress.

Hart and the other new liberals, however, seem to be seeking a future without a past—a chrome future which, as a campaign theme, plays like electronic music: all metallic beeps, no deep harmonics. In the Iowa debate, Hart declared that we must "leave the past behind," perhaps the oldest "new idea" of all. (The greatest continuity in American thought is precisely the persistent faith in novelty.) In their wholesale condemnation of the past, the new liberals seem ready to cede all human experience to Reagan. McGovern is their political father, but they tend to deny any parentage. Only lately has Hart begun to acknowledge their relationship. (In the upper echelon of the Hart campaign, some campaign aides refer to McGovern as Obi-Wan Kenobe, the last Jedi Knight, who vouchsafes to a younger man the secret of the Force needed to defeat the dark side. But is Gary Hart a Luke Skywalker?)

Walter Mondale, for his part, doesn't seem to grasp the weight of the new-politics constituency within the party. He has carefully built a New Deal–like coalition at the organizational level without thinking much about these people, who tend to be unorganized. He may win the primaries without the constituency McGovern fostered, but his neglect of it could lead to indifference in the fall. There's a dangerous precedent: Humphrey, Mondale's mentor, lost partly because of its abstention. Now this group is numerically larger, more established, and nearly as volatile. Lack of enthusiasm for Mondale is most apparent here.

Mondale offers a paradoxical unity, for he doesn't account for any of the schisms in recent Democratic history. The only discontinuities to him are Republican presidencies. He's the party insider who wants all conflicts settled on the inside. In this he is outside the Progressive creed, which considers economic and political conflict to be a universal fact and the motive force of progress. McGovern views the party as the appropriate channel for conflict, whereas Mondale sees it as the expression of consensus. The difference is crucial. Mondale's instinctive avoidance of antagonism may account for why he sometimes hesitates so long before clearly taking sides on controversial issues. "Fritz never bled over the Vietnam issue," says McGovern. "It did not tear at his soul. I don't quite know why. The issue was divisive, disrupting the fabric of the Democratic Party. I don't think he likes controversy, to do battle over a moral issue that disrupts the peace of his own party." He pauses, and adds: "Fritz is a good decent man with liberal instincts. I'd certainly do everything I could to get him elected if he's nominated."

McGovern doesn't have the iron lantern of the party anymore, but he can light a flame. Mondale, meanwhile, is marching victoriously across the country holding a cold lantern. In the Iowa debate, the frontrunner attacked Reagan as a "radical," but in so doing only underscored the President's strength of conviction. The name-calling confronts Reagan without engaging his ideology. In a corollary criticism, Mondale has been chiding Reagan for his "management style." By echoing the characteristically Republican notion that government should be run like a business, Mondale inadvertently casts Reagan as the populist, the expansive visionary. "Reagan intimidates some of the candidates," observes McGovern.

More than any Democrat, Ronald Reagan rallies behind himself the inspirational Progressive themes, arousing enormous moral and political energy. It is partly the tincture of Progressivism that distinguishes Reaganism from traditional Republicanism and gives it a broader appeal. Reagan's utopia, like Bryan's, is in some golden age of the past. The old populists defended a society passing away under the onslaught of industrialism; Reagan wants to restore that society, which he believes has been undermined by big government. He uses Progressive rhetoric against Progressive values, projecting a dramatic struggle of the people against the establishment. Only in his version the special interests are the many and the oppressed are the few. He expropriates the liberals' symbolic heritage, without any of them explicitly calling him to account.

Except George McGovern. "The populist and Progressive traditions have so much insight into our contemporary problems," he says. "Reaganism is an appeal to selfishness, a direct antithesis to social justice, the Judeo-Christian ethic to feed the hungry, clothe the naked, house the homeless. There are two competing feelings in each of us. Each of us is grasping and greedy. Reagan appeals to that. The Democratic Party has to stand foursquare for a more humane tradition. You don't separate yourself from history."

Controlling the image of the past has immediate practical consequences, as Reagan has proved. He sets the thematic stage for the liberals, just as Carter did for the conservatives. The Progressive interpretation of history may not be so anachronistic after all. Come home, America.

(March 1984)

PART III

1984

Statecraft as Spacecraft

As autumn 1983 turned brisk, Walter Mondale took to accusing his rival, John Glenn, of not being a real Democrat. Glenn responded by accusing Mondale of being the candidate of special interests. To Scott Miller, who is playing a crucial role in shaping Glenn's media strategy, this competition is highly reminiscent of the Pepsi Challenge.

Until recently, Miller was the creative director at McCann-Erickson, the advertising agency, where he handled the Coca-Cola account. More people have seen his work than have seen any single film or television program. "Have a Coke and a smile." That's Miller's slogan. "Coke is it!" That's his, too. To counter Miller's spots, Pepsi-Cola contrived the Pepsi Challenge, a taste test in which consumers were shown preferring Pepsi to Coke. This gave Miller one of his best ideas. It occurred to him that "if everyone's challenging us," if Coke was the standard by which other soft drinks measured themselves, then Coke must be "the real thing." Soon, under Miller's direction, friendly Bill Cosby, speaking for Coke, was on television, challenging the Pepsi Challenge. "People were glad we were fighting back," says Miller. "That's the way I feel about Glenn and Mondale. You demoralize people if you don't fight back. The greatest danger for Glenn is that if he doesn't do it himself, Mondale will describe what he's all about. And if Mondale doesn't take Glenn on, he looks weak. My worry is not Glenn being on the wrong side, but not being strong."

Mondale and Glenn often appear on the same platform to challenge each other, but their campaigns are conducted on wholly different planes. The former vice president is collecting the endorsements of elected officials and interest groups in the belief that their support will translate into a majority of the convention delegates. Glenn's campaign is asymmetrical to Mondale's. He is attempting to nullify the strength of traditional organization through media. "Glenn does best against the broadest possible electorate," explains Miller. "He's best in a general election, second best in a primary, third best in a caucus, and last among party activists. He's got to appeal to the most people he can. Mondale is running the ground game, three yards and a cloud of dust. Glenn's got to go to the air. He's got to play the air game."

The nerve center of the "air game" is a Manhattan political consulting firm called DHS, which stands for David H. Sawyer. The firm's clients have ranged from Jane Byrne, the former Chicago mayor, to Shimon Peres, the leader of Israel's Labor Party. DHS is John Glenn's media NASA, launching him into political orbit. And within that complex, Scott Miller, 38 years old, is the creative talent. He and Sawyer have worked together since 1976. "He's a brilliant person," says Sawyer. "He writes all the television spots. Scott's a very good strategic thinker. He has a superb sense of positioning. We work in a very, very close collaboration." Greg Schneiders, Glenn's press secretary, says, "The success or failure of the campaign depends on communicating the message on television. The Sawyer operation is extraordinarily important, a very large piece of the whole. Within that, Scott is one of the most important people. He has a solid sense of politics. For Scott, it's somewhat intuitive. He understands Glenn's style. He has even contributed to the basic stump speech."

On rare occasions an image maker and a candidate are ideally matched. Miller's main strength is his "intuitive" grasp of American popular culture. And Glenn's main strength—his status as an all-American hero—happens to be cultural as well. Moreover, Miller, like Glenn, was born and raised in small-town Ohio. Miller understands the candidate's sensibility. "I have pretty average tastes," he says. "The middle of the country, for better or worse, is the middle of taste. It helps me in advertising. A lot of commercial imagery is placed in middle America. To have come out of that gives you a certain advantage. You don't have to imagine what it's like. With Glenn, it eliminates the cynicism I might have about his sincerity. He's the kind of people I grew up with."

What makes Miller's involvement in the campaign such a potent factor is not just his empathy with the candidate but also his instinctive perception of the great themes implicit in the John Glenn story. The frontier, the future, and the pathfinder—the campaign draws on the same compelling material as the movie version of Tom Wolfe's *The Right Stuff*, fortuitously released as the campaign begins. *The Right Stuff* is the basic text. After Wolfe, Scott Miller is the chief interpreter. He provides the commentary, telling us how to think about Glenn after we've left the theater. "The movie is the promo," he says. "It reinforces what everyone knows about Glenn. Our job is to connect it with where he's going." The campaign is the sequel.

The slogans from the movie and the campaign neatly segue into each other. The slogan for the film: "How the future began"; the slogan for the campaign: "Believe in the future again." It's hardly surprising that in the Glenn campaign the most important place is the frontier and the most important time is the future. That's where Americans have been; it's where we're always going. Believe in the future *again*. John Glenn knows that the frontier and the future are realities. Unlike the rest of us, he's actually been there. "The movie is already in the public mind," says Miller. "We've got to link the positive side of Glenn and the political program. We have to try to create some clarity of image. You use symbols to talk about ideas."

The Glenn campaign occurs on the high frontier of symbolism. This doesn't make Glenn a synthetic character—"a celluloid candidate," in the words of New York's Governor Mario Cuomo. For most Americans, the imagery confirms Glenn's authenticity. Long before people flew in airplanes, let alone rockets, Americans gave credence to the set of symbols Glenn now embodies and projects.

Scott Miller's commercial and political advertising amount to an extended essay on American heroism. Time and again, he has dramatized heroes to sell a product or win an election. The Glenn campaign is the logical culmination of Miller's work, and in order to understand it one must understand his other campaigns. They are vivid in his own mind as he helps produce the Glenn spots.

"You've got to let people know that they're supposed to think about the product," Miller says. It perturbs him that what many advertising executives "let people know" is cynical, an expression of disdain. "It really bothers me that they have contempt for ordinary people," he says. "Why portray a husband and wife who yell at each other or a kid who's stupid? Why not teach people about human relationships and ideals?"

When he took over the Coke account, the "promise of the product had gotten a little high," he says. "It was going to change your life; you were going to play volleyball on the beach with a lot of young Nazis." Soon ads appeared featuring thirsty construction workers. "Have a Coke and a smile." Another Miller spot was like a cheerful version of Hitchcock's *Rear Window*. A camera focused on a Manhattan apartment building. When the camera entered each window it showed each person engaged in a different activity, but all drinking Coke. "Coke," says Miller, "is a little thing you have in common."

His most memorable spot for Coke starred Mean Joe Green of the Pittsburgh Steelers, a very large, very rough football player. He comes down the tunnel leading from the field to the locker room. He is dirty and sweaty. Clearly, things are not going well out there for the Steelers. A small boy, who just happens to be in the tunnel, offers Mean Joe a Coke. Mean Joe brushes him off with a growl, but the boy insists. Mean Joe drinks it in one gulp. Now he's smiling. The boy, however, is glumly walking away. He doesn't see Mean Joe smiling. "Hey, kid," bellows Mean Joe. And he throws the boy the sweatshirt off his back. "Wow! Thanks, Mean Joe!" "The idea," explains Miller, "was a kid meets his hero and what they have in common is Coke." Mean Joe is an unapproachable hero, and that's part of the message. "The way Mean Joe sold Coke was to sell an idea of what life can be like, what a human exchange can be like. A product ought to have a leadership quality, make you feel good. Mean Joe and the kid was a moment that had over two hundred million people in tears. In the most crass way, it could have been an astronaut. Coke is a symbol we have in common. It breaks down barriers. Glenn represents without any question some common ground. We can all agree that this man, in America's shining moment, was the ideal. That's common ground. Secondly, he belongs to nobody. He can therefore bring people together."

Miller has created other commercials about heroes, including spots for Miller Lite Beer, starring Joe Frazier, "famous heavyweight singer." But Miller did not move from Lite Beer to heavy political campaigning overnight. All along, he was working at DHS in numerous races. He worked for Senators Warren Magnuson and Daniel Patrick Moynihan; he worked for Governor Bruce Babbitt of Arizona. And, during the Chrysler crisis, when the United Auto Workers had to give up wage gains and benefits, he worked for the union, "putting the retreat in heroic terms," he says. His slogan: "Working hard, working proud." In 1982, he worked on the campaign of the Democratic National Committee. His slogan: "It's not fair. It's Republican."

Perhaps the most polished, effective, and conceptual political campaign he worked on was that of the mayor of Boston, Kevin White, in 1979. White's pollster asked Bostonians: "Does Kevin White care about people like me?" The favorable response, according to Miller, was "zero." White had already served two terms; he was charismatic, but idiosyncratic and controversial; and the busing crisis which tore apart the city was a fresh wound. "The obvious suggestion," says Miller, "was to show the human side of Kevin White." But that wasn't the strategy adopted. "The question posed wasn't who you like, it's who loves the city," says Miller. "Kevin loves the city, he's going to make it work; he's crazy, but he loves it." The advertising depicted a romantic image of the urban mayor, making urgent telephone calls at 2 A.M. Miller's slogan: "The Mayor." His other slogan: "The loner in love with the city." White was reelected—proving, among other things, that by playing from existing strengths a tough battle could be won. "It bears on the Presidential campaign," Miller contends. "People don't have to love John Glenn. There are symbols in a political campaign. We can say this guy can set an example. This guy can be our face to the world as he was in 1962. He can be America. You don't have to love him. Just understand him and admit that this is the kind of leadership we've got to have. Strength of character is what people are looking for in a leader."

"John Glenn is our Eisenhower," the speaker of the House has said. Besides the startling physical resemblance, Glenn, like Ike, is a military hero, seemingly above partisanship, who promises national unity. But there the similarity ends. The heroisms are dissimilar; the astronaut is not the general. Glenn was a pilot, a "single-combat warrior," in Tom Wolfe's phrase. Eisenhower, on the other hand, won power long before he was president at least partly because of his skillful manipulation of a Byzantine official bureaucracy. He commanded the largest American army in history; he led the invasion of Europe. Millions of Americans had a direct relationship with Eisenhower (Yes, sir!). When he was elected president, his enormous accomplishments reassured voters that he would deal confidently and prudently with the cold war. For John Glenn to be Dwight Eisenhower he would have had to have organized and executed the space program, not just have participated in it.

Glenn's strategists, in fact, do not see the candidate in the Eisenhower mold. The contrast between the two points to the central problem of the campaign: How can a hero be a leader? Glenn's deed compels our admiration, but we stand at a distance from him as spectators on the curb. "Glenn is not standoffish with people. People are standoffish with him," says Joseph Grandmaison, chief of field organization. "There's an aura about him. Mondale, however, is eminently approachable." How can the voters establish a relationship with their hero so that he becomes their leader?

Glenn's media advisers have decided not to work against the obvious themes in his story, but to work with them. Glenn will be presented as the pathfinder who can lead us into the future—statecraft as spacecraft. "His relationship to the masses is the same as the pilot to the passengers," says Miller. "They say: 'Take the controls, we'll go with you.' As president he would say: 'I'm going to set an example of courage and discipline. I'm going to set an objective. I'm going to tell you what to do. But, most important, I'm going to do it.' Glenn will set an example. It's clearly a different kind of leadership. People want to follow, to believe in him, to have him set a direction. That's his image. That image in itself can be leadership if he sets a path."

The Glenn campaign will highlight the theme of the future in three ways. First, it will project the candidate as the pilot of the ship of state. Second, it will stress his association with President John F. Kennedy. And third, it will publicize his specific policies to demonstrate how he will get us from here to there. These notions are not purely the products of cogitation by Glenn's strategists. They also have emerged from the extensive survey research conducted by the campaign's pollster, William Hamilton, and from the discussions of focus groups of representative voters conducted by a social psychologist, Ned Kennan.

The polling data, according to Scott Miller, shows that "people are hopeful about the new technologies, but they're fearful. The captain speaks to you in a calm tone. The pilot image is consistent with the computer age. It's consistent with an age of new technologies, of electronic media, rather than speaking in union halls. If you lay out Mondale and Glenn, Mondale does represent the past in a certain way. In that equation, people want to believe Glenn can lead them into the future."

The survey research shows something else. "The identification the press makes with Glenn is Eisenhower," says Miller. "The identification the public makes with Glenn is Kennedy. They identify him with a sense they had about the country, when the country really believed in itself. John F. Kennedy theoretically said to Glenn, 'We've got to get off the mark, and we need a giant symbol.' Glenn was willing to sit on a booster rocket and show the way." Glenn was the living symbol of the New Frontier. And wasn't space the reality of the New Frontier? "When people think about Kennedy they think about how they felt about America at the time," says Miller. Aligning himself with Kennedy is a way for Glenn to cast the still-luminous past upon the future. We're going back toward the glowing light in order to go forward. The future becomes familiar territory.

The campaign's private polls have discovered that Kennedy is a door into the future in another way. Voters have been asked: "Which President would be most appropriate to deal with the problems of today?" Kennedy wins nearly 40 percent of the vote. The next nearest president is Eisenhower, who comes in at 8 percent. Kennedy, therefore, is a much better running mate than Ike.

But what has Kennedy's pilot friend been doing all these years? By offering detailed programs, Glenn's handlers hope to prove, according to Miller, that "he's been getting the background to be president. If he gets something intelligent on track, people will say, 'Ah, that's what he's been doing for twenty years.' You can't say future, future, future. Glenn's character to lead has to be program-specific."

On the night of October 15, all the images and themes were packaged in a five-minute advertisement, broadcast nationally on CBS. It starkly positions Glenn, on his own terms, against Mondale. The word "Democrat" is not mentioned once. The spot opens with these printed words on the screen, read by a narrator: "At a time when most politicians are caught up in the policies of the past or the issue of the moment . . . only one man is talking about the future." Glenn appears, talking about "a whole new time period" we're entering, and the need to "set goals and go for it." He quickly discusses computers and education. He's courageous, too, as he tells a group of hard hats that he's against protectionism. "He doesn't play to the special interests, he doesn't play the old political game," says the narrator. Now Glenn is talking about how he had to write letters to the wives and mothers of his friends who were killed in combat. "It sears your soul." He's for peace. Finally comes the image we've been anxiously awaiting. Blastoff! *"Godspeed, John Glenn."* "They call him one of the true American heroes," intones the narrator. "He represented America in one of its finest hours, fulfilling the pledge of a young president." Enter J.F.K., followed by Glenn. This sequence is in black-and-white, dreamlike, a projection of our yearning, our wish-fulfillment. Then: "Believe in the future again."

As adroitly constructed as the imagemaker's version of the Glenn campaign may be, one must concede it would not resonate so powerfully if it were not playing off *The Right Stuff*. We haven't had a shared experience with Glenn for more than twenty years. In order to "believe in the future again," we must remember "how the future began." Because the film is so faithful to the book, Tom Wolfe has provided the essential framework for the campaign. He has understood the themes coursing through the Glenn story more explicitly and profoundly than anyone else. He has, after all, received his doctorate in American studies from Yale. The American studies treatment of the story is the most penetrating, and it has immediate political importance.

The line to John Glenn in mythology begins in the primeval American wilderness. The line to John Glenn in the movie begins with a man on horseback, Chuck Yeager, the early test pilot, Leatherstocking redux. *The Right Stuff* is another Leatherstocking tale, after

James Fenimore Cooper, of isolated, stoic heroes on the frontier, or, as the fraternity of pilots puts it, "pushing the outside of the envelope." Leatherstocking forsakes the town for the forest, polite society for a band of Indians and trappers who live by natural law, not "legal law." No matter what Leatherstocking must do in blazing trails, his integrity is inviolate; he continually plunges ahead toward Eden, moving back to innocence. Like Leatherstocking, the astronaut lives among a band of brothers, but not really in society. He abides by a code of natural law which determines whether or not he has "the right stuff." The most significant things he does are done alone. In order to succeed he must keep politicians, bureaucrats, and scientists—encroaching civilization—at bay. He is an uncompromising figure. The blackness of space seems to demand his white purity.

Chuck Yeager, the first man to break the sound barrier, personifies "the right stuff." All the astronauts seek to emulate his manner and live according to the code; they express themselves through action. Glenn alone among them expresses himself through speech. Unlike Leatherstocking, Glenn can be both a pathfinder and live in society. Compared to a professional politician he might sound flat and laconic, but to his fellow astronauts he was initially suspect because he was considered loquacious. When he jabbers about the flag at a NASA press conference, the other astronauts roll their eyes. But Glenn, it turns out, has a worthy motive for talking. His wife stutters badly; she's a virtual mute. Glenn is giving voice to the voiceless. When Lyndon Johnson demands to be let into the Glenn house with a battalion of television cameras in tow, terrifying Annie Glenn, John bucks not just the NASA bureaucracy but L.B.J. himself and tells his wife to keep the door sealed. His fierceness is in the service of his tenderness. It is the ultimate confrontation between the brotherhood and society. All the politicians in *The Right Stuff* are depicted as creeps, with the exception of Kennedy, who appears in the film only in a newsreel clip. This sequence is in black-and-white, an imposition of reality that is somehow dreamlike. L.B.J., the professional politician, is Glenn's greatest rival outside of the brethren. (Symbolically, L.B.J. is the stand-in for Walter Mondale, whose patron was Hubert Humphrey, whose patron was Lyndon Johnson— all three of them senators who became vice president.) In defending his wife, Glenn holds off intrusive officialdom. He keeps the home and the fraternity sacrosanct. He is not only accepted by the brotherhood, but tacitly acknowledged as their public face; he can speak for them, too. His speech doesn't detract from his coolness—it's just him. Appropriately, Glenn's space shot is the most wildly celebrated by the public. He can exist in both worlds. He doesn't suffer the fate of

Leatherstocking, who can only live in the anarchic forest (or the wild blue yonder), beyond society. Leatherstocking constantly presses on into the wilderness. Even after the astronauts have flown, Yeager tries once again to reach the transcendental frontier. Leatherstocking is incorrigibly restless. He wants to move from the Old World to the New, from age to youth, from the past to the future. Back in society, Glenn gives these ancient themes a political spin; he remains true to the code, but doesn't become an anachronism. His campaign themes are a restatement of some of the most enduring notions in our culture. They are at the heart of many American dreams. It is, after all, the incumbent president's dream that we have a "new beginning," that we return to our roots to restore our power. At the edge of the myth, John Glenn encounters Ronald Reagan.

A contest between Glenn and Reagan would pit myth against myth. In the American studies version, this would be a race between a James Fenimore Cooper hero and a Horatio Alger hero. Reagan presents himself as the self-made man. He tells us that he's just like us and that through the free market we can succeed as he has. For decades, Reagan has been surrounded by image makers in Hollywood and in politics. But ultimately he has been his own mythmaker: the self-made man invents himself. In Hollywood, Reagan never made the transition from person to persona. He was a player in other people's dreams. He was known as the "Errol Flynn of the Bs"; there was no "Reagan type." Jack Warner, asked what he thought of Ronald Reagan for governor, is reputed to have said: "Jimmy Stewart for governor, Reagan for best friend." Stewart was a superstar, an archetype. Moreover, he had been a U.S. senator in two movies—*Mr. Smith Goes to Washington* and *The Man Who Shot Liberty Valence*. Warner understood Reagan only in the context of moviemaking, where a "best friend" couldn't be a brilliant leading man. A "best friend" in politics was altogether another matter. Reagan's failure to rise high in the Hollywood firmament has been crucial to his political stardom. If he had been a superstar, his celebrity would have been blinding; we wouldn't be able to see his ideology. Reagan, however, is ordinary enough to make his message sound trustworthy. He achieves his real stardom by bringing Reaganism to us, by asking us to go back with him to where dreams began in the free market. Reaganism was the star vehicle Reagan had been waiting for all his life, the ultimate treatment of conservatism. Great acting that electrifies audiences is born of conviction. And while Reagan exalts the individual he stands at the head of a mass movement.

Glenn has no mass movement. Yet his myth is a powerful weapon against Reagan's. Reagan met the stars on Sunset Boulevard. John Glenn rocketed to the stars, where no American had been before. He is the American none of us can be. There was nothing incomplete about his mission, his celebrity, before he entered politics. While Reagan was making movies, Glenn was doing things people make movies about. That is why Glenn, alone among the Democratic candidates, can raise the "actor issue." "I wasn't doing *Hellcats of the Navy* on a movie lot," Glenn said at the candidates' forum in New York, referring to the Ronald Reagan–Nancy Davis vehicle. Scott Miller says, "I'm convinced that Glenn thinks Reagan is a complete wimp." Glenn did not need us to become a star. His actual individualism makes Reagan's rhetorical version seem pale. But which has more political power? And can Glenn bring himself to say that he needs us?

The astronaut is not Everyman. But Glenn's media advisers are trying hard to make him an approachable hero. In a thirty-minute spot shown in late October only in Iowa, Glenn appears informally before about thirty ordinary Iowans sitting on folding chairs. There's no podium separating the candidate from the people. He responds to their spontaneous questions; it's not prepackaged. (That's the packaging.) Glenn gives some long, detailed answers, a three-point plan to reduce the federal deficit, for example. He's a little rough around the edges. In the middle of the spot, someone asks Annie Glenn a question: What kind of a president would her husband make? She wonders aloud if she should stand in front of the group alongside her husband. He urges her to come forward. She speaks with great deliberation; she still has a faint stutter. She tells us the intimate John Glenn story he's too modest and too proud to tell about himself. She talks about how his war experiences make him devoted to peace. "He has not had to watch late-night TV. He knows how horrible it is." She tells how deeply he cares about the poor, too. After speaking for about five minutes she sits down to applause. Glenn pauses. "Not for the cameras here," he says. But the cameras keep filming. "You don't know what this means for Annie to get up and give a speech like that." But we do; we remember the scene from the movie. Now Glenn gently explains to the neighborly Iowans that she has conquered her handicap. "That's sort of an aside from the program," he says. He takes the next question. But the "aside" is not peripheral. The love story subplot makes Glenn approachable.

His media strategists have been careful not to embellish his natural, unaffected style, which some feel may be terminally dull. "He's not flamboyant," says David Sawyer. "He gives a sense of straightness, directness, strength, integrity. Anytime you try to cloud those characteristics it's a mistake." To embellish "the right stuff" would be to undermine the iconography.

But will "the right stuff" fly in presidential politics? The fact that the myth fits the man doesn't mean he must be president. In the end, Glenn will still have to court constituency groups. He will have to debate Walter Mondale. He will have to prove that the activity and interest generated by the movie and the advertising can be effectively marshaled by his organizational apparatus. He will have to demonstrate that media translates into delegates. Only if he can meet these tests, and if he has not been left behind, can he face Ronald Reagan.

In the darkness of the family theater in the east wing of the White House, the president of the United States is participating in the great national experience of viewing *The Right Stuff*. "Imagine," says Scott Miller, "Ronald Reagan is sitting there watching someone playing John Glenn. The thought has got to flash through his mind: What a great part! It puts *Kings Row* to shame."

(November 1983)

Over and Out

John Glenn rehearsed for the New Hampshire debate for days with his media advisers, videotaping, reviewing, and perfecting his performance. On the stage at Dartmouth College on January 15, Senator Glenn waited patiently for the appropriate moment to attack Walter Mondale. At last the opening appeared and Glenn unloaded: "gobbledygook . . . ridiculous . . . promising everything to everybody . . . I'm disgusted." Then the Glenn campaign waited anxiously for the public to acclaim their candidate's boldness. Within twenty-four hours *The Washington Post*–ABC News poll showed that Glenn's ratings had plummeted. At 11 percent he trailed Mondale by forty points and latecomer Jesse Jackson by two. It later emerged that the poll was based on a sample of only fifty-seven people who saw the debate; its margin of error was arguably 100 percent. Nevertheless, it was an unreliable indicator confirming a reliable notion, that Glenn is auguring in for a crash. Within the campaign the mood turned from apprehension to panic.

By his own calculations, Glenn was supposed to be closing in on Mondale by now. In Glenn's private survey research, Mondale seems startlingly vulnerable. He is too much a politician, too closely identified with Jimmy Carter, too liberal, too uninteresting. Mondale's great organizational strength could be finessed by media experts. Glenn would concede the ground to Mondale if he could control the air. His early advertising, created by Scott Miller, the Coca-Cola ad man, and David Sawyer, the political consultant, presented the ideal Glenn. Outer space, John F. Kennedy, ticker-tape parades—it was all there. Glenn was crisp, caring, and charismatic, dropping words like "new technology." But there was no lift-off.

Glenn's advisers now blame the failure of his image partly on *The*

Right Stuff, the cinematic epic touted by the press and feared by Mondale. By recalling Glenn's heroism at the zenith of American optimism, it was thought, the movie would make us embrace him as the one to lead us bravely into the future. Instead, according to David Sawyer, the movie had "a basically negative effect. It looked like we were running the campaign solely on the fact that he's an astronaut." Everybody knows Glenn was a spaceman; not everybody knows that he's a senator, and many of those who do know it tend to discount it. In the American mind he lives only on the tip of a booster rocket. The campaign attempted to solve the problem by connecting his mythology with his political career. The slick ads worked well, perhaps too well. They contrasted sharply with the candidate on the stump, who has been typically stumbling, inarticulate, and boring. The contradiction between his person and his persona had made voters hesitate to support him. And it wasn't just that he was perceived exclusively as an astronaut that gave pause. His prosaic qualities hurt him more than they would another candidate precisely because of his cosmic deed. He has seen the globe as a big blue marble, but he offers no global insight. We know he went up to heaven; we don't know what he learned there. He's the most earthbound candidate of all. He has little notion himself of how to apply his myth to his candidacy. His advertising does it, but that only widens the gap.

Candidate Glenn reminds one of the old *Life* magazine's version of the space program as a mind-numbing procession of dreary applecheeked cadets. By contrast, the filmic John Glenn has an ironic self-consciousness. "I'm a lonely beacon of restraint in a squall of car crazies," Glenn says wryly in the movie. A good line, but it was Tom Wolfe's. The movie's producers put it in Glenn's mouth because they know that the public gags on unrelieved self-righteousness. But that was the movies. This is reality.

When Glenn's image failed to move significant numbers of voters into his column by the late fall of 1983, his handlers decided to carry the battle to the ideological plane. Mondale was on the offensive; every other day he seemed to boast a new endorsement. Glenn's frustration rose. He knew he ought to be winning. And his pollster, William Hamilton, produced numbers to support that feeling. Hamilton presented voters with two constructs, one labeled the "old party" and the other the "new party." The old party—the party of Walter Mondale—was traditionally liberal and wanted to reverse Reagan's policies. The new party—the party of John Glenn—wanted to reform Reaganism, but not to go back to the old Democratic policies; it would seek arms control but maintain a strong defense; and it would challenge interest groups on behalf of undefined "new goals." A majority of those polled favored the "new party." Bewilderingly, a majority also favored Mondale. Glenn's advisers concluded that their campaign would have to make these distinctions evident if the "new party" voters who backed Mondale were to be won over to Glenn.

In mid-November, Glenn assailed Mondale as being weak on defense, a captive of special interests, and wedded to the "failed policies of the past." Mondale counterattacked, accusing Glenn of not being a "real Democrat," a charge he underlined by pointing out Glenn's 1981 Senate vote in favor of Reagan's economic program. Glenn's campaign waited for the ratings. But rather than marking his rise, Glenn's ideological outburst provoked his precipitous decline. What happened?

Many of Glenn's supporters were young professionals, women, and liberals who hoped that he would indeed be a progressive candidate of new ideas. When he revealed himself to be an ordinary conservative Democrat, they instantly deserted him, some going over to Mondale and others swelling the ranks of the undecided. Glenn had closed the door on those most intrigued by his mythology. He locked himself into a politics-as-usual candidacy, driven by arbitrary categories created by polling. The paper new party, Glenn's vehicle, in fact served to obfuscate his weakness. According to a private poll conducted by Patrick Caddell, Glenn's support of the B-1 bomber and nerve gas production makes 60 percent of Democratic voters nervous about his attitudes toward "defense spending and arms control." Thus his attack on Mondale for being "weak" on defense only called attention to his own liability. Instead of transcending the confines of ideology through charisma, he imprisoned himself.

The premise underlying his campaign has been "electability": Glenn's centrism would attract Republicans and allow him to triumph over Reagan. In one way this notion is rigidly linear, viewing a candidate in the middle as occupying more ground than anyone else. In another way the notion is circular: Glenn is electable because of his positions, which make him electable. But of course it is Glenn's mythology, not his ideology, which constitutes his appeal. Had he blended that mythology with more liberal positions he might very well have lured Mondale voters to his side. So far, "electability" has proved to be a restrictive rationale. It is such a thin motive for presidential campaigns that candidates of both parties who have founded their efforts upon it have always proved precisely unelectable. (Where have you gone, George Romney? A nation turns its lonely eyes to you, Birch Bayh.) Most voters do not think the way political consultants and columnists do; they rarely sacrifice their emotions to expedient reasoning—and those who do think this way, this year, are supporting Mondale. In addition, support for a candidate in broad polls doesn't necessarily translate into support in partisan primaries. The most motivated voters are the most issue-oriented, they are the ones who dominate party elections. Some sort of artificial "center" may be fabricated out of polling data, but finding it in actual politics is another matter.

Moreover, a collection of positions pasted together into a political profile doesn't make for an ideology. The absence of a salient or at least a salable idea at the core of the Glenn campaign distinguishes it fundamentally from the most successful unconventional presidential campaign of recent times, that of Jimmy Carter in 1976. Carter, like Glenn, relied upon images rather than organization to win the nomination. But unlike Glenn, Carter advanced two powerful ideas: first, restoring integrity to government after Watergate, a commitment demonstrated by his religious authenticity; and second, solidifying racial and regional reconciliation, a commitment demonstrated by his being a southerner devoted to civil rights. These were genuine longings, to which Carter, above all other candidates, laid claim. In no substantive sense does Glenn's candidacy, despite its media-based character, resemble Carter's.

Glenn's ideological attack served a highly useful function for his opponent. Glenn became Reagan's surrogate, a sparring partner for Mondale. By punishing Glenn, Mondale prepares for the championship fight. Glenn's mechanical performance at the New Hampshire debate, where he reiterated the arguments he had already made and lost points on, provided another healthy workout for Mondale. Mondale needs Glenn, just as Reagan needs Mondale.

The Glenn campaign has few remaining options, and they have all been tested in controlled discussions of representative voters called "focus groups" conducted by a social psychologist. It was discovered that if people learn more nice things about Glenn's political career, they're more likely to vote for him. Conversely, if they are told nasty things about Mondale they're less likely to vote for him. There's a catch: because Glenn is perceived as an all-American hero he's not supposed to say anything nasty. Unless his positive ratings can be improved enough to give him a cushion, he risks losing it all by using negative television spots. This is the conundrum now preoccupying the managers of Glenn's campaign. It appears to have pushed them close to the edge.

On the one hand, there's a notion that Glenn can be reinvented. "Given the image Glenn has right now in the press, and the image Walter Mondale has," says Miller, "people are looking actively for an alternative." Who's the alternative? "We'll be presenting John Glenn as the alternative to John Glenn and Walter Mondale." According to this extraordinary formula, Glenn I is lost in space. Glenn II is on the launching pad. Miller conjectures that if Glenn had just begun his campaign he would be hailed as a deliverer. "Seeing Jesse Jackson made me wish Glenn had entered the race three weeks ago." Still, he believes that Glenn II can fly. "I think he can erase 'dull-and-stupid' on the air." Once the new probe is aloft, we can forget about that first one—dull-and-stupid.

On the other hand, maybe the campaign should go negative. "My instinct," says Miller, "is to take out Mondale's kneecaps. I don't want to be there on February 29 [the day after the New Hampshire primary] and find I've still got ammunition in my belt." A slew of negative ads have already been produced. One of them is reminiscent of the lurid segments in *The Right Stuff* about the Russian space program. It uses blurry black-and-white photos of Mondale, Lane Kirkland, and the Diplomat Hotel in Miami Beach to "expose" the alliance between Mondale and the AFL-CIO as if it were a scandal that had just been uncovered.

Both Glenn and Mondale have accepted the conventional wisdom that this is a two-man race. Glenn's advisers believe that voters deserting Mondale because of Glenn's negative advertising would of course turn to Glenn. "Mondale's loss is always Glenn's gain," says Miller. But if the problem is as bad as the Glenn negative spots say, then the solution must be more dramatic than Glenn.

For the moment, his status as runner-up has stabilized. But if he sinks more, the entire complexion of the contest would quickly change. Mondale would be deprived of his straw man. Glenn's demise and Jackson's emergence would create an opening for a Great White Hope. But can Gary Hart, the obvious contender, fill the role he has set for himself as leader of the "new generation" any more than Glenn has become leader of the "new party"?

The strategy of manufacturing Glenn II to replace Glenn I has a precedent. In Ohio, Glenn A lost his 1970 bid for the Senate; he was effectively branded a lightweight, not a real Democrat. In 1974, Glenn B won the Senate race by directly challenging his opponent, establishing his credentials as a real politician. In 1984, Glenn I has been a combination of Glenns A and B. The heat shield on Glenn I, however, has burned off. In presidential campaigns there are rarely second chances. The most righteous right stuff, one remembers, is about the glory of facing the end gracefully.

(February 1984)

Hart's Big Chill

"Mondale is mush," said Gary Hart in a recent conversation. "He's weak, and his managers know it, and they're scared. Mondale's argument is inevitability, but Muskie was more inevitable than Mondale." Hart's analysis may yet be proved correct; but if it is, why should he be the beneficiary? The Hart campaign has so far disappointed the hopes many liberals held out for it. The handsome, youthful senator from Colorado was going to be the candidate of excitement. With the best young public policy thinkers in America at his side, he would stride out of the West to lead the Democratic Party into the future. John F. Kennedy, Hart's model, had taken the generation first mobilized by Adlai E. Stevenson and brought it to power by giving it a harder edge. Gary Hart was going to do the same for the generation awakened by J.F.K., the generation that created the candidacies of Eugene McCarthy and George McGovern. The cohort that brought in and fought against the war in Vietnam, now grown to maturity, would fulfill its promise at last, and Gary Hart would stand at its head.

By now, according to the scenario, Hart would be marching toward victory with the aroused generation in massed formation behind him. There is no sign of that yet; so far his campaign has been a lonely crowd. Like Jerry Brown before him, Hart is in danger of being seen as one more in a series of false messiahs of the new generation. Hart has seemed unable—or perhaps unwilling—to connect with the dormant feelings of his potential supporters. Over and over, in Washington, one hears the same plays on the candidate's name. All Hart but no heart. Too much Hart, not enough soul. Hart broken. As 1984 began, the political community tended to dismiss the Hart campaign as a thing cold and inert.

Yet Hart himself is curiously insistent that his campaign is very much alive. It doesn't worry him, he says, that in the Gallup poll he is under 5 percent. He knows that in 1972 and 1976, at similar points in their campaigns, George McGovern and Jimmy Carter had similarly negligible ratings. "The public polls are meaningless in nomination politics," he says. "They mainly measure name recognition." So he doesn't mind that most voters may never have heard of him.

Hart is encouraged by his private polls, which tell him that 84 percent of prospective Democratic primary voters declare that they would vote for a candidate who would "bring new ideas and fresh approaches" to governing. Though polls do indeed show that there is still an opportunity for him or someone like him, they say nothing about whether he is capable of seizing that opportunity.

The opportunity lies in the fact that among the candidates only Gary Hart is potentially a generational politician. In 1984, Hart alone is positioned to become the leader of the generation born during the 1940s and 1950s—the generation that shaped and was shaped by the hopes, conflicts, and disillusionments of the 1960s and 1970s and that, because of its vast numbers, will eventually command politics well into the twenty-first century. Generational politics in America isn't new. Throughout the twentieth century each burst of liberal reform has had a strong generational impulse behind it. Theodore Roosevelt, at 42 the youngest president in American history, opened the new century. Franklin Delano Roosevelt, who said, "This generation of Americans has a rendezvous with destiny," brought a phalanx of young reformers to Washington. John F. Kennedy, elected at 43, campaigned in 1960 on an explicit generational theme, and announced in his inaugural that "the torch has been passed to a new generation of Americans." Hart, who is 46, seems convinced he can make a similar appeal. "I can win," he says quietly. "It can be done." Perhaps, but clearly Hart has not done it yet. Why?

The answer may lie in the contradictions of his character, which is of a sort that is unusual in his profession. Unlike the kind of politician who seeks love and acceptance from crowds and eagerly divulges his private stories to strangers, Hart is self-conscious and self-contained. He has an almost mystical belief in his personal destiny, yet exalts rationalism in politics. He is a self-proclaimed generational chieftain who is a full decade removed from those who would be his followers. He offers the hope of making liberalism once again the country's dominant doctrine, but categorically refuses to make any emotional appeal. He believes passionately, without allowing himself to show passion. One of the traits that has been crucial in making him a United States senator—his immense political self-control—may incapacitate his presidential campaign.

In talking casually with people about Hart, I've found a widespread assumption that he is the product of a privileged childhood—the son of some prosperous Episcopalian minister, perhaps, or even a scion of some western ranching dynasty. The reality is different, and more intriguing; but few people know it because Hart talks about himself only with the greatest reluctance. He is Gatsbyesque in the way his smooth, self-created persona blurs his origins. There's something impenetrable about him that both attracts and perplexes his aides. One of them told me that on his first day on the job, he discovered that nobody on the staff was completely sure about the senator's precise background, or even about his real name.

Gary Hart grew up in Ottawa, Kansas. His father was a railroad worker who, he says, never earned more than $100 a week. Both of his parents came from large, poor families. Neither graduated from high school. Both were evangelical Protestants, and Gary was "raised in the Church of the Nazarene, faithfully." During the summers he worked on railroad gangs, where most of his fellow laborers were black and Hispanic. He went to Bethany Nazarene College, an unaccredited school in Oklahoma. There he had the good luck to study under Prescott Johnson, the school's one-man philosophy department, who recruited a few select incoming students each year. "That shaped me as much as anything else," Hart says. "It was a whole new intellectual world." Under Johnson's tutelage he studied the classics, and he aspired to become a philosophy professor like his mentor. He grew ambitious enough to apply to the Yale Divinity School. When he left for New Haven, it was his first trip East.

The working-class provincial approached the Ivy League with a sense of "adventure and a little awe, apprehensive about people talking differently than I did." He felt, he says, "woefully inadequate." In his second year he decided he didn't want to become a professor after all, yet he put in the three years necessary to receive his divinity degree. He regarded it as an opportunity to get a "really good college education." He took courses in three departments—religion, philosophy, and literature. "I put together one hundred great books for myself. A lot I did on my own. I read the Russians, Tolstoy and Dostoyevsky and the others. I read Hugo, all of Faulkner, Hemingway, Melville, Hawthorne, the Greeks."

In 1960, Hart, then 23, received his political baptism as a student volunteer for John F. Kennedy. To this day Kennedy, the highborn intellectual politician, remains Hart's ideal. (While some politicians still celebrate their log-cabin origins, many liberals, since F.D.R. and J.F.K., try to make their personal stories fit the aristocratic model.) "John Kennedy activated my generation politically," says Hart. "Most people my age weren't interested in politics, because that's what guys who smoked cigars did; it was unsavory. Anyone in grad school interested in politics was considered an oddball. Kennedy legitimized politics, even before there was a cause. He created the cause. Now public service was an honorable thing."

Kennedy's emergence on the national stage helped resolve Hart's personal crisis. "Here was a bridge to the real world, an idealistic and honorable bridge," he says. He decided that he would attend law school and eventually settle in Denver. "It never crossed my mind to stay in the East," he says. "It would mean abandoning my roots altogether." While he was at Yale Law School, his father changed his name from Hartpence to Hart, the Senator claims, which was the original family name. The son did likewise, assuming a new, dashing name that was an old name at a time when he was establishing his identity.

By his mid-twenties, Hart embodied the tension of three major transformations. He was a midwesterner who had gone East; a young man of the fifties who embraced the sixties; and a self-made intellectual striving to test his beliefs in the public arena. Going from East to West is the classic American odyssey; but going from West to East is an equally significant, if mostly unheralded, mythic journey. (*The Great Gatsby*, of course, is the definitive book on the theme.) It means to go from anonymity to power, from roughness to sophistication, and, perhaps, from authenticity to artificiality. Hart aimed to be both an easterner and a westerner, a man with two advanced degrees from Yale, yet the representative Coloradan.

Hart was in law school during the Kennedy years. The ethos of the 1950 was still very prevalent, according to his campaign manager and classmate, Oliver Henkel. "It was a sleepwalking existence," says Henkel. "If you put one foot ahead of the next, then you would get ahead. In law school that began to break down. People started to talk about freedom marches and sit-ins." The hipsters of Hart's era had been beatniks, rebels without a cause; one could try to escape, but not to a community. Individuals were "on the road," but that was not for Hart. Hart was what David Riesman, in *The Lonely Crowd*, called inner-directed, and his earnest striving was exactly what beats denied. Hart understood hipness in the sixties, but he could never be truly hip in the '60s manner because he had always been too cool, too alone, too rational. He was a committed member of the silent generation coming of age in the 1960s, a generational anomaly.

Hart's severe education also set him apart. He was rigorously schooled in philosophy and law, closed systems of logic which work explicitly from premises to conclusions and are steeped in mistrust of irrationality. But political society, where Hart chose to live, isn't the land of pure reason. The distance between thought and action is always treacherous.

After John Kennedy's assassination, Hart went from law school to Washington to serve in Robert F. Kennedy's Justice Department. Hart doesn't see Robert Kennedy, as many others do, as an existential hero, defining himself through intense commitment. In Hart's view, J.F.K.'s assassination "created Bobby's commitment. He was a captive of events. He was not his own man; he was his brother's brother. He was called on to respond to commitment. Bobby is almost Greek, a tragic figure, a man thrust into a role." To Hart, R.F.K.'s passion can't be reproduced, even if one wanted to, because he was possessed by circumstances.

When R.F.K. left to run for the Senate, Hart went to the Interior Department where, as Stewart Udall's special assistant, he helped draft some of the early environmental laws. When Richard Nixon was elected president, Hart moved to Denver and set up a private law practice specializing in natural resource issues. In 1970 he wrote a long memo to Senator George McGovern outlining how he should organize his campaign in the western states. McGovern asked the unknown Denver attorney to be his campaign manager.

Hart wrote a book about the campaign, an inside account of how a relatively obscure senator came from nowhere in the polls at the beginning of an election year to win his party's nomination. In *Right from the Start,* Hart describes these extraordinary events through the prism of Tolstoy's deterministic theory of history, citing General Kutuzov's injunction in *War and Peace*—"time and patience." The brilliance of the primary campaign, however, was in sharp contrast to the muddle of the general election effort. Here, too, Hart perceives the hidden currents of history. For despite all the egregious political errors, especially the Eagleton affair, Hart believes that his side "lost the election on the issues." He argues that the ideological springs of the Democratic Party had run dry by 1972. Although the campaign brought forward a new generation of organizers, it failed to produce a similar group of young thinkers. "American liberalism was near bankruptcy," he writes. But for Hart the McGovern campaign was a beginning, not an end. If change was to come, then a new generation must assume power. But, Hart observes in his book, power is not passed like a torch from one generation to the next. "While one generation has power, it also has strength, and some fleeting claim to immortality. It relinquishes power only under duress, because the loss of power is a blunt reminder of mortality." And even the will of the young isn't enough to seize power. The historical moment must be right.

After writing *Right from the Start*, Hart decided to run for the Senate. He was 37 years old. His campaign slogan was, "They've had their turn, now it's our turn." It was 1974, the Watergate year, and the reference was obviously to Nixon. But there was a subtext. Hart's standard stump speech was entitled, "The End of the New Deal." In it he pointed out that while the architects of the New Deal were not doctrinaire, "the pragmatism of the New Deal has become doctrine." Hart asserted his belief in the liberal principle that "government is the guarantor of equal opportunity and individual liberty," but he warned that the "marriage of bureaucracy and technocracy," big government and big business, was "leading us to a two-class society— the rich and all the rest of us." His speech was suggestive, not definitive. He admitted he didn't have all the answers. He argued that only by recovering the original experimental method of the New Deal could we be released from imprisoning "old premises." He wasn't retreating from liberalism or his association with McGovern (who, in any case, wasn't a liability in 1974), but elaborating the insights he had gained during the 1972 campaign. He won big.

In the Senate, Hart received a seat on the Armed Services Committee, where he grew frustrated with the narrowness of the debate over defense policy. "Gary intuited that the choices before him weren't sound," says Larry Smith, his former legislative assistant, who is now director of Harvard's Center for Science and International Affairs. "It was fallacious to talk about defense only in quantitative terms. One had to focus on goals and objectives rather than on the percentage of growth in the budget. More is not better. Less is not better. Only better is better. The debate had to be reconceived." Hart's military reform policy had four principal aspects: first, officers should be trained as group leaders, not as bureaucratic managers; second, in the European theater, military doctrine should stress maneuver, not attrition; third, global strategy should emphasize naval forces, a post-Vietnam notion that deemphasizes land encampments; and fourth, weapons should be designed to work in battle. This is the school of thought popularized by James Fallows in *National Defense*. Hart's advocacy of military reform won him praise as an innovator and criticism as a technocrat more interested in instrumentalities than in goals. Hart says he never intended military reform as an isolated initiative, removed from larger considerations of foreign policy, but rather as a complement to a position in favor of arms control.

By 1980, according to Smith, Hart considered military reform as the "prototype for a series of policy redesigns." Reagan had won the presidency partly because of his promise of the prosperity that would be wrought by supply-side economics and partly because of the older liberals' ideological exhaustion. Hart set out to reframe the economic debate on the Democratic side, scouring academia in search of young intellectuals. He discovered the prophets of industrial policy—Robert B. Reich, Lester Thurow, and others—long before any other Democrat. Hart's intense interest in the subject was crucial in making it a major public issue. He sees industrial policy—an explicit and coherent government role in economic development—as a way to accelerate growth, meet foreign competition, and minimize the human costs of technological change. He regards the free market of Reagan's imagination as a myth. Instead of passive reliance on the "magic of the marketplace," he would chart the trends of international markets, restructure industries, and retrain workers. Hart feels that the post-industrial revolution we are experiencing is an upheaval every bit as profound as the first industrial revolution. His frequent statements on the potential value of high technology have often been interpreted as indifference to declining regions and industries. Lately, he has been saying that he favors a "balanced" policy, one that applies high technology to basic manufacturing. Still, he eschews protectionist measures, such as the automobile "domestic content" bill advanced by labor, believing them to be attempts to preserve the past and avoid the inescapable future.

Hart's recasting of military and industrial strategy began to mesh with his presidential political strategy in November 1980, after he had won a difficult reelection contest for the Senate. He began with the premise that for the Democratic Party to win and govern well it would have to distinguish itself both from Reaganism and from its own ossified past. The key test of a presidential candidate must be his vision. If the test were how many endorsements one could garner, Walter Mondale would prevail. But if the test were a new perspective, Mondale would falter.

Hart's strategy suggested two stages. In the first stage, the notion would be advanced that for the party to triumph again it must offer fresh approaches. In this stage, Hart would position himself as the candidate of new ideas. In the second stage, he would integrate the various issues thematically. Mondale, who deals exclusively in particulars (interest groups and specific policies) would be pressured to operate on a higher conceptual level. The idea was to create a non-conditional campaign, forcing Mondale onto terrain where he was unsteady.

Hart sought to advance his strategy at the midterm Democratic conference in Philadelphia. He presided over a panel called New Ideas for the '80s, with Reich, Fallows, and others, which attracted a large crowd of party delegates. It was the successful culmination of the first stage of his campaign. The second stage was foreshadowed by his speech to the full conference. It was a lackluster performance, and Hart failed to emerge from the pack. His panel had engaged the minds of his audience, but his speech did not engage their hearts.

Because Hart was not the orthodox old liberal, the "neoliberal" tag was applied to him, and after an article appeared in *Esquire* on the subject, he couldn't shake the appellation. In the short run, the label gained Hart a few early supporters. But in the long run it pigeon-holed him in a way that restricted his appeal. "We didn't have anything to do with neoliberalism," says Larry Smith. "Somebody came along and put it on Gary's forehead. It was a term he never would have chosen. The term was a political liability, a code word for a point of view insufficiently passionate about the goals and values of the traditional liberal movement. In the contest for ideas, it came too quickly, before Gary could mount his own definition." Hart himself says laconically, "Neoliberalism is irrelevant."

The second stage of the campaign, the thematic phase, was supposed to be launched with the publication of his book, *A New Democracy*, in the spring of 1983. The central theme of the book reiterated what he had said in his presidential announcement speech: "Far too many candidates and too many Presidents have been running against the very government they seek to lead. Government is the instrument by which we solve our collective problems." In a review in the *New Republic*, Arthur Schlesinger Jr. hailed the book for its "authentic intellectual curiosity"; but as a campaign tactic, the book was a flop. Unlike Hart's first book, it failed to link specific programs to larger themes. It was, as Schlesinger also noted in his review, a "laundry list." "The second stage has been much harder than the first" said press secretary Kathy Bushkin. "And the book didn't do it."

All through 1983 Hart was unable to repeat the success of his midterm panel, creating his own events, setting the terms other candidates would have to respond to. Instead, Mondale's traditional campaign of endorsements set the pace, as he attempted to present his victory as an accomplished fact even before a single ballot was cast. By fostering the image of inevitability, Mondale hoped to make it a reality. Hart, in the meantime, had his own difficulties. As always, he found it hard to ask people for help, whether old political friends or potential financial supporters. He appeared aloof, passionless. Above all, he was not offering the poetry of his own experience—the story of the rise of a working-class midwestern boy who went to Yale, committed himself to civil rights, the environment, and peace, and now embodies the future. He seemed curiously constrained, as though he would lose himself if he let go.

My first interview with Hart occurred after a long, exhausting day of campaigning in New Hampshire, where he toured a garbage dump, the Wilton General Store, the Milford town square, and the ethnic clubs of Manchester. He ended his campaigning at an American Legion Hall, where he spent a half-hour quietly watching a football game, drinking a beer, and talking with the patrons. There was no stir in the room. He didn't call attention to himself. His presence was discreet, but not remote.

Later, at ease at the home of a supporter, he talked freely. "I know I wouldn't get the endorsements of the AFL-CIO, NOW, the NEA," he said. "They're like banks. They play it safe. It's the nature of human institutions not to take risks. Most of the factions of the Democratic Party in 1960 didn't support John Kennedy. And I have been doing something very unconventional, laying out greatly detailed policies. By April or May, this campaign will have to get down to policies. There will come a time when memorized answers won't work," he said—a jibe clearly aimed at John Glenn. "I will be so much better prepared that I will win."

Why doesn't he tell his story? "Any time a candidate talks about himself I get turned off," he replied. "It's old-style politics. It's commercializing your personal life. It's so hackneyed and trite. There's a point beyond which you can sacrifice your individuality for ambition. I don't have to sell myself. I have to sell the need to change generations of leadership. I figure if people want to know my story, they'll ask. Why does it have to be personal?" To Hart, egotistical displays are sins of pride. If his ideas are correct, and the forces of history are in proper motion, he will be president. If they're not, he won't be. "You can't force change on a society that doesn't want change," he remarked. "If the Democratic Party wants security and certainty, it will nominate Mondale. I can't make the Democratic Party do anything." Instead of personal charisma releasing voter enthusiasm, he sees emotions springing from a logical course of events. "Emotion in nomination politics," he says, "is the product of success. The day I win my first primary, this will be the most emotional campaign of all. And I won't be doing anything different. Success liberates emotion."

Hart, who declined to become a philosophy professor, still holds to the philosophic ideal of the rule of reason. In Plato's *Republic* the philosopher-king enthrones reason in the state. He banishes the poet, who in Plato's scheme is a theatrical dramatist. The poet's inspiration doesn't derive from a logic whose steps we can trace. His appeal is to feeling, not to reason. "The dramatic poet," writes Plato, "sets up a vicious form of government in the individual soul: he gratifies that senseless part which cannot distinguish great and small, but regards the same things as now one, now the other; and he is an image-maker whose images are phantoms far removed from reality." By playing on the illusions he has conjured, the dramatic poet corrupts the character of society and overthrows the reign of true principles. When the president himself is an actor, a dramatic artist who governs through appearances, Plato's nightmare seems wonderfully up to date. The great philosopher's utopian *Republic*, however, was no democracy. In a democracy, even putative philosopher-kings must be dramatic artists. If politicians reject the drama, they reject the stage, and that is tantamount to rejecting the audience. And to do that is to deny the true principles of *this* republic.

In my second interview with Hart, I asked him about the quandary of a philosopher-politician in a democracy. "What I'm resisting is what Plato feared, the role of unreason, the cheap emotionalism in politics," he said. "I overreact to it. I think politics ought to involve human emotion. But I'm against the manipulation of emotion for human gain. Maybe if I were better at it I'd feel differently. Also, I don't find talking about myself easy. I'm constantly on guard against the manipulative use of my background. I can't use my upbringing to sway votes for me. I can use it to make a point. I keep looking for ways to reveal myself, but I can't do it unless it comes naturally. If I do it on a calculated basis, I can't do it. Phoniness drives me nuts, and politics is loaded with phonies. I consciously try to avoid what turns people off about politics—hypocrisy and shallow emotionalism. I am not an entertainer."

Hart wants to lead not by appearances but by ideas. His brand of liberalism, though anchored in enduring ideals, is experimental. His willingness to risk advancing unorthodox policies makes him a liberal in the manner of the young New Dealers. In this light, Hart's politics are traditional, for the traditional fundament of Democratic success has always been new ideas.

Hart's liberalism is a distinct departure from Mondale's. Mondale rallies the fractured Democratic coalition by waving the bloody shirt of the New Deal. He seeks to restore the status quo of the immediate past, which is the dictionary definition of conservatism. Reagan, for his part, is the atavistic Adam Smith liberal. He attempts to restore the free market of the pre–New Deal era without allowing theoretically for the modern corporation, thereby clearing the way for greater concentrations of economic power and undermining his own stated goal. But in a contest between Walter Mondale and Ronald Reagan, Reagan, even as the incumbent, still appears as the candidate of change, the innovator, because Mondale casts himself as the defender of the old regime, and because Mondale's inherent caution highlights Reagan's risk-taking on behalf of ideas.

Yet both men are custodians of visions of the past. Curiously, both claim the mantle of F.D.R. The original New Deal was a fusion of vision and policy. Reagan, the old New Dealer turned reactionary, understands the visionary element better than any other politician of recent times. He appropriates it for his own ends, frequently invoking F.D.R. Mondale has appropriated the programmatic aspect, harnessing policy to a coalition of interest groups. He asserts that this is the true tradition, and charges that Reagan is the aberration, the "radical." The split of vision and program is at the heart of liberalism's ideological crisis. Can they be reunited by the rediscovery of the experimental method that animated the New Deal? That is Hart's ultimate promise.

If Hart could somehow awaken this excitement and win the nomination, he would be in a position to mount a general election campaign unlike that of any other Democrat in the field. Mondale, the candidate of inevitability, promises a traditional party campaign. Glenn, the candidate of electability, promises a campaign of image. Hart, who is not at all inevitable, may actually be highly electable. Among other things, he would instantly raise the age issue to prominence. While Mondale's stolidity allows Reagan to look youthful, Hart's real youth would highlight Reagan's real age. Then, Hart the Coloradan would challenge Reagan in the West, the redoubt of conservatism. This political challenge would strike at the core of Reagan's image as an authentic westerner. It might unnerve Reagan to run against a young man who wears cowboy boots and stakes a claim to the future. Most important, Hart's politics of ideas meets Reagan's greatest strength. Against an opponent without vision, Reagan would be free to run against liberal "special interests." But against a candidate of ideas, *Reagan's* special interests might become the issue. Also, because Hart really does have ideas, not merely policies, and because they're central not only to his campaign but to his personality, he might at last be able to make Reagan's cavalier use of facts an issue for the first time. Candidates who deal in particulars concede ideology to Reagan, and no matter how many facts they marshal they can never project as compelling a vision as his. But a candidate who engages Reagan on the high frontier of ideology concedes nothing and may force him onto the defensive.

Just as Kennedy focused the scattered energies of his generation, Hart, if he is to succeed, must reassemble the younger generation for a new crusade. He must cast the election as a contest not between a Democrat and a Republican, but between the new generation and the old leaders, a continuum that runs from Mondale through Reagan.

The post–World War II generation is not a coherent whole. It contains three distinct parts. In order to forge it into his political base, Hart would have to appeal to all of them. He must speak to those his own age, who "gave life to the midlife crisis," as his friend Oliver Henkel puts it. "By the time we reached our late 30s and early 40s, the world we had expected to come into at middle age wasn't there at all." Hart must also speak to those at the center of the generation, those whose sensibilities were shaped in the 1960s. They're now iced in the big chill. Many are frustrated in second-level jobs, squeezed financially as they begin families, wondering if the hope of their college years was simply a naïve delusion yet still yearning for commitment and community. Finally, Hart must speak to those currently in college, the new silent generation, whose vivid memories are only of Watergate, inflation, "America Held Hostage," and Reagan; they have yet to learn the virtue of public life.

The present moment strangely echoes the late '50s, when Hart himself was awakened to politics. The young are mute. There's no great cause, and narrow careerism is an overriding obsession. Hart's detachment seems superficially to reflect the temper of the time. But he is beyond the moment in his devotion to an ideal of public life, so clearly at odds with the avarice avidly promoted by Reagan and the power without purpose emanating from some of the other Democratic candidates.

Reason alone, however, doesn't make presidents. There is, for instance, the mundane matter of money—of which Hart has little. And when there's no money there's no television, without which his message may not reach the voters. Even then, he would have to confront the voters' widespread resignation in the face of what's being presented to them as inevitable. Moreover, to take advantage of his natural assets, Hart must do what he's resisted thus far: he must reveal his passion, demonstrating his politics are not bloodless and abstract. That may be a price he will refuse to pay, because, as he sees it, he has protected his authenticity by holding back. What he wants most may be what he's incapable of having. If he fails, he will have recapitulated the essential experience of the rebels of the 1950s: he will have become an isolated individual unable to make himself heard while older men drone on.

(January 1984)

Mr. Smith Goes
to Washington

The most popular Democratic presidential candidate in the private polls now (February 1984) is a certain Senator Smith. Among likely Democratic caucus voters in Iowa he beats both Walter Mondale and John Glenn by two-to-one margins. Against Mondale alone, he wins again, 34 to 30 percent. And 71 percent would seriously consider supporting him rather than their current choice. In New Hampshire, 54 percent of the voters who say they will cast ballots in the primary for Mondale also say they would switch to Smith. Given his impressive showings, it's not surprising that Smith is admired on Capitol Hill. "God, I wish I knew Senator Smith," says Senator Joseph Biden of Delaware. "He's a helluva guy." Many representatives and senators want to emulate Smith because of his sudden rise. But there's only one insider in the Smith campaign—Patrick Caddell, the pollster. The reason is that Caddell made Senator Smith up.

Who is Smith? He is, according to a secret Caddell poll and a massive Caddell memo, a moderate liberal in his early 40s who has served in the Senate for a decade. He has bold solutions for the future; he doesn't support the past policies of either party. He calls for a new generation of leadership that will restore shared sacrifice and will put the national interest above particular interests. Caddell charts Smith's appeal by setting up a race in which his fictional candidate (disguised as "C") runs against two other fictional candidates, "A" and "B," who happen to have the exact characteristics of Mondale and Glenn. Then Caddell runs the fictional Smith against the real Mondale and Glenn. Smith always wins.

In Frank Capra's classic movie of all-American populism, *Mr. Smith Goes to Washington,* the old politicians count on Senator Smith, the neophyte legislator played by Jimmy Stewart, to be a nonentity, thus allowing them to go on playing politics as usual. Caddell's Senator Smith really *is* a nonentity, but that doesn't keep him from being dangerous to the entrenched leadership. Caddell, through his influence with a politician who doesn't exist, has gained influence with politicians who do. To them, Smith has credibility, that impalpable but essential quality sought by all candidates. They understand that Smith is an ideal; but they also see him as an instrument by which Caddell has discovered the hidden weaknesses of the front-runner, Mondale, and by which he has located the volatile primary voters and figured out how they might be moved. In the Democratic wasteland, Smith routs the hollow men. And the seer is the figure everyone seeks.

Caddell argues that there's an "emotional vacuum" in the 1984 Democratic presidential campaign, a "disconnect" between what the candidates offer and the voters want. This vacuum is what led Caddell to create Senator Smith in the first place. "If we substitute our version of the past for Reagan's, our placebos for his, our interest groups for his, we'll lose," Caddell says. "If we play neo-Reaganism, we'll lose; the public will buy the real thing. If we win without a vision, we'll relive the horror of the Carter Administration, and we won't be back in power for the rest of the century." Doom, in Caddell's view, is at hand. The curse can be lifted only through the advent of a potent young knight. Caddell scans the desolate scene and offers the scenario.

Who is Caddell? He is a 33-year-old political operative with more experience in national politics than anyone of his age. The last election in which he didn't "have" the Democratic nominee was in 1968, when he was a 17-year-old high-school math "nerd" in Jacksonville, Florida. In 1972, he was the principal pollster for George McGovern; in 1976 and 1980, for Jimmy Carter. He has become something of an independent factor in presidential politics. "Pat is a greater force than most Senators," says Biden, his friend and client. "People listen to him because of his track record and his great persuasive abilities. All he needs is a candidate." Since Carter's defeat, he's had many, including Harold Washington, now mayor of Chicago; Wilson Goode, now mayor of Philadelphia; Michael Dukakis, now governor of Massachusetts; and Mario Cuomo, now governor of New York. Caddell also has his detractors. In their view he is simply a manipulator, someone on a power trip who uses numbers to get politicians and even a president to do his bidding. Or he is a bogus philosopher, a con man who believes his own pitch. In Washington this winter, Caddell has frequently been tagged as a member of the Jockey Club, whose members are politicos without a horse to ride. Rather than watch the race from the grandstands, he would conjure up a steed. (Caddell, however, insists that every presidential campaign state except Senator Ernest Hollings's has held serious discussions with him, some firmly offering him positions.)

With his physical bulk and white-streaked black beard, Caddell resembles an excitable giant panda. When he becomes engrossed in conversation, he will pace the floor, pointing his finger dramatically, his voice becoming gradually more intense over a period of hours. But the real source of his influence is his mode of thought, which is not that of the ordinary pollster. Most pollsters are literal-minded and backward-looking; what counts is what happened yesterday. But Caddell operates on the principle that anything the mind can imagine is real—a real possibility—and therefore can be acted on. With polling, he's able to show that if the public were presented with the product, they would buy it—polling as prophesy. "The future happens while we're watching the past," he says. "If what everybody says about 1988 is true, that it's going to be the battle for the future and produce a whole new generation of leadership on both sides, then something must be occurring right now. The future is right now."

Caddell's new strategy is partly an attempt to learn from Carter's political demise, which Caddell thinks was rooted in Carter's inability to translate the themes that elected him into a conceptual guide for governing. As Caddell tells it, Carter was a brilliant candidate in 1976, "talking about positive values, looking at problems in new ways. He was elected to be leader of the society, but failed to become leader of the government. So the bureaucracy churned out policy after policy, choking the process. There was a total lack of priority of agendas; there was everything for everyone, but no one stayed bought. Then Carter ran up against economic reality." In July 1979, as gas lines lengthened and Carter's popularity plummeted, the administration's political crisis came to a head. Carter suddenly withdrew to Camp David for almost two weeks. In the council of state at Laurel Lodge, Caddell and Vice President Walter Mondale argued heatedly. Caddell demanded a transcendental "breakthrough" that would recapture the 1976 Carter. Mondale regarded Caddell's semimystical talk of a national crisis of the spirit as literally insane. Mondale thought the problem was gasoline, not malaise; he urged the president to speak at more labor conventions. Carter listened to Caddell. He came down from the mountain and delivered an address replete with morally uplifting themes. It was his last attempt to be born again. And for a few days he did in fact recapture some of the early magic of '76. But the abrupt and messy firings of cabinet members less than a week later—according to former Carter aides, the work of neither the Caddell nor the Mondale factions but of vengeful White House Georgians—dashed all hope. The Mondale-Caddell breach that opened during this episode foreshadowed the Smith-Mondale race of Caddell's 1984 polls. Two strains of the Carter administration—themes, represented by Caddell, and interests, represented by Mondale—are at war.

While the Carter administration was bleeding from inside, Reagan and the conservatives sharpened their knives. In trying to develop themes for the 1980 race, Caddell held meetings with the top policymakers, asking: "What is our vision of the future?" He recalls: "In the White House there was silence, shrugged shoulders up and down the line. The only way to win the election, since we had no vision to offer, was to offer the danger of Reagan." It didn't work. The principal lesson Caddell learned from Carter's loss to Reagan was that "we have to campaign on principles and ideas. Reagan is a man of convictions and belief. You can only best him when you put forward ideas that you fervently believe."

As Reagan enacted his economic program and the Democrats retreated, Caddell ruminated about the future. In mid-1983 his thoughts began to crystallize. Together with Senator Biden—whom he was beginning to think of as a potential president—he put together a speech that Biden delivered on September 13 to the New Jersey Democratic state convention. The 40-year-old senator told these party regulars that the Democratic "vision has been blurred," that the party has become "the broker of narrow special interest." To challenge Reagan, the "false assumptions of his philosophy" must be challenged and a "national vision" advanced. He closed with an emotional summons to the post–World War II generation, saying, "Our party must mend the broken hearts of my generation with the same tonic that fired its political activism two decades ago, and end the political apathy and alienation that have characterized it for too long." The speech electrified the crowd. Biden repeated the performance later that month at the Maine state convention. More electricity. Caddell decided to write an analysis "that would speak to the possibilities."

On October 25 he produced a 150-page memo portentously entitled "The State of American Politics," a critique of the Democratic Party and a strategy for launching a new presidential candidacy. In the memo, Caddell sees "national degeneration—greed, special pleading, unfairness, myopia, cynicism, stagnation, and disunity." The Democrats are "wandering in a political desert" and on the edge of becoming "a lifeless force." No candidate in the field can rejuvenate "the fading promise of the American future." In the meantime, Reagan "maintains the political initiative." His great advantage is his "ideological conviction."

Within the Democratic Party, power has been redistributed to the "Capital Beltway party of Congress, lobbyists and interest groups." The Beltway party has engineered what amounts to a "political coup d'état." The danger is that the Beltway party, to guard its interests, would stymie innovative ideas and nominate "narrow-based candidates doomed to eventual defeat." Moreover, the real party is ideologically distant from the Beltway party. Both are liberal, but the real party is hostile to the "establishment" modes of thinking of the Beltway party, whose favorite son is, of course, Walter Mondale. The result is a "public vacuum," with, Caddell estimates, perhaps three-quarters of the party's activists not participating. But he sees how they might be mobilized. "Presidential campaigns," he writes, "are won first and foremost on ideas." It's still possible, the memo argues, to mount a candidacy.

Caddell then describes an ideal candidate who would speak urgently for the "national interest," be explicitly "generational," and take risks which would certify his credibility. His salient theme would be that the "future is at risk." We face a "twin peril"—Reaganism and a Democratic Party lost in a fog of nostalgia and interest groups. The candidate would propose a new "social compact to seize the future." Caddell then elaborately details policies that might comprise such a compact, ranging from tax reform to industrial policy. Finally, he writes, the hope of "revitalizing America" falls to the new generation. Caddell dreams that its activism can be reignited, its commitment reinstilled, that the "apathy and alienation that has shrouded it for too long" can be lifted.

But like his earlier formulation of American "malaise," Caddell's statement is a diagnosis without a cure. He attempts to draw a vision from a critique, presenting his themes as if they were a coherent, fully formed ideology. But the notion that "the future is at risk," however true, is not an ideology. It is not even a concept; it is a fear. The "national interest," moreover, is a vaporous container that can be filled with almost anything. The weakness of Caddell's intellectual method is that one cannot adduce an ideology from studying the short-term anxieties of the electorate, however useful that study may be for designing particular campaigns. The policies Caddell describes and his call for a "social compact" don't necessarily flow from his logic. Mondale, just as easily as Smith, could support Caddell's program—and, for the most part, he does. In the end, Caddell's argument is a plea for a motivating idea in politics rather than the idea itself.

About a dozen copies of Caddell's mammoth memo were made, stamped "confidential," and circulated to his friends, mostly younger political operatives. In late November, Caddell tested his notions in a poll of Iowa Democrats. He posed two initial questions. The first stated: "While there is not a crisis in the country now, things are slipping out of control and we need new and fundamentally different solutions if we are to solve America's problems." Seventy-seven percent agreed. The second: "While there are problems in America, things are not more serious than they have been before and the solutions we've used in the past will work again." Only 14 percent agreed. Did Walter Mondale have "fresh ideas"? Only 18 percent said yes. And 56 percent agreed that both Mondale and Glenn "spend too much time arguing about the past; we need a Presidential candidate who will look to the future." Caddell discovered that the most volatile votes are liberal "baby boomers," among whom the men tend to be angry and the women depressed. Into this potentially unstable situation, which to those on the outside may appear calm and certain, Caddell introduces Senator Smith. It's no contest, at least in the computer printout.

In mid-1983 Senator Dale Bumpers was approached. He gave some serious consideration to making a run, but decided in the end against it. Senator Christopher Dodd was also sounded out, but he felt unready for the leap. Then the question was raised with Biden, for whom the themes were second nature. To Caddell, Biden more than anyone else was Smith. Biden mulled it over—would he give up his Senate seat, which is up in 1984? Was this the right time for him?—and decided in early January not to do it.

By now Caddell had taken another poll, this one for the Citizens Coalition for Arms Control, a group that favors the nuclear freeze. Glenn's support among New Hampshire voters was fading, the poll found, but it wasn't drifting over to Mondale. The ranks of the undecided were swelling. Moreover, by a 48 to 43 percent margin, voters felt that a new candidate should enter the race because "the current ones are not offering any new ideas or real solutions." Before the poll was commissioned, Representative Edward Markey of Massachusetts, a prominent advocate of the freeze, had been urged by a few prominent movement leaders to consider a presidential bid. When he saw Caddell's poll he paused for a moment but quickly decided to pass. Still, in theory, the ground was fertile for Smith.

Caddell had now figured out another crucial piece of the Smith puzzle—how to finesse the "frontloading" of the delegate selection process, the bunching of primaries early in the race that would seem to favor an established front-runner. "Frontloading," says Caddell, "has a perverse potential, a possible mutation. The distance between Iowa and New Hampshire has been closed to a week, maximizing the momentum factor with a surprise. If you surprise in both, come in a surprise second in Iowa and on that momentum win New Hampshire, you move into a situation with two weeks to Super Tuesday [the 'national primary' day in mid-March]. This candidate is riding momentum, mounting a blitzkrieg of free media. And there's probably not enough time for the party establishment to regroup and counterattack effectively." And then Smith would win. But the filing deadline for the New Hampshire primary, January 3, came and went, and Smith did not materialize. By a process of elimination, only those already in the race remained to claim his mantle.

"The irony is that I haven't been with Gary all along," says Caddell. After all, it was Gary Hart, as McGovern's campaign manager, who hired Caddell, then a Harvard undergraduate, in 1972. Later Caddell assisted Hart in both his Senate campaigns in Colorado, and the two men maintained a close if sometimes strained friendship. But for '84, Caddell was looking for someone with more fire. For his part, the self-contained Hart had difficulty asking for help. As 1984 dawned, Hart's campaign appeared stalled, partly because of his seeming inability to project emotional intensity. Caddell had run out of Smiths, and Hart was all that was left; for Hart, Caddell's strategy was the new departure his campaign desperately needed. Mutual friends insisted that Hart and Caddell talk. So Caddell found himself in New Hampshire, in a room at the Hanover Inn, on the campus of Dartmouth College, helping Gary Hart prepare for a three-hour, nationally televised debate.

Though Hart is the nearest facsimile among the eight Democrats in the race, he does not measure up to Smith. If Hart were Smith, then Hart, like Smith, would be running ahead of Mondale. In last Sunday's debate, Hart, like Smith, spoke of the future, of a new generation of leadership, of transcending politics-as-usual. And in Monday's papers, Hart got good reviews. But Hart, unlike Smith, has not vaulted out of the second tier. Smith had been the imaginary personification of None Of The Above; Hart is very much one of the above.

The story of the 1984 campaign of Senator Smith thus ends rather inconclusively, without a tidy resolution. Its anticlimactic finish, however, doesn't deter the drawing of at least one lesson about Smith's flesh-and-blood colleagues. Every study shows that voting participation appears to be on the increase, especially in groups traditionally loyal to the Democratic Party. Plainly, voters want to vote. But as Smith's strong showing demonstrated, they do not yet much want to vote for the available Democratic presidential alternatives. The gap between the public and the field is still huge. And freebooters like Patrick Caddell are pulled into the vacuum, where they can exercise their special influence. If there were no wasteland there would be no clamor for the seer.

(February 1984)

Mondale's Days of Rage

It took less than a month for Walter Mondale to go from one kind of inevitability to another. Time and again before New Hampshire he had declared, "This is the sweetest primary ever." He had expected to have the nomination in hand by Super Tuesday, March 13, 1984. When the day of his anointment rolled around, the issue was still inevitability, but it was no longer victory that was inevitable. Mondale reacted to his sudden reversal by passing into the first two stages of mourning: denial and anger. He expressed disbelief that this could be happening to him. He had, after all, constructed the most substantial organization, amassed the most money, collected the most endorsements. Politics to him was a subtle technical craft, and he had spent virtually his entire life learning it. Was everything he knew wrong? Gary Hart, his rival, struck him as something like "a Cabbage Patch doll," a "fad," whose politics were based on "hype" and "tinsel." But what appeared to Mondale to be overwhelming realities were not compelling the allegiance of most voters. The inescapable truths of Washington, where the Mondale campaign was carefully nurtured over three-and-a-half years, lacked resonance in the country. None of the constituency groups Mondale had counted on really delivered. What happened to organized labor? Where was the beef?

Mondale's politics have been commonly considered to be traditional. His rise from the lowest level of local precincts to the apex of national prominence was a classical odyssey. He is staunchly partisan, a loyalist, a "real Democrat." And his campaign has rested upon a coalition of all the usual groups—and some new ones. Mondale's campaign, however, is in its own way every bit as novel as Hart's. Both are responses to the collapse of the old party system, where the bosses actually could deliver what they promised. Within the Democratic Party, George McGovern's and Jimmy Carter's candidacies were proof that the traditional party had departed. Mondale appreciated Carter's shortcomings, but not the cause of his initial elevation. In 1984 Mondale wanted to re-create the traditional party whose last hurrah was the 1968 campaign of Hubert Humphrey, Mondale's mentor, who was almost elected president on the strength of organized labor's last-minute effort. Mondale's image of the party was drawn from the past, but he saw its reality in the self-enclosed world of Washington. His campaign ultimately has been based on wishful thinking, which he feels is utterly practical and realistic. "So," James Johnson, his campaign chairman, told a friend in 1981, "if it's a normal year, we win."

The essential premise of the campaign was to bend the selection of delegates to the Democratic convention to fit Mondale's strengths. To succeed, the campaign also had to bend the perception of the process. Mondale's most valuable resource was his Rolodex of contacts. He knew all the party people, the interest groups, the financial angels, the national political reporters and editors. His mastery of the Washington culture was complete. After Carter's 1980 defeat, Mondale could easily have reestablished his identity back home. He never gave a second thought, however, to running from anywhere but Washington. Mondale of Washington eclipsed Mondale of Minnesota; the establishment figure overshadowed the populist. Mondale felt no tension between these poles; he believed that he resolved the contradictions in himself. He considered his views to be a logical progression from those of his prairie populist father, the Rev. Theodore Mondale. To Fritz, liberalism was at once a movement of the dispossessed and a movement of a temporarily supplanted establishment. He conflated ideals and interests, which aren't necessarily in conflict but also aren't necessarily the same.

Throughout 1981, after the Carter debacle, a vast network of lobbyists and lawyers gathered around Mondale. In fact, almost every person in a top campaign position was a lobbyist, from Robert Beckel, the campaign manager, to Anne Wexler, the dominant member of Mondale's political action committee, Citizens for the Future of America. Mondale himself became a lobbyist when he joined the law firm of Winston and Strawn, whose chief partner is his good friend, John Reilly. As vice president, Mondale had served as Carter's legislative liaison to Congress, in effect his lobbyist. Carter had roots, Mondale had connections. He was the outsider's insider. Like many liberals who came to Washington to do good, he stayed to do well—a phenomenon so common that the formula has become a cliché. The Mondale campaign was the Mondale lobby.

At its heart was James Johnson, Mondale's longtime aide, who set up a lobbying outfit called Public Strategies, Inc., at 2550 M Street, N.W., the same address as Winston and Strawn. Johnson lives in a spare apartment across from the office. His life is largely circumscribed by a few blocks on the edge of Georgetown. His intelligence, according to those who have worked closely with him, is incisive, narrow, and cautious. As early as 1981, he was using the word "inevitability" to recruit political operatives.

Johnson conceived of the Democratic Party as a legislative body and of Mondale's nomination as a bill that would be enacted into law. With the divisive civil rights and Vietnam issues in the past, the campaign tried to express a new consensus. In the attempt to forge this consensus, Mondale implicitly accepted the symbolic claims of the interest groups headquartered in Washington. The AFL-CIO was working people, NOW was women, and the NEA was teachers. He had a vision of The People, Inc. And when he won an organizational endorsement he believed he had won a segment of public opinion. He understood public opinion only in a hierarchical and institutional form. By achieving a consensus in Washington he believed he had achieved one in the country; by mediating among Washington leaders he would become the leader of American society. Mondale designed a party that would appreciate his special appeal.

Like Edward M. Kennedy, he had considerable influence over the Hunt Commission, which rewrote the party rules. Both Kennedy and Mondale were insiders who used the rules to create an inside track to the 1984 nomination. Who would win the race would be decided later, but they took similar approaches. According to the Mondale view, the ideal delegate was someone who could be lobbied. What was publicly called "inevitability" was based on the submerged principle of "lobbyability," the notion that delegates would play the game Mondale had framed on the Washington model. By helping to shape the new rules, the Mondale campaign constructed a bureaucratic drama to drive the lobbying enterprise.

Its progress would be marked exclusively in quantitative and linear terms: number of delegates courted, dollars pledged, bumper stickers printed. The rest of the Democratic field was viewed mechanically. If the pace set by the Mondale benchmarks kept the opposition candidates' press coverage, interest group support, and funds low, they would eventually have to drop out. Then their supporters would have no choice but to support Mondale. No attempt was made to compete for the others' real or potential constituencies, particularly the essentially unorganized cohort of younger voters that came to be called the "new generation." Mondale operatives believed that they would crush all resistance by outlobbying the other candidates for the support of the party insiders.

The strategy was to present the candidate as experienced in the byways and folkways of Washington and thus more effective. But the strategy had a subtext. It was also an ideology, a justification of the key Mondale operatives' status within Washington.

By the end of 1981, the Mondale lobby was thriving and the candidate was emerging publicly. Jim Johnson started to use a new word: "chits." Mondale would compete against Kennedy in 1982 by picking up chits to be cashed in later. He endorsed more candidates, slept in more Holiday Inns, ate more rubber chickens than any other candidate. He was educating the party about the Mondale lobby. His appearances were tightly regulated by his scheduler, Rebecca McGowan, who exercised enormous control over his person and through it over his persona. The private Mondale is informal, warm, and humorous. But when some Mondale operatives brought up the idea of somehow showing this side, McGowan objected. "That wouldn't be *vice presidential,*" she reprimanded. Johnson backed her up, and Mondale stayed buttoned down.

On December 1, 1982, Walter Mondale, who had been appointed to every public office he ever held, from attorney general of Minnesota to senator to vice president, was appointed front-runner. The person who appointed him was Edward Kennedy, who did so by bowing out. Mondale had never won a position through conflict, and he hadn't run a truly competitive campaign under his own name since 1966—a full generation ago. His luck seemed to be holding. He rose in the national polls and the money flowed in; new quantitative measurements gave the campaign new credibility. Moreover, the path to the AFL-CIO endorsement, the crown jewel of endorsements, was now unobstructed. With Kennedy on the scene, an internal debate within organized labor would have ensued. Kennedy's withdrawal, however, stopped discussion. Labor was overtaken by circumstance and Mondale was duly appointed labor's candidate. The inside track, created by the Hunt Commission, appeared clear.

If 1982 was the year of the chit, 1983 was the year of the straw poll. On February 21, Mondale announced his candidacy, using the phrase "I know" more than a dozen times in his last dozen sentences: "I know what I'm doing." He was running as the unabashed insider, seeking the restoration of budget cuts *and* the Washington players ousted in 1980. He didn't explain, however, what shortcomings of liberalism might have helped bring about Reagan's ascension to power in the first place. To him, Reagan was an aberration, a "radical," whose rise could be explained only by external causes such as the Iranian hostage crisis. Mondale's understanding of history was exclusively partisan; it had just one dimension.

In state after state, the Mondale lobby contrived a series of straw polls, orchestrating contests where likely delegates would be present. The campaign would compete for and win interest group favor in forums of its own making. The straw polls were new benchmarks fostering the perception of "inevitability." It was a phony war that conveyed the image of success.

In the spring of 1983, there was an ominous sign. Mondale, thinking he would pick up a valuable chit, endorsed Richard Daley Jr. for mayor of Chicago. Daley ran the campaign of a front-runner and insider, evoking the names and legacy of his father, buried seven years earlier. Daley lost to a black insurgent, Harold Washington. Mondale was disturbed; he worried that part of the black vote might now be lost to him. Beyond that, he saw no lessons for his own campaign. He moved on to more straw polls.

And to John Glenn. The former astronaut was a shadow Reagan. Glenn's effort seemed to offer the perfect test. He matched Mondale's campaign asymmetrically at almost every point. He was conservative, Mondale liberal; he relied upon media, Mondale upon organization. By the end of the year Glenn had begun his long descent. Mondale appeared more inevitable than ever.

As Mondale marched toward victory, a feeling of resignation quietly grew among Democrats. He seemed to be the only candidate available to oppose Reagan, but he also seemed doomed. An NBC poll in Iowa showed that three-quarters of the voters shared these sentiments. Mondale fit neatly into the story Reagan wished to tell, a story of big government vanquished and free markets revived. With Mondale in the picture, Reagan could project his Manichaean vision; Mondale would play the "failed policies of the past." In a sense, he was Reagan's justification. For many young voters, Mondale stood for a closed system in which everything was known and had been tried before. He represented the end of the horizon, the death of hope. The undercurrent of frustration was extremely powerful.

On the eve of the New Hampshire primary, Mondale's dream party was almost a reality. On January 27 one of his top aides told me: "Interest groups, the establishment—they're almost not there as factors. Anti-establishment feelings don't turn up in the presidential race." Mondale had neglected just one group: almost everyone under the age of forty-five. In voting for Gary Hart, many in the new generation had a sensation of empowering themselves.

In New Hampshire, Mondale went through the looking glass. The tools he had forged and polished, and which he had flourished before an awestruck press, were suddenly worse than useless. At first, he was bewildered. Then he was filled with fury. His days of rage followed. On March 9, in a prepared speech at Emory University, he made a sour appeal to the new generation. "To appeal to your suspected cynicism, he would market himself as an outsider gunning for the establishment," he said about Hart. "To play toward your alleged insecurity, he would build a platform with plenty of room for self-interest and a little space for generosity. And to exploit your rumored taste for tinsel, he would drape himself in newness." And in Boston he said, evidently referring to Hart's separations from his wife, "I haven't stayed with public life to get away from my family. I've got a good one." Mondale failed to understand Hart's politics or his special generational knowledge. Hart was a mystery.

In the meantime, Mondale attempted to reinvent himself. His ads had previously ended: "This President will know what he's doing." Now they concluded: "This President will fight on our side." But could Mondale be the candidate of change, against the one who changed everything? A new ad featured black-and-white photographs of a farmhouse, a general store, and a rural church congregation while the narrator intoned: "Working on small farms in Minnesota, Walter Mondale learned that the strength of America comes from the land." Not from the Beltway.

Mondale now had harsh negative ads on the air, slamming Hart's "new ideas" as fraudulent and misguided. But according to private Hart polls, these spots served only to double Mondale's negative ratings. Mondale's greatest personal asset, polls show, is his "decency" and "compassion." By turning to negative advertising he risked his positive image, much as John Glenn had done when he ran negative ads against Mondale.

Super Tuesday was the reductio ad absurdum of the Mondale campaign. He had reformed the party rules to prevent another outsider, another Carter, from capturing the nomination. Mondale was caught in the devices of his own making. By front-loading the primaries he had created a mechanism that could destroy him. In order to save himself he traveled to Georgia, where he was embraced by Carter. Without this endorsement, he would have lost Georgia and with it, perhaps, his ability to stay in the race. Because of Jimmy Carter, Mondale could continue. It was the only endorsement that ever delivered anything significant to him.

"I am ready—I am ready to be President," Mondale told us. But Americans' image of the president differs from his. They don't want a president who is merely effective in Washington terms; they want one who's independent of the legislative process. So long as Mondale represented himself as the candidate of the congressional caucus, so long as his home state seemed to be Capitol Hill, the public wouldn't accept him as commander-in-chief. The more the Mondale lobby pushed its image of the presidency, the less the public saw Mondale as president. The separation of powers is an idea the public carries in its bones. Americans know what a president is, but Mondale has been telling them that they need a prime minister. Thus, even his "experience," his final rationale, is flawed. The people and the campaign have fundamentally opposing conceptions of the presidency. Americans are always ready for a president. They just haven't been ready for Mondale.

The Mondale campaign may go on, but his phantasmagorical effort to resurrect the traditional party has failed. The Mondale lobby was unable to rebuild the old organization on a new basis. Instead it constructed a political Potemkin village. The real political organization of the United States in the 1980s is not the network of mediating groups, with letterheads and mailing lists, on which Mondale relied. It is the gigantic web of electronic filigree, of broadcasting and receiving, that places a television set in every inhabited space in the land. To use *that* organization a politician must have a message. In recent days, on the stump and in advertisements, Mondale has become a full-throated populist. He has a message now, but the time may be too late for it. The public's ears still ring with the echoes of three years of lobbying, of caution, of the inside track. By denouncing Hart as the manufactured candidate of media, Mondale is running against what has become the real political process—a process Hart did not create but merely has understood. And by trying to convince Americans that "newness" is inherently wrong, Mondale is running against the entire culture.

(April 1984)

All in the Family

New York

Walter Mondale, Norwegian though he is, was a *landsman* in New York. Gary Hart was a Martian. "There's no box I fit in, no category for me here," Hart told me the day before the voting, downcast by foreknowledge of his impending defeat. Hart had come to New York thinking he had to supplicate the votes of Jews, who constitute about 30 percent of the Democratic electorate here. So in a major speech proclaiming his support for Israel, he came out unconditionally for recognition of Jerusalem as its capital—a shift in his position. When questioned, Hart blamed his staff for his previous position, which he then said he hadn't really changed. As in Illinois, he slid down a spiral of errors. Instead of reassuring New Yorkers, he confused them; and by appealing to Jews simply as a narrow interest group he abandoned his special political appeal.

No fundamental issue separated Hart and Mondale. Hart, in fact, stressed this point during a locally televised debate on April 1, saying, "We're all very close together on what ought to be the values of this society." In the absence of a defining issue like the Vietnam War, the candidates' styles became the salient issues. The New York backdrop highlighted their differences in a unique way. It was here, after all, that the New Deal was invented. The squire of Hyde Park, Franklin D. Roosevelt, united two great progressive concepts of government: government as instrument of a transcendent public interest and government as instrument of political coalition. New York also has a European-style socialist and social-democratic legacy evident in trade unions, journalism, and politics. New York happens to be the most highly unionized state, and organized labor is regarded by many, at least in theory, not as mere business unionism but as the principal agent of social change. The great days, the days of Wagner, Lehman, Roosevelt, are not forgotten. The emotions of many New Yorkers are still engaged by an old dream, the dream of class struggle leavened by patrician uplift. Walter Mondale evokes that dream. His promise is its restoration.

Still, the concepts F.D.R. once fused were divided between contending candidates. Hart asks for a government above interests. The Coloradan is a product of space, solitude, and vistas. He is separate—so separate that a lot of New Yorkers wonder if he is real. He is too alone, too autonomous. Mondale, on the other hand, is a familiar figure. He's the subway conductor, surrounded by a straphanging mass of party leaders. The Democratic coalition is his identity; he's the sum of its fractions and factions, and to him a consensus of these parts equals the public interest.

Mondale had responded to his initial primary defeats with shock and fierce anger. By the time his campaign moved to New York, his disciplined organization had channeled his emotion into a deliberate negative campaign intended to demonize Hart. Particular issues, such as Hart's positions on windfall profits and the Chrysler bailout, were raised less for their intrinsic importance than as counters in a larger strategy of undermining public perception of Hart's whole character and brand of politics. "We knew we weren't going to get 2 percent more support from windfall profits, and 2 percent from this issue or that," James Johnson, Mondale's campaign chairman, told me. "These issues were raised for the reason of creating a large question mark about who Hart was and where he was coming from. As long as Gary Hart was going to sail along as some kind of cosmic star in the stratosphere, we were not going to win. In Illinois we had the great benefit that the points we were making, the mistakes Hart was making, and the media we were using all played at the same time. That's luck."

In the New York TV debate moderated by CBS's Dan Rather, Mondale pressed the strategy hard. His television ads, crafted by New York's renowned political consultant, David Garth, were now on the air. One spot said: "Gary Hart voted against the Chrysler loan . . . but it was the same chance we took when we saved New York City from bankruptcy." Actually Hart voted *for* the New York loan guarantee. But by drawing an analogy with the Chrysler bailout, the ad depicted him as having been somehow against it. (Hart to City: Drop Dead.) In the Rather debate, Mondale emphasized the points already promoted in his ads. He aggressively moved against Hart before his opponent could establish his own tone. "Rat-a-tat-tat," said Jesse Jackson. It may not have been an enlightened examination of the issues, but that was not its purpose. "In terms of a contrast between Mondale and Hart as someone unsure of himself," Jim Johnson said later, "yes, it was very beneficial."

Inside the Mondale campaign, Governor Mario Cuomo's lieutenants assumed virtually all of the command posts. Like many other liberal Democratic officeholders, Cuomo had endorsed Mondale when it appeared that the contest within the party would be between him and John Glenn. The idea was to prevent acrimonious division, wrap up the nomination early, and unite for the battle against Ronald Reagan. In Cuomo's mind as much as anyone else's, Hart's sudden rise raised grave doubts about Mondale's political strength. Cuomo even quoted his mama as calling Fritz *"polenta,"* an Italian word meaning corn mush. Cuomo, however, would show Mondale what political commitment really meant.

All happy families, Tolstoy wrote, are alike. The "Democratic family of New York" (Cuomo's phrase) is one big unhappy family. Mayor Ed Koch dislikes Cuomo, and vice versa. Koch dislikes the unions and City Council President Carol Bellamy, who once compared him unfavorably to Dr. Seuss's Yertle the Turtle. Almost everyone in the leadership of the New York Democracy dislikes each other, regardless of race, creed, or gender. But they all assembled in a temporary consensus behind Mondale. Cuomo was the grand marshal. His warm voice, reading radio commercials he had written himself, draped the aura of the great tradition once again around the chosen candidate. Of all the thousands of endorsements Mondale has received thus far, Cuomo's was the most significant. It gave Mondale ideological vitality and historical legitimacy.

Even as Mondale mobilized, Hart's advisers observed his seemingly inherent weakness. Fully half of the Mondale vote remained "soft," not firmly committed. The stage appeared set for an independent insurgency, a classic Hart upset of the establishment insider. In New York, political insurgency has a history of its own, a tradition as old as a yellowing Thomas Nast cartoon of the Tweed Ring and as new as Cuomo's own upset of Koch in the most recent Democratic gubernatorial primary. Hart never found his place in that tradition. He made some gestures at assimilation, some attempts at becoming a native. For example, he stole Cuomo's most famous metaphor— "the family of New York"—turning it into "the family of America." This bit of rhetorical legerdemain, however felicitous, wasn't sufficient to make him one of the family. On the Friday before the primary, a private Hart poll revealed that 35 percent of the voters couldn't rate Hart. They didn't know enough about him to venture an opinion. He was an *auslander*. The problem wasn't the message; it was the messenger.

His identity crisis was aggravated by his campaign, which seemed to lack a strategic center. All too typical of his campaign was the chaos surrounding the production of a half-hour television speech, where he would at last make his case without Mondale carping at him. First there were tumultuous arguments among his advisers about whether to have such a spot. Then they argued about the script. Then an entire day was spent working on it, rushing production, completing it barely in time, and thereby missing all the press deadlines for breaking stories. Alas, no free coverage. On the air, the exhausted candidate resembled Raskolnikov in a business suit. Choppy images made his thoughts seem disjointed. He remained a mystery.

The one issue difference that Hart successfully sustained for a time dealt with Mondale's statement that he would commit American troops to Honduras until certain stipulations were met by the Nicaraguan government. On television a burning fuse appeared. "Remember Vietnam?" asked the narrator. "Our sons as bargaining chips. Will we ever learn?" By raising the memory of Vietnam, Hart's advisers hoped to arouse his natural base among younger voters and cut into Mondale's liberal support. Their research showed that they were on solid ground. But throughout the weekend before the election, Mondale inched closer to Hart's position, and a lot of voters inched back to Fritz. In the meantime, Hart was declaring his fealty to the same values as Mondale, noting that they disagree only on "methods."

Most voters may not have recognized it, but for Hart this disagreement was crucial. It went to the heart of their dispute, the heart of Hart's politics, the heart of his notion of Democratic history. On the question of methodology, Hart connected himself to the liberal tradition. "Policies fail," he told me. "Times change. Society grinds to a halt because the methods don't achieve the old ends. A transition figure comes along who's innovative and experimental. Some methods don't work. Some do. They become dogma—the New Deal. A religion is built around it. The transition figure never worships his methods because he knows they're experimental. Those who follow, though, build the religion. The religion isn't wrong. It's still equality, justice, and opportunity. But people worship the methods. This campaign is about finding new methods to preserve the values. Mondale is testing my religiosity, my purity on how I voted on these programs—like the Chrysler bailout. I want to find new methods. You can destroy almost anybody, especially a new figure. I'm trying to reinvent political language in thirty days. I'm not just trying to win an election."

Jesse Jackson, too, was trying to reinvent political language. "Nobody has a hegemony on originality," he observed in one of the debates. He was the true beneficiary of Hart's and Mondale's negative campaigns, partly because he was spared from being a target and partly because he could posture as a healer, even as he was inexplicably elaborating his views of "Jewtown" for *Newsweek*. ("If you can't buy any suits downtown, you go down to Jewtown on Maxwell Street, and you start negotiating with Hyman and Sons," etc.) The deep feelings he aroused among blacks, however, were affirmative. He was voicing their concerns in presidential forums, getting equal time on prime time. In New York he served as a rallying point against Mayor Koch, who is engaged in a vituperative feud with many black leaders. By arousing blacks to register and vote, Jackson is the forerunner of a black mayoral candidate. He builds the local base, even as he furthers his own aims.

On April 3, Mondale smashed Hart's base in New York, winning almost every constituency, including the fabled "Yuppies." It was, in a sense, the New Deal coalition revived, with one notable exception—it claimed very few blacks. Jackson is creating enormous fervor throughout black America; among his constituency, his momentum appears unstoppable.

Unlike Connecticut, which Hart swept along with the rest of New England, New York is still very much part of the older economy: only 6 percent of New York's jobs are related to high technology, according to the U.S. Bureau of Labor Statistics, compared to about 20 percent in Connecticut. For the Mondale base, the Chrysler bailout and protectionism are not just symbols of compassion; they express the anxieties of blue-collar workers in traditional manufacturing. Mondale's New York victory is the high-water mark of his effort—and perhaps of Mondalism itself. In 1988, New York will fall behind Texas in population; it will lose thousands of jobs in smokestack industries and gain thousands in high-tech and knowledge-intensive sectors. The New York that supported Mondale today will be more like New England in four years' time.

The conflict between Mondale and Hart is something more than an ordinary political clash; it represents worlds in collision. "It's two countries here," Hart told me. "The industrial country and the post-industrial country. What most people haven't figured out here is that the post-industrial economy of new technology is the salvation of the industrial economy."

(April 1984)

The Prime Minister
and the Monarch

The Democratic convention started the day after the California primary, when Walter Mondale fell across the finish line the apparent but shaky victor. He retreated to North Oaks, Minnesota, to conduct the important business of the convention. By selecting a vice president, he named himself the indisputable presidential nominee. Almost everyone in the party and the press accepted his premise. A week after California, according to the Gallup poll, he was 9 percentage points behind Ronald Reagan—within striking distance.

The North Oaks scenario had been written into Mondale's script years ago by James Johnson, his campaign chair. It was his idea that Mondale should purchase a new house, secluded and yet near the Minneapolis airport, where the candidate would reestablish his roots after winning the primaries. At home, Mondale would receive party luminaries and constituency groups. By demonstrating mastery of coalition-building in the post-primary period he would provide evidence of the superiority of his leadership. Now he had an open field; there was no opponent to hinder him. His slogan would be put to the test: "This President will know what he's doing."

Seven vice presidents appeared in turn on his driveway: three women, two blacks, two Texans (one Anglo, the other Hispanic). When Mondale interviewed Wilson Goode, the mayor of Philadelphia, who had held office for six months, the credibility and gravity of the procedure was cast into doubt. Mondale had brought the world of Washington to suburban Minnesota. In order to attract his attention, the constituencies began playing the game they believed Mondale had set up. They began demonstrating and speechmaking on the floor of the media convention. Judy Goldsmith, president of the National Organization of Women, declared that there would be a "thunderstorm" if Mondale didn't choose a woman. She threatened a convention floor fight; but what she threatened was what she was doing. Mondale raised feminists' expectations by delivering a speech at the NOW convention. Choosing a woman had been drained of its possibilities; its meaning had been inverted. A dreadful alchemy would make Mondale's gallantry into pandering. A moral decision had been transformed into one of spoils.

The press added a new element of volatility. Mondale had announced his goal to be party unity. Any discontent was therefore magnified, measuring the candidate against his own standard. SPECIAL INTEREST QUESTION ARISES AS MONDALE SEEKS V.P., read the front-page headline in the *Boston Globe*. The lead editorial in *The Washington Post*, headlined MR. MONDALE'S PROBLEM, said that the candidate resembled "the great importuner rather than the great leader," trying to "appease every group," who "repeats too many hack phrases." He must "establish his independence." Columnist Mary McGrory decried Mondale's "failure of imagination."

By the end of June, according to the Gallup poll, Mondale was trailing Reagan by 19 points. During his sojourn at North Oaks he had dropped 10 points.

Before the polls disclosed Mondale's predicament, his managers believed the vice presidential exercise had been a success, mainly because it was being depicted nightly on television. They thought the message was: Mondale in control. When political operatives with close ties to the campaign urged that Mondale communicate a larger message than politicking, they were told to wait for the acceptance speech. The campaign is seen by its chief designers as a series of discrete events and tasks. Each building block would be put into place at the right time. If the candidate is behind, have patience. It's not the moment for the big message. After the convention, after more construction according to the blueprint, Mondale will stand taller. Mondale's senior advisers did not grasp that the symbolic ritual they had created was conveying a theme, and that the theme was: see the "special interests." Mondale lamented privately that the criticism was unfair. He was just trying to build a coalition—and isn't that what the Democratic Party is all about? On July 6, escorting interviewee Martha Layne Collins, governor of Kentucky for six months, down his driveway, Mondale said, "I don't know how else to proceed."

Ronald Reagan, however, demonstrated another method. Before a crowd of cheering auto workers, he unveiled who's running with him. "Remember when it was fashionable to claim that God is dead? Well, today I think we're seeing that He is alive and well in the hearts of our people." God, in fact, is the source of the recovery wrought by Reaganomics. "We're grateful to Him," said Reagan, "for the many blessings He has showered upon us." No "failure of imagination" here. Claiming the mandate of heaven is a divine right of presidents.

Whereas Mondale campaigns as the leader of party and perhaps of government, Reagan runs as the leader of society. In Britain these functions are divided between the prime minister and the monarch. "Unfortunately," Mondale wrote in *The Accountability of Power*, "the world's greatest democracy has allowed the trappings of monarchy to overgrow the office originally intended to be a protection against monarchial rule." In that 1975 book, Mondale argued for a regeneration of the party system. The parties, in his view, had been undermined by the imperial presidency and the "electronic media." He proposed new party caucuses in Congress, a mixture of caucuses and primaries to winnow the presidential possibilities, and a "Presidential leadership which continually recognizes the role of strengthening and consulting the party in the exercise of that leadership." He called this vision his "ideal."

Mondale was writing in the wake of Watergate and Richard Nixon's compulsive effort to quell his resentments against the universe with the ruffles and flourishes of a uniformed palace guard. Reagan serves as monarch without the Nixonian atmospherics. When Reagan greets Donald Duck's voice at the White House, as he did recently, on the fiftieth anniversary of Mr. Duck's debut, it's a meeting of equals. Both live in the fantasyland of the American psyche, and thus are more popular and enduring than any party politician. Reagan implicitly comprehends this better than any recent occupant of the presidential office. Mondale disagrees in principle with this reality, which places him at a disadvantage against his otherworldly-wise opponent. While Mondale gladly labors in the profane realm, Reagan reserves the sacred for himself.

In this contest, Reagan's stance has proved more sustainable against the third party in American politics, a party with its own hierarchy, conflicts, and ideology: the press. Reagan's armor hasn't yet been pierced by the press. Mondale, by contrast, has pitched his tent in the middle of its firing range. The press has now assumed the role Gary Hart played during the primaries—the constant critic of "politics as usual." How the press treats these candidates reveals as much about itself as it does about the politicians.

In the mid-nineteenth century, almost every American newspaper was affiliated with a political party; the press was an extension of the partisan culture. During the Progressive era, the press developed a new function, as an extra-constitutional check and balance. It saw its task as exposer of the gap between ethics and interests. The press began to regard itself as a force for objective truth above the interests and against the parties, at best institutions of partial truth. The new journalistic method was "realism," the accumulation of shocking unadorned facts, which by themselves establish a point of view. Just as muckraking challenged the parties, professionalism conflicted with the old partisanship. By the time of Watergate, investigative reporting had become completely professional, justified by its ideology of strict, objective empiricism. The press rose to new heights of influence, and its ancient antagonist, the parties, declined. In the vacuum have appeared politicians whose careers are elevated by means of images and ideas. The absolute expression of this new political culture is Ronald Reagan. The press, for its part, has become more central in a system that its own ideology—an ideology of piecemeal factual accumulation—prevents it from fully describing.

When confronted with Reagan, the orthodox method has been confounded. Reagan's politics aren't a composite of particulars. He starts with unalterable assumptions, from which he derives his facts. The press exposes the errors of his details, but is constrained by its orthodoxy from systematically interpreting Reagan's ideology, the most important thing about him.

With the economy soaring, thanks to the largest and most perverse Keynesian stimulus ever, Reagan can claim his supply-side doctrine is vindicated. His performance allows him to operate on any level he chooses. And he chooses to float beyond any conventional press construct. He refuses to enter into the pigeonhole of partisan figure, having campaigned since 1965 as a "citizen-politician." Like the press, he's against "politics as usual."

The first artist to be elected president isn't diminished when the artifice is disclosed. Sometime soon a reporter will get his hands on the script for the Republican convention and excerpts will be printed in the newspapers. The exposure of the script, however, will not damage Reagan. Most of what he's said and done since January 20, 1981, has been scripted. The point is that his script has enabled him to outmaneuver his opponents, including the third party. Reagan can afford to ignore the tests the press poses for him. Instead, he creates new *tableaux vivants* in which there are no tests. He can fail on his own terms only if the scenery falls on him.

Reagan's range is both higher and lower than Mondale's. Right now he's perceived as the triumphal head of state. But he's also the leader of the conservative faction that's seized control of the Republican Party. If the election is posed as a race between partisanship and monarchy, the monarch will win. But if it's a party versus a faction, the party has a larger moral claim. Fortunately for Mondale, when the roles of monarch and factional chieftain clash, Reagan usually chooses faction. His Achilles heel is exposed when his loyalty to the conservative movement overrides the presidential image. That's when the scenery falls on him. On July 3, for example, he held a peacemaking luncheon for environmental leaders at the White House—an apparently fail-safe tableau. But the environmentalists were outraged by the appointment the day before of Anne Gorsuch Burford, the discredited and ousted head of the Environmental Protection Agency, to the National Advisory Committee on Oceans and Atmosphere. The president's patronage of a movement cadre, in spite of her previous indiscretions, tarnished his shiny crown, at least for a day.

Reagan's factional commitment has long been a potential political liability of intense concern to his handlers. It was the very weakness that his campaign had to mask in the 1980 election. Since September 1980 he has been surrounded by an extensive apparatus set up to protect him from his "gaffes." What's generally not appreciated is that these so-called mistakes are almost always flashes of Reagan's heartfelt beliefs, emblems of his factional identity. Reagan understands that the press must report the story that's presented to it. So the press has been presented with Reagan the king and denied access to Reagan the factionalist.

Meanwhile, Reagan campaigns as monarch. "Gentlemen, start your engines!" he declared regally from Air Force One through the loudspeakers at the Firecracker 400 stock-car race in Daytona, Florida, on the Fourth of July. *Roar!* saluted all the machines and people.

In Mondale, the press finds what it has been denied by Reagan. Mondale is openly attempting to put together a classic political party. Whenever a squeaky wheel demands more grease, the incident can be flatly reported in the revelatory mode. The press maintains its objectivity while telling a story with a moral—a moral about the partisan and the "special interests." The intrinsic merits of the policies of these interests have been nearly irrelevant in the media judgments made so far about Mondale. What has been crucial is his inability to lift himself above the interests; his actions are always reported as the reflection of material forces. Throughout the primaries, Mondale refused to believe that "special interests" was a real issue. How could it be wrong to demonstrate loyalty to groups that had demonstrated loyalty to him? His defense confirms for the press that he is nothing more than a party politician, someone without a mystique. For political journalists—unable to report on even genuine conflicts of ideas except as clashes between personalities or constituencies—Mondale is a congenial subject. "What you see is what you get," he's boasted. When Reagan is Reagan, the hounds of the press are thwarted. But when Mondale is Mondale, the pack always catches the scent.

Curiously, Mondale tried to establish himself in the post-primary period by repeating the vice presidential search scenario of that extra-partisan politician, Jimmy Carter. Mondale replayed Carter's novel process as though it were a tradition that must be upheld. He evoked Carter but didn't resemble him. In his own pre-convention period in 1976, Carter struck deep organ notes. And he was beyond the familiar categories favored by the press. In Plains, Georgia, he didn't seem besieged; the prospective vice presidents he summoned to his exotic yet representative small town seemed to be seeking him out. At the 1976 convention, Carter stood before the delegates as a religious white southerner who had learned from the civil rights movement and would apply its lessons of healing to the post-Vietnam, post-Watergate nation. He appeared larger than the coalition supporting him. The coalition seemed to be a natural coming together, moved by the spirit. It didn't seem the result of a deal that had been hammered out. Thus the convention unfolded as a liturgical epiphany of the democracy, concluding with a benediction by Martin Luther King Sr. and the singing of "We Shall Overcome" as tears misted the eyes of even the most hardened reporters. The power of this incantatory moment has been unmatched at a Democratic convention. Amazing grace indeed. It left Carter with a gigantic lead, a lead of more than 30 points. And even though he squandered nearly all of it, it was just enough to carry him into the Oval Office. Mondale must hope he will gain in the polls what Carter lost.

Reagan is forcing the pace of the campaign by slowing it down. With a slower pace, less can happen; his lead can remain unsurmountable. The subliminal message is that everything is going splendidly. Disturbing the calm he's created is inappropriate behavior. "We don't have to be engaged in the hectic, rapid, almost frantic struggle for the nomination," says James Lake, communications director of the Reagan-Bush Committee. "We maintain our Presidential character. And Mondale solidifies the perception that he panders to special interests."

Tick-tock, tick-tock. Mondale needs a new story, fast.

(July 1984)

Norwegian Wood

Minneapolis

On the eve of the Democratic convention, Walter Mondale revisited his childhood home, Elmore, Minnesota, population 882. He had left as a poor preacher's kid; he returned in glory, accompanied by the submachine-gun toting Secret Service, a traveling carnival of reporters, and a radiant vice presidential choice, Geraldine Ferraro. Yet he insists he has remained the same, someone whose past is plainly displayed in the present. "What you see is what you get," he has informed rallies across the country. But what do you see? A mostly inexpressive man in a gray suit, whose closest friends in the Senate had to learn the most elementary details of his personal life, such as his boyhood poverty, from newspaper stories. What do you get? A man who has climbed from obscurity to international fame, from a tiny village to the head of the largest political party on earth, from nowhere to everywhere. What you get, therefore, is more than what you see. "It's quite incredible," Hubert Humphrey once remarked on the surprising abruptness with which Mondale has progressed at every stage in his career. The qualities that have put him in public office and sustained him there are qualities that are largely invisible to the public. His flaring ambition and his extraordinary tactical shrewdness have been shielded from view. Mondale often seems to be wearing a mask. But his very inexpressiveness is a clue to the political culture that has made him. That culture explains much of what enabled him to arrive victorious at the Democratic convention. Equally, it suggests what he lacks—what he must find elsewhere, or fail.

In Minnesota the ultimate goal of politics is the achievement of an unspoken consensus. This constant quest derives mainly from religious and ethnic sources. The dominant religion is Lutheranism, which stresses ritual, authority, and social obligation. And most people are Scandinavian, like Mondale, who finds the poetry of life fishing in the silence of the north woods. The work ethic is deeply ingrained and often revalidated. If one works hard and adheres to the rules, success naturally follows. Good intentions are regarded nearly as highly as results. Trust is taken for granted.

Tocqueville wrote of an American society based on "individualism rightly understood." Minnesotans believe in what might be called community rightly understood. Virtually everyone believes that the helping hand of fellowship must stay the harsh, invisible hand of the market. This implicit belief can be seen in the unexampled philanthropy of Minneapolis businessmen, who give more to charity and the arts than any comparable group in the nation. And it is apparent in the assumption shared by both political parties that government must do things that individuals acting alone cannot. The Democrats and the Republicans (who are more liberal than many Democrats elsewhere, and don't even call themselves Republicans, but "independent" Republicans) rarely debate first principles. The argument is over how, not whether, government should serve. The parties debate means, not ends; issues, not ideology.

Long ago, when Mondale was still living on the Elmore homestead, the native search for consensus assumed opposing forms. One was the crass boosterism and small-town conformity acidly described by Sinclair Lewis in his novels *Babbitt* and *Main Street*. The other was the social solidarity practiced by the Farmer-Labor movement. Mondale does not figure in the beginning of this story, during the heroic days of class struggle, but in the middle, the period of consolidation and maturity. He moved into the house his fathers built.

The party that fostered Mondale began as a movement. Early in the century, across the plains of the upper Midwest, embittered farmers organized the Nonpartisan League to counter the grain elevator operators and railroad barons who ruled their fates even more capriciously than the weather. The League sought public ownership of the elevators and flour mills, and to attain that goal it endorsed political candidates. Most of its leaders were ethnic Germans, and during the virulently anti-German crusade at the onset of World War I many were arrested. After the war, the battered remnants of the League joined with the Minnesota Federation of Labor to make endorsements under a new name. This new amalgamation was called the Farmer-Labor Party. By 1930, galvanized by the Depression, the party came to power in Minnesota. Its platform scourged capitalism and called for the creation of a "cooperative commonwealth." Its champion, Floyd Olson ("I am not a liberal, I am a radical"), was elected governor. Olson was simultaneously ideological and pragmatic. He quietly welcomed Communist Party operatives into the fold, believing that an alliance of "progressives"—the Popular Front—was essential in the face of conservative reaction. The communists were used for their organizational skills; Olson wasn't led by them. For he also cut a deal with Franklin D. Roosevelt. In return for his party's support of F.D.R. in presidential elections, federal patronage flowed through it instead of through the local Democrats, who sank into a third-party marginality.

In 1936 Olson unexpectedly died, and the Republicans moved into the resulting vacuum. In 1938, Harold Stassen, the "boy wonder," founder of the modern Republican Party in the state, swept to the governorship at the age of 31. He was for "good government," replacing most of the patronage system with a civil service. Most important, he accepted the New Deal; and he implemented his own social welfare, mental health, and environmental programs. The Republican renaissance under Stassen provoked a self-defeating factionalism within the Farmer-Labor Party, which fell out of favor with the voters for years.

Not until 1944 did the gravitational pull of consensus become stronger than the centrifugal motion of factionalism. It was then that the Farmer-Labor Party and the Democrats merged, becoming the Democratic Farmer Labor Party—the New Deal coalition writ small. The internal mechanisms making the new party tick were precinct and county caucuses, forums which elected delegates to the state convention, which in turn bestowed its coveted endorsement on candidates. The Farmer-Labor wing of the party was initially fearful that without its old endorsement process the old Democratic hacks and scalawags would surreptitiously gain control. A stigma was attached to politicians who spurned the endorsement's authority by challenging it in a primary. To act outside the rules was an affront to solidarity; it made one an ambitious wrecker, a rebel without a cause. It courted the risk of going back to the days when the fractured Democrats and Farmer-Laborites roamed the wilderness.

The broker of the marriage between the Farmer-Laborites and the Democrats was a young political science instructor at the University of Minnesota, Hubert Humphrey. He infused the D.F.L.P. with his energy, buoyancy, and commitment. Only in the beginning was charisma necessary. Later, because the party gave life and support to the politicians, few really needed to be, or have been, truly charismatic. Personality did not have to carry the weight of politics. The party was the image; public discourse was party discourse.

Humphrey was a founding father, but not much of an analytical thinker. His doctoral thesis was a celebration of the New Deal; he assumed the basics. He operated in an ad hoc manner, often improvising his positions as he spoke. He was the great tinkerer, who showered his enthusiasm on every project. After Humphrey, the politics of the D.F.L.P. have been typically marked by figures for whom technique is substance and structure is style.

Few politicians in the D.F.L.P. tradition have maneuvered as skillfully as Walter Mondale. He has advanced his career by a series of adroit tactical adjustments. Within the state, he has been viewed as someone never quite possessed of his own persona, the protégé of one elder or another. Yet his appointments to a succession of offices were not gifts, but the result of energetic campaigns—campaigns, however, that were conducted out of public view. Mondale never presented himself to the Minnesota electorate as anything less than the incumbent. He has thrived by leaving as little as possible to chance. He makes no mistakes, except perhaps that he makes no mistakes.

In 1947, Mondale's political science professor at Macalester College took the class to the Minneapolis City Hall to hear the new mayor speak. Mondale was thrilled by Humphrey. He was caught up in a movement of academics in politics. Virtually all of the D.F.L.P.'s founding fathers (and a few mothers) came from the university mileu; they might have had humbler origins, but when they wrote the party's constitution they were neither farmers nor laborers.

Mondale entered the D.F.L.P. at a critical juncture. Anti-communist liberals and Popular Fronters were locked in a fierce civil war— the national Democratic scene writ small. Almost all of the commanding figures of the D.F.L.P. made their marks in this battle— Professor Humphrey; Professor Eugene McCarthy; Professor Arthur Naftalin (later mayor of Minneapolis); a son of the University of Minnesota Law School dean, Donald Fraser (later congressman and the current mayor of Minneapolis); and University of Minnesota scholastic and football star Orville Freeman (later governor and U.S. secretary of agriculture).

The tumultuous internecine conflict over a great principle mostly turned on tactics such as packing caucuses. Young Mondale became a leader of the student auxiliary. His first political success, in fact, was achieved by importing patronage workers to a caucus to win control of a county Young D.F.L.P. group.

For the founders, the civil war involved personal and philosophic convulsions. Humphrey, for example, had worked closely with some communists and came reluctantly and slowly to his anticommunism. "When Mondale arrives, this struggle is behind us," says Arthur Naftalin. "It's a derivative matter for him. I don't recall any baseline ideological test for Mondale. The programmatic is a given. Mondale gets high points on managing. That's a key to Mondale."

Working as a field organizer in Humphrey's 1948 Senate campaign, Mondale acquired a reputation as a crackerjack technician. He went to law school and joined Freeman and Fraser's firm. He was the bright young man—the safe new generation of leadership.

Humphrey remained the most eminent figure in the D.F.L.P., but Orville Freeman was the most powerful. Though the 1950s were a dreary decade for the Democrats nationally, in Minnesota it was a time of resurgence. In 1954 Freeman was elected governor; in 1956 Mondale was his campaign manager. He soon set his sights on a state senate seat, but his assiduous preparations were upset when the state attorney general quit in a fit of pique at Freeman. An election was held to fill the slot, an election in which only one person voted— Orville Freeman. But the campaign for that single vote was hard fought. The struggle pitted the labor wing of the party against the university-based wing. Labor leaders resented Freeman's reliance on a new class for his staff and advisers. They backed for promotion the colorless but loyal George Scott, the deputy attorney general. Humphrey, distant in Washington, would almost certainly have urged Scott's appointment over Mondale's, according to a close associate. But he was never consulted. Mondale organized rapidly, down to the level of Minneapolis ward committeemen. Labor spokesmen, however, told Freeman that Mondale was too young, too inexperienced. What they really objected to was that he wasn't their handpicked candidate. In the end, Freeman voted for Mondale in the belief that he represented the future.

Upon becoming attorney general, Mondale told a friend: "I'm never going to smile in public." He felt that an emotionless expression was the most convincing expression.

In 1964, Mondale arrived at the Democratic convention in Atlantic City certain that Lyndon Johnson would pick as his running mate one of Minnesota's senators—McCarthy or Humphrey. Mondale was ready in any case. In his briefcase were the addresses of every member of the D.F.L.P. executive committee and the text of a telegram urging them to support Mondale for the Senate appointment.

First, though, there was an obstacle. Johnson created a test for Humphrey that he would have to pass before receiving his reward. It was the year of Mississippi Summer, the year of moral courage and martyrdom. Now the Mississippi Freedom Democratic Party was demanding to be seated as the rightful delegation, supplanting the lily-white contingent. Someone had to work out a tactical accommodation to prevent the incident from sullying L.B.J.'s pristine nomination. Humphrey decided that someone should be cautious yet committed, lawyerly yet political. Humphrey administered Johnson's test to Mondale. Both their careers depended upon his ability to find a middle way between absolutes. Mondale passed the test brilliantly, managing to contrive a formula that, while unacceptable to the Freedom Democrats, was overwhelmingly approved by the convention; it was clear that the civil rights forces would be granted more than symbolic power at future conventions. Within hours, Humphrey was on the platform before the cheering throng, holding Johnson's upraised hand.

Although Humphrey was indebted to Mondale, he was not especially close to him. Moreover, Humphrey thought highly of Congressman John Blatnik, also in the running to take his Senate seat. But Humphrey's influence over the selection of his successor was negligible. The only opinion that mattered was that of the governor—stolid Karl Rolvaag, son of Ole Rölvaag, author of *Giants in the Earth,* the epic novel of Scandinavian immigration to the New World. Mondale happened to be one of Rolvaag's closest allies. The attorney general had a larger staff than the governor, and Mondale had put it at Rolvaag's daily disposal. Unfortunately, Rolvaag suffered from alcoholism. In June 1964, on a fishing expedition with Mondale, he had smashed up a motorboat while drinking. Mondale helped the governor back to the cabin, but he didn't report the accident to the police. Rolvaag owed Mondale for his tactful handling of the affair.

After Mondale was appointed by Rolvaag to the Senate seat (over the muted objections of labor, which favored Blatnik), he could no longer act as inside conciliator. Without Mondale as buffer between the partly incapacitated governor and party activists, the D.F.L.P. lapsed into momentary disarray. Rolvaag lost the 1966 endorsement, but won the primary. With the consensus disrupted, the path was cleared for a Republican.

The split within the D.F.L.P. after Mondale left for the Senate was not a conflict of principle. Just as it was being smoothed over, however, Lyndon Johnson escalated the Vietnam War. Humphrey emerged as an enthusiastic apologist. The D.F.L.P. split again, a deeper split than any since the battle with the Popular Front. Humphrey, for his part, tended to see the Vietnam War as another aspect of his earlier confrontation with the local communists. Mondale, the freshman senator, stood by Humphrey, at first from conviction that the war was righteous and then, as he became very quietly disillusioned, from personal loyalty. However, the other senator from Minnesota, Eugene McCarthy, a Catholic intellectual who had always been a singular character in the D.F.L.P., was not so passive. He broke the tacit rules and challenged his party's incumbent president for the nomination. His strong showing in the New Hampshire primary helped trigger L.B.J.'s withdrawal from and Humphrey's entry into the race.

By the time Humphrey declared his candidacy, it was too late for him to enter the primaries. He had to win through endorsements from strategic governors and mayors, who could deliver their delegations. To gain the support of the party establishment and at the same time try to appeal to the new generation, Humphrey appointed as his campaign co-chairs two youthful senators, Fred Harris of Oklahoma, and Walter Mondale.

Humphrey's style and Mondale's clashed. Mondale was always prepared and concise, whereas Humphrey was disorganized and effusive. And Mondale had what amounted to contempt for Humphrey's penchant for suffering fools gladly. "He was not in awe," says Harris. At the meeting where Humphrey asked Harris and Mondale to run his campaign, Mondale pointedly asked, "Are we figureheads, or are we going to run this?" "You're going to run it," the vice president replied. "You say that now, Humphrey," said Mondale. "but do you mean it?"

Not really, as Mondale suspected. Humphrey's campaign became a hydra-headed beast, with the heads snarling at each other. "The older advisers thought we were boy scouts," says Harris. One operative told Mondale and Harris about bribes he wanted to pay various influential state officials. "Out, out, out!" shouted Mondale. Then a friend of Humphrey's attempted to use the campaign as a scam for personal profit. "If that man ever shows his face in this campaign again, I'll walk out," Mondale threatened the sheepish Humphrey.

"It was the new politics versus the old," Harris recalls. "Mondale and I were more in tune with the new." The battle between the campaign factions was most intensely joined over the Vietnam issue. Mondale and Harris urged Humphrey to break with Johnson on the war. Humphrey prepared a major speech calling for an unconditional bombing halt, which he showed his managers. "Don't change a word," Mondale advised. Humphrey agreed. Then, as he left the vice president's splendid office, Mondale stopped in the doorway. "Do you have to clear a speech like that with Johnson?" he asked.

"Oh, no," said Humphrey. "This is a speech I'll give as a candidate. But as a courtesy I'll tell the president." The speech was never given.

Johnson was still in charge; his power included control over every aspect of the convention in Chicago he could not physically attend because of his disgrace. Mondale and Harris had an ominous feeling that the convention would be L.B.J.'s *Götterdämmerung*, with Humphrey playing the one who was immolated. They pleaded with Humphrey to have the site changed. But they were overruled by Humphrey's cronies. Once again, at the convention, Mondale and Harris got Humphrey to support a Vietnam statement that would separate him from Johnson. But the White House fell on Humphrey, and he hastily retreated. Out in the streets, chaos and violence prevailed. Humphrey was consumed by the flames. "I didn't leave Chicago, I escaped," Mondale said.

For Mondale, the grueling Humphrey campaign had clear lessons. He did not want to repeat the mistakes the tenderhearted and weak founding father had made. "Mondale worries about a person being too open like Humphrey," says Harris. "If he shows his emotions, he feels it might get him in trouble."

In 1972, Mondale was reelected to the Senate. At the celebration, an ebullient Humphrey prophesied that Mondale would be president. Mondale looked startled. By 1974, however, he was stumping the country, making the familiar campaign noises. Then he announced that he wouldn't run after all. Humphrey, who now saw Mondale as his extension into the next era—his political immortality—was disappointed. He made his famous remark that his heir lacked "fire in the belly."

When Jimmy Carter named Mondale as his running mate in 1976, Humphrey was elated. Mondale got the job not by impressing Carter as a pale Humphrey, but as someone much more like Carter. Cool, calm, and dry, he prepared carefully, as usual, for his interview in Plains, even noting the similar points in his and Carter's books. Mondale combined Humphrey's constituencies and Carter's managerialism. Carter became the last in a long line of political leaders to discover in Mondale precisely the qualities he needed.

Mondale's elevation was followed swiftly back in Minnesota by the D.F.L.P.'s fall. With Humphrey's death in 1978, it was as if the party's magic died, too. Wendell Anderson, who won every county as gubernatorial candidate in 1974, had appointed himself senator to fill Mondale's place—in Minnesotan eyes, an act of unseemly ambition. He was ignominiously defeated for transgressing the unwritten rules. Donald Fraser, who won the D.F.L.P. endorsement for the other Senate seat, was overturned in the primary by a former Humphrey friend, Robert Short, who appealed demagogically to the growing anti-abortion vote. He lost to the Republican. The governorship was lost as well. By now, Mondale's relation to the local political scene is more nostalgic than immediate. He is a favorite son, but no longer a real factor within the D.F.L.P.

Mondale's presidential campaign was predicated on the idea of making everything he understood work to perfection—doing what comes naturally. The kernel of his politics was the D.F.L.P. model. Mondale would get the endorsements and the labor backing, and would weld together the kind of coalition that he believed was the foundation of party success. And he would campaign as an incumbent, as he always had: "I am ready to be President." There would be no mistakes. In New Hampshire, Mondale faced the voters for the first time on his own as a nonincumbent. The winner was Gary Hart, who upon entering the Senate had remarked: "We're not a bunch of little Hubert Humphreys."

Throughout the campaign there have been eerie echoes. Humphrey had to disentangle himself from Johnson; Mondale from Carter. Humphrey had to prevail over McCarthy, who appealed to the young, independent, and moderate Republicans, like Hart. But Humphrey entered no primaries and had no need to attack his opponents. Actually, McCarthy was undermined by Robert Kennedy, whose campaign's range included the highest notes and some of the lowest. In California, in order to halt McCarthy's drive after his overwhelming victory in Oregon, Kennedy willfully distorted McCarthy's record. It was reminiscent of the hardball campaigning conducted by John F. Kennedy against Humphrey in the 1960 West Virginia primary.

Mondale stopped Hart's momentum just as the Kennedys stopped Humphrey's and McCarthy's. Hart claimed the Kennedy image, but Mondale, with old Bobby Kennedy's operative, John Reilly, close at hand, claimed the ruthless tactics. Mondale found every fissure in Hart and relentlessly broke him apart. Once again, Mondale's tactical talent was proved.

Now Mondale's micropolitics confront Reagan's macropolitics. In this contest, Mondale's experience and background are insufficient for victory. "When one comes to the thematic is when one first runs for an office," says Donald Fraser, mayor of Minneapolis. "When you're running for reelection you're less likely to do that. You're running on your record. Fritz hasn't had that first election experience. He has never been driven to that thematic necessity. He was forced to shift his posture in going after Hart, but he wasn't into a thematic approach in the whole primary campaign."

In running against Reagan, Mondale is inexperienced. He must show us what we haven't seen yet. For American politics is not Minnesota's writ large. The presidential political culture more nearly resembles that of California, where candidates, even for assembly races, are sustained by images and ideology. No politician there trusts his fate to party.

Mondale, the Minnesotan, never had to struggle to establish his political philosophy. Reagan, the Californian, is a founding father in his own right. He is the foremost leader of a conservative movement that has been transformed from a sect into a ruling elite. He has undergone a personal change from a leftist into a rightist, and therefore operates on a politically self-conscious and explicit level. He always casts his position in terms of first principles, while Mondale discusses discrete policies. Reagan's free-floating politics match his economic vision of an America without rules. Mondale, for his part, still assumes the centrality of the consensus Reagan has shattered.

At the opening of the San Francisco convention, Mondale seemed mired in the sort of politics he must rise above in order to win. As he deliberated over a vice presidential selection who would play Mondale to Mondale, he was barraged by a flock of competing constituencies. He ended the clamor by choosing Geraldine Ferraro. He graced her with the force that had graced him, the force of appointment. And her appointment, like his, was the outcome of an orchestrated insiders' campaign. Yet even though it was a calculated interest-group move on Mondale's part, the historic Ferraro choice carried him inexorably beyond interest-group politics, past the prosaic and predictable. The sexual politics at the center of the Democratic Party ultimately defied conventional categories. Through the power of appointment he moves into the unknown, the shadowland of hope; whether he fully appreciates it, he has entered the future. Mondale's promise can now be fulfilled only by transcending the career that has brought him to this moment.

(August 1984)

The Family Way

The Republican Party is a business; the Democratic Party is a family. Togetherness, not efficiency, is the greatest virtue, perhaps because strife is so recurrent. Only family members know how to help or hurt each other most. One must be privy to the intimate history to be able to produce true misery. Throughout the long presidential primary campaign of 1984, the pursuit of unhappiness seemed to be the Democrats' purpose. When they convened in San Francisco in August, the fear of yet more schisms had not yet been dispelled.

From the platform of Moscone Center, speaker after speaker accused Ronald Reagan of having fostered divisions among the classes, races, and sexes. Their description of what Reagan has done to the country was a portrait of the fractured party. By advocating a united America, the speakers expressed their wish for a united democracy. As in a fable, the dream assumed literal form. To unite the discordant family, a marriage took place, a marriage in which the man and the woman can't hold hands. By making a choice that was highly unorthodox, Mondale challenged the Republicans' claim to traditionalism. The convention became a sacrament of union.

The events had a classic four-act dramatic structure. Each act featured a soliloquy by a leading player, touching in some way on the theme of the family. It wasn't until the final act that the meaning of the theme was clarified—or, rather, that the next level of confusion became apparent.

The prologue was spoken by Governor Mario Cuomo of New York. He reestablished the founding myth; he told the tales of heroic ancestors. The performance, the man, and the message were all of a piece, a gestalt, a deeply personal, and nontransferable, vision offered as a universal vision. He presented the poetry about the past that Mondale himself never could manage through the cold months of being assailed as yesterday's man. Cuomo's evocative rhetoric, however, didn't diminish Mondale. Instead, it gave him a background against which he appeared more vivid, less abstract.

All the elements in Cuomo's vision are timeless. "It's an old story. It's as old as our history," he said. His imagery has Old World overtones: he speaks of a country divided "into the royalty and rabble" and of a new president, "a Democrat born not to the blood of kings." Reagan's policies are nothing more than greed, creating a "tale of two cities." This is a view of Manhattan from Queens. And if greed is eternal, rebuked before by Americans, why is it now embraced? The people have fallen through trickery: "glitter . . . showmanship . . . smoke and mirrors . . . illusions." The people are decent, but have lost "their senses." Reagan's election in 1980, in fact, was "won under false pretenses." The Democrats must offer such a compelling "logic" that not even a "slick Madison Avenue commercial" will "muffle the sound." What the party must adhere to is a "credo," whose first principle is that of community: "the idea of family." Once Democrats reaffirm this value, they can command the future because they will be in touch with the past. The path ahead lies through memory. "We can do it again. If we do not forget. . . . Please make this nation remember how futures are built." They are built by "the family of America, for the love of God."

During his speech Cuomo gesticulated with his right hand raised in the customary benediction of a priest. With his first two fingers raised and his second two folded against his palm, he distinctly made the sign of the cross, a subliminal gesture impressing itself on the subconscious of millions. Cuomo blessed the audience, his physical movements uniting them in one faith. Only through the Democracy could they find salvation.

Salvation, too, is the goal of Jesse Jackson, the speaker of the second night. Many Democrats worried that he would fabricate a crisis that only he could resolve. Jackson indeed came to resolve the crisis of anxiety. He presented himself as the outcast son, who wears a crown of thorns. And he invoked his own metaphor of the family, the Rainbow Coalition, which must include "the damned, disinherited, disrespected, and the despised" or else there can be no "redemption."

Jackson addressed himself to the problem of how an imperfect party and an imperfect people can fulfill a "perfect mission." His speech operated on three levels—the religious, the political, and the personal. And it was divided into three discernible parts—the cruci-fixion, the passion, the resurrection.

Images of death and martyrdom pervade the first section. Jackson speaks to Hubert Humphrey on his deathbed who counsels him on the need for forgiveness. Jackson measures the price of progress in the suffering of Jews and blacks together: Schwerner, Goodman, and Chaney. Tears of rage, tears of grief. Jesse is on the cross. He has sinned, driven a wedge between blacks and Jews. Hymie, Hymie, why have you forsaken me? "Charge it to my head and not to my heart." By our forgiveness he is born again.

Then, the passion of the dispossessed. Poverty, hunger, broken homes. Jackson understands that what Reagan is about is more than greed. "Reaganism is a spirit," he says. It is a "false prophecy." Reagan's failure is moral, not just economic. "Apparently he is not familiar with the structure of a prayer. You thank the Lord for the food you are about to receive, not the food that just left" (because of Reagan's cuts in food programs).

Finally, the resurrection. He recalls a childhood memory, hearing a preacher speak of Jesus: " 'If I be lifted up, I'll draw all men unto me.' I didn't quite understand what he meant as a child growing up. But I understand a little better now. If you raise up truth, it's mag-netic." Jackson becomes Jesus: "I too was born in a slum." And as he becomes the leader of "divine inspiration," the congregation sees its identity in him. "If one of us rises, all of us must rise." Suffering will nurture faith, and faith will defeat "false prophecy." "Our time has come. No grave can hold our body down." He is risen. *Hallelujah!*

The third night belonged to Gary Hart. His critics wanted him to praise Mondale and disappear for good. But though he declared that he would support the nominee, he remained an unrepentant son—no filial piety here. At the moment he spoke, he still held the loyalty of almost half the electoral party. To introduce him, Aaron Copland's "Fanfare for the Common Man" broke into a rock tempo and segued into the theme from *The Magnificent Seven* as the screens in the hall showed pictures of Hart on horseback. This *son et lumière* show was somewhere between a Marlboro commercial and MTV. Then Hart appeared, the high plains drifter. "Promises are cheap, rhetoric is hollow, and nostalgia is not a program." *Make my day.* His woodenly delivered speech was a barely concealed critique of the regulars. "For the worst sin in political affairs is not to be mistaken, but to be irrelevant." He presented a completely coherent position, his method of experimentalism and program of post-industrialism. He was the only major speaker to discuss industrial policy explicitly, and he was also the only one to mention the Vietnam War. Few really heard him. They saw, instead, his icy defiance: "We will prevail." Later that night, Mondale was nominated. Hart might have been. He avowed that if he had, he would have selected as his running mate Geraldine Ferraro.

Ferraro had been Mondale's fourth choice. When the vice presidential selection process contrived by his inner political family disintegrated into a public relations absurdity, the pressure on Mondale to pick a running mate before the convention became intense. He was initially smitten with the rather stiff San Francisco mayor, Dianne Feinstein. Some of his senior staff favored Los Angeles Mayor Tom Bradley. Others wanted San Antonio Mayor Henry Cisneros. Mario Cuomo and Tip O'Neill wanted Ferraro. For a variety of reasons the other contestants were eliminated. And Ferraro stood alone. Her selection was tactical, but what began as an expediency turned into a phenomenon. The arranged marriage blossomed. "This is an exciting choice," said Mondale twice, in introducing his running mate in the red dress and pearls.

Ferraro's speech on the culminating night of the convention was laced with the language of marriage: "Love, caring, partnership." She used the word "faith" seven times. She presented herself as the personification of change and yet against certain recent changes. She harmonized with Cuomo's theme of traditionalism. Her dream is of the restoration of the world before Reagan, although that world didn't have feminists on the ticket. Reagan has violated "the rules" handed down from "our parents." The "rules" work well for them and for us, and they can work well for "our children." "Tonight," she said, "we reclaim our dream." She means both a dream of the past and a dream that never was.

At last, it's Mondale's turn. He talks about "recapturing the best in our tradition." But this isn't a flat summary; it's time for a surprise ending. To begin with, Mondale repudiates Cuomo's logic. No, Reagan didn't win because he fooled people. He won because of "our mistakes." Just as Jackson confessed his personal transgressions, so did Mondale. He is chastened by Reagan, and he has adjusted his position accordingly. He advocates "no defense cuts that weaken our security; no business taxes that weaken our economy; no laundry lists that raid our treasury." Mondale will reduce the budget deficit by two-thirds by the end of his term; he'll cut spending, *and* he'll raise taxes. The crowd thunders approval.

This promise to tax us seems to be an extraordinarily forthright and strong statement. Actually, Mondale's rhetoric and Reagan's practice have passed each other going in opposite directions. For decades the Democrats attempted to convince Republicans that the federal budget ought not to be confused with the household budget. Now Mondale has dispensed with the old-time Keynesian religion. While everyone, including Reagan, views the current deficit as too large, Mondale takes an extreme position; he seems to have turned against deficits per se. Reagan's political popularity, in the meantime, is buoyed by military Keynesianism and tax cuts which, though advertised as supply-side, have as their main consequence burgeoning consumer demand. Senator Edward Kennedy, in his introduction of Mondale to the convention, derided Reagan as a "California Coolidge." Mondale's program, however, is almost literally a reiteration of Hoover's—tax increases, a balanced budget, and protectionism. He is trying to sell a policy of austerity in a boom. Moreover, he's promoting retro-Hooverism to an electorate accustomed to thinking of him in terms of largesse. But the image of Mondale playing against type was precisely what captivated the convention. He's the new Mondale, with the old values. "And now," said the head of the family, "we leave San Francisco—together." The thousands of delegates waved thousands of flags, sang patriotic hymns, and bopped to "Beat It." Gerry Ferraro boogied across the platform. Mondale stood smiling—the husband who doesn't dance.

The Democrats' rediscovery of traditionalism is a heartfelt tactic aimed at recapturing their working-class constituency, much of which defected in 1980. The Democrats' tolerance for diversity, they can now say, flows from their orthodoxy; they're open because they're close-knit. The Mondale-Ferraro nuclear family at the party's center is proof of the claim. Reagan's orthodoxy, by contrast, is threatening to those who don't share it. With Ferraro, the Democrats may have the "social issues" coming and going. Can this compensate for Mondale's befuddled economics?

More than anyone else, Geraldine Ferraro embodies the ambivalence of the party toward change and tradition, a conflict that dangerously fragmented the party during the primary campaign. The success of the ticket may depend upon her ability to maintain the balance. No other vice presidential candidate has been the focus of such tension. She cannot do it alone. Mondale must be a good provider and at the same time support her independence. They must make this modern marriage work—if nothing else, for the sake of the children.

(August 1984)

The GOP "Me Decade"

Dallas

Ronald Reagan's hypocrisy works so effectively because he doesn't know he's a hypocrite. At least that's how some of his senior advisers explain it. While he rails against the breakdown of traditional values, his political operatives point to his daughter Patti, the antinuclear activist married to her yoga instructor; his son Ron, the ballet-dancer-turned-freelance-writer; and First Daughter Maureen, the divorced feminist. Reagan's handlers understand that in the eyes of voters the president's public intolerance is softened and contradicted by his private tolerance. Without his hypocrisy, they assert, he would be perceived as brittle and threatening. And because he lacks self-consciousness about his inconsistency, he can perform his political chores with convincing sincerity.

The hypocrisy that works so well for him on social issues also helps him sell his economic policies. His federal deficit encapsulates his hypocrisy here. He religiously condemns the sin, but it's what's making him happy. He has "MasterCarded" the recovery: reelect now, pay later.

To conservatives such as Reagan, Keynesianism has been more than an economic doctrine; the cultural consequences of Keynesianism meant the destruction of the Protestant ethic and the self-regulating market. If Keynesianism worked, then the old gospel of success must be humbug. By deficit spending, one could get something now and never be punished. Prosperity no longer could be traced to the moral character of striving individuals as in Horatio Alger's novellas, the kind Reagan grew up on. Thus, only by suppressing big government could America be restored. Then wealth would again be dependent on positive thinking. Reaganism is the mind cure for the bad dream of Keynesianism. When we believe, the good dreams of the past will come true. While Reagan waits for utopia, there's a free lunch.

Reagan is more a hero of consumption than production. Old-fashioned production means sacrificing oneself to an impersonal process, while modern consumption means personal transformation through appearances. Reagan represents consumption without guilt. And through his rise in the entertainment industry and the leisure class, he's been ironically able to convince us that he embodies the old ideology of a productive class. His free-market rhetoric gives a license to unfettered consumption. The clue is that pain and denial, the stock-in-trade of economic puritanism, never figure in Reagan's formula. Some of his top aides appreciate that this juncture between his words and results accounts for much of his political magic. He allows us to have whatever we want so long as we give credence to an obsolescent ideology. He's a permissive father. Ask Patti.

The two sides of Reagan don't invalidate each other, but exist in a comfortable coalition. Only he holds the disparate themes together, as the Republican convention demonstrated. The parade of 1988 hopefuls signaled that the party will splinter when Reagan moves on. And more than future factionalism was obvious: the incoherence of Reaganism itself was revealed. When not enveloped by Reagan's most relaxed persona, the raw themes stood out in frightful relief. For the first three nights of the convention, intolerance and greed were on conspicuous display. Then Reagan abandoned his attractive hypocrisy and joined in the spirit of conservatism triumphant.

The Republican convention in August 1984 was the apotheosis of the "me decade." For the Republicans, the rich have the same function that the poor have for the Democrats: they are objects of compassion and even pity. Since a majority of the GOP delegates had annual incomes in excess of $50,000, their concern was empathetic. For them, a vote for Reagan is a vote for immediate gratification. In this respect, they are true legatees of the 1960s.

The 1960s promised both self-fulfillment and community, but a community without any sense of duty or public virtue, a community whose ethereal harmony was natural. Since this harmony was elusive, it couldn't be sustained. The impulse for community remains, however, in partially bureaucratized form in the Democratic constituency groups. In the meantime, the self-fulfillment aspect has triumphed within the Republican Party. And Reagan has emerged as the avatar of a new age of narcissism, where the pursuit of happiness has been reduced to the ruthless pursuit of money. What hedonism and unbridled capitalism have in common is the repudiation of the social contract. When the conservatives say "me," they don't say it like the "me generation," satirized by Tom Wolfe, who meant a supra-consciousness beyond the material world, a cosmic union in the noösphere. When they say "me," they mean me, myself, and mine. They don't mean anything as altruistic as an interest group, which inevitably means others. They're not an interest group, but America; and they define America as themselves. Others can join them by becoming them. All one needs is the membership fee.

Dallas was an inspired choice for the convention. The town's boosters depict it as a wide open frontier, but it's tightly controlled at the top by a self-perpetuating élite. It's a city of blinding heat, freeways, and mirrored-glass buildings; it makes Los Angeles look like Cambridge. (One wag said, "The only reflective thing here is the glass.") Most important, Dallas is both a place and a fantasy. There's Dallas and there's *Dallas,* the television soap opera. After the Republican platform committee finished bashing the remnants of moderate Republicanism—just as J.R. crushes Cliff Barnes every week—its members basked at an exclusive party at Southfork Ranch, the set of the mythical Ewings. Southfork, a shrine to greed, has become Dallas's most popular tourist attraction, more popular now than Dealey Plaza.

The convention opened with the bombastic presentation of Olympic gold medalists. "U.S.A.! U.S.A.!" Just as U.S.A. wasted the opposition in the Olympic games, the Republicans would waste the Democrats. Thus began a systematic effort to portray the Democratic Party as somehow illegitimate and un-American. The intent was not merely to discredit Walter Mondale. In order to build a Republican majority, the Democrats would have to be thoroughly smashed. Through almost every major speech ran a theme of the Democrats' suspect patriotism.

The true keynoter was Jeane Kirkpatrick, the United Nations ambassador. She traced virtually all foreign policy problems to "the last Democratic administration." Reagan's inauguration marked "a reaffirmation of historic American ideals" and "confidence in the legitimacy and success of American institutions." (Did Jimmy Carter believe American institutions were illegitimate?) All the Reagan administration's foreign policy difficulties were attributed to external causes. And making matters "dangerous" is the "blame America first crowd"—namely, the "San Francisco Democrats," whose convention wasn't that of real Democrats. Kirkpatrick, not Mondale, is the legitimate heir of Hubert Humphrey. We must end "endless self-criticism," stop feeling guilty, and defend ourselves.

The next night, former President Gerald Ford suggested, "Let's save a lot of time and make the reelection of President Reagan unanimous!" (That would be one way to end "self-criticism.") But Ford was too lily-livered for many conservatives. On his special evening, the National Conservative Political Action Committee, a New Right group that targets liberals for termination with extreme prejudice, held what amounted to a counterconvention at Nelson Bunker Hunt's Circle T Ranch, a Texas Bavaria. This was not the Dallas Museum of Art crowd. Sides of longhorn steer—the hors d'oeuvres— were basted over hot coals. Indians in war bonnets danced. Cowboys performed rope tricks, a stagecoach rolled guests around a trail, and a huge brahma bull was saddled up for rides: *Yahoo!* (Honest—one woman, on the bull, yelled *"Yahoo!"*) Celebrities circulated. "I loved you in *Planet of the Apes,*" a woman gushed to Charlton Heston. "Moses, Moses!" beseeched another fan.

After gorging on barbecue, the almost two thousand guests entered a gigantic air-conditioned white tent about as big as Texas Stadium for dinner. At the tent's entrance a NCPAC videotape of the history of the world, ending in its salvation by Reagan's election, was on sale. Suddenly, in slow motion, we see Reagan shot by John Hinckley: "A gunman's bullet almost did what the president's critics have not been able to do." But soon Reagan's smiling again. Jerry Falwell of Moral Majority walks by and catches Reagan's face on the screen. "Is that real?" he asked. Or is it Memorex? "Oh, he's not here yet?"

Inside the big top, plates of cold tenderloin were served, followed by NCPAC leader, Terry Dolan, with short hair, manicured moustache, tight knit shirt, stacked-heel boots, and tight jeans, a pair of sunglasses with aviator frames inserted neatly into his back pocket, who pranced up to the microphone. He delivered a diatribe against the press, featuring a personal attack on *Washington Post* columnist Mary McGrory, a representative agent of demonic forces. To these conservatives, the press is the moral equivalent of communism. Pat Boone, the singer, tried to lighten things up: "How do you like this air conditioning? Who said Republicans don't care about the environment? If we don't like it, we change it." Then Chad Everett, star of "Medical Center" and a genius-level cretin, made a speech: "I want you to help me to invite you to welcome me." Finally, Bob Hope appeared: "Four, three, two, one. I'm just testing the microphone. We bomb in five minutes. I hope I don't." Hope led the crowd on a tour through the mausoleum of popular culture: *Thanks for the memories*. And then there was a mad rush for the valet parking.

The next day, Republican women held a proper luncheon for the First Lady at the pharaonic Anatole Hotel, whose three marble atriums are sufficiently large to serve as a museum for the pyramids. The main speaker was Joan Rivers, the laughing hyena of Republicanism. No pathos about capital shortage here. When Reagan talks about a "city on a hill," she knows he's talking about Beverly Hills. "I never do housework," she said. "That's the fun of being a Republican." The ladies tittered nervously. They weren't sure whether to laugh or express shock. Rivers's heartfelt vulgarity was shattering the veneer of hypocrisy.

That night, Barry Goldwater, who suffered the lowest moment of recent GOP history, crowed at the highest moment. He labeled every war in the twentieth century a "Democrat war," and charged: "Don't you Democrat leaders try to tell me that Americans don't honor and love America!" His argument was, in substance, no different from Kirkpatrick's, although it lacked her artifice. Still, he was there first.

After Goldwater's fulmination, Reagan was nominated. Thousands of red, white, and blue balloons descended from the ceiling. Within minutes the delegates committed genocide in a burst of enthusiasm and popping. Not a single balloon was taken prisoner. Reagan had come to Dallas, to the Anatole Hotel, that afternoon. He proclaimed the GOP to be "America's party," like that model of corporate efficiency—the Dallas Cowboys. But if the Republican Party is America's, then what's the Democratic Party? Why should we even have another party?

The next morning, August 23, Reagan addressed a prayer breakfast of more than ten thousand supporters. In his speech he offered a profoundly confused political theology. He claimed that the Founding Fathers "saw the state, in fact, as a form of moral order." But, in the 1960s, "we began to make great steps toward secularizing our nation." The secularizers are "intolerant" and "care only for the interests of the state." (But wasn't the federal government "a form of moral order"? Did it lose its moral underpinnings in the 1960s? How can those who believe the American identity is not reflected in the national government also assert that that government was invested in the beginning with divine purpose? Does it follow that if there's prayer in public schools, conservatives will believe that government possesses an imminent morality?) Reagan then declared politics and morality, which has its foundation "in religion," to be "inseparable," contradicting Jefferson's injunction against theocracy. "Without God," Reagan said, "there is no virtue." (It must follow that those who are "secularizing" are without virtue. They deprive America of virtue. They are against God.) "America's party" is attempting to restore our rightful relationship with God. Reagan's fellow worshippers roared approval of the logic of holy war.

By the time of Reagan's acceptance speech, replete with more Democrat-bashing—"unconscionable . . . cease its obstructionist ways"—some of his political advisers began to think that the harsh tone of the convention was not working for them. The Democratic Party, after all, is still the majority party. To succeed, Republicans must cajole the opposition to their side. By focusing the brunt of the attack on the party, the convention speakers may have reminded Democrats—and independents—why they are not Republicans. When the first post-convention polls came in, Reagan gained virtually no ground—an extraordinarily poor performance, even with his large lead. He had apparently reached his limit. Some Reagan advisers worry that his hard-edged stance on social issues might prevent some Democrats from voting for him. Reagan the laid-back, Reagan the tolerant hypocrite, Reagan the "me decade" dreamer, is the Reagan who wins biggest.

Mondale in his call for a "new realism," celebration of "hard work," and insistence on new taxes, seems to believe we must punish ourselves for our binge of self-indulgence under Reagan. Mondale's problem isn't that he overpromises, but that he underpromises. Liberals used to be the advocates of leisure, not misplaced puritanism. Even farsighted labor leaders such as Walter Reuther thought cogently about how leisure would liberate the working class. Now, through a weird alchemy, conservatives under Reagan have appropriated leisure from the liberals. While Mondale presents work as bitter medicine, Reagan says it's the road to self-fulfillment, even superstardom. Reagan is "Miller Time," Mondale is the factory whistle. Reagan promises that just possibly, if you dream hard enough, you can be rich, famous, not work hard, and live almost forever—like him. In the end, Americans want the pursuit of happiness, not blood, sweat, and tears. Almost always, the party of leisure wins elections. In recent history, that is usually the party of deficits. Reagan condemns what sustains him, and dreams on.

 About a month before the convention, according to a top political aide, Reagan screened the movie *Ghostbusters* at Camp David. "That was great!" the president said. "It was better than movies when I was making them. You know why? If they had made *Ghostbusters* back then, the whole thing would've been a dream and the guy would've woken up at the end."

All power to the imagination!

(September 1984)

Spurious George

Philadelphia

The morning after his debate with Geraldine Ferraro, George Bush stood before a crowd of cheering longshoremen on the docks of Elizabeth, New Jersey, while Floyd Patterson and Joe Frazier outfitted him with enormous boxing gloves. *"Fantastic* individuals," chirped Bush. Then he whispered to a union official, man to man, "We tried to kick a little ass last night." But his sly smirk rapidly contorted into an expression of embarrassed rage when he realized that his microphone was still on. "Whoops! Oh God, he heard me! Turn that thing off!"

With this crude display the vice president accomplished the opposite of what he intended. His strained effort to be one of the boys proved nothing so much as his distance from them. He defended his gracelessness as "an old Texas football expression," only underlining his inauthenticity. Bush never played "Texas football." He was captain of the baseball team, and the team was Yale's. One of the boys is one of the many things George Bush is not.

Bush is a Yankee who tried to make it as a cowboy, and the Stetson makes him a very peculiar-looking Yankee indeed. He's too conservative to be a New England Republican, yet he's not a blood-red Sunbelt conservative, and he's not a moderate, either. He votes in Texas, his only home is in Maine, and he works in Washington. The vice presidency, a job that demands no independent identity, compounds his identity crisis. Even larger-than-life figures such as Lyndon Johnson were diminished by it. What happens to someone who is not larger than life?

Bush is the Reagan understudy without the Reagan audience. He's not at home within his party. Yet he was to the Republican manor

born, unlike Reagan, the former left-wing Democrat who comforta-
bly toodled through Ohio in Harry Truman's campaign train. How
much money, one wonders, did old Prescott Bush give to Dewey?
Bush's lineage is too old-Republican—it goes back way before Democrats for Nixon—so he must constantly prove himself as a Reaganite.
His political trademark is to appease the right wing without endear-
ing himself to it. He cultivates those who hold him in greatest contempt. He is the patrician Willy Loman; he wants to be not just liked
but well-liked. He desperately craves acceptance by his lessers in
order to get ahead. But no matter how much the Skull and Bones
member panders, he fails to gain admittance to the outsiders' club.
"I'm a conservative, but I'm not a nut about it," he has said. He can't,
it seems, stop himself from being inauthentic. Bush embodies all of
the contradictions of the Republican Party without Reagan, but he
is not the resolution.

Bush's is an all-American story that defines him as out of place. He
had the good fortune to have had as his father Prescott Bush, the
managing director of Brown Brothers Harriman, the investment
bank, and later a U.S. senator from Connecticut. George escaped the
fatherland, Connecticut, for the frontier, Texas, where he succeeded
as an oilman. He could claim that he lived the virtues of inner-
directedness—he had made himself through willpower (and, incidentally, family money). Like the ambitious eldest son of a hereditary
peer desiring a parliamentary seat in his own right, he ran for the
House, finding a rotten borough in Houston and serving two terms.
Once he was credentialed as a genuine Sunbelt politician, his eastern
establishment connections advanced him forward from job to job.
Like Frank Merriwell, the fictional Yale hero, Bush was always a
winner, but never transformed by experience. His jobs didn't shape
him; they merely exalted him. In the meantime, he edged away from
Republican tradition. He sought to shed the old skin by becoming a
conservative. He began to take his cues from the outsiders' world,
whose rhythm he didn't quite grasp. He tried to establish his right-
wing bona fides early. In 1964 he endorsed Barry Goldwater for the
Republican nomination. When he decided to run for president himself in 1980, he gathered around him a tight group of conservative
cadres, as well as some blue-blood CIA types. One of the conservatives was Vic Gold, press secretary to Goldwater and Spiro Agnew.
"I knew what Bush's positioning was," says Gold. "John Anderson
defined him as Ronald Reagan in a Brooks Brothers suit. He was
correct, except that Bush doesn't wear Brooks Brothers suits. His
great appeal was that he could represent the conservative virtues we

stood for in the Goldwater campaign in a way that could be sold without the sharper edges. It was just presented in a way that was more acceptable to the so-called moderates."

Bush ran for president on his résumé, not on his ideology. His slogan—"a President we won't have to train"—was aimed not only at Jimmy Carter but at Ronald Reagan. Bush even attempted to sanitize his résumé. He dropped his memberships in the Trilateral Commission and the Council on Foreign Relations, centers of "insider" conspiracy in right-wing demonology. He called attention through indirection to Reagan's weakness, his age, by jogging in every primary state. Still, Reagan beat him. For Reagan is not only a man, but the embodiment of an ideology. Bush supported "conservatism" but denounced "voodoo economics." His instincts kept him several paces behind the natural leader.

As vice president, Bush has quietly romanced the right, trying to ingratiate himself with conservative activists across the country, attending their events and returning their phone calls. He has also given many of them, including evangelical new rightists, access to the White House. Jerry Falwell, who seeks status at least as much as salvation, has emerged as an outspoken admirer of Bush. Yet the New Right is never satisfied. No administration can fulfill all its demands, which are always changing. Reagan, however, isn't a profitable target of attacks because of his popularity among the rank and file. Thus, Bush has become the symbol of the enemy within, the "insiders," who have prevented the attainment of conservative perfection. His defense of Reaganism is a defense against the right. Clearly, to Bush, the price is worth it. The prize is the presidency.

In 1984, an unexpected obstacle has loomed in his path. In competing against Geraldine Ferraro, Bush would be measured against new standards. The immigrant's daughter speaks too fast and too loudly. She is indisputably female, but hardly deferential. Her money is too crisp. She hasn't waited enough generations to transform the primitive accumulation of capital into ennobling public service. Her rise has been too swift. She hasn't held enough jobs. As president, she would have to be trained, like Reagan. But, unlike Bush, she is not disoriented within her party; she is not trying to assimilate. In partisan terms, she makes *him* look like an immigrant.

Thus Ferraro became the object of his resentments and frustrations. Barbara Bush, the white-haired proper dowager, called her a "$4 million—I can't say it, but it rhymes with rich." ("Why is that nice old lady calling me a bitch?" Ferraro asked an aide.) Then Bush's press secretary, Peter Teeley, called her "bitchy." The Bush team's tacky psych warfare was the opening round of the debate.

Here at last was Bush's big chance to show himself as the un-abashed Reaganite, to defend Reaganism better than Reagan. For the first half of the debate, he had great difficulty establishing a consistent tone. His voice, birdlike, ranged from fluttery to screechy: "Whine on, harvest moon!" His cheerleading was so breathless that some of his locutions came out unintentionally ridiculous: "We think of civil rights as something like crime in your neighborhoods." He conde-scended to Ferraro: "Let me help you." And he was met by a steely feminist fury that he is not likely to have encountered at home: "I almost resent, Vice President Bush, your patronizing attitude."

Bush's patronizing of Ferraro, however, was mild compared to his patronizing of Reagan: "I wish everybody could've seen that one—the president giving the facts to Gromyko in all of these nuclear meetings—excellent, right on top of that subject matter, and I'll bet you that Gromyko went back to the Soviet Union saying, 'Hey, listen, this president is calling the shots. We'd better move.'" Did Bush mean that those who didn't see that one—i.e., the entire elector-ate—might quite reasonably believe that Reagan doesn't know the facts, is not on top of the subject matter, and isn't calling the shots? Does this president need more training? And did Bush himself have all his facts straight? He declared portentously that both Mondale and Ferraro had asserted that our marines in Lebanon "died in shame." Was Bush on top of that subject matter?

Bush's performance still far outshone Reagan's. He remembered to claim the economy as a success, to assail the Carter-Mondale record repeatedly, and to hail The Future. But his rendition of the conserva-tive vision wasn't like Reagan's wide-screen, Dolby-sound vision. Bush's was more like a Chamber of Commerce pamphlet. He talked of "opportunity" and the "American dream," but the only specific dream he mentioned was one he described as his own: "I know what it is to have a dream and have a job and work hard to employ others." In the debate, his debilitated ideology passed as adequate. Many of the television network commentators instantly declared him the vic-tor. And the polls, partly reflecting the Heisenberg effect of media influence, showed Bush a slight winner.

Bush's favorability rating appeared to increase dramatically only among one group—the New Right, which dislikes him in principle. Richard Viguerie, a guiding light of the movement, sent Bush a telegram: "Congratulations. Super job. You almost sounded and acted like a populist." But Bush's flawless defense of Reaganism hadn't really won any true converts. "Conservatives aren't going to feel different about Bush in the future," says Viguerie. "He knows the words, but he doesn't know the tune. I couldn't black-talk, jive, and sound natural."

"Whoops!" Bush's locker-room towel-snapping at his opponent made the "winner" suddenly appear to be a gaffe-master. Declining to apologize, he stumbled backwards into the "died in shame" controversy again. Nobody, it turned out, could support his claim that either Mondale or Ferraro had ever made the slur he accused them of. Standing before the networks' cameras, Bush frantically quoted from dictionaries to prove his point by word association. Then he got *Webster*'s and the *American Heritage* dictionaries confused. His spontaneity in the 1984 campaign was at an end. Vice presidents live on short leashes. The Reagan campaign terminated all his press conferences and unrehearsed appearances. He had achieved forced isolation—the final stage of Reaganization. Turn that thing off!

(November 1984)

The Reagan Millennium

The October terrors were over. Ronald Reagan's momentary exposure to spontaneous debate had almost unnerved us; this was not the awesome Great Communicator we had come to worship. After the second debate, with Walter Mondale vanquished by a joke, the reassuring image could be restored. On the stump, every detail and word was artfully arranged by advance men and speechwriters. And in the television advertising, there was no hint of the confused fellow muttering about "Armageddon" and a "time capsule."

A large, menacing grizzly bear, lumbering through the woods, suddenly appeared on our screens. "Some people say the bear is tame. Some say it's vicious." Close-up on huge claws. "Since no one can be sure who's right, isn't it smart to be as strong as the bear?" The bear comes face to face with the shadowy silhouette of an isolated hunter, and takes a step backward. There is no mention of the Soviet Union, or the defense budget, or Mondale, or Reagan. The meaning of the ad is already in the psyche of the viewer. And we know that the steadfast hunter symbolically must be Reagan.

"Good emotional advertising isn't designed so much to think about, to understand, so much as to feel. It's the most powerful part of advertising. It stays with people longer and better," says Phil Dusenberry, a creative member of the "Tuesday team," the advertising group assembled especially to produce Reagan's commercials. In ordinary life, Dusenberry produces ads for Pepsi. "We believe Pepsi people have a special spirit, optimism, good feelings for life and living." For the Reagan campaign, he says, "patriotism is the feeling." "The ads work," claims Doug Watts, media coordinator for the Reagan-Bush Committee. "I mean they produce results—faith and confidence." But these emotions are invested in a personality, whose victory must be personal, ruling out the surpassing loyalty of voters

to a party. "Reagan is bigger than the party," says Jim Travis, manager of the Tuesday team. "He's a radical president."

Reagan does not craft his own ads, but they are a clear embodiment
of his message. From the mosaic of individual ads, we can begin to
see the coherent shape of Reaganism and its appeal. Like the bear ad,
the implications need not be obvious, or stated, to be real. In Reaganism, the upbeat mood sustains itself; consciousness dictates circumstances. Reagan's unique selling proposition is his identification with
our desires. If we reject him, we deny ourselves. Our manifest destiny is his election. We are in control because we have placed our
trust in him.

Reagan fosters nostalgia for the present. Our current happy days
are depicted through a gauzy lens. Reagan persuades us that thinking
about the present is an act of remembrance. He erases time. "We
shouldn't be dwelling on the past, or even the present," he said
during the second debate. "The meaning of this election is the future." But, he added, we know "nothing" about it. No past, no
present, no future—we have only an enduring sense of place. Reagan
has faith that we are always the same and that the place remains the
same. Except that before him, somehow, our vision was blocked. His
slogan: *America's coming back.* But what is coming back? The change
Reagan sees is visual; it's a change in scenery. He defies time, both
in his person and his policies. To him, the future is not urgently
pressing. He's relaxed, unlike the fretful Mondale. The mode of
"coming back," as his ads repeatedly explain, is dreams—timeless
scenes of where we want to go. And the dreams Americans have are
recurrent; they never fundamentally change. They are always about
the familiar and perfect place, an America of the mind.

Reagan beckons us by themes and dreams to a millennial community of permanent prosperity beyond the business cycle and over the
rainbow. But he describes no specific new frontiers to conquer. We
are not on an errand in the wilderness. We can go home again. His
campaign is driven by ideology without ideas. Among the virtues of
the promised land is its vagueness. If the process of reaching utopia
could be charted by linear logic it would seem mundane and, therefore, not utopia. Our faith, however, can hasten the great day. Elections, which are measures of faith, are an encouragement to increasingly fervent missionary work, especially among Democrats. The
more we convert, the sooner the perfection of the world. Reagan, by
transforming religious motifs into political myths, acts as the sacred
secularizer.

The president extols traditional values, but he exists on production values. Voters believe they agree with him on issues, even when they don't; his talent is to get them to convince themselves. His "talking head" spots are marvels of nuance. He has total confidence in the camera and the microphone; they are his old friends. In one ad, he establishes eye contact with us and talks about "a clear choice." Then he looks away, dipping his head for a second, projecting the appearance of natural thoughtfulness and intimacy, although he's reading a script. With this small gesture the distance between the viewer and the performer is closed. "And it's a very simple choice." The camera is slowly, almost imperceptibly, moving toward him. We are physically getting closer to Reagan; we are being taken in. "It makes you wonder if they remember how things used to be." This line, delivered with conviction, has no meaning, but it's evocative and affecting. "There's a better life ahead. But only if we look ahead." It's a place, not a time. But what's "clear" about what we see? We see only Reagan. His triumph is one of manner over matter.

In his arsenal of techniques, his radio-trained voice is among his most effective weapons. He narrates most of his ads. "Reagan is the strongest means we have," says Doug Watts. "At a focus group that tested spots someone said, 'I just love that guy's voice.' Then he was flushed with embarrassment when he realized it was the president's voice." In a series of ads, Reagan narrates scenes of happy Americana. Without any break in his narration, we see him speaking before the Republican convention. His voice has been electronically augmented by a slight reverberation, making it huskier and warmer. We sense the presence of the delegates by their sound, but we don't see anyone, except Reagan. He speaks directly to us. In terms of visual structure, we are members of the responsive crowd.

Reagan is an icon for people weary of stress. It's comforting to see the president's utter absence of anxiety about the most terrifying problems. In his ads, he never works hard. He works hard only at play on his ranch. Otherwise, he's cool. He's strong, but he never sweats. He attacks the welfare state, yet his spots have a subtext of leisure. He conveys the image of success without effort. The cuts from scene to scene are often slow dissolves. There's no technical acknowledgment of conflict, as there is in the jerkily cut Mondale ads. Reagan consoles us. The mood is underscored by the welling of flutes and strings. He tells us a bedtime story, tucks us in, and promises us sweet dreams. We're asleep before we know it.

An inspirational leader must be the master of more than technique. He must have experienced what he preaches. Reagan wants to unite heaven and earth, a millennial image. In the 1960s and 1970s, the

American body politic was corrupted and the soul drifted to another place, a place of malaise, a Slough of Despond. Reagan himself has gone through the division of body and soul three times. In his most famous movie, *Kings Row,* his legs were cut off at the knees, and he cried out, "Where's the rest of me?" Then, he was divorced by Jane Wyman and married Nancy Davis. "I have found the rest of me," he wrote in his memoirs. Finally, in the early days of his presidency, he was wounded by an assassin's bullet, forcing him to experience the physical divorce of body and soul and their reunification. He became the personification of his program to bring together again the American spirit and place. America's coming back—it's coming back home, coming back from death.

Nowhere is this theme of redemption more vividly explored than in the Tuesday team's eighteen-minute film shown at the Republican convention and subsequently extended into a thirty-minute ad, "January 20, 1981." Reagan takes the oath of office. Images of morning: a kid delivers newspapers, suburban commuters pile into a station wagon. "Yes," says Reagan, "it was quite a day, a new beginning." George Bush agreed, "The mood is different." Factory workers and blacks concur. A Hispanic proclaims, "God bless America!" Images: a wedding, a young family moves into a new house, a kid salutes the flag, the Statue of Liberty. Then Reagan stands before a flag-draped coffin. A soldier hugs his mother, grasping a flag in her hand. "I can't forget the men who died, who gave that right to me," sings country-western crooner Lee Greenwood. "There ain't no doubt I love this land. God bless the U.S.A." "Yes," says Reagan, "there's a lot of talk of renewed patriotism." Images: Air Force One, Reagan at the Korean demilitarized zone. A young woman testifies: "If anybody has any question of where he's headed, it's their fault. Maybe they don't have a television." Seeing is believing.

Suddenly, shots ring out, and bodies fall to the ground. Reagan is hit. "I didn't know I was shot," he says. He recalls Cardinal Cooke, "a wonderful, a most dedicated man . . . he said . . . God must've been sitting on my shoulder. Well, He must've been. . . . Whatever time I've got left, it now belongs to someone else." He looks down. Slow dissolve. He has not only been elected by us; he is now one of God's elect. Vigorous again, he strides the world stage. Images: Reagan in Japan, Reagan in China. Flags wave.

Shots ring out. A grainy black-and-white newsreel depicts the D-day assault on Normandy—the good war. ("It's real," Phil Dusenberry, principal director of the film, tells me. "No scripts. It's a real-life dream.") "These are the boys," says Reagan, as the camera scans a group of old men, wiping away tears, the Rangers who took the beachhead in 1944. "The best darned kids in the world," says Reagan about men his own age. He, too, is one of the "kids."

A young woman sits among the ancient kids. Her father was one of them. But he died before he could make the pilgrimage to Normandy. Reagan reads a letter she's written to her father, bringing him back to life. "I'll feel all the things you made me feel through your stories and your eyes," he reads, his voice heavy with emotion. The daughter weeps. "I'll never forget what you went through, Dad, nor will I let anyone else forget. And, Dad, I'll always be proud." Reagan has become the father. The World War II veteran who serves in a Culver City movie studio is now battle-scarred. Without the sacrifice there could be no redemption, no recovery. Fate is obligated to us. Will we forget what he went through? Will we feel the things he made us feel through his stories? Aren't we prouder?

Images: Reagan on horseback, Reagan chopping wood. The scene slowly dissolves from the ranch to the Oval Office, where the President sits calmly and passively. He is a comforting, not a punitive, father. Compared to him, everyone else seems brash and troubled. Now we're in the White House's Roosevelt Room, where battle streamers hang from flags. "My fondest hope," says Reagan, "is never again to add another streamer."

"I'm proud to be an American," pipes up the song. Images of movement, up, up, and away: white-water rapids, skyscrapers, a flag-raising, a space shuttle blast-off. These images take us away but bring us back home; even the space shuttle returns to earth. More images: the Normandy veterans—the kids—stand with hands over hearts. Reagan stands with Olympic medalists, his arm paternally wrapped around Mary Lou Retton. Dissolve to the Statue of Liberty—he's her father, too. Then Reagan walks in the White House, his arm around Bush. He's even *his* father. And if he's our father, this must be home. Close-up of Reagan, hands clasped above his head in the victor's pose. The presidential seal. Ruffles and flourishes. "Ladies and Gentlemen, the president of the United States."

America's coming back. But who or what is it coming back from? To Reagan, Mondale is less a person—"What's his name" he once called him—than a condition to be overcome. Mondale is a pole of negative energy that gives Reagan his magnetism. For Reagan's purposes, Mondale has been the best of all possible opponents. In the absence of an ideal Mondale, Reagan's preconceived ideology would work less than ideally. "The reason Mondale is perfectly constructed as an opponent is not because he's dull and boring," says Doug Watts.

"Reagan has always run with a cynical eye on government, the outsider against the system. Every one of his opponents has been Mondale."

America's coming back from more than the Carter-Mondale years. We are overcoming time to return to place, a place of our dreams. If the place weren't familiar, we wouldn't know when we had arrived. Reagan assumes that everyone knows what home feels like. And if this is home, he must be our father.

If we're coming back, where were we? We were in "an America that wasn't working," according to a Reagan ad. Why wasn't it working? "People were losing faith in the American dream." The crisis in the material world was only a manifestation of a spiritual crisis. Images: an old woman hobbles down a weed-covered path going nowhere. An empty, silent factory. A door swinging on an abandoned farmhouse opening onto a barren, parched field. Then a cowboy wipes the dust off himself. "We rolled up our sleeves and showed that working together there is nothing we Americans can't do." Images: a station wagon in front of a suburban home. Workers streaming into a factory. Smiles. The sun. Sparks from a welder's torch. We have progressed from infertility to insemination to fertility. "The springtime of hope for America," says Reagan. "Greatness lies ahead of us."

America's coming back. But are we redeemed already? Reagan presents no particular problems to solve, besides overcoming the condition called "Mondale." "Today," says a Reagan ad, "the dream lives again. Today jobs are coming back. The economy is coming back. And America is coming back, standing tall in the world again." Images: construction workers reconstruct the Statue of Liberty. The workers, however, aren't building anything new. They are engaged in an act of restoration. "President Reagan, rebuilding the American dream."

Reagan's media campaigns present him as the fulfillment of American ideals and his version of the "new patriotism" as the only possible interpretation. But Reagan's broadcast ideology is nostalgia without the function of historical memory. He promises a "city on a hill," without a social covenant. He never echoes the visions of John Winthrop: "The care of the public must oversway all private respects . . . for it is a true rule that particular estates cannot subsist in the ruin of the public. . . . We must be knit together in this work as one man." Reagan's message resonates with his reverberating voice, but it does not resonate deeply in our history. Unlike the Founding Fathers, who had an overwhelming sense of time, Reagan's time is weightless. With Reagan, we escaped history; we achieved grace and redemption through an act of blind faith.

But what if Election Day isn't the consummation of history? Then Reagan must confront the age issue in its most meaningful sense— the sense of time. For when time enters the picture, timeless millennial kingdoms fail. Such kingdoms, in fact, always fail in history, each in its own way, especially those bound together by visions without plans. After Election Day must come the Day of the Locust, because the narcissistic dreams of self-interest, being bottomless, can never be fulfilled.

The flaw in Reagan's vision is that the place he believes is eternal is defined by time. "America is change," wrote James Bryce, the English Tocqueville, in the *American Commonwealth*. This, after all, is not a static republic, where the future is past, and the present is forever. Reagan's call to glory calls us to a place out of time, to a synthesized mood of perpetual self-satisfaction. The dreams he evokes are dreams without prophecy. Yet America is always a prophecy. America is not a resting place. We are never redeemed from history. We make history. America never comes back. America is change.

(November 1984)

The Passing of the Passé

Walter Mondale committed many errors, but his principal one was so fundamental that it can appropriately be rendered only in the form of a blunt statistic: 525 electoral votes to 13. The lopsided result could be partly attributed, of course, to Reagan's personal popularity and to economic prosperity. But Mondale was not such a cipher that he can claim no credit for his demise. The extent of his failure exceeded Reagan's planning for triumph. Mondale's campaign was an endless anticlimax, a year-long free-fall. By November 6, he had become "inevitable" for the last time.

Mondale's greatest flaw, apparent from the beginning, was that he was Mondale—that is, the quintessential establishment Democrat. What was most striking about him was how little originality he possessed. He appeared as a faithful reproduction in the picture gallery of party history; he was an original copy.

Mondale stressed that his authenticity came from the party establishment. He created a test for others—who's a "real Democrat"?—that in turn created a standard by which he would be judged. His insistence on the exclusive nature of the party and by implication the magnificence of his own status made most people into outsiders. Until his final days on the stump, the "people's Democrat" communicated the fearful condescension of a defensive élite.

Mondale saw the rationale of his campaign as the restoration to power of the New Deal coalition. But he was forced by repeated upsets to notice that bonds had been loosened and energy was dissipating—the definition of physical entropy. Mondale could feel that these bonds were weaker in his own relationship with the Democratic electorate. And he projected the entropy he detected within the party to society at large, viewing everything as falling apart and breaking down. He peopled this dismal vista with the heroes of the past—F.D.R., J.F.K., and Truman. By identifying himself with them, he hoped to reawaken primal memories and thereby strengthen voters' allegiance to his cause. He acted as if brandishing these symbols would restore the great days. Yet the candidate of entropy could not offer gifts great enough to make the coalition strong again. And, although he evoked the iconography, he did not explain where the initial spirit of attachment came from. Because he couldn't dramatically demonstrate how the gods had won their power, he could not be invested with it himself, no matter what his geneological claim. He portrayed himself as the curator of a tradition, a role ruling out the creative master stroke.

While the least effective element in the 1984 Democratic coalition was Mondale, the most important element in the New Deal coalition was Roosevelt. Roosevelt's power flowed from the social debts he was owed. He seemed to be a figure of almost mystical dimension because tens of millions felt that his indispensable leadership had transformed their estates and status. He gave the New Deal constituencies life and fire, gifts which could never be excelled. While mass organizations such as the industrial unions felt their very existence had required F.D.R.'s tenure, individuals felt an intensely personal connection to the president. When they heard his warm voice on the radio calling them "my friends," they could sense the Depression lifting. For the immigrant workers, being a real American meant being a real Democrat; they were included at last. The arrangements Roosevelt established were permanent, but the feeling of indebtedness was not easily transferable from generation to generation. When the New Deal was no longer new, when it became the matter-of-fact condition of daily life, the ardent loyalty of the founding period faded. It could be temporarily called from the deep by ritual, but it could not be sustained without the creation of new social debts. Thus the insurgency was calmed. Yet the bureaucratic stratum whose prestige and power had been built upon it flourished, assuming an autonomous existence of its own. The interests of labor, women, and blacks are not necessarily narrow or "special." The legitimacy of their claims and rights, however, doesn't mean that an independent establishment doesn't exist. Its center is Washington, and its purest political expression was Walter Mondale.

Mondale had a fervent institutional following, but no personal following. He was a noble functionary, a member of an aristocracy independent of the older sources of established power such as big business. He was part of an élite with its own peculiar pecking order and rights. He was a technocrat among the policy élite, an organization man among the organizational élite, a lawyer-lobbyist among the lawyer-lobbyists; he was *the* placeman of placemen. And his elevated status was due to his membership in the party élite, not his standing with the broad electorate. He had always been selected, then returned, but never simply elected. He received his rank by appointment. His renowned caution derived partly from the protective embrace of the establishment that cosseted him. This élite preserved the old deal in ossified form, excluding a new deal.

After the shocks of the outsider candidacies of George McGovern and Jimmy Carter, the party insiders set about creating special privileges for themselves in the presidential nominating process, privileges that would exempt them from the unsettling fluctuation of popular opinion. The agents of Edward Kennedy, Mondale, and the AFL-CIO wrote new party rules. The new rules front-loaded the primaries, ostensibly giving an advantage to the candidate who amassed the most formidable organizational endorsements and resources; supplanted many primaries with caucuses, again favoring the organizational choice; and revived the congressional caucus— "king caucus"—by ennobling officeholders as "super delegates," whose instincts would be partial to whichever insider candidate emerged. By forging these rules, the establishment believed it would bring back to life the world as it ought to have been, the ideal past in the present. Their distorted image of the future was based on an equally distorted reading of the past. Only eccentric interlopers, in their view, had prevented the party from its natural self-expression.

The candidate who garnered the establishment endorsement, supposedly making him best suited to run successfully according to the new scheme, was the "real Democrat." The slogan was an ideological justification for a fixed position, and Mondale used it as a rhetorical bludgeon to beat his opponent. In doing so he articulated the hauteur of the Washington establishment, an imperious claim to superior status and legitimacy. He had no realization that the capital élite's independence led to isolation, that its haughtiness and presumption led to political ineptitude.

After the recession of 1981–82, Mondale regarded Reagan as a spent force, a bankrupt ideologue. He was simply "Hoover with a smile," as Tip O'Neill put it. In approaching this familiar enemy, there was no need to rethink; the old verities would be more than sufficient. Mondale had no sense that the politics of 1982 led away from the politics of 1984, that the politics of recession led away from those of recovery. His adherence to the 1982 model, which was the 1930s model rephrased but not updated, permitted him to hold the notion that when the traditional case was stated, his faction of the party would be restored to its proper station: the White House.

The establishment that had been deposed by Reagan in 1980 was soon under assault within its own gates by Gary Hart and a new generational constituency that did not fit any of the conventional categories and could not be organizationally brokered. After initial disorientation, Mondale responded to the challenge with a relentless campaign of distortions of virtually every aspect of Hart's record. Mondale's face disappeared from his ads, replaced by instruments of fear—a blinking red telephone and a handgun aimed at the viewer. (Hart would either blow up the planet or blow your head off.) To be sure, Hart's failings undermined his own effort; the reality of Hart was less than the idea of Hart. But after New Hampshire, Mondale never offered himself as a positive alternative. His campaign was one of almost sheer negativity. He jammed Hart's message without ever engaging it. Perhaps no candidate of either party has ever run a bleaker or emptier campaign. It destroyed Mondale's favorability rating with millions of voters, including millions who later reluctantly voted for him. Reagan campaign officials were surprised to discover after the primaries that Mondale's unfavorable rating in Massachusetts, bastion of liberalism, approached an astonishing 50 percent.

In his moment of maximum crisis, Mondale fell back on one element of his coalition, the AFL-CIO, which had fallen back on him to rescue it from its own crisis. No Democratic candidate, not even Hubert Humphrey, has been so materially indebted during the primary to one group and one interest. The labor federation's money was essential for more than field organizing. It helped finance Mondale's polling and media advertisements. Without this aid the thinness of his campaign would have been transparent, and it might have drifted away from its own lack of weight.

The traditional party was based on long-held loyalties and customs. One of these customs was that organized labor did not endorse a presidential candidate until after the conventions of both parties. Labor, its leadership believed, would be best served by rewarding those who constantly bid for its favor. Lane Kirkland broke with this tradition. He lined up labor on the side of one candidate against others, in Hart's case a candidate with a strongly pro-labor record. Kirkland was bidding for more than the support of candidates; he was attempting to secure dominance over the party itself. Thus labor preempted the already skewed election process, which it had helped shape, subsuming the function of the party itself through the shell of the Mondale campaign, which became its dependency.

Labor's early endorsement was an effort to arrest its general decline. In 1983, at the time of the endorsement, the unionized segment of the work force stood at about 17 percent, down from a high of about 30 percent in the early 1950s. The AFL-CIO had become backward and incompetent in many of its essential tasks, including basic organizing. If the federation had been a vital force of growing influence in its own right, it would not have felt the compulsion to create a de facto labor party. Its endorsement was a sign of its weakness, not strength; its entropy in the economic realm led it into the political. Mondale represented an external solution to labor's internal crisis, a way to achieve change without really changing anything. He was a shortcut back to the old deal, whose restoration would allow the AFL-CIO to avoid going through the pain of renewing itself.

In the past, the party appealed for the support of all citizens as an autonomous institution, perhaps serving some interests more than others but the captive of none. Mondale's reliance during the critical primaries on 135 delegate committees, financed mainly with millions of dollars from labor political action committees, removed his claim to traditionalism. He proposed a radical new mode of partisanship by securing the nomination through paths directly controlled by a single interest. Mondale postured as a party savior, but he undercut its Van Burenism, its independent mediating stance above all contentious interests. Are the parties merely different agglomerations of interest, competing sides of the means of production, or do they have identities of their own? When Mondale fell from grace, he became the candidate of one interest over the party. His recovery then raised the question of his independence. His individuality was blurred, and he could not credibly project a strong persona.

The image his campaign finally did project was that of the Chrysler bailout. This economic imagery had a latent function, for it applied to both the Mondale campaign and the AFL-CIO executive board. The reason they were so aroused by the symbolism of Chrysler was that they too needed bailout.

Throughout the primary, Mondale's high command asserted that independents and moderate Republicans were peripheral to victory in November. Kirkland, especially, disdainfully dismissed Hart for his appeal to them. These voters weren't real Democrats—who wanted them? Kirkland, in fact, has been unheralded for his unexampled pioneering of the arguments that would help motivate Hart's voters to cast ballots for Reagan. Hart, said Kirkland, was "unacceptable" to labor. If Hart was unacceptable, his voters must be too. By this line of reasoning, Kirkland—and his candidate—must then be unacceptable to them. Hart, Kirkland continued, had a "microchip mind." This was intended as an insult. Hart's constituency took it as a compliment, interpreting it to mean that his mind, unlike Mondale's, couldn't be organized by Kirkland. (Computer users voted for Reagan over Mondale, 62 percent to 37, according to the *New York Times*/CBS poll.) Then, clinching the case, Kirkland declared that choosing between Reagan and Hart would be choosing "between two Liberaces at the same piano." So there was no difference between them after all. It made perfect sense—Kirkland's sense—for 34 percent of Hart's voters to support Reagan.

In mid-spring, when Hart momentarily appeared finished, Mondale attempted to incorporate Hart's theme of The Future, as if it were another constituency group mustering into the coalition. His speech on the subject was one of his finest statements on entropy. "The future was made in Heaven for America," Mondale said on April 19. If that were so, human intervention would seem to be beside the point. "We have everything we need for the future," he said, "except a leader to take us there." But if we need a leader, it must be because we need him to do things that aren't being done. "Instead of building our future, Mr. Reagan is dismantling it." Mondale saw Reagan and Republicanism as the source of decay, and he enumerated in great detail the many things that were running down. Government, to Mondale, was a bulwark against these almost random forces in the universe. But Mondale didn't promise to reverse all that Reagan had done. He admitted Reagan's power and our weakness as a united people. For Mondale was saying that even with all of us behind him, we could only stop the tendency to decay. The conclusion of his speech was the image of his own retirement. "When we reach the year 2000, I hope to be a 72-year-old, happily retired former President." The implied comparison to the active seventy-three-year-old Reagan only made Mondale seem passive and decrepit—another image of decay. Then Mondale added that we must "invent the future," an intrusion into his logic. His notion that America is fulfilled, except in the leader department, and at the same time decaying, was incoherent. What he communicated was that he had little idea what the future was about, and he would be the ideal leader for this future.

The best and most coherent summary of Mondale's position was made by Mario Cuomo. In his keynote address Cuomo became the best of all possible Mondales. He depicted Reaganism as timeless greed and America riven between haves and have-nots. Reagan was interchangeable with Hoover, except for his deceptive salesmanship. And if Reagan is an old-fashioned Republican, then the New Deal coalition *redivivus* could defeat him. Everything is as it was, if we could only penetrate Reagan's veneer. The future has already occurred, and we could get back to it. "We can do it again," said Cuomo, "if we do not forget."

The convention regenerated Mondale. For an instant, he was almost even with Reagan in the polls. Most important, the convention had given him Geraldine Ferraro, a running mate who offered the chance for thematic renewal. Together they were America's anchor team. Unfortunately, Mondale had no idea how to handle this sort of ethereal material. Immediately after he named Ferraro, he attempted to defenestrate Charles Manatt, the chair of the Democratic National Committee, while welcoming good old Bert Lance at the front door. Manatt declined to be pushed and Mondale wilted. The affair was a perfect recapitulation of the chaotic indecision of the Carter administration. Lance was once again disgraced; this time his crime was loyalty to Mondale.

The euphoria of the convention was quickly dashed. Ferraro, revealing her tax returns, was cast by the press as the hanging victim in *The Ox Bow Incident;* in her famous press conference, she rewrote the script as *High Noon,* with herself as Gary Cooper. Mondale's instinct was to lie low, to be cautious, to wait and see. He passed up the opportunity to defend Ferraro's honor, and thereby to defend the fragile mythology that was beginning to grow around the couple. He returned to the scene only when the coast was clear, like the timid townsfolk who come out after the shooting stops, blinking in the sun. Ferraro had faced the gunslingers alone. In a curious symmetry, when Secretary of Labor Ray Donovan was indicted shortly afterward, Reagan immediately assailed the "lynch mob" atmosphere, proving that he was still the sheriff. Voters may have been more sympathetic to Reagan than they intended to be because his impetuous loyalty contrasted so strongly with Mondale's faintheartedness.

Many of the issues Mondale seized upon were opportunistic, but not opportunities. His pledge in his acceptance speech to raise taxes was not a new deal. It was neither a program nor a philosophy. It was not even a strategy; it was a tactic. Its only purpose was to counteract the image of Mondale as overcautious, as a man afraid to give offense. Once that purpose was served, the issue had no value, except to Reagan. But Mondale cleaved to it long after its odor was high. The issue was not the merit of the issue, but Mondale's insistence on its salience. He had given Reagan the one issue Reagan would have had to prove. If Mondale didn't exist, Reagan couldn't have invented him.

Mondale, moreover, did not grasp the symbolic undertow of the tax issue. He believed that sensible policy would bring Americans back to their normal political positions. Carter was an aberration; Reagan was an aberration; Mondale was normal. Yet he never comprehended Carter's anti-establishment appeal. Nor did he understand that Carter had threatened Americans' need to dream. By urging acceptance of pessimistic complexity—limits to growth, the zero-sum society, and, of course, malaise—Carter was demanding the end of the dream function. Americans vote to solve problems. In 1980, voters solved the problem of the death of dreams by electing the dreamy Reagan. As his alternative, Mondale offered a return to grinding reality, more grinding than that aberration Carter had offered. Instead of conveying the sense of possibility, he communicated the closing of frontiers. Reagan was unchallenged as the candidate of dreams.

Mondale appeared to reinvent his "strategy" every day, signaling ineffectiveness, instability, and insecurity. His views seemed to reflect the metabolism of his erratic schedule. Every day marked the announcement of a different issue: if it's Thursday, this must be toxic waste. It didn't look as though he was generating issues; the issues were making the man. And they were presented as a series of tactical adjustments, not as conceptual premises. Mondale racked up issue upon issue, trying to win a war of attrition by a process of addition. What it added up to was Mondale, who was less than the whole. Because it was all said by the same person, he expected it would somehow all be coherent. By constantly shifting issues, he helped convince voters that he accommodated his thinking to short-term pressures. His confusion was a sign of inadaptability. He was trying desperately to evolve, but he couldn't transcend himself. Reagan, in the meantime, was thrown off balance only by the first debate. His strength of conviction and tight campaign management team then conveyed a sense of stability—a return to normalcy.

In the closing two weeks of the campaign, Mondale abandoned issues and sought to regain the Democratic past from Reagan, a political kleptomaniac. In September, Reagan even unveiled a bust of Hubert Humphrey at the White House, with Muriel Humphrey and Joan Mondale present as props. Once Hubert had been stolen, what was left? Mondale, however, continued as the candidate of the party of memory. "I remember the first campaign I was involved in. . . . Harry Truman in 1948," he shouted to larger and larger crowds. And he produced a letter Reagan wrote to Richard Nixon in 1960, comparing John F. Kennedy to Marx and Hitler. Mondale convinced us that, yes, he had voted for Kennedy. But he never showed us why he deserved J.F.K.'s endorsement. Actually, Kennedy's grandest new idea—Keynesianism—was one Mondale had jettisoned for his tax plan. What innovation did he propose in Kennedy's spirit? Reagan, for his part, didn't wait for others' endorsement. He endorsed those whose aura he coveted—Kennedy, Truman, Bruce Springsteen. Reagan was myth, Mondale anti-myth. Mondale reclaimed Kennedy and Truman; and Springsteen, still alive, announced that he was a Democrat. But it made no difference. No matter how hard he tried, Mondale couldn't help but be Mondale.

The final scene of the final act was at hand. Everyone in the audience knew what the denouement would be. Too late, in adversity, Mondale's character became strong. It was a grace note. Then his campaign was overthrown, releasing all Democrats from his faint spell. Mondale, the perennial protégé, was without protégés. The curtain was drawn.

The Mondale campaign is the last word, at least for now, in a political outlook that may be called "passéism." Its credo: anything that has been superseded has proved its worth. If it's gone, it's good. Nothing can be tried that hasn't already failed. Repetition is the road to perfection. The future is the endless rehearsal of the past. All that was missing from Mondale's version of liberalism was the concept of progress.

After Election Day, the passéists offered their commentaries. Mondale, some argued, was an insufficient Mondale. If he were Mondale squared, more of a traditional Democrat, a real real Democrat, he might have beaten Reagan. Others argued that he simply had a poor personality. The apologists had justifications, but not answers; there was no evidence of self-criticism.

Mondale's candidacy was a barely sustainable rationalization of the position of the Washington establishment throughout 1984. Among the truths revealed by the campaign is that the party lords do not have the keys to the kingdom. But even with Mondale's defeat, they retain a unique power: the power to destroy any presidential candidacy they wholeheartedly endorse.

(December 1984)

Once Upon a Time
in America

Geraldine Ferraro declined to campaign for the United States Senate in order to mount an even more desperate campaign. She was driven to her decision by the pain principle. For when she made her reluctant announcement on December 11, she gave as her motive a Justice Department investigation of her finances. "I have absolutely no doubt," she said, "that I will be vindicated." Perhaps she will be. But what she ultimately would have risked in a bruising fight with the incumbent, Alfonse D'Amato, an expert in kidney chops, is still at stake. It is the myth of Ferraro—an apotheosis of both the immigrant and the feminist myths. The sacred history Ferraro is trying to establish may be threatened by the exposure of a profane past. Her campaign for eminence may turn out to be more arduous than a campaign for office, her status as a meta-historical figure more insecure than ever. The first and most important salvo in this campaign to preserve her iconography began with the publication of her book.

Some world-historical figures dream of going to the Finland Station. When Geraldine Ferraro was chosen as the first woman vice presidential nominee, she wanted to go someplace else. "I realized," she writes in *Ferraro: My Story* (Bantam), "I had a long night before me and had better go to the ladies' room."

Ferraro's book alternates between passages of self-trivialization and self-importance. Her writing is far more vivid indulging in the former than the latter. The ladies' room is a recurrent theme. On the campaign press plane, Ferraro thinks about it as reporters demand answers about her finances: "The only bathroom was in the rear. To use it I had to run the gauntlet of the press every time; they, of course, seized the opportunity to ask me more questions. The pressure was intense."

The scarcity of female Secret Service agents contributed to Ferraro's concern, creating what she describes as a "minor crisis": "The agents would . . . have to 'secure' the ladies' room, going in and peering under the stalls to make sure there was no one lurking inside. . . . After a while I started going into the ladies' room ahead of them, bending down to check out the stalls myself and then yelling, 'All clear!' " (One can only hope that Jeane Kirkpatrick fills her forthcoming book with similarly revealing passages: "Blame America second. First . . .")

Reading *Ferraro: My Story* is a long day's journey into mindlessness. The author has the sure literary instinct for the intimate non sequitur. For example, her immediate worry after her selection was that her slip showed as she waved to the crowd. "Male candidates have it easy," she writes. "My problem as a woman was how to look vice presidential." What to wear? Her acceptance speech provoked what she calls "the first clothing controversy." She wanted to wear the white dress that "looked dynamite." But Joan Mondale was also "planning to wear white, a new suit she had bought just for the occasion." So Ferraro's daughters were "dispatched to the department stores." Six dresses were tried on: none would do. Back to the white one she "bought on Orchard Street." And guess what? "Nobody cared—least of all Joan Mondale."

On the basis of these extended portions alone, Ferraro's book might have been appropriately titled *To the Ladies' Room*. The taffeta touches must be seen as a calculated appeal to *Redbook* readers, an essential constituency if Ferraro is to make back her one-million-dollar advance for her publisher. Yet these superficialities appear no more calculating than the dull boilerplate on the issues. In these dreary paragraphs, Ferraro seems to have confused her current role as memoirist with that of her former role as Democratic platform chair. Here Ferraro appears to be presiding over her ghostwriter, who has churned out much obligatory prose no one should feel obliged to read. This is where Ferraro really loses Bantam's advance.

If she had difficulty during the campaign maintaining a consistent tone, wavering between "I Am Woman" and "Sono Femine" ("You people who are married to Italian men, you know what it's like"), Ferraro succeeds at last in her book. The campaign is portrayed like *Scenes from a Marriage*, a marriage in desperate need of a counselor. And she presents herself as the battered wife—the Tina Turner of the Democratic Party. Even her own memoir is more abuse heaped on her. "I never realized," she wails, "that writing a book would force me to relive the campaign over and over."

Ferraro defiantly claims her victimhood as proof of her innocence—political, moral, and economic. She insists on being judged by comparison with her wickedly motivated opponents. Then, she apparently believes, readers will identify with her story. And what a wonderful story it is! It is a pulsing immigrant saga, from Ellis Island to Fire Island, from black dresses to white. "For hundreds of years," she writes, "America had held out a promise to those who reached her shores: if you were willing to work hard and live by what you believed, you could earn your share of this country's great blessings."

Ferraro, however, is thin precisely as autobiography. The book is not a proper life and times. Her rise is duly noted and so are the obstacles to her further success, which are mostly blamed on an accursed sexism. But the problem of her parvenu splendor is glossed over as an inappropriate topic for inquiry. Her explanations of where all the cars and houses came from remain murky. She prefers that the subject not be changed from sex to money. She wishes that readers imagine the romance of her family's humble beginnings, not how she finally arrived.

Perhaps more than anyone else during the campaign year, Barbara Bush, the vice president's wife, recognized intuitively that Ferraro's vulnerability was her recently amassed capital. Mrs. Bush, expressing the resentment of established wealth, announced that she and her husband would not hide that they had money, "not like that four million dollar—I can't say it, but it rhymes with 'rich.' " In her assertion of social superiority, Mrs. Bush flung herself toward the gutter. By turning the central question about Ferraro into a question of manners, she helped to obscure it.

Yet Mrs. Bush seems to have grasped the problem more readily than the Mondale campaign. Though an effort was made to vet Ferraro, it was rushed and inadequate. The exigencies of the campaign, especially Mondale's weakness, dictated that he secure Ferraro as his running mate quickly. The speed, however, was not deliberate. And Ferraro was hardly an exemplar of cooperation. In her memoir, she tells the tale of campaign treasurer Michael Berman hurriedly flying to Queens to check the Ferraro-Zaccaro finances. At the time, the prospective candidate was preparing to leave for the San Francisco convention. She informed the anxious Berman that his visit was "inconvenient." Why? "I had made an appointment to get my hair cut." Would the new woman rather be bobbed than audited? To accommodate her, Berman flew in before her rendezvous with the hairdresser. Time was short, her hair was long. Or was there another reason for this avoidance drill?

Ferraro's acceptance of Walter Mondale's proposal apparently inspired her to think like Molly Bloom: "Yes, I decided. Yes." On Ferraro's night to remember, she was our bride, "the one standing in for millions and millions of American women." Her infatuation with the wedding overshadowed the plainness of the groom. When Ferraro awoke the morning after, the marriage was not what she expected. She felt she was being arbitrarily ordered around; submission was demanded. Mondale's insensitivity included asking her to travel to California, where he believed he might have a chance. No, she replied. Instead she wanted to "go over the issues first." (According to a senior Mondale campaign aide, Ferraro spent the evening after this meeting sobbing.) She began to have vivid daydreams about herself as a man. If she were Senator Lloyd Bentsen of Texas, "they would have said, 'OK, Senator, we'll see what we can do to accommodate you.'"

Yet this quandary did not descend upon Ferraro like a cosmic destiny, kismet at the Moscone Center. It was a fate she avidly sought. Her nomination was partly secured by a group of influential women politicos she calls "Team A": "They were friends. They were savvy. They were brilliant political tacticians." Just as Mondale conducted his campaign like a lobby, before he was shocked by Gary Hart in New Hampshire, those who wanted something from him followed his cue. So the Ferraro lobby badgered Mondale until he privately admonished its leaders to proceed more discreetly, please. He wanted to look strong and they were interfering. Let me do what you want without nagging me in front of everybody, he promised. Typically, Mondale showed scant self-awareness that he had helped set in motion the politics that revolved around him, at least according to the Ferraro account.

And yet Ferraro herself sees no irony when she is subjected to pressures from Jesse Jackson, the master of bait-and-switch demands. "Politics is filled with all sorts of power games," writes Ferraro. "I don't play those games, and I don't want anybody playing them with me." ("Why am I working so hard for women and everyone is still mad at me?" Mondale lamented, after a meeting with the Ferraro lobby.)

As Ferraro tells it, the high-handed treatment by Mondale was merely a foretaste of the abuse that followed. "Bam. Bam Bam. Sud-

denly I was getting hit from all sides." Every day the press was filled
with stories about her husband's real-estate business. And after she
denied Reagan was a "good Christian," there were furious counterat-
tacks by a coterie of partisan Republican clergymen, including New
York Archbishop John J. O'Connor. Of course, Ferraro had launched
the first strike, misfiring on the ground. Suddenly she appeared to be
the crusader, mixing politics and religion. It also seemed that she
wasn't really seeking a secular office, but an ecclesiastical one. Perhaps she aspired to sainthood by martyrdom?

Election Day was both an ending and a release, "more like a wake.
One by one, the elected Democratic officials stopped by to pay their
condolences." Mondale was dead. The bad marriage was over. And
Ferraro proceeded as if her troubles had a statute of limitations.
Now, she writes, "the future is whatever we want it to be."

Ferraro fervently believes in the power of self-invention, identifying with the most prominent self-invented figure of the age—Ronald
Reagan. She praises one of his stock speeches "promoting the idea
that with effort we can lift ourselves up by our bootstraps. I have no
quarrel with that. It's my own story." Yet in her acceptance speech,
she assailed the Reagan administration for breaking "a lot of the rules
about what was decent and fair." Reagan, moreover, is an "anecdotal
president," impervious to the facts, maintaining his leadership by
illusory appearances.

The theme of broken rules haunted her campaign. Her August
1984 news conference, intended to dispel the suspicions raised about
her finances, in fact raised more questions than it answered. She
created the sense that she was fearlessly confronting the issue, clearing herself by appearance—the very thing she charges is false about
Reagan.

But her future can stretch on limitlessly only if her past is "whatever we want it to be." During the campaign, the press relentlessly
searched for the absolutely certifiable crime that would put Ferraro's
name on the police blotter. The dictate of investigative journalism,
the Watergate syndrome, demanded that reporters deal with her in
this way. If she claimed, "I am not a crook," then the task was
obvious. Curiously, while the dragnet was moving through the available records, the autobiography she advanced went generally unchallenged. To be sure, many journalists did pursue the story; for their
meritorious service, the *Philadelphia Inquirer* and the *Wall Street Journal* were banned from the Ferraro campaign plane. Many of the facts
have already been published, sporadically sprinkled through scores
of stories. Like handcuffs, they have been tried on and shaken off;

they are merely facts, not crimes. Does she have to be guilty, however, for us to know who she is?

Dozens of questions about Ferraro's finances are still unanswered. These are not minor questions, the questions of political opponents seeking partisan advantage. Her principal defense was her ignorance, that she didn't know the details of her husband's business. This was why she claimed an exemption in a congressional financial disclosure statement that permitted her to avoid revealing John Zaccaro's holdings. Yet the House Committee on Standards of Official Conduct investigation reported that her own statements contained "numerous errors and omissions"; that "she failed to disclose or incorrectly disclosed a significant number of items relevant to her total financial concerns"; and that she "did not meet the three standards necessary for claiming the exemption from disclosure of her husband's financial interests."

All the important issues raised by the House report turned out unfavorably for Ferraro. Her finances are still largely an enigma. In her memoir, she presents herself like the hero in a Hitchcock film, entangled in a plot she doesn't understand but must unravel to be free of it. But the deeper one explores the Ferraro story, the less convincing she seems. Time and again, there are appearances by organized crime figures. Despite her personal attractiveness, her support of worthy causes, and her admirable compassion, her story can be understood only by taking the Mob milieu into account. Ferraro may be a paragon of legality, but this reality has been crucial to her life. What's love got to do with it?

During the Prohibition era, Newburgh, New York, was a center of bootlegging and gambling, gaining a reputation as the "Barbary Coast on the Hudson." One of the Newburgh kingpins was Michael DeVasto, owner of breweries and speakeasies, a local legend for pistol-whipping Jack "Legs" Diamond. (Eventually, DeVasto joined Al Capone in the Atlanta penitentiary for tax evasion.)

In 1926, Dominic Ferraro came to town to work for DeVasto, first, according to one account, as a driver, and then as the manager of the Roxy nightclub. In 1933, at the height of the Depression, he bought the Roxy for $21,255, a grand sum. Two years later, Geraldine Ferraro was born above the nightclub. In time, her father moved the Roxy to a more central location and opened a storefront. He listed himself in city records as "clerk." But in 1944, the Ferraros were arrested for operating a numbers racket. A grand jury indicted them as "common gamblers." Dominic died the day he was to appear in court, and the charge against his wife was dismissed.

Salvatore Profaci, brother of Joseph Profaci, boss of one of the original five New York Mafia families, was among the underworld figures who did business in Newburgh. Much of the money Joe accumulated by illegal means was invested in legal businesses. Sal ran many of these enterprises, and his business partner was Phillip Zaccaro, John Zaccaro's father. Together they owned a realty company, called Bowery and Spring Realty Corporation, and a clothing manufacturing company in Newburgh. (In 1959 a special Senate investigative committee, spearheaded by Robert F. Kennedy, ferreted out Joe Profaci's hidden interest in the Newburgh firm.)

In 1954, while Sal was sailing his yacht off Asbury Park, New Jersey, it exploded. He had many enemies, but Zaccaro was a friend. In fact, Phil had been a character witness at Profaci's citizenship hearings. "A person of good moral character . . . well disposed to the good order and happiness of the United States," he testified. Phil also signed as a character reference on Sal's pistol license, an act of friendship that resulted in the New York Police Department's confiscating his own pistol license.

After Sal's demise, Bowery and Spring Realty was dissolved to settle the estate. Phil, as company president, folded his assets into the P. Zaccaro realty company. At P. Zaccaro, Phil was the president and his brother, Frank, was the vice president. In 1960, Frank and the company itself were named in a 103-count indictment, for demanding kickbacks from contractors working on the properties Frank managed for the city. "He received kickbacks on every single contract he had," said Manhattan District Attorney Frank Hogan. Frank Zaccaro pleaded guilty to five counts and paid a fine.

In the summer of 1961, Geraldine Ferraro applied for and was offered a job in the Manhattan district attorney's office. But when she informed her prospective employer that she would begin work after returning from her honeymoon, the job was immediately withdrawn. In *Ferraro! A Woman Making History* by Rosemary Breslin and Joshua Hammer, Ferraro attributed the cause of her rejection to sexism: "A major concern was that training would take a certain period of time, and being a woman, I would start to have babies and it would all be wasted." She failed to note that this very office had successfully prosecuted the P. Zaccaro company just a year before, and that this may have been the reason the job was withdrawn. (Thirteen years later, Ferraro was hired as an assistant district attorney in Queens, where her cousin Nick was the district attorney.)

In 1978, Ferraro ran for Congress. Her campaign manager was Carmine Parisi, who later served as her congressional assistant. His son also worked for a while as an intern in her office. Parisi's father happened to be Camillo Parisi, a capo, or captain, in the Genovese crime family, according to congressional testimony. Before working with Ferraro, Carmine had worked with Anthony Scotto, the president of the Brooklyn International Longshoreman's Association (ILA). Scotto also served as the president of the New York Maritime Port Council, a group representing 150 unions, which he used as an instrument to gain political influence. His appointee on the council was Carmine Parisi. Scotto inherited the ILA position from his wife's father, Anthony Anastasio. Another position Scotto inherited from his father-in-law was that of capo in the Gambino crime family, according to the Senate Subcommittee on Investigations. (In 1979, Scotto was convicted of accepting bribes and sentenced to five years in prison.)

Ferraro's 1978 campaign was financed by her husband. But the Federal Election Commission ruled that $110,000 of the campaign loans were made illegally, and he was fined $750. Ferraro was therefore forced to repay her husband. (Later she would claim an exemption on a House income disclosure form, swearing that she had no direct knowledge or benefit from John Zaccaro's wealth. Yet she is listed as a secretary of a number of the corporations they owned. And on a New York State Insurance Department form, she listed herself as the vice president of P. Zaccaro.) To compensate her husband, Ferraro sold properties, shares of which were also owned by a businessman named Manny Lerman. She took out two personal loans, which she in turn loaned to her campaign committee.

After she won her House seat, she set up a finance committee to raise money to repay her campaign debt to herself. Ferraro installed as her finance chair Nicholas Sands, a.k.a. Dominick Santiago, president of a carpenter's union local, convicted in 1975 of labor racketeering, and previously indicted for embezzling $500,000 in pension funds. Sands was said to have been brought into the Ferraro operation by Parisi. In late 1979, a year after the successful Ferraro gala, billed as "An Evening with Geraldine," nine bullets were fired at Sands and his Mercedes in a gangland-style assassination attempt. Incredibly, he survived, and has maintained an extremely low profile ever since. (Ferraro claimed not to have known anything about Sands' background.)

In the meantime, Manny Lerman, the Zaccaro-Ferraro business partner, was revealed, during the 1984 campaign, to have a stake in a building at 200–202 Lafayette Street, a building half-owned and managed by John Zaccaro, located a couple of blocks from the storefront headquarters of P. Zaccaro in Little Italy. At the Lafayette Street property, the prime tenant was Star Distributors, the largest pornography distributor in the country, an enterprise controlled by the DeCavalcante crime family, according to Senate Judiciary Committee hearings. The business had been under investigation by state and federal law enforcement agencies since the early 1970s. (When the Star Distributors issue arose, the Ferraro campaign, on August 20, 1984, released a statement: "Mr. Zaccaro took immediate steps to determine whether these allegations were true. . . . The media reports were the first indication Mr. Zaccaro had received of the nature of the materials stored by the tenant.")

Shortly after this controversy flared up, another name surfaced: William "the Butcher" Masselli. Masselli was one of the largest contributors to the Ferraro campaign debt retirement fund. His record includes convictions for kidnapping, drug conspiracy, and truck hijacking.

Masselli, however, had no business connection to P. Zaccaro. Michael "the Baker" LaRosa, another big contributor, did. The LaRosa tie was an inheritance from Phil Zaccaro. Between 1957 and 1971, the Zaccaro family lent him more than $250,000 for real estate ventures. John Zaccaro became the president of P. Zaccaro in 1971, but the firm continued to manage LaRosa's properties until 1977. He gave generously to Ferraro's campaign. In 1981 he was convicted of labor racketeering, apprehended in an FBI sting operation. According to an undercover FBI agent, LaRosa was a key liaison among the five families that made up the New York Mafia. Moreover, law enforcement sources described him as a "soldier" in the Lucchese crime family. (During the 1984 campaign, Ferraro said, "I've known Mr. LaRosa. He's a businessman in New York and beyond that I'm just not going to comment.")

Another big contributor to the Ferraro congressional campaign was Edward "Eddie" Tse Chiu Chan, who was identified in testimony before the President's Commission on Organized Crime by a Federal Drug Enforcement agent as a leading underworld figure. He was one of the chieftains of the On Leong business group, which was reported to have forged links to the Ghost Shadows, a murderous tong gang that law-enforcement officials believe has carried out "hits" in New York, Canada, Washington, D.C., and San Francisco.

When Eddie Chan gave a maximum contribution of $1,000 to the

Ferraro campaign, he listed his occupation as owner of a Chinese restaurant at One Mott Street, a building owned by a company called Frajo Associates. "Frajo" stands for Frank and John Zaccaro. And the associates today are John Zaccaro and his mother. All the Frajo properties, incidentally, are managed by P. Zaccaro. Prominent among the Frajo buildings was one located at 232 Mulberry Street, an address used as the official residence of Aniello Dellacroce, the number two man in the Gambino crime family. (According to the New York police, in the late 1970s, after Carlo Gambino's death, Dellacroce fought for control of the national crime syndicate with rival mobster Carmine Galante, whose murder he ordered in 1979.) In fact, the Mulberry Street tenement was not Dellacroce's residence. He lived in style on Staten Island. Dellacroce used the apartment for arrest forms, among other things. It is a common practice among Mafia bosses to have a Mulberry Street address, typically requiring a trusted landlord, as a condition for establishing a front.

In 1971, after John Zaccaro assumed control of P. Zaccaro, he sold the Mulberry Street building. Geraldine Ferraro acted as the attorney for a group of four buyers. But she dealt with only one of them—Lawrence "Joe" Latona, a buyer and seller of corpses, a "body broker," who ran his business out of the next-door building. (In 1938 and again in 1974, P. Zaccaro represented Latona's sister, Angelina, in a real estate investment.) Latona sold the Mulberry Street property in 1982 to Joseph "Joe the Cat" LaForte, named in Senate testimony as Dellacroce's underboss. LaForte's property holdings were extensive and included a Mulberry Street building, facing the original Frajo-owned building, that housed the Ravenite Social Club, the Gambino family headquarters. Latona was an incorporator of the club and the managing agent of the building. And it was at the Ravenite that Dellacroce was arrested for income tax evasion, a charge of which he was convicted.

LaForte was no stranger to John Zaccaro. Among the properties that P. Zaccaro managed were two buildings owned by a Chinese doctor named Yat Tung Tse. In 1979 Tse asked Zaccaro to find him a buyer. On May 8, Zaccaro wrote: "Dr. Tse, you must take this offer because I will never get another buyer like this." The buyer was Joseph LaForte, who had been indicted a month before for tax evasion. A month later, Tse sold his buildings to LaForte, who was soon sent to the Atlanta penitentiary.

Zaccaro had another tie to LaForte. They shared an attorney,

Murray Michenburg, who was merely one of the many lawyers working for Zaccaro. And Zaccaro's accountant, until as late as August 1984, Jack Selger, was also retained by Salvatore Profaci.

Though Ferraro has given the appearance of revealing all, the income tax returns she has displayed are merely personal and summary documents. She has not disclosed full-partnership or corporate returns. Undoubtedly, much more remains to be known.

It was clear, even before Ferraro's announcement that she would not run for the Senate seat, that she was a liability. Governor Mario Cuomo, running for reelection, seemed aware of the danger when he gave her a sharp elbow, saying that he would have little time to help her campaign. An archaeological press corps would have feverishly unearthed more of her past, and Cuomo might have been somehow tainted, too. After all, she would have been seen as his running mate. His immigrant saga might be overshadowed by hers. His talk about "the family of New York" might be canceled out by revelations about very different families. If she had decided to run, she would have been a truck bomber headed straight for the New York State Democratic Party.

Though Ferraro has chosen not to run, there has not yet been a true reckoning. In her book, Ferraro derides Reagan for turning history into fable. But what is really absent from her own story is detail, the texture of her background, which she claims is her greatest strength. She is one of the best-known Americans, and one of the least-known. Before she was chosen, Michael Berman, the Mondale campaign treasurer, inquired whether there was anything that she and her husband had done that could conceivably embarrass herself, Mondale, the Democratic Party, and the country. She firmly assured him of her impeccable past. So it is understandable that the former Mondale staff is today deeply embittered about Ferraro. They are convinced that she deliberately misled them.

But an assessment of the political problem may extend beyond her dissembling. Mondale constructed a selection process governed more by external labels than by personal qualities. Ferraro fit many of the categories that Mondale needed. She was female, Catholic, Italian, from a big state, and an organizational Democrat. He was, moreover, almost forced to take a risk in choosing her because of his dim prospects. The rush of history also seemed to be in her favor. The women's movement felt stymied by Ronald Reagan, and many of its leaders felt they could impose their will on Mondale. Thus a historic moment arrived: deus sex machina. "Go for it!" advised her husband. This was a credo that had served them well over the years. Why shouldn't their particular American dream apply to the highest office?

The aspiration to legitimate power is an old story. In *The Godfather*, Michael Corleone, the Al Pacino character, the firstborn, college-educated American son, resisted taking part in the family enterprise, but exchanged his moral nerve for blood loyalty, becoming what he had attempted to escape. Ferraro's die was cast when she married her husband. Though she projects herself as a kind of Horatio Alger heroine, that story never happened. Instead, she married well within a certain circle, fulfilling her initial ambition. But she could never reject her past without rejecting her husband—and most of her life.

Because of the opportunities suddenly opened to her, she attempted to become completely legitimate in a telescoped period of time. Other families had achieved the power she sought. But the Kennedys, for example, took generations to move from ward politics to bootlegging to the presidency. If Joseph Kennedy Sr. had ever run for president, as he once wished, the subsequent climate for his children unquestionably would have been inclement. He was much too close to the primitive accumulation of the family fortune to take full advantage of it. But the Kennedy money, at least, was vast enough to support the sons' ambitions.

By itself, the Ferraro-Zaccaro fortune was too narrow to fulfill her desires. For that, she required a unique historical warp—a strong feminist push, a weakened Mondale, and a faulty selection process. But Mondale was too weak to lift her into the vice president's mansion. And her fortune could not protect her from the problems arising from it. Her ambition cannot bear its own burden. While she struggles to protect her myth in the future, there is still the matter of her past.

(January 1986)

PART IV

The Reagan Persuasion

The Righteous Empire

"We thank you, Father, for the leadership of President Ronald Reagan." With this prayer of thanksgiving, the Reverend James Robison opened the 1984 Republican National Convention. Robison, a new right evangelist with a syndicated television show emanating from nearby Fort Worth, has met with the president frequently over the past years. In being allowed to bless the convention, Robison himself received the blessing of the Republican Party. He is a man of unequivocal opinions. An anti-Semite, he has said, "is someone who hates Jews more than he's supposed to." And: "The non-Christian can't understand spiritual things." After Robison draped the Republican delegates with the mantle of divine election, the chosen party proceeded with its predestined agenda.

On the fourth night, the anointed president delivered his acceptance speech, and then bowed his head for the benediction, intoned by the convention's final speaker, the Reverend W. A. Criswell, pastor of the immense First Baptist Church of Dallas. This was not Criswell's first campaign. In 1960 he was foremost among those assailing John F. Kennedy because he was a Catholic. *Can a Man Be a Loyal Roman Catholic and a Good President of the United States?* was the title of a pamphlet written by Criswell. The answer, emphatically, was no. The Catholic Church, he declared, was "a political tyranny." And Kennedy's election would "spell the death of a free church in a free state." Now, standing next to President Reagan, he armed the Republicans with moral righteousness.

Robison's and Criswell's prominence at the Republican convention was not a testament to the negligence of the convention's organizers. The Dallas affair was the most tightly controlled party event in years, scripted word for word from beginning to end, and approved by the White House, the Reagan-Bush Committee, and the

Republican National Committee. Robison's and Criswell's elevation to the honored party pulpit was a testament to the rise of the evangelical new right. "It was not at all surprising," said a former presidential assistant, Morton Blackwell, who served as Reagan's liaison to the religious groups and the conservative movement through early 1984. "It made perfect sense." On the morning of the convention's last day, Reagan attended a prayer breakfast, hosted by Criswell, at which he pronounced politics and religion "inseparable."

Walter Mondale seized on Reagan's declaration, making the separation of church and state the first major issue of the campaign. The debate was abstract and philosophical. But the motivating force behind this controversy is something that is not abstract: the evangelical new right, a political élite that has been transformed in less than a decade from an almost irrelevant fringe into a centerpiece of the conservative movement. The "movement evangelicals" have a far-flung organizational and communications network, a uniquely compelling ideology, and a trained, committed cadre of thousands. Unlike other religionists, from Billy Graham to the Catholic bishops, who place some demarcation line between religion and politics, the movement evangelicals quite deliberately refuse to distinguish between the flag and the cross, a position encapsulated in their notion of America as a "Christian nation."

Because of their centrality in conservative movement politics, the president, who considers himself at least as much a movement figure as a party leader, has been unwilling to distance himself from them. Throughout his first term, he has briefed them, encouraged them, deployed White House resources to coordinate them, and thereby magnified them. It may not be the establishment of religion, but it is certainly the cultivation of cults. Reagan is using the evangelical new right apparatus to register millions of new voters, who may give him decisive margins of victory in southern states. And on one issue—abortion, on which the movement evangelicals have made an unlikely alliance with the Catholic hierarchy—the president has made a solid promise in exchange for their support. At private meetings at the White House with conservative militants, he has pledged that he will appoint Supreme Court justices who will act to overturn *Roe v. Wade*, thus recriminalizing abortion. His pledge has been reiterated by the Republican platform. It's hardly a secret; it's a certainty.

Reagan regards the evangelical new right as an auxiliary force, a division of Christian soldiers in the conservative army. But their goals extend beyond his finite career. When he goes, they stay. As Reagan has said: "You ain't seen nothing yet." They can see past the second term to the Second Coming. They have a conception of history's end. The present is merely the period of pre-tribulation tribulations. What follows are the real troubles, then the rapture, when the born-again are physically whisked up to heaven in time to avoid Armageddon, the ultimate battle between good (us) and evil (them, the evil empire), which will clear the air and usher in Christ's return. In preparing for the universal apocalypse, the movement evangelicals are eagerly pursuing an ideological apocalypse. The business of soul winning has become the politics of takeover. The evangelical new right, for example, has systematically seized control of the leadership of the Southern Baptist Convention, the largest Protestant sect, with more than fourteen million members, altering long-held theological positions for political advantage. And state by state, from Minnesota to Texas, movement evangelicals are succeeding in taking over local Republican organizations. According to Gary Jarmin, director of the evangelical new right group, Christian Voice, "The Republican Party is a tool."

The appearance of the Reverends Robison, Criswell, and Jerry Falwell at the Republican Convention was a sign to the new right evangelicals that the party is on the path of political salvation. Their ascending importance is due to the confluence of two long-term trends within the conservative movement: first, the effort of a splinter to move into the mainstream; and second, the effort by conservatives to capture for the Republican Party constituencies motivated by the noneconomic "social issue." The Democrats, since at least the New Deal, had been able to unite a coalition of groups as diverse as rural southern Baptists and urban northern Catholics, mainly by a common economic appeal. Perhaps, conservatives reasoned, it would be possible to undermine both the Democrats and moderate Republicans by shifting various groups into the GOP on a basis other than economics. As it turned out, the evangelical new right became the hard edge of the "social issue."

In 1964, Barry Goldwater's campaign managers believed that widespread backlash against the civil rights movement and the burgeoning youth culture could be mobilized on behalf of the Republican candidate. A "documentary" half-hour film called *Choice* was produced, featuring a kaleidoscope of images, including rioting blacks, topless models, and nightclub denizens dancing the twist. A front group, Mothers for a Moral America, was created to act as its sponsor. The film's producer, Rus Walton, said its intent was to "take this latent anger and concern which now exists, built it up, and subtly turn and focus it."

In 1968, presidential candidate George Wallace, and to some extent Richard Nixon, sought to enlist "this latent anger." Kevin Phillips, a young aide to Nixon's campaign manager, John Mitchell, saw the election returns as evidence of a profound political realignment, bred in great part by cultural hatred of eastern liberalism. Phillips's book, *The Emerging Republican Majority* (1969), was the first theoretical work on the social issue. According to Phillips, a "populist revolt" of the recently arrived middle class, driven by resentment of the "mandarins of Establishment liberalism," had sustained Wallace and helped elect Nixon. By playing off ethnic, regional, and cultural polarizations, a new realignment could be forged. This kind of politics also happened to be ideally suited to Nixon's temperament.

On the surface, Phillips's analysis seemed to be an electoral strategy aimed at taking advantage of the harsh tensions of the 1960s and the growing geopolitical strength of the Sunbelt. But on a more immediate and effective level, he offered a factional strategy within the Republican Party for displacing Yankees in the interest of the conservative movement. *The Emerging Republican Majority* was less a party-building plan than an intraparty realignment strategy. Conservatives didn't just want to bring new groups into the party; through another door they drove others out. And by enforcing party rules that tilt against the large states, which are bastions of traditional Republican moderation, participation by Yankees and their potential allies could be reduced.

In 1970, another book on the social issue appeared: *The Real Majority*, by Richard Scammon and Ben Wattenberg. It argued that Democrats had been set on the defensive by the Republicans' manipulation of the social issue, which they defined as the "more personally frightening aspects of disruptive change." They predicted that voters were moving to the left on economics and to the right on social issues. Therefore, they prescribed that Democratic politicians should appeal to the "unyoung, unpoor, and unblack" by seizing Nixon's thunder (when the going gets tough, the tough get going). Only then would Democrats recapture their straying partisans and thus the center.

The Real Majority was assiduously read by Nixon's political operatives, who tried to appropriate a strategy intended for Democratic use. The point man for the Republican exploitation of the social issue in the 1970 midterm election was Vice President Spiro Agnew, well configured for this task: he was neither Catholic nor Baptist, but a border-state ethnic. He stumped the country, urging "workingmen" to join the "New Majority" against "the pampered prodigies of the radical liberals."

After Nixon's 1972 landslide, he toyed with the notion of changing the name of the Republican Party to the "new majority party," a reflection of the realignment he was seeking. Watergate, however, intervened; Agnew pleaded nolo contendere, and the presidency fell to a traditional Republican, Gerald Ford. In 1980, after repeated attempts, Ronald Reagan, much more the man of the conservative movement than either Nixon or Agnew, secured the GOP nomination. Some observers saw him as the one who would use the social issue as the method to complete Nixon's work. As the new administration assumed office in January 1981, the neoconservative essayist Norman Podhoretz, in an article in *Commentary* entitled "The New American Majority," argued that Reagan's success was significantly due to a "wave of cultural disgust" at the "new culture" typified by "Gay Lib and abortion." He was "perfect" to "reconstitute the new majority that Nixon had coaxed into emerging but that he had never had a chance to consolidate."

Reagan's political team, however, believed that the Republican Party risked its own destruction to the degree that the social issue became prominent. The senior White House aides embarked on a journey toward realignment by other means. They decided that just as the Democratic coalition had unified around the economic issue, the Republicans could do the same, and without the debilitating side effects of the social issue. Moreover, there was little sentiment among the senior staff for a moral crusade, especially on abortion. Even Edwin Meese, the aide closest to the conservative movement, personally (and quietly) favored the pro-choice rather than the anti-abortion position, says a colleague.

A strategy of repressive tolerance was adopted toward the social issue and the constituencies aroused by it. According to a senior adviser, the strategy worked like this: the evangelical new right and its allies rallied followers around constitutional amendments on school prayer and abortion. The White House staff, fearing Republican fragmentation and the galvanizing of new opposition, offered insincere gestures of support while desiring continual frustration. With tacit White House agreement, Senate Majority Leader Howard Baker granted time for the various social issues to be ventilated. The bills lost and were sent back into limbo. Any White House aide who seriously tried to keep the social issue bills on the front burner was also sent into limbo. For example, Faith Whittlesey, director of the

Office of Public Liaison, campaigned fanatically for evangelical new right goals—even haranguing bewildered corporate executives on tuition tax credits—and quickly became a nonentity. In the meantime, a presidential assistant, Morton Blackwell, was assigned to look after the constituency, which was to be maintained in a state of perpetual mobilization. The flaw in the strategy was that the White House served as an incubator for the movement it was trying to contain. Reagan, for his part, never wholeheartedly cooperated with the containment strategy; he insisted on encouraging the movement evangelicals whenever he was given the chance. And he sometimes created opportunities, especially "photo opportunities," against the advice of his staff.

Spokesmen for the evangelical new right invariably depict their movement as the spontaneously defensive response of traditional folk to the intrusive designs of a liberal élite. To be sure, certain Supreme Court decisions have stirred up a reaction. But movement evangelicals are not simply reacting to the jackboot march of liberalism. Their leadership has ambitiously, deliberately, and aggressively planned their rise to influence for years. This movement is not just another manifestation of historic populism, despite the frequent invocations of Andrew Jackson—who happened to be a radical and vigorous advocate of church-state separation. Social issue conservatism's claim to populism is based mostly on wishful history.

Nor is the evangelical new right in the mainline tradition of evangelism itself. In the eighteenth century, evangelicals believed adamantly that the realms of spirit and state were separate, a principal reason many Baptists fought in the Revolution. They associated the ecclesiastical establishment with the party of the rich and the well-born, an unholy alliance against the individual conscience. In the late-nineteenth century a new strain of evangelism, which came to be called fundamentalism, employed the revival technique to rally the faithful against a corrupting modern society. Fundamentalism stressed a literal interpretation of the Bible, conversion, and warfare against worldly trends. This warfare mainly took the form of separation from the evil world; withdrawal and abstinence was the way to purity. The evangelical new right is an aberrant and relatively new form of fundamentalism, rooted in anti-Catholicism.

In the 1950s, Carl McIntire was an obscure preacher who belonged to a religious denomination he himself had organized. He rode McCarthyism to fame and fortune, combining anti-Catholicism with anticommunism. In communism he discovered an international conspiracy to match his conception of what he labeled "the harlot church." He also attacked the mainline Protestant churches as "apostate, Communist, and modernist." In 1960, he joined W. A. Criswell in the crusade against the papist Kennedy. The fervor of the cause didn't prevent McIntire's bright young apostle, Billy James Hargis, from splitting off to form his own group, the Christian Crusade. To McIntire's perspective, Hargis added the element of racial fear. In 1964, Hargis built a movement around a constitutional amendment to overturn the Supreme Court ruling on school prayer, an amendment endorsed by Senator Goldwater. McIntire and Hargis constructed empires of radio stations, seminaries, real estate holdings, publishing houses, and direct-mail operations, models for what was to come.

Among the myriad right-wing fundamentalist groups roaming the wilderness was the Christian Freedom Foundation (C.F.F.) begun in 1950 with money from Howard Pew of Sun Oil. Its goal was to train and elect "real Christians" to public office. In 1975, C.F.F.'s funding was assumed by Richard DeVos, president of the Amway Corporation. (In the early 1980s, DeVos became finance chairman of the Republican National Committee.) To propagate its ideas, C.F.F. created Third Century Publishers, which issued *One Nation Under God,* by the former Goldwater operative Rus Walton, laying out the notion of America as a "Christian Republic" based on "Christian principles" ranging from the elimination of taxes supporting public schools to the return of the gold standard.

The director of C.F.F. was a voluble former sales marketing manager for Colgate Palmolive, Ed McAteer. To him, selling was akin to spreading the gospel. "We had truckloads of hair spray to sell," he says. "That's ideal training." McAteer had devoted his life to evangelism, becoming a well-known layman on the circuit, even attending international conferences. "I was like a scientist attending science meetings." He knew virtually everyone, from the backwoods pastors to the television preachers. His contacts suggested to him the possible scope of the movement.

In 1976, McAteer left the C.F.F. for a more promising job as field director of the Conservative Caucus, a new group that was part of the burgeoning new right nexus. At its helm was Richard Viguerie, who had parlayed George Wallace's list of contributors into a huge computerized direct-mail operation, building a movement on single-issue causes, such as opposition to the Panama Canal Treaty. Viguerie's righthand man is Howard Phillips, Conservative Caucus head, who hired McAteer as his right hand. "Ed was the most important person in making the religious right happen," says Phillips. "He took me around to meet a lot of people. His role was that of Johnny Appleseed." "I was crossbreeding," says McAteer.

In 1978, McAteer took Phillips to lunch at a motel outside Lynchburg, Virginia, to meet an unknown pastor, Jerry Falwell. They proposed a plan. Falwell should be the head of a new movement group that would draw in the religious minded. Phillips even had a name: the Moral Majority. Falwell wasn't fully convinced. "There was skepticism from his people that there wasn't enough money," says Phillips. At the next meeting, however, Falwell was converted.

"McAteer didn't stop there," says Phillips. "There were more meetings." "I introduced everyone to everyone," crows McAteer. "I was introducing Phillips, I was introducing Viguerie." There were meetings, for example, with Pat Robertson, the oleaginous prophet of God, owner of the Christian Broadcasting Network, and chief of his own political outfit, the Freedom Council. Links were established with Christian Voice, a new group which pushed legislation to declare America a "Christian nation" and issued a "biblical scorecard" rating legislators on "Christian issues," such as funding for the Department of Education and support for a balanced budget amendment.

And then there were meetings with James Robison. By 1980, McAteer was head of his very own organization, the Religious Roundtable, with Robison serving as vice president. The Roundtable rounded up thousands of evangelical preachers for a convention in Dallas to be addressed by the Republican presidential candidate. The group was little more than a letterhead; Robison, however, placed his personal staff and money at the Roundtable's disposal to organize the big event, an event Morton Blackwell calls "a major turning point in the history of the United States."

"You can't endorse me," Ronald Reagan told the throng. "But I endorse you." His appearance gave the evangelical new right a legitimacy it had previously lacked. Without the sense that they had the approval of a major party's presidential candidate, many evangelicals would not have been drawn into the network. "Vast numbers of religious leaders were considering whether to get involved," says Blackwell. "As a result of that meeting they decided to." The religious right was at that moment in a nascent stage, and the Roundtable gathering was like a movie lot façade. "There was no organizational context in 1980," admits Phillips. "It was largely rhetorical. But the Dallas meeting sent the message that there were a great many people who were greatly respected who were involved." McAteer's brilliant contrivance, pasted together at the last minute with crucial aid from Robison, created a stage setting for Reagan, whose "endorsement" was indispensable in turning appearance into reality. And he in turn appeared to dominate the social forces set in motion by the social issue, trumping the born-again Carter.

The movement's evangelicals justified their spreading network by more than the imprimatur of Ronald Reagan. Every movement requires a theorist. If McAteer was the essential organizer and Falwell the publicist, then Tim LaHaye, a prolific author, played the role of popular philosopher. His 1980 book, *Battle for the Mind*, sold more hardcover copies than the best-selling *Megatrends*. He interprets American history according to the Book of Revelation. Most important, he names the enemy: secular humanism, our unacknowledged but official religion. "Secular humanism puts man at the center of all things," LaHaye explained to me. "It came to America by way of graduate schools. The guy who was the most influential was Robert Owen [the English utopian], who came to the conclusion that the American people were too religious to accept socialism. He and a group of transcendentalists, Unitarians, and atheists decided to make public education compulsory. That's when they brought in Horace Mann, the Unitarian. What Mann did for secular humanism in the nineteenth century, John Dewey did for the twentieth century. Now education is on a purely secular basis. And where do you get all your teachers? The Columbia University Teachers College. John Dewey was there. It is the strongest citadel of secular humanism in America. The total secularization of the public school system is only a small part of what will happen. They're almost in total control."

LaHaye sees a fusion of conspirators which includes the illuminati and the Trilateral Commission but inexplicably omits the Masons. The secular humanists and their fellow travelers, he writes, number 275,000. They "control America"—the press, the government, the movies. (This last part works against Reagan, but it doesn't matter in such a grand theory.) America was founded as a "Christian nation," but our leaders and institutions are imposters. (This makes sense because the anti-Christ always assumes the guise of moral spokesman, which is one of the signs by which we can recognize him.) LaHaye writes: "They label it democracy, but they mean humanism, in all its atheistic, amoral depravity." He aims at piety revealed by acts of faith. Public education, the "anti-God" fount of secular humanism, aims at critical intelligence revealed by acts of reasoning. We cannot reenter the original covenant unless we are willing to be born again; those who do not are somehow false citizens. And America itself can be born again and enter sacred time through the institutions of the evangelical new right, a counterculture that will restore true doctrine. "This is," LaHaye says, "essentially what the President is saying."

LaHaye, a co-founder of the Moral Majority, has in fact been a welcome guest at the White House. "I've heard secular humanism discussed with Reagan," says Blackwell. "I've heard him use the term. It was once discussed in the Cabinet Room. He responded affirmatively to the comments that were made." (Better to nod, no doubt, than to nod off.)

Blackwell, a former new right operative employed by Viguerie, was the key contact for the movement evangelicals in the White House. As he worked to develop support for the president, he helped coordinate the new right's leadership. He shepherded them regularly through the White House, helped shape their events to enhance the administration's agenda, and circulated drafts of legislation among them. He contends that "we could do better if there had been re-peated initiatives" on the various social issues. "The grass-roots groups can't get the full level of enthusiasm. They aren't about to activate their people unless there are public policy battles going on." Yet Blackwell, according to a senior adviser, understood that the social issue was secondary to the economic. He played the game, says this source, "to get the cadres trained."

When Sandra Day O'Connor was nominated for the Supreme Court, Blackwell wrote long memos to the president urgently con-veying the sentiments of the anti-abortion activists. And he brought them in to meet with Reagan. O'Connor passed the anti-abortion test that Reagan himself administered.

In his function as ambassador to the new right, Blackwell de-pended heavily on Ed McAteer. "He'd call and ask if he should go to certain meetings," says McAteer. "I told him who was important and who wasn't. I'd tell him whom to see on what."

One of the subjects about which McAteer kept Blackwell informed was the conservative effort to wrest control of the Southern Baptist Convention (S.B.C.) leadership. This denomination has historically supported a radical division between church and state because it was founded in rebellion against oppressive state religion. Baptists tradi-tionally have placed their trust in the priesthood of the believer, not imposed dogma. From this theological tenet flowed its positions on abortion and school prayer. At the S.B.C. 1971 convention, a resolu-tion passed almost unanimously upholding the right of abortion if a mother was in any physical or emotional peril. And over a period of two decades, the S.B.C. affirmed support eight times for the Supreme Court ruling that school prayer was unconstitutional. S.B.C. convention delegates are "messengers," individuals proud of not being part of organized factions. But a small group of dedicated movement evangelicals changed all this.

One of their nerve centers is the Criswell Center for Biblical Studies, housed in the Dallas First Baptist Church and led by Paige Patterson, a Criswell associate. "We got together fifteen or twenty people to redirect the denomination," he says. "First, we located all the conservatives we could. Second, we needed to counteract the one-sided information put out by the state Baptist newspapers. We started our own, the *Southern Baptist Advocate*. Third, we agreed to elect a solid conservative president. His appointive powers determine who goes on the boards and agencies." In 1979, the movement's evangelicals organized and financed enough messengers at the convention to elect a president—Ed McAteer's home-town preacher, Adrian Rogers. (By now, Patterson was on the Roundtable's board.) In 1980, the conservative faction elected Bailey Smith, who announced: "God does not hear the prayer of a Jew." In 1982, James Draper, a Criswell associate, was elected. At that convention McAteer was adviser to the resolutions committee. "I pushed, I did," he says. "We got that abortion thing hammered out." Thus the S.B.C. did a complete about-face on the issue. Then the S.B.C. reversed its position on school prayer. "McAteer told me the convention was going to do that," says Blackwell. "We were delighted." At the 1984 convention, the S.B.C. passed a resolution against the ordination of women as ministers because "God requires" their "submission." Then Charles Stanley, a Moral Majority board member, recruited into the network by McAteer, was elected president.

Tactics similar to those used within the S.B.C. are being used by the movement's evangelicals within the Republican Party. "The Republican Party is going through a catharsis," says Tim LaHaye. "It will become a magnet to conservative America." The force drawing people in is not one of nature; it's organized. "We've taken over the GOP in many areas," says Gary Jarmin of the right-wing Christian Voice group. "In Minnesota we've taken over more than half the party. At the Texas state convention in July, Christian Voice brought in 1,500 delegates out of 5,000. This is a major change. We intend to use the Republican Party as a vehicle."

John Buchanan, an eight-term moderate Republican representative from Alabama, was among the first to be singed by the movement evangelicals' fire. In 1980, a group of about twenty-five people appeared in his office. "They introduced themselves as 'the Christians,'" says Buchanan. "They said, 'We're here to help elect those

who support the Christians and defeat those against the Christians.' "
Buchanan, a Southern Baptist minister, rejoined: "I'm a Christian
myself." He recalls, "The first issue they brought up was the Department of Education, which they said was trying to destroy Christian-
ity and establish the religion of secular humanism. I asked if that was
an issue on which Christians could disagree. They said no." So the
Christians, mostly Moral Majority members, fielded a primary candidate against Buchanan, registered five thousand new voters for the
sparsely attended election, and unseated him. "The Republican Party
has abandoned its tradition and history, the principles of Lincoln,"
says Buchanan. "What was once a lunatic fringe has become a driving
force in the party. They beat my brains out with Christian love."

But morality in one congressional district is not enough. The evangelical new right is playing off the 1984 presidential campaign in
order to expand its political machine, broaden its base, and prepare
for the future. "Within each church," says Jarmin, "we form a structure, identify who's registered and who isn't, put our literature
through the pipeline. After we register you, we have to educate you."

At the Republican Convention, the president himself unveiled the
evangelical new right's worldview. He portrayed the movement as
a defensive counter to liberal usurpers, those who are "secularizing
our nation . . . intolerant of religion." His speech was not novel. He
had voiced the same opinions in March at the National Association
of Evangelicals meeting, where he attacked those "who turned to a
modern-day secularism." The Dallas sermon, however, aroused a
furor. Suddenly, the tone seemed to shift. Reagan made more remarks, trying to clarify the previous ones. He declared that the "wall
of separation" between church and state had been broken down by
"irreligionists." He claimed that they "twist the concept of freedom
of religion to mean freedom against religion." He complained that
his Dallas utterance had been misunderstood, and in a sense it was:
it was not generally understood that he was offering up his version
of the secular humanism theory.

No matter how low Democratic presidential candidate Walter
Mondale's standing in the polls, he rates high in the demonology of
the evangelical new right. After all, his brother, Lester Mondale, a
Unitarian minister, actually signed the 1933 manifesto of the American Humanist Association. This is no ordinary election, but a battle
with the beast itself. "Mondale admits he's a humanist!" exclaims
LaHaye. "I've documented this! What he's said will be distributed to
the millions of Christian people."

The evangelical new right sets its political revivals according to the electoral calendar. But while it rides Reagan's candidacy, it runs its own race. Its fixation on the social issue has begun to disturb the younger members of the Reagan high command. They believe that the social issue is indeed becoming more salient. But now it's working against the populist scenario envisioned long ago. The "unyoung" of 1970 are a declining share of the electorate; those who were young in 1970 (and still are) are in the ascendance, even if they haven't elected one of their own as president yet. Although older voters may be responsive to populism, the younger are strongly libertarian. Reagan's politicos fear that whatever mandate the president wins may be eroded swiftly by social issue conservatism. They nervously contemplate Reagan winning a majority of the voters under forty, then triggering a generational war they would lose. "Younger voters are pro-choice on everything," says Robert Teeter, a pollster who's a key Reagan campaign strategist. "In terms of voting groups available to us, the New Deal is gone. We've got to have these new groups coming in. We can't take secondary issues and turn them off. It gets tough for whoever follows Reagan. The Republican Party can't institutionalize this. We can't live with it."

Reagan in his first term was able to postpone the reckoning over the social issue mostly because of his good luck with the economy. But by offering constitutional amendments, so successful a strategy in his first term in holding off the righteous militants while exploiting their energy, Reagan has trapped the GOP into a long-term crisis.

The party may crack, but the movement's evangelicals will flourish. That would be the ultimate fulfillment of social-issue conservatism. The divisions this sort of politics engenders are inescapable. And the party that enacts sectarian doctrine into law in the attempt to regenerate a lost world will pay a steep political price. The true believers will be neither surprised nor disappointed. They place the highest value on ideology, which they are certain foretells the fate of America and the Second Coming. They believe that their bursts of enthusiasm are bringing them closer to the end of time, but they are paradoxically promoting the movement which worships above all the god of worldly power.

(October 1984)

Saint James

When James Watt, Ronald Reagan's former secretary of the interior, was crucified, sent to his cross by his own testimony, his prophetic mission was fulfilled. The story of his self-sacrifice, *The Courage of a Conservative* (Simon & Schuster), is a most peculiar contribution to the vast literature of martyrology. There are, after all, few accounts of a martyr's passion written by a martyr himself; by definition the genre should rule out autobiography. We are therefore lucky to have Watt's effort, unique in so many ways.

This is a book by a man waging a relentless war against complexity and ambiguity. He sees contemporary politics as a Manichaean struggle between absolute good and absolute evil, between conservatives and liberals; or, as he once put it, between "liberals and Americans." We must return to simple virtues. To reanimate them, Watt simplifies politics, transforming it into an eschatological religion. "The contest between liberals and conservatives," writes the conservatives' conservative, "is a moral battle. It is a contest over who is right and who is wrong."

This "battle for America" is ultimately beyond politics, beyond the realm of profane worldliness. It can, Watt asserts, "be described in theological expressions." His tale is all weird Christology, about a father (Ronald Reagan), a son (Watt himself), and a holy ghost (the conservative spirit). In this pageant of Washington, Watt comes to the corrupt capital preaching the truth. Playing the role of the beast of Rome is the liberal establishment, whose pharisees of the press conspire to effect his demise.

The plot is familiar. So is the writing. The cadences of *The Courage of a Conservative* are not those of the King James Version, but of the losing entry in a high school essay contest on patriotism: "We walked the beautiful coastal areas, the magnificent plains, the towering mountains, the lush valleys, the colorful deserts and the mighty forests. To see this land in all of its dimensions is inspiring." (Zzzzzz. Watt's tone covers virtually the entire range of D-minus banality. There is patriotic banality. There is absurd banality.) "We are Jews, we are Christians, we are whatever religion we want to be—or none at all. . . . We are pluralistic, championing individualism."

What's especially wonderful about this last statement is that Watt doesn't really believe any of it. Pluralism is not one of his strong points. Above all, he wants Americans (no liberals need apply) to share in the fellowship of belief—his belief. But he's apparently overcome by enthusiasm for cliché; this one happened to wander into his head at the moment of literary creation. Watt's writing is to language what strip-mining is to conservation. Clearly, his manuscript was barely improved by his Manhattan publisher. Was this neglect—seemingly a deliberate attempt to allow his actual voice to be heard—another clever ploy by the eastern liberal media establishment to expose him to more persecution? Watt's book, however, should not be judged solely by its frequently meaningless passages. *The Courage of a Conservative*, though filled with cant, is intended to serve a higher cause—the resurrection of our "spiritual freedom."

Watt traces the American fall to 1857, when the McGuffey *Eclectic Readers*, grammar school textbooks "loaded with Bible verses," were rewritten. "Meanwhile, in Europe, the German philosopher Friedrich Nietzsche was declaring flatly, 'God is dead.' " Marx and Darwin, Watt notes, were making mischief too. "When the modern liberal political movement was born in the 1930s, there was still no conscious intention of supplanting America's Judeo-Christian culture." The army even dispensed copies of the New Testament. (Onward, Christian Soldiers!) But the progress of liberalism opened an "intellectual vacuum" into which stepped Jean-Paul Sartre and existentialism—"the rage on liberal college campuses." Then in 1973, the *Humanist Manifesto* was issued, whose signatories included, yes, Lester Mondale, the brother of you-know-who. Two religions— "the Judeo-Christian and liberalism of humanism"—are locked in a cosmic struggle. But the liberals have the upper hand, in control of government, which is "shamelessly advancing a philosophy of humanism."

The national government is merely one of the instruments wielded by the satanic liberal establishment. "Labor, big government, big business, education, the media and the many special interest groups" are all under its aegis. "They rule America." While Watt has a fearful contempt for almost every American institution, he claims to be a true upholder of the "American system," which turns out not to be a system at all. Instead, it is a metaphysical dream, with "Judeo-Christian roots."

More than nuance escapes him. Even the most obvious distinctions are invisible. He sometimes gets so carried away with his excited discoveries of liberal plots against authority that he forgets that he has previously declared that the liberals "rule America." Watt's dissociation from his own thinking is particularly evident in his attempt to uncover the ultimate liberal goals. The "threats to our government," he writes, "have a chilling similarity to events following more recent revolutions in other lands." (Which revolutions does he have in mind? Is liberalism communism? Or does "recent revolutions" refer to Islamic fundamentalism? Why not Nazism? Why not, indeed?) Liberalism, according to Watt, draws upon "Nietzsche and the European philosophers who believed that the 'superior race' or 'superior people,' not the individual citizen, should make the decision for society." ("Europe," in Watt's book, is very evil, the Old World of vice and decadence. "European" ideas infect and contaminate an otherwise pristine America.)

At last, in 1981, riding in from the West to save America from the "loss of absolutes," come Reagan and his sidekick, Jim Watt, rancher and sagebrush rebel. But that Watt has little to do with another James Watt, a Watt who was never a rancher, but always lived in town. This Watt spent most of his adult life in Washington, slowly and frustratingly trying to carve out a career among the conservative élite. He was a Chamber of Commerce functionary of the second rank, lifted to leadership of a right-wing legal foundation by a wealthy benefactor, the brewer Joseph Coors, and on the basis of this sponsorship placed in charge of the Department of Interior. This Watt is an inside-the-Beltway kind of guy, who is never mentioned by the other Watt, the rugged individualist. His inability to reconcile his life with his ideology is a triumph of ideology. Recognizing his own worldliness would be a traumatic shock. If he did, he might have great difficulty sustaining his belief that all wrongs can be ascribed to an external force, an omnipotent liberal establishment.

The press is that establishment's most fearsome weapon, because it focuses on him. His description of the journalists assigned the task of covering him is the essence of the conservative paranoid style that the right has supposedly cast aside in the Reagan era:

They followed me everywhere I went, recording dozens and dozens of hours of my speeches, sometimes as many as ten speeches a week. . . . They were, by their own admission, looking . . . for a gaffe, recording thousands and thousands of words in search of a few that could be used against me. . . . What was of interest were their efforts to embarrass me for daring to state the truth.

Reagan's overriding of Watt's effort to banish the Beach Boys from the July 4th celebration on the Mall was a conspiracy. "Members of a liberal press saw an opportunity to create a controversy by censoring the facts and avoiding the real issues." The problem, really, was drugs and rock 'n' roll. Watt just wanted to ban *that* on the Mall—not the Beach Boys. They happened to be scheduled to play; their bouncing by his dictate was incidental.

As for Watt's joke about a new departmental panel—"a woman, a black, a Jew, and a cripple"—the press response was only a prelude to congressional persecution:

> The majority of the members of almost every committee sought to embarrass, ridicule and demean the Reagan administration and its spokesmen. . . . The attack was directed against me personally. That was how they got headlines. . . . But how much more could I take?

His chauffeur dropped him off at the Interior building. In his office he "confronted" [a] "simple framed item . . . General Douglas MacArthur's last address to his West Point academy. Across the top are these large words: Duty Honor Country. . . . There was no personal sacrifice too great. . . ." So Watt gave himself for America—James of Montana, the king of the Judeo-Christians:

> I bowed my head and gave a silent prayer to Him from Whom my strength and courage come. My discouragement ebbed away, a smile welled up from inside. I was again ready to make decisions in the next round in the battle for America.

Watt's conservatism is not shared by all conservatives. But it is espoused by millions, who have increased in numbers over the years and mobilized behind Reagan, the conservative standard-bearer since 1968. What happens when President Reagan departs, and the forces he has built up are loosed within the Republican Party?

Watt, who steadfastly refuses to make elementary distinctions, would erase the distinction between the civil and the religious, a separation he construes as a liberal lie. Thus he imports his theology into his politics, which he organizes around the idea that to be born again one must first experience a kind of death. "I knew the personal price," he writes.

Watt's example might yet prove to have grave consequences for Republicans. But for those Christian soldiers, an army of martyrs, eager to ascend to paradise, the end is not the end. Rather, it's the price of resurrection.

(March 1986)

Reaganism on "Fast Forward"

"Special orders" used to be the dead zone of the House of Representatives. After official business is finished, any legislator can hear his words echo in the deserted chamber to his heart's content. Last year, it dawned on a group of aggressive young conservatives that even when the day is done the camera is still on. They realized that if they filled the "special orders" time slot, they would have their own nationally televised show on C-SPAN, the cable network which broadcasts House sessions. "The best Arbitron rating we have," says Representative Newt Gingrich of Georgia, "is that a quarter-million people are watching at any given minute."

Gingrich and his confederates had been trying hard to influence Ronald Reagan, but were having difficulty gaining access to him. Except in carefully managed situations they were kept away by wary aides, who wished to protect their chief not only from inflammatory visitors but from overwork in general. In the afternoons they sent him upstairs to the White House living quarters, where he did what he usually does when left to his own devices: he turned on the television. One day, flipping the channels with his remote-control tuner, the great communicator made a connection: *Live* from Capitol Hill, the Not-Ready-for-Prime-Time C-SPAN boys! The president, to whom flamboyant conservative rhetoric is pure protein, grabbed for his telephone. "The White House staff protects him from us by sending him upstairs, and he watches us on television," smirks Gingrich. "It saves us the cab fare."

The moment that Reagan met the C-SPAN boys, a spark of electricity leapt across the generational divide of the conservative movement. For two decades, conservatives have battled with traditional Republicans for primacy within the Republican Party. This fight is increasingly taking on a generational cast. "When you think about political action, don't think about what John Wayne would do," Gingrich tells crowds of cheering young Republicans. "Think what Indiana Jones would do!"

The C-SPAN boys are one corner of a bigger picture. A great struggle is coming, and some of the most influential younger Republicans—in the White House, the Reagan-Bush Committee, the Congress, the political consultant firms—are devoting a great deal of thought and energy to understanding its shape. Many of them look to Representative Jack Kemp as Reagan's true heir. But they are not much concerned with individual politicians, including Reagan. They uniformly believe that beyond the intraparty strife lies a more momentous contest for the loyalty of the volatile new generation. The ultimate conflict, as they see it, is not within the parties between generations. It is between the parties within the new generation.

The first generation of conservatives to which the contemporary movement can trace its lineage emerged in the 1940s and early 1950s. It was a fringe of isolated figures, such as Whittaker Chambers, the messianic communist turned messianic anti-communist; Frederich von Hayek, the Austrian free market economist; and Russell Kirk, cultural conservative who yearned for the feudal past. Like medieval monks, they kept the illuminated manuscripts in what they saw as a long dark age. Some were certain the West was lost to a new "serfdom"; all viewed the future as utterly bleak. The second conservative generation, spanning roughly the mid-1950s to the mid-1970s, felt impelled to make its case to a broader public. Advocates such as William F. Buckley Jr., editor of the conservative *National Review*, and Senator Barry Goldwater still considered liberalism dominant; yet they believed it could be challenged. They knew they had a political base, and they thought they could take over the Republican Party. They weren't sure, however, that they had a majority in the country. In the mid-1960s, a dazzling star rose on the horizon when Reagan became governor of California. As president, he has become the fulfillment of the conservatives' wish for redemption; he is their justification, their roots. To the third generation of conservatives, liberalism is decadent, obsolete, on the brink of being eradicated. The future, they believe, belongs to them.

That future appears in three guises. First, there's "the future"—"a vision of a very different America," according to Gingrich. The young conservatives are enraptured with the laser light show of high technology. And they believe that this technology can somehow revive traditional society, turning the global village into one giant straitlaced small town. This is back to basics with microchips, Reaganism on fast forward.

Then there is the future under Reagan. They must reelect the president, or risk losing their legitimacy. "Reagan has to have a successful second term, or else a lot of us will be retired for a long time," says Jeffrey Bell, an official of Citizens for America, a conservative activist organization. Yet Reagan, for them, is not the culmination of history or the end of ideology; he is the beginning. And after Reagan looms the tumultuous succession crisis of 1988. The past and the future are sacred to the young conservatives; it's the present that's profane.

Almost all of the C-SPAN boys arrived in Washington as a result of Republican sweeps in 1978 and 1980. They were initially dubbed "Reagan's robots" because they mechanically voted the party line. Last year, however, the robots came to life and started running wild in the House. "We're moving from *Advise and Consent* to *Flashdance,*" says Representative Vin Weber of Minnesota, one of the group's key strategists.

Baiting that white-maned bear, Speaker Tip O'Neill, is the C-SPAN boys' favorite sport. During one of the C-SPAN shows, in mid-May, Gingrich denounced by name House liberals he claimed were soft on communism. The next week O'Neill retaliated by having the cameras scan the empty galleries, puncturing the illusion that the conservative orators had the ears of their colleagues. Then O'Neill charged that Gingrich's assault on members' "Americanism" was the "lowest thing that I have ever seen in my thirty-two years in the House." Because his attack was personally aimed at Gingrich, the speaker was declared out of order. That night this extraordinary incident elevated the C-SPAN boys from the cable ghetto to the network news. They were ecstatic. "Tip O'Neill," says Gingrich, "is an arrogant, overbearing boss. He sounds like a 1930s movie. Our policies of confrontation have begun to achieve results when policies of reasonableness have not."

But there's reason to their madness. Given the propensity of voters to split their ballot, votes for Reagan can't be expected to translate into votes for other Republicans. Moreover, according to the calculations of an influential House Republican leader, "We'll lose 45 seats in 1986 in the normal course of events." The frustration of perennial minority status has led six senior Republicans to refuse to run for almost certain reelection. Imbued with the spirit of triumphal Reaganism, the C-SPAN boys reject this fate.

In February 1983, a group of less than six young congressmen began meeting regularly. "We were not close friends," says Weber. "We observed in each other a more confrontational style towards the

Democrats." Soon the group expanded to more than a dozen committed members. Each week they discuss books (John Naisbitt's *Megatrends,* Alvin Toffler's *The Third Wave,* Paul Johnson's *Modern Times*) and plan their provocations. The notion of turning C-SPAN into an ideological instrument is only one tactic. Another is constantly to force votes on polarizing issues such as school prayer or trade with communist nations. The C-SPAN boys don't actually anticipate winning. They want to build a record that Democrats would have to take some pains to explain to voters. If these divisive roll calls also happen to place moderate Republicans in a precarious position, so much the better.

The C-SPAN boys are conducting an experiment in consciousness raising. Gingrich, a former history professor at Western Georgia State, mixes references to Zen Buddhism with talk of the Founding Fathers. He is the group's acknowledged philosopher-king. "There are very long-term rhythms of nature in Taoism," he explains. "I have a real sense of history, in the sense that I'm comfortable with a ten-to-fifteen-year process. The rhythm I'm establishing drives my colleagues crazy. When you permeate the culture with your ideas, the culture will govern itself. It goes back to Lao-tzu. If our ideas are better and generate energy, we'll have more recruits to govern America than the old, closed, passive party. Our ideas will achieve primacy. That's part of the Taoist tradition." As such talk paradoxically shows, this is a peculiarly American brand of conservatism. Its animating notion isn't preservation but change, a legacy of a movement that was virtually born yesterday.

The name the C-SPAN boys prefer to travel by is the Conservative Opportunity Society, a label and a goal. "We believe the country and the world are in a tremendous state of transition," says Vin Weber. "The global economy, the technological revolution—we look at that and we think it requires a major political change. The experiment launched by Franklin Roosevelt, that concept of the liberal welfare state, is no longer appropriate. Basic assumptions have to be rethought. The Democratic Party has become the defender of the institutions it's built and of the coalition that's grown up around those institutions. When the earth moves, that party finds it hard to adapt to change. For them to rip loose, appraise things objectively, and become the party of transition is hard. Gary Hart was right on target. The message of his defeat is that that party is interwoven with the status quo and that its candidate can't react to the changes happening. Our party has the flip side of that problem. We have been the party of opposition for fifty years. Moderate Republicans have accepted all of the Democrats' premises. Their normal reaction is a modification of the agendas. The Democrats say paint the room yellow. The moderates say paint it pale yellow. The conservatives say don't paint it. We depend on the Democrats for our existence. If we're going to take advantage of the transition we have to change our role. We know the minority mind-set and the Democrats' ideology are bankrupt. Our party hasn't fully responded to that bankruptcy."

To fill the intellectual vacuum, Gingrich has just published a futurist's manifesto entitled *Window of Opportunity*. He unveils a conservatism nobody has ever seen before. For his book is a hymn to post-industrialism, as he understands it. He lays out a vast government-initiated industrial policy for outer space, where he dreams of moon factories and travel to the "Hiltons and Marriotts of the Solar System." He hails the "information-age work ethic," worker self-management, even worker ownership. And he disparages hierarchical management as typical of counterproductive "linear thinking." "The opportunity society," he writes, "calls not for a laissez-faire society in which the economic world is a neutral jungle of purely random individual behavior, but for forceful government intervention on behalf of growth and opportunity." Gingrich asserts that the consequence of the "scientific marvel" will be a "resurgence of traditional values." His argument is marked by a confusion of realms. He seeks the Holy Grail through the computer, as though endless invention will lead us to a society sanctified by Jerry Falwell. Technology always disrupts the conditions that have sustained tradi tionalism. Machine culture is value-free, and this neutrality itself has a secular bias. Gingrich, however, is unfamiliar with the classical conservative pessimism about technology; he offers no lament about the Virgin and the dynamo. So he seeks a devil, and finds it—"a liberal élite" of "deviant beliefs." He wants to purge both the economy and society of decadence, which apparently has its origin in liberalism. Gingrich wants fair-minded consideration in the marketplace of ideas, but he practices a self-indulgent paranoid style in characterizing those with whom he disagrees. His is an astounding fusion of imagination and lack of imagination. Still, his rendering of the future carries the conservative movement's parsecs beyond their conventional categories. Turn on, tune in, take over!

Meanwhile, in a different region of the galaxy—Buffalo, New York—Rep. Jack Kemp is preparing for a more earthbound future. Occasionally he attends the C-SPAN boys' meetings, but he has his own agenda, all of which they've embraced. Kemp, however, tends to disdain their futurism and their harsher tactics. "I think Gingrich is wrong going after Tip on an ad hominem basis," he says. "It should be less personal and more on the ideas." He wants to be both a radical and a team player. Despite his early attachment to the supply-side cause, he has a natural caution, having passed up two good chances to run for higher office. And he would like to avoid a pigeonhole. (He substitutes "American" for "Conservative" when discussing the "opportunity society.") He's several years older than most of the C-SPAN boys, and he came to the House in 1970, an eon ago. He is a bridge between conservative generations, a Young Turk to the elders and an elder statesman to those younger.

More than any other politician, Kemp changed the way Republicans think about economics. His blue-collar suburban district has forced him to appeal to the traditional Democratic base. He has had to contend with urban blight, declining smokestack industries, and racial friction. The old Republican remedies were insufficient for reelection. He sought another rationale. He discovered the supply-siders, a sect of economists preaching a doctrine of tax cuts, free markets, and boundless growth. Almost at the instant that it was explained to him, he became its leading political exponent. The supply-siders, in their enthusiasm, wanted to run Kemp for president in 1980. He played Hamlet with such unintentional skill that Reagan's campaign manager, John Sears, became nervously preoccupied with his ambition. At the time, Reagan was peddling the bitter Republican medicine of austerity. He had always liked Kemp, who once served as his aide in California. In the movies, Reagan's favorite role was the Gipper, because he once aspired to sports immortality. Kemp had been an authentic professional quarterback, the young hero Reagan himself had wanted to be. Kemp is Reagan's cultural and ideological son. He became the seller, Sears the distributor, and Reagan the buyer of the sunny supply-side prescription. Kemp renounced the campaign he never really mounted, and Reagan became the candidate of new ideas. Kemp kept building the movement, and inducted into the supply-side cabal a young congressman named David Stockman. Partly through Kemp's influence, Stockman was appointed director of the Office of Management and Budget. In the early Reagan years, when recession and deficits appeared instead of the predicted boom, Stockman became disillusioned. Kemp, who had ridden the Laffer Curve to national prominence, was shut out of the White House. Then came the recovery, and the doors opened again.

Kemp argued that the recession had been caused by the incompletion of the supply-side program. Tax cuts were only half a loaf. The economy had declined because the Federal Reserve, following the monetarists' doctrine of progress through pain, strangled the money supply. In its place, he urged the return of the gold standard. Only then, he believed, would his populist economics be whole and prosperity assured. "Fed-bashing" became the order of the day, with the central bank the symbol of the élite against the people.

Whatever the merits of Kemp's critique of the Fed, his solution is an atavistic version of monetarism. Gold is the M1 of the past. The populists of the last century railed against the Cross of Gold and advocated the free coinage of silver. And whatever the merits of their case, this solution was a monomaniacal panacea which crushed all other reform issues. "Free silver is the cowbird of the reform movement," wrote the populist journalist Henry Demarest Lloyd. The gold standard is the cowbird of the conservative movement today, Bryanism rewound.

Kemp's economic plan—no tax increases, a flat tax, and the gold standard—have become articles of faith for the young conservatives. Just as Kemp gave Reagan a program for his first term, he hopes to do so for his second. And this would place Kemp into position for the next term.

For Republicans, Reagan is now Mao. Everyone speaks in the name of the helmsman, quoting the *Red Book*. But behind the huge poster, behind the cult of personality, a hundred factions bloom. When Mao went on his long retreat he was planning another leap forward, another cultural revolution. But when Reagan goes on retreat, he rests, to return as the vehicle of others' ideas.

For the young conservatives the debate over the 1984 Republican platform has been a chance to demonstrate their firepower. Walter Mondale's call for tax increases enormously enhanced their position. To them, Mondale has roughly the same economic program as their traditional Republican nemesis, Senator Bob Dole. In 1976, vice presidential candidates Mondale and Dole debated hotly. Now their convergence neatly fits the conservatives' theories and needs. By digging in against tax increases, they deepen the schism within the party to their advantage. Moreover, this foreshadows another round of confrontations in the House, which also serves their purpose. On August 13, 1984, at a platform subcommittee at the Republican National Convention, the young conservatives engaged the opposition, including the agents of Ronald Reagan, who wanted the platform to give the president ambiguous leeway on taxes. Gingrich, Weber, and Kemp emerged triumphant. In a sense, this was the first primary of 1988. "Intellectually the establishment has been defeated," says Kemp. "The question is who will win politically."

Reagan, of course, isn't superannuated yet. His victory is a necessary precondition to the young conservatives' rise. He made possible their existence in the first place, shattered the party establishment, and remains the father. They must compete for the new generation through his campaign. According to the Reagan-Bush committee's private polls, the president is making inroads. Males under the age of 45 favor him over Mondale by about a 20-point margin. About a third of the Hart voters have drifted over to him. Since Mondale won the Democratic nomination, voters under the age of 24 have overwhelmingly flocked into Reagan's camp. They have known only two presidents, and Reagan does not suffer in the comparison. While the Democratic convention bolstered Mondale with his traditional constituency, younger voters, especially males, were almost completely unmoved. The Reagan-Bush committee is trying to hold these voters through a special appeal: Reagan is the first candidate ever to purchase advertising time on MTV, the music video channel. Reagan is a man for all media. His attractiveness to the young is mostly a function of his personality and of the economic recovery. But whenever Reagan, or any other conservative, emphasizes social issues, younger voters immediately desert. The split within conservatism between technological progress and social reaction keeps the new generation beyond the conservatives' grasp and thus makes a conclusive political realignment elusive.

The Reagan-Mondale election contest, however sharply defined, masks a coming generational civil war, an irrepressible conflict. The conservatives' standing will mainly depend upon how convincingly they make their case among their contemporaries. They have a purchase on the new generation through their rendition of the future and their anti-establishmentarianism. But they are culturally retrograde—not because they extol traditional values, but because they receive new perspectives second-hand. Gingrich's Zen, for example, is trickle-down counterculture. The young conservatives are cut off from the leading edge of the new class, the mass of knowledge-based professionals, at least partly because of their hostility to feminism and their remoteness from blacks. And to be alien or antagonistic to these sensibilities severs the conservatives from the most culturally strategic white males. Also, what happens if the Reagan recovery goes seriously sour?

The new generation has a self-image as a chosen generation, destined to make a great transformation. It may be too radical a step for many to permit those whose credentials were gained in the reaction to the popular generational movements of the past to lead them into the future. But by playing on disillusionment and unfulfilled hope, the young conservatives plan to realize their project of ruling twenty-first-century America. "There's a world view fight going on, a *weltanschauung* fight, at all levels," says Gingrich. "We agree with the younger liberals that the future is coming. But we fundamentally disagree about the nature of reality. The baby boomers are likely to split. It's unknowable who wins." What would Indiana Jones do?

(September 1984)

Gregory Fossedal's Flight
to the Stars

Ten days before leaving for Geneva, Ronald Reagan and those most responsible for launching the Star Wars idea gathered in the cabinet room. Among the guests: Edward Teller, inventor of the hydrogen bomb; retired Lieutenant General Daniel O. Graham, generalissimo of High Frontier, a group promoting Star Wars; and Lewis Lehrman, multimillionaire president of Citizens for America.

And then there was Gregory Fossedal, editorial writer for the *Wall Street Journal* and chief publicist for the cause, whose writings had issued the call to arms. Later, Fossedal gave this account of the conversation:

"I have something to help you prepare for the summit," he told Reagan. "I've had made a special model of Mikhail Gorbachev for you to study. *This* is the man you'll be up against." And he placed in the president's palm a Darth Vader doll, complete with light saber.

"You know," said Reagan, "they really *are* an evil empire."

"I'm glad to hear you say that again," Fossedal replied.

"Well, I've never had any regrets or retractions about that."

And they shook hands.

In Reagan's other hand, he held Darth Vader and a gift from Lehrman—Fossedal and Graham's book on Star Wars, *A Defense that Defends.* Recalled Lehrman, "The president was grateful. He suggested he was going to take it to Geneva with him."

"I was hoping that I could throw a wrench in the summit," says Fossedal, twenty-seven, the solar system's foremost practitioner of conservative parajournalism.

Even last spring there had been rumors that Fossedal was giving briefings at the White House, promoting Star Wars—what the administration calls the Strategic Defense Initiative, or SDI. Then the *Journal*'s Washington bureau came into possession of written proof: Fossedal was guilty as whispered. He had transgressed journalistic ethics. Moreover, he was a repeat offender.

Smoking gun in hand, Albert Hunt, the newspaper's bureau chief in Washington, telephoned Robert Bartley, who runs the editorial board in New York, where Fossedal is based. Relations between reporter and opinion writers, between Washington and New York, had long been tense. *L'affaire* Fossedal only confirmed Washington's worst suspicions.

This was no mere turf fight or clash of personal ambitions. Since Bartley assumed command of his post in 1972, the *Wall Street Journal*'s editorial pages had become the ministry of ideology for the conservative movement. "This is where you learned about supply-side economics and 'Star Wars,'" says Bartley. Both ideas became linchpins of the Reagan administration, and the manner of their advancement in both cases provoked internal battling within the *Journal*.

On the right, Fossedal is widely regarded as his generation's most promising journalist, propitiously placed at the heart of the nation's largest-circulation newspaper. His career has been brief, but it crosses an amazingly broad swath of the conservative movement, from the jejune *Dartmouth Review* to the thunderous *Journal*. His opinions are sought by many of his elders. He is a confidant of ex-President Richard Nixon, a friend of conservative leader Lewis Lehrman, an adviser to Republican presidential hopeful, Representative Jack Kemp of New York.

He even made a guest appearance on national television during the 1984 presidential campaign. Bartley had decided Fossedal needed some reportorial seasoning, so he sent him to cover the press conference in which Geraldine Ferraro, the Democratic vice presidential nominee, was defending her convoluted finances. Fossedal asked a question. Unsatisfied with the answer, he fumed as Ferraro moved on to another topic. Soon, he couldn't contain himself. *"Answer it!"* he shouted. *"Answer it!"* Other journalists present erupted with sustained boos. ("I thought it was legit," says Fossedal. "They were biased. . . . But I think there ought to be more booing at press conferences.")

Fossedal's rise may have a certain novelty, but his method is firmly in the *Journal*'s tradition. Fossedal brought Star Wars to the newspaper much the way one of his mentors, former *Journal* editorialist Jude Wanniski, brought supply-side enthusiasm. And just as Wanniski seemed to cross the line separating the observer from the participant, so did Fossedal. Wanniski resigned to move from supply-side theory to practice. Would Fossedal be next?

When Hunt called about the White House briefing, Bartley said he'd investigate; he eventually took responsibility himself. "In fact," he said, "I'd approved it along with a bunch of other Star Wars talks. It's hard to hold that too much against him. That won't happen again."

"Bartley," says Fossedal, "looks at me as a very potent explosive that needs to be handled with care. He has to use this explosive strategically."

Fossedal wears yacht-sized boat shoes and argyle socks that don't match his too-short pants—which clash with a blue suit jacket worn as a sports coat. He is tall, lumbering, and has clearly laid off the "lean cuisine." He has the sort of pale coloration cultivated under fluorescent lights, suggesting fabled Norwegian charisma. He punctuates his remarks with self-appreciative, deep chuckles. But this is not yet another cord of Norwegian wood. Fossedal is the Hunter Thompson of the right-wing "nerds."

For years, Fossedal has been campaigning for the big new idea that is literally out of this world. "He's obsessed," says a friend. Even his wife Lisa works for a new right-wing group devoted to this ultimate nuclear defense—the space fortress that would shield America from Soviet missiles forever.

The scientists come and go, murmuring of feasibility studies. But, Fossedal argues, "It's not a scientific debate. It's political." In such a debate, says Fossedal, "the most important weapons are ideas."

Fossedal wrote articles and books for High Frontier, the group that brought the notion to Reagan's attention. He pushed the idea in unsigned *Journal* editorials and signed opinion essays. He advised other conservative groups, like Citizens for America, on how to adjust their Star Wars' pitch. All the while, he roamed Capitol Hill, buttonholing legislators, lobbying for support.

The ubiquitous Fossedal has left a distinct impression. A friend says he's "abrasive." "Rough edges," says a colleague; "you have to check some of the facts." "Irrepressibly energetic," declares Lehrman. "A lightning rod," says Bartley. "That's his appeal."

"I *am* abrasive," Fossedal declares.

Among his most ardent supporters is Richard Nixon, who, according to a source close to the former president, regards Fossedal as his bright young man, his link to the new generation of conservative thinkers. "I have concluded," Nixon wrote in a letter to Fossedal's publisher, "that he is one of the soundest and most intelligent foreign policy analysts in the country today."

Greg Fossedal grew up almost everywhere.

His father Donald was a marketing expert, a hotelier, a roller-skating rink and car-wash owner, and a pinball-arcade operator. (He's now the superintendent of documents for the U.S. Government Printing Office.) The family moved from Williamsport, Pa., to Lewisburg, Pa.; to Buffalo; to Long Lake, Minn.; to Sylvania, Ohio; to Roseville, Minn.; to St. Louis; to Wilmette, Ill.; to Twin Lakes and then Salem, Wisc. While most children might feel they were uprooted just as they were making friends, Fossedal says, "I liked it. Usually I was leaving town by the time my enemies were catching up with me."

In 1977, Fossedal entered Dartmouth College, at that time opening up to women and many more blacks—and jettisoning its hallowed Indian symbol. Conservative alumni answered these changes with sputtering rage at the liberals they believed were besmirching traditional values.

Fossedal emerged as the editor of the *Daily Dartmouth.* He had fallen in with a small crowd led by Ben Hart, son of Jeffrey Hart, an English professor and an editor of the *National Review,* the flagship conservative journal run by William F. Buckley Jr.

Buckley himself had achieved an early prominence by publishing *God and Man at Yale,* attacking his alma mater for liberal decadence. Aided and abetted by the Harts, father and son, Fossedal sought to replicate the Buckley experience. He used the *Daily Dartmouth* as his voice, editorializing in favor of an alumnus running for the board of trustees on a platform of resurrecting the Indian and killing affirmative-action admissions.

His talent for making enemies was soon proven. In 1980, the editorial staff of the paper revolted and forced his firing. Fossedal & Co. immediately gave birth to an alternative, the *Dartmouth Review.* The first issue was funded with Fossedal's student loan. "One·of the points," he said, "was to be outrageous."

DISCRIMINATION IS A VIRTUE, read one headline. WHY WHITES ARE SORE, read another. DIS SHO' AIN'T NO JIVE, BRO, ran the most infamous *Dartmouth Review* headline. "Today," went the piece, "the 'ministration be slashin' dem free welfare lunches for us po' students."

"There's this situation," Fossedal explains now. "They started letting kids into the school who have a hard time getting by. Some wind up committing crimes . . . Let blacks enter, but don't lower standards. To merely talk about that you are branded a racist. You needed someone to shake things up, to say what everyone knows to be true."

The recalcitrant alumni responded with a flood of subscription orders. George Champion, the former chief executive officer of Chase Manhattan Bank, provided thousands of dollars. But support was not restricted to Dartmouth graduates. The newspaper was seen as a right-wing prototype by conservative foundations, which began subsidizing dozens of similar campus ventures, seeking to clone the Fossedal model.

Fossedal himself was looking beyond the campus. Jeffrey Hart advised him to become a "right-wing muckraker," Fossedal says. As he contemplated the role, he moved to Ronald Reagan's Washington in search of ideological patronage.

Fossedal secured an appointment in the Department of Education in the belief that his mission was to bring about its demise. "I thought people should resign or call for the department to be abolished and get fired," he says. He wrote an article in the conservative *Dallas Morning News* ripping his employer. The piece was instantly reprinted by *Human Events*, the old-right weekly avidly read by Reagan. With this article, Fossedal says, he succeeded in achieving his goal: "I was fired on Thanksgiving Day."

Mustered out of government service, he found a reporting job on the Charleston, W.Va., *Daily Mail*, then covering a controversy into which Fossedal promptly inserted himself.

"A local right-wing kind of guy," says Fossedal, was campaigning against the incumbent Democrat, Senator Robert Byrd. In an attempt to bolster his chances, the National Conservative Political Action Committee (NCPAC) tried to put television ads on the air slamming Byrd—which the TV stations rejected. When a right-wing group demanded that the NCPAC ads run, Fossedal happily put his name on the letterhead. "I knew nothing about journalism or the rules," he says. "So I was fired."

Yet another opportunity beckoned. The *Washington Times*, the conservative newspaper funded by the Unification Church of the Rev. Sun Myung Moon, was seeking a young editorialist. Fossedal, his previous experience a superb credential, was hired. "A lot of people didn't like me," he says. "I'm sure I rubbed them the wrong way personally."

His writing was not restricted to the *Washington Times*. For NCPAC, he produced a 187-page tract, "Reagan: A Record of

Achievement," used as a fund-raiser. "I've been told," says Fossedal, "they raised a lot of money. Everybody underpays me."

His horizons broadened. He blasted off to the very edge of the ideological universe: High Frontier. Daniel Graham and his group claimed that Star Wars would eternally change the nuclear balance of terror, but it was a cause restricted to true believers.

"Star Wars," says Fossedal, "was dead in the water. They needed some excuse to keep writing about it. Graham was looking for someone to popularize the stuff. It's not an idea that will bubble up through a bureaucracy on the sheer merits. So I met Graham and told him he needed a Suslov, a propagandist." Thus, Fossedal proudly acknowledges his model for promoting Star Wars was the late Soviet commissar of ideology, the overbearing Mikhail Suslov.

Fossedal may be a new type on the right, but not in politics. He is what was called in the old left "a reliable"—the versatile ideologue capable of generating workmanlike prose in anticipation of the party line on virtually any subject. Articles began pouring out, under the Fossedal-Graham byline. In 1983, *A Defense that Defends* was published. By now, Graham and Edward Teller had managed to win Reagan over to the idea.

For more than twenty years, the right-wingers had wearily fought in the trenches against arms control, considered the fundament of immoral détente. They argued that by accepting the theory of deterrence, the fearsome potential of Mutual Assured Destruction (MAD), the United States was imprisoned within the long twilight struggle, the endless cold war—forcing it to do business with the Soviet Union. Young Fossedal brought an excited tone to a Utopian cause: *Eureka!* Star Wars was the high-technology escape, resolving the MAD dilemma that made the United States accept the evil empire. By erecting a "peace shield" in outer space America could, wrote Fossedal-Graham, remove "nuclear fear"—free at last.

"As long as you've got this nuclear sword over your head, you can't change the Soviet system," says Fossedal. "The goal is to peacefully dismantle communism." With total defense, he argues, you can do away with all offensive missiles. In this way, Fossedal claims, Star Wars complements the nuclear freeze. "Nobody," he says, "wants to be the party that sits around the planet Earth and worries about the federal budget deficit."

After his year at the *Washington Times*, augmented by outside work, Fossedal applied to the *Wall Street Journal*, coming to Bartley's attention as the protégé of Jude Wanniski. "I was muttering to Bartley," says Wanniski. "There was no spark [on the editorial page]. But Bartley said he wouldn't hire him because he was too young."

Instead, Fossedal took a job at the *San Diego Union* as an editorial writer and columnist. As soon as he settled in San Diego, Bartley called. "Fossedal was no longer young," says Wanniski. "He was six months older."

Robert Bartley had long been an opponent of arms control. "Star Wars is not a new issue to me at all," he says. He had become especially close to Richard Perle, the hawkish assistant secretary of defense.

Fossedal gave the old anti-arms control arguments a new twist. "Until Greg started pushing Star Wars, Bartley wasn't taking it all that seriously," says Wanniski. "Bartley had to be convinced that it would hold up to the assaults he knew would come from the establishment." Once convinced, Bartley unleashed Fossedal. And the *Journal* became the Star Wars' starship.

Fossedal began holding press conferences and lectures of his own, touring the country on behalf of Star Wars. He gave two such speeches in the White House, which aroused the *Journal*'s vigilant Washington bureau.

Kosta Tsipis, M.I.T.'s eminent physicist, has debated him twice. "Debating him is meaningless," says Tsipis. "He does not understand the physical facts. He has a set of numbers and he mentions them without knowing what they mean or being able to support them. He engages in ad hominem red-baiting. Fossedal is really a propagandist. I'm alarmed that the *Wall Street Journal*, which is a serious paper, is allowing this to happen. My concern is with recklessness."

"I do know the facts," counters Fossedal. "This is a political disagreement."

Fossedal's prolific polemics gained him entrance to certain inner sanctums. Nixon called and asked Fossedal to arrange a dinner of young conservatives. They began an extended correspondence, speak on the phone, and occasionally meet.

A similar relationship was established with Jack Kemp, the choice of many conservatives as the next Republican presidential nominee. Meetings, phone calls, dinners—Fossedal is a regular on Kemp's schedule.

Fossedal was becoming a one-man echo chamber; almost every conservative publication—and even magazines like the *New Republic*—have been graced by his byline. Yet he still found time to write a book manuscript—*My Dear Alex: Letters from the KGB*—coauthored with his old *Dartmouth Review* comrade, Dinesh D'Souza, the managing editor of the Heritage Foundation's *Policy Review* and later a White House domestic policy aide.

This fiction, published in 1987, purports to be a collection of letters from a KGB control agent (Vladimir) in Moscow to his man (Alex) in America during the Reagan years. The Moscow epistemologist constantly berates his operative for his failures to emulate American journalists in their subtle attacks on Reagan and, therefore, America.

"We name names," says Fossedal about the book. Indeed, many, including NBC's Tom Brokaw, "All in the Family" producer Norman Lear, the *New York Times'* Tom Wicker, and former U.S. ambassador to Russia George Kennan, are among those mentioned in Vladimir's correspondence to Alex. "I think they're pro-Soviet," Fossedal insists. "I'm not really interested in why they think what they do."

In one of Vladimir's missives, he writes, "Your amateur suggestion we work out a way to assassinate the president I find most implausible, indeed laughable. No, Alex, we must use the four years we have to generate deep divisions among the American people and encourage hatred for Reagan's policies among the intelligentsia. Curiously, the best tactics for doing this have been developed by Americans, not by us. I suggest you begin reading the works of Michael Harrington, Mary McGrory, Arthur Schlesinger, John Kenneth Galbraith, Garry Wills and Lester Thurow. Anthony Lewis of the *New York Times* is an absolute must."

This is conservatism without the Reagan smile. Indeed, the introduction to the book was written by Richard Nixon.

The Fossedal file, at least at the *Wall Street Journal,* is closing soon.

Fossedal has learned that he will have more time to enjoy the leisure of the theory class—he has been accepted at the Hoover Institution at Stanford University. The conservative think tank has agreed to take him on as a visiting scholar and media fellow, starting in January 1986, where he plans to devote himself to longer articles and "The Pozner Letters." He will also write a column for the Copley newspaper chain. At the *Journal's* Washington bureau, official silence reigns.

"Being at Hoover," says Fossedal, "I can be a consultant to all these effective little political coteries. I'll be in Washington more."

(November 1985)

Chief Justice Rehnquist

The appointment of William Hubbs Rehnquist as the chief justice of the United States is the crowning touch of the conservative movement. When Ronald Reagan's charm no longer exercises its potent spell, Rehnquist will remain in Washington, a philosopher-king, safe from the electoral tides. Unsurprisingly, conservatives have rejoiced at the prospect of the ultimate conservative making good on his legal philosophy. In equal measure, liberals have lamented that if only his judicial views had been really understood during the hearings, his confirmation might have been thwarted.

But those who seek the heart of his thought in his jurisprudence will search in vain. The farther one travels along the great conservative principles that supposedly guide Rehnquist, the more elusive they become. What appears to be a smoothly paved road veers into a series of blind alleys.

Conservatives may praise Rehnquist for his devotion to federalism, or states rights. Yet the principle fades in the face of state actions he disapproves. He may be upheld as a true believer in strict construction, but he is free-wheeling in his tactical rejection of judicial restraint to advance his activist convictions. He may be hailed for his deference to the "original intent" of the Constitution's framers, yet his history of the United States is so idiosyncratic that his colleagues on the Court have felt compelled to dispute him in an effort to straighten the record. Acclaim may be offered for Rehnquist's exemplary legal reasoning. Yet, in the absence of logic or precedent, he has frequently resorted to homiletic non sequiturs or sardonic jokes to clinch a point.

Could it be that his renowned legal dogma is a smokescreen for a slippery pragmatism? But Rehnquist is no cynical fraud. And the discovery of black holes in his jurisprudence does not mean that his philosophy is ersatz or even inconsistent. Rehnquist's true philosophy is encompassing enough to unite his legal tenets and his glaring exceptions to them—pro and anti-federalism, strict and loose construction, original and imagined intent. But this philosophy is derived less from a theory of the Constitution than from a vision of power. With Rehnquist rises a kind of conservatism very different from that projected in Reagan's rhetoric. Rehnquist is a rare species of Republican, one who espouses a creed that has few open adherents in the age of Reagan: conservative statism.

"Government," said Reagan in his first inaugural address, "is the problem." His appeal has been as the champion of the individual against big institutions, the promise of liberty against the oppression of government. In Rehnquist's ideology, however, the uninhibited power of the state is the solution. To get the political results he wants, Rehnquist turns to government—on either the state or national level, depending on where the politically dominant are in tune with his views. This he justifies as majoritarianism, almost always casting minorities—whether political or racial—into the profane realm of submission. His final appeal is to authority, as he interprets it at the moment, not to legal artifice; he appoints himself as the diviner of majority sentiment.

Rehnquist delivered his most audacious brief for conservative statism in a 1980 lecture entitled "Government by Cliché." The "cliché" he set out to debunk is that the Constitution is "a charter which guarantees rights to individuals against the government." On the contrary, he stated, the Constitution is "certainly not a 'guarantee' of individual liberty." Its purpose is to establish a government "to have direct authority over the individual citizen."

Rehnquist's philosophy is the product of neither an inadvertent nor a haphazard evolution, but has been fixed for decades. He has been a conservative statist at least since 1952 when, as a clerk to Justice Robert H. Jackson, he wrote in a memo that *Plessy v. Ferguson*, the Supreme Court decision upholding racial segregation, "should be reaffirmed." Might, argued Rehnquist, makes right: "in the long run it is the majority who will determine what the constitutional rights of the minority are." His career has been an elaboration of that sentence.

And his appointment as chief justice comes at a critical juncture for conservatives, who are investing much of their hopes for continuing Reagan's work when he departs in the jurists he has named. But substituting Rehnquist for Reagan may have unforeseen consequences for conservatism itself. Reagan's warm persona has performed miraculous feats, particularly in convincing the common man that conservatism is not the exclusive property of the rich and powerful. Will Rehnquist's regime of cold realpolitik remove the benign image that Reagan has tried so hard to attach to the right?

Already Rehnquist has fostered disillusionment among the libertarians, conservatism's mine canaries, who are often the first to sniff the fumes of an impending ideological cave-in. At almost the instant that Rehnquist was nominated, the Cato Institute, a libertarian think tank, issued a withering blast, *The New Right v. the Constitution,* a book by Stephen Macedo, a professor of government at Harvard. "The New Right's position," he concluded, after examining the writings of Rehnquist and other like-minded jurists, "is diametrically opposed to the ideas of the framers, to the text of the Constitution, and to morality itself."

Are the libertarians forerunners of a conservative fragmentation? Or will the right collectively decide to overlook the principles that Rehnquist enunciated in that 1980 speech in order to justify their support of him? In it, Rehnquist asserted that people were "better off for having formed governments even though the governments themselves proved to be tyrannical. . . . It is better to endure the coercive force wielded by a government in which they [ordinary citizens] have some say, rather than risk the anarchy in which neither life, liberty nor property are safe from the 'savage few.' "

Rehnquist cited as his authority the work of Thomas Hobbes, the seventeenth-century English philosopher, author of *Leviathan* and a philosophical father of big government. Against him, Rehnquist pitted another English political thinker, John Locke, advocate of natural rights and father of classical liberalism. Unhesitatingly, Rehnquist ruled in favor of Hobbes—"much more of a realist."

Rehnquist's skepticism about Locke is longstanding. In an article in the *Indiana Law Journal* in 1973, for example, he criticized Locke for his belief that "the right to express one's views on a political subject is a fundamental 'right of man.' " The mocking quotation marks around "right of man" were Rehnquist's own.

Locke, to Rehnquist, is a dreamy idealist, who justified government "only because it could protect these rights and only so long as it did so." But the highest principle, according to Rehnquist, is "majority rule," embodied in the state. Unfortunately, he argued, this simple principle has "tended to become distorted by attention paid to the Bill of Rights and the Civil War Amendments."

Seen in this light, his advocacy of states' rights is an instrument to promote whatever he decides the majority's goals happen to be. And his assertion of federalism suddenly appears to be something other than a way to attain the Jeffersonian dream of liberty; it is revealed as a wish for unchecked power.

Rehnquist's jurisprudence is a mélange of contradictions that makes little sense without reference to his underlying theory of political power. In his 1976 lecture, "The Notion of a Living Constitution," he laid out his belief that the Constitution and federal statutes must be interpreted narrowly, in line with "the intent" of the framers.

But he makes new rules at will, often overriding Supreme Court precedent, without reference to the Constitution. Such a case is *Regan v. Wald.* In it, Rehnquist fell back on a reading of the current geopolitical situation as his rationale. He upheld executive authority—"justified by weighty concerns of foreign policy"—to restrict the right to travel. Justice Harry Blackmun, writing in dissent, called Rehnquist's view "utter confusion."

And as for original intent, consider *Wallace v. Jaffrey,* in which the court ruled unconstitutional an Alabama school-prayer statute. "It is impossible," Rehnquist dissented, "to build sound constitutional doctrine upon a mistaken understanding of constitutional history." He offered a quirky alternative history of the establishment clause of the First Amendment, which he claimed has been wrongly interpreted because of "Jefferson's misleading metaphor." Jefferson had called it a "wall of separation between church and state." (But if Jefferson was "misleading" and Rehnquist was right, then what happened to original intent?)

Sometimes Rehnquist completely ignores precedent, rendering judgment without apparent constitutional foundation. This trait was evident in *National League of Cities v. Usery.* In this case, he asserted the grounds of states' rights in arguing to invalidate a federal law extending minimum wage coverage to state and municipal employes. But in doing so, he forgot about strict construction, the narrow interpretation of the Constitution. The only constitutional reference he made was to the Tenth Amendment in a brief note. Yet this amendment does little to support his point, since it does nothing to limit the powers that are granted to the federal government. (In order to defend one principle—states' rights—he violated the other—strict construction.) "Thus the rejection of his own theory in this case seems complete and unqualified," wrote David Shapiro, a Harvard law professor in the *Harvard Law Review.*

On the question of states' rights, further confusion ensues. In *Taylor v. Louisiana,* the court struck down a state law excluding women from juries. Rehnquist's dissent expressed his principled position on states' rights. But in *Allied Structural Steel Co. v. Spannau,* he declared unconstitutional a Minnesota pension reform law as an "impairment" of contract law—another higher principle. And, in *First National Bank v. Bellotti,* a case involving a Massachusetts restriction on corporate participation in election campaigns, Rehnquist objected, too.

His logic is often tortuous. In a political memo to the White House when Richard Nixon was president, offering arguments against the Equal Rights Amendment as a travesty of federalism, he wandered into appeals to authority and poetic quotations. The ERA, he wrote, would usurp the "power of decision" naturally invested in the husband. And, citing "an English poet," he said it would turn " 'holy wedlock' into 'holy deadlock.' "

Occasionally, in attempts to wriggle his point through the law, he has supported in theory that which he opposes in practice. In *Bob Jones University v. the United States,* for example, the court upheld the Internal Revenue Service's denial of tax-exempt status to schools that practice racial discrimination. Rehnquist's dissent supported the notion of IRS criteria, but he reasoned that these would be applied only in extreme cases to schools of either Dickensian or Qaddafian horror: "I have little doubt that neither the 'Fagin School for Pickpockets' nor a school training students for guerrilla warfare and terrorism in other countries would meet the definitions contained in the regulations." Certainly, he argued, the racially segregated Bob Jones University did not fit these categories.

Perhaps the most controversial case involving Rehnquist's judgment that arose during his confirmation hearing was *Laird v. Tatum.* In this instance, Rehnquist cast the deciding vote in rejecting a challenge to the constitutionality of military surveillance of political protest. As memos from his tenure as head of the Justice Department's Office of Legal Counsel in 1971 revealed, Rehnquist had been an important player in the case on which he ruled—a violation of the American Bar Association's code of ethics, a code he vowed to follow during his 1971 confirmation hearings as a Supreme Court justice. Moreover, when questioned this summer about his participation in drawing up plans for domestic military intelligence operations against dissidents, he denied all knowledge, providing evidence of either concealment or amnesia.

Rehnquist's role in *Laird v. Tatum* has been considered a matter of ethics. To be sure, it is that. But it is also revelatory of his view of power. In the months immediately preceding his nomination to the Supreme Court, the Nixon administration sent him on a speaking tour of the country, making the case for an expansive state power—a system that would eventually be signified by the word "Watergate." Rehnquist defended executive privilege and military surveillance; he called openly for " 'qualified' martial law"; and he argued that "the First Amendment does not prohibit even foolish or unauthorized information-gathering by the government."

Ultimately, though, the case which best explains Rehnquist's philosophy is what might be called *Hobbes v. Locke.* In his judgments here, Rehnquist has gone to the root—the Declaration of Independence and the long struggle in English political thought that produced it. As the historian Bernard Bailyn observed in his book, *The Ideological Origins of the American Revolution,* Hobbes was a discredited figure whom even the Tory loyalists to the crown refused to cite. Locke, of course, was a direct inspiration to the Declaration's author, Thomas Jefferson, who borrowed his phrasings and concepts. It is noteworthy that Rehnquist has set himself to the right of those who opposed the American Revolution. But his position in *Hobbes v. Locke* is not an antiquarian matter; it is about the future, when he is chief justice.

In the drawing room at Jefferson's Monticello hangs a large portrait of John Locke. Now, Rehnquist will attempt to remove the philosopher of natural rights from the national gallery of American ideas. At last, the conservative movement has empowered someone who truly despises liberalism.

(September 1986)

The Courtier: George Will

George Will once compared himself to Walter Lippmann, the model philosopher-columnist, for his "various relationships with presidents." In *Statecraft as Soulcraft*, Will wrote: "My thesis is that the most important task confronting Americans as a polity is, in part, a philosopher's task." With little reluctance, Will has wrapped himself in the philosopher's mantle and taken up a relationship with President and, especially, Mrs. Reagan. He has served the Reagans as a social liaison, as a political adviser, and as the first lady's occasional luncheon companion. Will has privately boasted of his association with the president's wife to distinguished journalists, who were taken aback by what they felt was crass status seeking. Perhaps he believed that the personal connection to Nancy Reagan was a measure of his standing at the apex of the Washington pecking order. Whatever his motivation, his tête-à-têtes with Mrs. Reagan at Galileo's restaurant on P Street or the Jockey Club in the Ritz-Carlton Hotel or the Middleburg Inn in Virginia hunt country do not certify him as a Lippmann.

While the real Lippmann may not have been all his admirers have said, he still towers over his pretenders. Unlike Lippmann, Will has proved his expertise in nothing in particular. He has written no original work of moral philosophy recognized by moral philosophers, as Lippmann did in *A Preface to Morals*. Will has made no original contributions to the study of public opinion or foreign affairs. He has written no book based on actual observation of events, as Lippmann did about the Scopes trial. Nor has Will helped promote the ideas of a more interesting mind, as Lippmann did with Keynes in *The Method of Freedom*.

Will's brief philosophical work, *Statecraft as Soulcraft*, with its clotted mass of quotations, reads in long stretches like Monty Python's shooting script of *Bartlett's*. The comic effect was underlined by Will's affectless piety. One random paragraph, for example, was filled with the sayings of David Hume, Benedict Spinoza, William Penn, Adam Smith, and Thomas Jefferson. The preceding paragraph cited Alexis de Tocqueville, William Blackstone, and Oliver Wendell Holmes. Though Will obscured his thesis in *Statecraft as Soulcraft* with promiscuous ancestor worship, it could be found by a dogged reader: government should act as society's moral tutor. This basic idea has enabled him to sustain a running commentary far more intellectually coherent than most columnists.

Since Will appeared on the scene, he has presented himself as a passionate advocate, a serious man engaged with serious things. One advertisement for *Newsweek* showed Will as he obviously wants to present himself, in his study, seated at his antique desk, Waterman fountain pen in hand, bone china cup and saucer nearby, with thick volumes of Churchilliana resting on the bookcase.

With the title of his new book, *The New Season: A Spectator's Guide to the 1988 Election* (Simon & Schuster), he no longer describes himself as the serious man, but as a casual "spectator," scorecard in hand, simply delighted to observe the competition. Baseball is indeed a wonderful game, and Will has rightly called it "noble," but his metaphor trivializes what he wishes to speak of solemnly and withdraws the gravity he implicitly imputes to himself.

The underlying message of the baseball metaphor is that there is no distinction between being a citizen and being a fan. Politics, in his book, is a cross between a spectacle and a sport. Will suggests that the ultimate claim of the American political system upon our participation is not natural law or hallowed tradition. Rather, it is merely pleasure for its own sake. He writes in his final paragraph:

> A philosopher once said: "People have more fun than anybody."
> Quite right, and Americans have more fun than any other people,
> in part because their politics—their collective conversation—is so
> astonishingly amicable and, all things considered, intelligent.

But the word "fun" gives away a fundamental problem, which is not that Will inflates his subject when he borrows others' phrases, but that he deflates it when he uses his own. In *The New Season*, spectator Will is Walter Lippmann as Mel Allen.

Much of this slight book is filled with commonplaces that can be gleaned from the daily newspaper: "In 1980 the nation was ripe for what Republicans do best. It was ripe for a campaign condemning the government." Or: "It is problematic for a party to come off eight years in power and present itself as an agent of change." Or: "A theme of this book is that politicians' words—the most public acts of public people—matter and should be taken seriously by serious students of politics." Most annoying of all, Will puts forth this boilerplate as if it were derived from a close reading of Aristotle.

Or others. Will stands like a butler at the door, announcing the entrance of distinguished guests: "No one knows more about American politics than Michael Barone . . . Now comes naughty Norman Ornstein to use history to rehabilitate Congress . . . Chris Matthews, a prodigy among Democratic political operators . . . Horace Busby, a wise political consultant whose pocket calculator never sleeps. . . ." Will presents their insights without acknowledging their differences. His authorities remain consistent, but he does not.

Will has done this before. In *Statecraft as Soulcraft* he argued that American conservatism, if it were to endure, required a more Burkean deference to established custom and institutions. In particular, he suggested, the right wing ought to take a more benign attitude toward the welfare state. But, Will claimed, what was also needed was a sense of moral absolutes. His tale of Western civilization's fall described the supplanting of worthy "ancients" such as Aristotle by cynical "moderns" such as Machiavelli, categories entirely derived from the work of philosopher Leo Strauss, but unacknowledged. The wholesale lifting of Strauss's semantics, without citation, by a writer who made a fetish of quotations, was a telling sign of Will's authenticity and originality.

Will's argument depended upon meshing Strauss and Burke. Yet Strauss, in *Natural Right and History*, cast Burke into the netherworld of despised moderns as one who "paves the way for the 'historical school.'" Burke's appeals to the glorious past undermined moral absolutes that, according to Strauss, existed independent of history. In *Statecraft as Soulcraft*, Will failed to face the central conundrum he had raised. If he had openly discussed Strauss, the problem of Strauss's and Burke's basic incompatibility would at least have been apparent. But Will neglected to acknowledge one of his principal sources. Instead, he tried to reconcile the irreconcilable by gratuitously assigning Burke to the "ancients." This merely revealed Will's frequent substitution of bald assertion for actual scholarship. In *Statecraft as Soulcraft*, the consequence was a shambles. As a work of philosophy, Will's book was unconvincing; but in explaining his continuing approach to column writing it was a success.

For all his quotesmanship, Will seems generally unfamiliar with much of the terrain of political science. *The New Season* neglects the difficult questions of, for example, dealignment, decomposition of the party system, the permanent campaign and its effects on governing, the influence of money, and the role of rising and declining élites. Many topics, in the meantime, receive superficial treatment: Will argues, without any supporting evidence, that political advertising cannot sway elections. Then he quotes "Mr. Dooley, Finley Peter Dunne's fictional barkeep, 'Politics ain't beanbag.'"

As Will sees it, the Republican and the Democratic parties are both stupid parties that fail to measure up to the standards of the Will party. (Or, more exact, the Will team, comprised completely of spectators.) The Democrats, among their other vices, are soft on communism. And the Republicans, among their other vices, are soft on communism. To Will, the Democrats must shed their permissive attitude toward immoral behavior and gluttonous constituency groups. Then they will gain back the voters they lost to Reagan. The Republicans, for their part, must relinquish their distaste for government and embrace the welfare state. Then they will keep the voters Reagan attracted. Both parties must be more resolute in confronting Moscow. If they follow this advice, they will move closer to the center of gravity: the Will party.

In spite of Will's absolutism, his prospectus of the upcoming campaign remains fundamentally cautious. He does not review any of the candidates; there never is heard a discouraging word. It is not so much that he is generously giving the candidates a clean slate as that he is giving himself one. The author of *The New Season* is attempting to show that he is a man for all seasons, particularly the one after Reagan.

Mostly, though, Will treads water, recycling the rhetoric of *Statecraft as Soulcraft*: "The infantilism; impatience; hedonism; inability to defer gratification that produced the cultural dissolution of the Sixties helped give rise to the inflation of the Seventies." This coarse relegation of an economic trend—inflation—to a state of mind—infantilism—is curious. Inflation, apparently, had nothing to do with the financing of the Vietnam War and the oil shocks. Will's passionate support of the Vietnam War, which precipitated the inflation of the 1970s, would seem to deprive him of capital to spend on this issue. But he does not pause.

His premise, if his explanation of inflation is to make any sense, must be that the private is the public: what happens in the bedrooms is directly reflected in politics and the economy. But one wonders, if there is a relationship between "a collapsing capacity for discipline" and America's fall from grace, whether it could be seen in statistics on personal turmoil. Will, however, offers assertion, not illustration.

In *The New Season,* Will more clearly reveals than in any other work that his analysis flows from a priori assumptions. Almost invariably, his conclusions are imposed at the beginning; his logic, or more accurately, his logic chopping, follows. Will's method is inimitable. On the contras, for example, he states his own position: pro. Then he quotes Lord Salisbury: "If you believe the doctors, nothing is wholesome; if you believe the theologians, nothing is innocent; if you believe the soldiers, nothing is safe." Finally, he holds the Democrats up to scorn: "it recently has seemed that if you believe the Democrats, nothing is vital." Thus the Will method, applied in case after case—first the verdict, then the trial.

To avoid being regarded as agents of appeasement, Will urges the Democrats to support the contras. Earlier in the book, he writes, "The Iran-contra affair involved various attempts to evade or subvert laws, established procedures, and intragovernmental traditions (thin reeds, these) of civility." But which laws?

Will's comment on the evasion and subversion of law is on the order of Vice President George Bush's passive and inspecific remark: "Mistakes were made." A bit of the scandal's background may cast some light on Will's attitude toward facts when they contradict his assumptions.

In January 1984, the CIA mined the harbors of Nicaragua without informing the Senate and House intelligence committees. As a result, the toughest version of the Boland Amendment was passed by Congress, saying that "no funds available" to any agency "involved in intelligence activities" could be used to aid the contras, "directly or indirectly."

After the Iran-contra scandal was exposed, in May 1987, Will launched an attack on the Boland Amendment—"unconstitutional in intent; pseudo-legal static in the system . . . a non-law"—far more vicious and emotional than any criticism he ventured about the scandal's participants. The conflict between the executive and legislative branches Will decried was precisely due to the administration's breach of "established procedures," to which the Boland Amendment was the response. And the diversion of funds to the contras was precisely intended to evade this measure. If the Boland Amendment was "a non-law," then what laws does Will believe were evaded and subverted? He does not say.

Like the politicians Will set out to study, his words must be taken seriously. Two words are key to his thought—"decent" and "civility"—his shorthand for different political mentalities. "Decent" arises in his language as something bad about Democrats: "There hangs about the Democratic party an aura of moral overreaching. A symptom is the use of words like 'decent' . . . as in 'a decent society requires this or that.' " "Civility," according to Will, is what will be restored when the Iran-contra scandal is swept away. But the meaning of these words, as Will uses them, is broader.

He uses "civility" to mean manners masquerading as morals, a category of form referring less to the rule of law than to the rule of etiquette; it is more an unspoken social, rather than ethical, code. Correct behavior may make the good possible, it is not goodness itself.

By contrast, "decency," which Will belittles, actually *is* about morals. And there is some history behind the word and its content. The introduction of the word "decent" into the political vocabulary can be attributed to George Orwell. In his essay on Charles Dickens, he defined the essence of the great novelist's sensibility as "decent." In an age of totalitarians, Dickens's message was still contemporary. Orwell wrote: "The central problem—how to prevent power from being abused—remains unsolved. . . . 'If men would behave decently the world would be decent' is not such a platitude as it sounds." Since Orwell's use of the word, a number of liberals, intellectuals, and reformers have taken it up. "Decent" connotes a tempered moral position, one that carefully avoids righteous absolutism; it also suggests compassion and patience. The word is precisely the opposite of élite condescension, the opposite of hauteur.

Oddly, Orwell's essay on Dickens was cited by Will in his column on the Royal Shakespeare production of *Nicholas Nickleby* in 1981. "Dickens's message," wrote Will, "which found an avid audience on Broadway, is that the worthiest cause is kindness, and it is timeless." But, in his preference for civility over decency, Will demonstrates that Dickens—and Orwell—did not make a lasting impression on him.

Will's tone of infallibility suggests that his expertise can be reliably followed on any subject from rockets to rock. He never acknowledges that he has changed a single imperious opinion. In his self-revisions, offered as fresh revelation, Will must be banking on his readers' amnesia.

For example, in 1986, in *The Morning After*, Will proclaimed the Reagan presidency a success. At home, Reagan was "saving" the welfare state "by tempering its excesses." Abroad, Will wrote in a 1986 column, Reagan achieved his "finest hour" at the Reykjavik summit, securing for himself "a high place in history." These accomplishments, he wrote in the book, translated into Republican control of the White House as far into the future as the human mind could contemplate: "At the presidential level, realignment is a fact."

As 1988 approaches, Reagan's fall from the Will firmament has been swift. In *The New Season*, he writes without a trace of self-consciousness or irony: "even allowing for the genial hyperbole of American politics and journalism, Reagan's consequences, although substantial, have not been as bold—as revolutionary, if you must—as those of FDR or LBJ."

Then there is Will's dauntless assessment of Bruce Springsteen. In *The New Season* Will asserts that Springsteen's "songs of stress, vulnerability, and precariousness are counterpoints to the Morning in America goo of overripe Reaganism." Consider now the Will of 1984, who tried to claim Springsteen for the Reagan campaign, an effort that resulted in Reagan's approving reference to Springsteen in a stump speech. The George Will of 1984 wrote: "Springsteen's fans say his message affirms the right values. Certainly his manner does. . . . He is no whiner, and the recitation of closed factories and other problems always seems punctuated by a grand, cheerful affirmation: 'Born in the U.S.A.!' . . . There still is nothing quite like being born in the U.S.A."

Never does Will weigh empirical evidence that might ruffle his dogmatic confidence. One seldom feels in the presence of an independent mind, one that considers factual counterarguments or unexpected events. Typically, he ascribes unworthy motives—"infantilism," and so forth—to those with whom he disagrees. *The New Season* is no departure for Will, but is written as if it were further proof of his 1969 doctoral thesis: "A specter is haunting American liberals, the specter of confident politics . . . the kind of open mind the liberal favors is a political menace." Will's method is unyielding—assertion, appeal to authority, snide dismissal of an opposing view. And so he continues his furious assault on the "menace" of the "open mind" and the "moral overreaching" of the "decent."

(October 1987)

The Overthrow of
Jeane Kirkpatrick

The neoconservatives rose to prominence largely on their claims to foreign-policy mastery. In dealing with revolutions that imperil dictators friendly to the United States—revolutions in places like the Philippines—they prescribed a definitive solution: Stand by your strongman.

But as the authoritarian Marcos regime fell, so did the neoconservative theory. Some neoconservatives made a last stand on the op-ed pages, apologetically defending Marcos. But the Reagan administration, confronted with one of its greatest foreign policy crises, eventually followed a strategy that ignored the neoconservatives' formula Though the neoconservatives offered themselves as the administration's instructors, their influence at the crucial moment proved to be virtually nil.

In 1980, Jeane Kirkpatrick, a scholar whose specialty was Peronist Argentina, presented a full-blown theory, published in *Commentary* magazine, attributing the fall of the Nicaraguan and Iranian autocrats to the Carter administration's "lack of realism." She derided the idea that "deep historical forces," finally beyond the control of American policy-makers, were at work. By failing to support Somoza and the Shah, Carter had contributed to the rise of hostile regimes.

Carter's policy fostered instability, Kirkpatrick wrote. She dismissed the "pervasive and mistaken assumption that one can easily locate and impose democratic alternatives" in the Third World and the "equally pervasive and equally flawed belief that change per se in . . . autocracies is inevitable, desirable and in the American interest." She argued instead for backing "positively friendly" authoritarian rulers. And she insisted that "right wing autocracies," unlike totalitarian ones, "do sometimes evolve into democracies."

Ronald Reagan was among the readers of Kirkpatrick's article. He was so impressed that he praised it during the 1980 campaign and named its author ambassador to the United Nations after the election.

In the 1984 campaign, during his second debate with Walter Mondale, Reagan reiterated Kirkpatrick's argument point by point. This time, he employed it specifically to describe the situation in the Philippines, asserting that failure to support "our friend" there would result in the triumph of "totalitarianism, pure and simple, as the alternative." Thus even after Kirkpatrick left the U.N. to become a syndicated columnist, Kirkpatrickism still had the status of a reigning doctrine.

The Philippines crisis, more than any other event of the 1980s, seemed made to order for the neoconservatives. All the elements present in the Philippines were also present in their theory. There was the "positively friendly" authoritarian dictator, the communist insurgency, the moderate "third force," and clear American interests—in the form of gigantic military bases. In this living laboratory, the theory was put to the test.

In December 1985, Kirkpatrick wrote a column ranking Marcos's Philippines in the top third of U.N. members in the good-government category. The unpleasantries uncovered by "American newspapers, newsweeklies and network newscasts" reflected an "obsessive intolerance" with "a nation of great strategic importance." The Shah and Somoza and other long-gone dictators were recalled. "The failings of each were magnified by people who played on American political purism."

The pattern seemed obvious to Kirkpatrick: "Once these rulers had fallen" they were replaced by "more tragically repressive, aggressive dictatorships." Kirkpatrick suggested that the "campaign against the government of the Philippines" might "produce similar consequences."

Early in March 1986, she prepared another column on the Philippines, at the very moment that its presidential election was taking place. "American liberals," she charged, were orchestrating a "campaign . . . to suggest the existence of an anti-Marcos 'consensus' inside the United States government." The result was "meddling" and "interference in Philippine politics." She denounced the "American role" as not "edifying" and cast doubt on charges of Marcos's election fraud—"it seems very unlikely."

American policy makers, she urged, must "cease" their "interference" or we would suffer the fate of the explorer Magellan, who was "hacked to death" by "the Philippine tribes." The Carter nightmare appeared to be recurring, only with Reagan in the White House.

But just as the Reagan administration was edging away from the weakening Philippine strongman, Kirkpatrick began edging away from her previously prepared column. Her line became muddy. As the column was being distributed by her syndicate, she rewrote it and sent out a revised version. In this one, she noted that "charges of fraud destroyed [the] perception" of "a creditable election."

A day after Kirkpatrick's original and altered columns simultaneously appeared in various newspapers, Reagan made the debate muddier. In an interview with *The Washington Post* on February 11, the president praised the emergence of a "two party system" in the Philippines and wondered whether the election fraud was really just "one sided." That evening, Reagan continued his musings at a press conference, at which he suggested "the possibility of fraud . . . on both sides."

Strangely enough, Reagan's comments had little connection with the policy pursued by his administration. On the morning of his press conference, policy makers at the White House had issued a statement expressing concern about Marcos's election fraud. The battle on the inside had already been won by those trying to extricate the United States from the Filipino dictator.

Most of the neoconservatives, however, were not taking their cue from the real administration position but from Reagan's remarks, which he had repudiated himself. Soon, from the neoconservative columns came a shower of praise for the new "two party system" now in place in the Philippines.

Something was happening that was "more important than whether Ferdinand Marcos or Corazon Aquino 'wins,' " wrote Ben Wattenberg, the neoconservative writer, in the *Washington Times*. "[D]emocracy has won a mighty battle." In this view, the election was more meaningful as an existential act than a political one.

The emergence of a "two party system" seemed to bear out the Kirkpatrick thesis that authoritarian regimes could evolve into democracies. But in fact there were not two parties and it wasn't a system. Marcos's organization was a party in the sense that the Gambino crime family is a party. And Aquino's party was a ramshackle affair, sustained by deep popular yearnings, expressed mainly in the streets.

On February 22, the neoconservatives found themselves in the unlikely and uncomfortable position of having the same line as Tass, the Soviet news agency, which attacked the United States for its "attempt to interfere in the internal affairs of the Philippines." To be sure, the conjunction of the neoconservatives and the Soviets as the last apologists for Marcos was a curious event. Certainly, their motives differed. The Soviets' action was a classic demonstration of cynical realpolitik. The neoconservatives acted out of ideological conviction. Yet both sought to put aside soft sentimentality about democratic niceties in the service of national interest.

The cardinal liberal sin, according to the neoconservatives, is "moral equivalence"—the equation of American and Russian short-comings. But in the Philippines' crisis, the neoconservatives exhibited a moral equivalence of their own—the equation of authoritarians and democrats. Because authoritarian regimes have been toppled and replaced by democratic ones—for example, in Greece, Portugal, and Argentina—the neoconservatives tend to see every permutation within authoritarianism as a step toward democracy. The conclusion they draw is that these regimes should be defended as if they were the seed of democracy, not the suffocating lid.

In the heat of the controversy, in the Philippines, no one articulated the neoconservative sensibility better than Owen Harries, the co-editor of the *National Interest,* a neoconservative quarterly intended to tutor the Reagan administration in foreign policy. On February 23, in the *New York Times,* he blamed the crisis on "the well-intentioned efforts of Americans of various political persuasions." He claimed the mantle of a higher realism: "Moral considerations . . . cannot be the decisive factors leading to demands for the removal of President Marcos." And he sketched a scenario in which Aquino's victory fostered "bloody chaos leading to the rapid growth of Communist power." Marcos, he concluded, must stay.

Blas Ople, Marcos's minister of labor, agreed. In the final days, Ople achieved a certain notoriety as Marcos's representative on television interview shows. On February 23, he appeared on "This Week with David Brinkley," where he pasted the last fig leaf on his regime: "I would like to paraphrase the distinguished ambassador to the United Nations from the United States, Jeane Kirkpatrick, who warned against a foreign policy of the United States, dedicated to the, literally, to the subjugation of a friendly nation. This is not the business of U.S. foreign policy."

But by the end, even a few neoconservatives seemed to question a theory that seemed to have so little relevance to what happened in the Philippines. Their advice had gone unheeded. They had been overrun by circumstances, unable to adjust, frozen in their past assumptions.

Charles Krauthammer, a *Washington Post* columnist with neoconservative sympathies, concluded that "the authoritarian-totalitarian distinction . . . as a guide for deciding which regime the United States will push toward democracy . . . has been superseded." Thus the old neoconservative doctrine was declared obsolete.

Perhaps the most apposite text on the neoconservatives' current condition is Kirkpatrick's famous *Commentary* essay. The "mistakes and distortions" of the Carter years were "all fashionable," she wrote. The liberals had "good intentions," but they were guilty of "idealism." They allowed the "blinding power of ideology" to govern their "interpretation of events."

(March 1986)

Norman Podhoretz's
Literary Standards

With the publication of his collected essays, *The Bloody Crossroads: Where Literature and Politics Meet* (Simon & Schuster), Norman Podhoretz, the editor of *Commentary* magazine, has achieved a tremendous, though narrow, feat of literary imagination. He has reproduced, down to the most exact nuances, the faded American Stalinist aesthetic. His accomplishment is doubly impressive because he has astonishingly managed to cast this rarefied, left-wing sectarian mentality as neoconservatism.

Unfortunately, *The Bloody Crossroads* is not the complete Podhoretz. Conspicuously absent are his fawning reviews of Edward Koch's *Mayor* and William F. Buckley Jr.'s *Overdrive*. Also missing are his enthralling columns excoriating President Reagan as a wimp and lamenting that Joseph McCarthy made the world unsafe for McCarthyism. Still, the pieces assembled in *The Bloody Crossroads* give a fair sense of the Podhoretz oeuvre.

The supreme litmus test by which he measures novelists, critics, and poets is whether they correctly answer the question: Which side are you on? Just as the Stalinists of the 1930s believed there were only two sides—either for or against the Soviet Union—so does Podhoretz.

His tone is at perfect pitch, veering from denunciatory invective to obsequious praise (on Kissinger's memoir: "What we have here is writing of the very highest order"), with few stops in between. He has adopted the pose of individual bravery, struggling against a ruthless ruling class, while declaiming the commonplace of the moment. He insists he speaks for the majority, an imperiled Western civilization, yet he maintains a relentlessly minoritarian sensibility.

Podhoretz calls the class enemy a variety of names: "the adversary culture," "the New Class," "the Left," "Bloomsbury." His piece on the English critic, F. R. Leavis, provides him an occasion for assailing "our own local variant of Bloomsbury, headquartered in the *New York Review of Books* and the *New York Times Book Review.*"

He permits no distractions in his clarifying vision. Communism, he is moved to write, has been "more dangerous than Nazism or fascism precisely because it exerted a much greater ideological appeal." Anyone who strays from the main task of battling the monolithic foe receives his scorn. Albert Camus, for example, showed "cowardice and hypocrisy" because of "his failure to side as clearly with the democracies as Sartre was siding with the Communists." Camus also failed to realize that "the truths of *The Rebel* were on the whole the truths of the 'Right.' " The Camus who was engaged and yet ambivalent, the actual Camus, should be relegated to the dustbin of history. The Camus "who should be revived," Podhoretz avers, is the one who unknowingly conveyed "the truths of the 'Right.' "

Podhoretz disdains Camus's ambivalence. The notion of art-for-art's-sake revolts him. "Most contemporary American novels," he writes, "invite the reader to join with the author in a luxuriously complacent celebration of themselves and of the stock prejudices and bigotries of the 'advanced' literary culture against the middle-class world around them." Even Saul Bellow "seemed always to be writing only about himself." Milan Kundera, the Czech writer, too, has fallen into this error, believing that he is not principally a political writer, but a novelist. The class enemy, called "the new aristocracy" by Podhoretz here, meaning other book reviewers, has taken Kundera's work as literature that "transcends political and ideological differences." "Why should you, of all writers," Podhoretz demands in an "open letter" to Kundera, "wish to be coopted by people who think there is no moral or political—or cultural—difference between West and East worth talking about, let alone fighting over?"

Like most neoconservatives, Podhoretz has little use for conservatism, which seeks in tradition a refuge from constant change. His writings on true conservatives are thin; but his essays in *The Bloody Crossroads* on Henry Adams and Alexander Solzhenitsyn address the subject. Adams is reduced to merely a crabbed, anti-Semitic personality. His *Education* is termed "repellent," and his *History of the United States during the Administrations of Thomas Jefferson and James Madison*, a magisterial work that places Adams in the same rank as Macaulay and approaches even Gibbon's, is dismissed as "covering only seventeen years of early American history." On the other hand, Solzhenitsyn is acquitted of all allegations of anti-Semitism and his "authoritarian coloration" is excused in the light of his anticommunist "prophetic mission." Once again, literature is judged mainly by an ideological—and perhaps anachronistic—criterion. If Adams had been born a century later and written about "the God that failed," instead of the Virgin and the dynamo, he might have received different treatment.

Podhoretz's hero is George Orwell, author of *1984* and the quintessential man of the democratic left, who, if he "were alive today . . . would be taking his stand with the neoconservatives and against the Left." To prove his point, Podhoretz quotes Orwell, an Englishman, stating his preference for America over the Soviet Union. Podhoretz, however, has expertly edited Orwell's statement so that the phrases—"In the end the choice may be forced upon us" and "if we fail to bring a West European union into being"—no longer appear. This airbrushing of Orwell to make him absolutely fit the correct line is wonderfully Orwellian, something Orwell, if "alive today," would undoubtedly have savored.

In the through-the-looking-glass decade of the 1980s, when Ronald Reagan presents himself as the latter-day Franklin D. Roosevelt, the figure Norman Podhoretz most closely resembles is Michael Gold, the literary commissar of the American Communist Party. In fact, in a 1930 essay, "Proletarian Realism," Gold foreshadowed Podhoretz: "Proletarian realism is never pointless. It does not believe in literature for its own sake, but in literature that is useful, has a social function . . . there are more intellectuals than ever who are trying to make literature a plaything. Every poem, every novel and drama, must have a social theme, or it is merely confectionery."

But Gold wrote more than essays. He was also the author of a novel, *Jews without Money*, one of the few of the "proletarian realism" school that can be judged to have had some literary merit. It cannot be said that Podhoretz has approached Gold's stature until he attempts fiction, too. In *The Bloody Crossroads* he explains that he has retreated from modernism: "Nowadays my taste in fiction runs strongly to the realistic." In the nonfiction world, the neoconservatives are battling the foreign service to remake U.S. foreign policy in their ideological image. Perhaps Podhoretz may attempt a novel depicting this class struggle entitled "Neoconservatives with State Department Appointments."

(May 1986)

Jack Wheeler's Big Safari

"Real weapons!" demanded Jeane Kirkpatrick.

Stormy applause erupted from thousands of black-tied movement conservatives.

"Real helicopters!" she continued.

"Real ground-to-air missiles!"

More stormy applause, and not merely for the former United Nations ambassador. The cheering was also for the international cast arrayed at the long table behind her. Here was the latest right-wing icon, Jonas Savimbi, the bearded Angolan rebel. Over there was the inexpressive Adolfo Calero, the contra *commandante*. The space between them was occupied by Vice President Bush, projecting a rapturous smile, and several grim Afghan *mujaheddin*, wrapped in turbans and captured Red Army belts. All were assembled in the Washington Hilton ballroom for the Conservative Political Action Conference in early 1986.

Roaming through the cavernous room, quietly passing among the two hundred tables, mostly unacknowledged, was Jack Wheeler, a forty-two-year-old man of medium height and strong build, wearing a somewhat ill-fitting gray suit. His long, thinning hair is swept straight back; his close-set, clear blue eyes have a piercing gaze. "The Indiana Jones of the right," said a reverent young conservative. "That's him."

Wheeler, a professional adventurer, glowed in the presence of this *tableau vivant* of the Reagan Doctrine; for his incredible explorations made it possible. Perhaps above all, the Reagan Doctrine stands for handing "real weapons" over to such "freedom fighters," making the cold war hot at the peripheries.

"Jack Wheeler lives the dreams the rest of us talk and write about," says Bently Elliott, the director of presidential speech writing. From another perspective, *Barricada,* the official Sandinista newspaper, has ominously warned its readers of "Wheeler's shadow." "The concept of 'freedom fighters' as an organizational principle," reported *Barricada,* "emerged basically from the work of Jack Wheeler."

In the history of the Reagan Doctrine, between the idea and the reality falls "Wheeler's shadow." By his deeds he has animated the doctrine that has become the catechism of the moment, promulgated by the columnists of conservative ideology.

"Now it's our turn," says Wheeler. "In the 1960s, we had this endless succession of Marxist guerrilla heroes—Mao Tse-tung, Fidel Castro, Che Guevara; all the Che posters on all the college dorm walls in the 1960s. Now there are *anti-*Marxist guerrilla heroes . . . the whole anti-imperialist liberation struggle is just all shifted around, 180 degrees . . . That's the gestalt."

On his journey to the contra way of knowledge, Wheeler has traveled for much of the past three years to the front lines on three continents. He instructed Angolans, Nicaraguans, and Afghans that they are allies in a united front. His voyages have not escaped notice in *Izvestia,* the Soviet newspaper, which featured him as an "ideological gangster."

When he returned from his first trip, in November 1983, he recounted his ideological adventure stories in the White House, where Ronald Reagan's speech writers were seized with enthusiasm. At last, someone was bringing the good news that a world-wide anti-Soviet insurgency was not a wish but a fact.

Wheeler was introduced to Lt. Col. Oliver North, the National Security Council's contact with the contras. Soon, Wheeler began advising his new friend. He also briefed William Casey, the CIA director, and he lectured Jeane Kirkpatrick in what might be called her metamorphosis from neoconservative into full-throated neo-contra. The president's speeches began to ring with tributes to "freedom fighters."

Wheeler has been brought into the councils of the conservative élite, but he is not essentially a political animal. "I just do not like politics," he says. "I don't like the backstabbing, the game playing. It's just endemic to politics, and I just don't like it."

He prefers jungle adventures—and his very name suggests a boy's hero. So does his "Dewar's Profile," an ad that appeared in 1980: "Past: Born in Los Angeles in 1943, Jack Wheeler climbed the Matterhorn, swam the Hellespont, slew the fabled Man Killing Tiger of Dalat and lived among Ecuadorian headhunters . . . Scotch: White Label."

Like Indiana Jones he seeks the treasure of wealth and power, but doesn't want to possess it; his is not so much the pursuit of happiness as the happiness of pursuit. "Because," says Wheeler, "ever since I could remember, I've had this sensation, a very intense awareness, that this is *it*. I mean, there will be only one me on this planet forever. You have one chance. One life. And some people collect stamps. Some collect rare china. I want to collect experiences."

Wheeler's quest began, he recalls, on a rainy Saturday afternoon, when he was 14 and opened Richard Halliburton's *Book of Marvels*—"my initial inspiration."

Halliburton was an American adventurer and writer who died at the age of 39 in 1939, attempting to sail a Chinese junk through a typhoon. His travels were captured in a breathless, exclamatory style. "I wanted freedom, freedom to indulge in whatever caprice struck my fancy," he wrote in *The Royal Road to Romance*.

"I'd never read anything like it," says Wheeler. "Place after place of romantic adventures. There was one chapter about Halliburton climbing the Matterhorn. I sat and stared at the picture, Halliburton on the Matterhorn. I just kind of found myself walking down the hall, finding my dad, putting the book down to the Matterhorn picture, and saying, 'Dad, I want to climb that mountain.' He saw that I was serious, not kidding around. 'Okay,' he said. 'Let's talk about it.'"

Jack Wheeler was a serious boy—in fact, at twelve the youngest eagle scout in the country, decorated by President Eisenhower at the White House. When his father, Jackson Wheeler, a popular Los Angeles television personality, took the family to Europe, he arranged for Jack to realize his dream. So, within months of reading Halliburton, Jack found himself triumphantly standing on the Matterhorn.

The Wheelers' grand tour included a brief stop in Moscow. "I remember a very oppressive atmosphere, like a very heavy wet wool blanket hung over the whole society," says Wheeler. He also remembers "a teen-age fantasy," antedating his Russian visit, "of going over there and forming a band of guerrillas. The Soviets could crush it, but not if the resistance spread."

Back home, he was elected student council president at the Hollywood Professional School (classmate: Annette Funicello, "mouseketeer"). Beyond school, his life was a series of amazing stories. During one summer vacation he wandered deep into the Amazon jungle, befriending a band of headhunting Jivaro Indians. As a token of esteem, they presented him with a shrunken head. (In 1961, when the precocious Wheeler was featured on the television program "This Is Your Life" at age seventeen, the chief headhunter appeared as a surprise from his past.)

At sixteen, Wheeler entered the University of California at Los Angeles, majoring in anthropology. During his freshman year he took a weekend off to fly to Turkey, just to swim naked across the Hellespont. Several expeditions later, literally to Timbuktu and back, he acquired a master's degree from the University of Hawaii and a doctorate from the University of Southern California, writing his thesis on Greek ethics.

There was also a short political interlude, immediately after his graduation from U.C.L.A.

"Dad, you know Ronald Reagan, don't you?"

"Why, yes," replied Jackson Wheeler, who had known Reagan for years as a Hollywood fixture. Now, in the fall of 1965, Reagan was preparing to run for the governorship of California.

"Could I meet him, Dad?"

The Wheelers ventured to the candidate's Pacific Palisades home, where Jack was anointed the state chair of Youth for Reagan. What he liked best about Reagan was that he was "not a professional politician."

By then, Wheeler had already dropped into the jungles of Vietnam, in 1963, wearing his U.C.L.A. varsity jacket. He was not tracking Viet Cong; his quarry was the Man Killing Tiger of Dalat. His rifle, a Weatherby big game gun, was a gift from Herb Klein, one of Richard Nixon's aides.

Wheeler's jungle guide knew not only where to find tigers. "He knew people who had cinnamon plantations." Jack wrote his father that "we might have a real opportunity here." The deal was struck, and Saigon Cinnamon International commenced exporting to spice brokers. Wheeler spent the mid-sixties shuttling between California and Vietnam. But as the business grew, the war escalated. He was not captivated by a Vietnam mystique; in 1967, feeling "very bitter," Wheeler simply withdrew.

"It was a war we had no intention of winning, and it was obscene," he says. "Vietnam was an obscenity, to murder fifty thousand American kids for nothing . . . Why we stayed is a real mystery. I think if Bobby Kennedy had been elected in 1968 things would have been really different."

The only tangible remnant of Wheeler's Vietnam days is a solid gold ring, purchased in the Chinese district of Saigon. He has not removed it from his finger for more than two decades. Engraved on the ring are two dragons, flanking a Chinese character. "It is," he said, "the Chinese symbol for happiness and virility, which to a Chinese is exactly the same thing."

After Vietnam, he made a business of his obsession. Wheeler Adventures was incorporated in the early 1970s, and since then has taken would-be explorers on safari—out of Africa and into Tibet, to the North Pole, and to the South Sea Islands. With his girlfriend, Jacqueline King, a former Las Vegas showgirl, he took four elephants along Hannibal's route across the Alps. "When you actually do it," he says, "actually take elephants over the Alps, the history becomes a part of your life. But I'd never do it again. Too risky, too risky for the elephants."

In 1976, Wheeler published *The Adventurer's Guide*, a mixture of philosophy, memoir and how-to. ("Exploring Outer Mongolia . . . You start by taking a boat from Yokohama. . . .") By chronicling his own feats of individual daring, he intended to stir the reader from his armchair with the call of the wild. "I want you to be a hero to yourself," he wrote. "To hell with the impossible dream!" To prove his point, in 1981 Wheeler made a daredevil parachute jump at the North Pole, a feat entered into the *Guinness Book of World Records*.

But Wheeler's personal dream shattered that year when Jacqueline King died of cancer. "She died in my arms," he says. "I didn't know whether I wanted to live or not. My life was pretty aimless. I became a hermit." He secluded himself for a time on a California beach, mesmerized by the ocean.

Back east, Ronald Reagan was moving into the White House. Wheeler felt himself pulled away from his grief and toward Washington. He reached out to an old pal from the Youth for Reagan group, Dana Rohrabacher, a presidential speech writer. "He felt a little left out," says Rohrabacher. "He wanted to be part of this great tide of human events. He wanted to do his part, play his role. He was calling me in dismay. I said, 'You have to credential yourself, make yourself a specialist.' "

Wheeler was blocked. He stared at a huge map of the world mounted on his wall. "And I just saw the map differently," he says. "You know where there are these pictures that have a whole bunch of black and gray splotches, and there's a figure in there. And you look and look and all of a sudden the figure just pops out at you. And you never look at it the same."

What he saw was a world in flames, "a whole family of guerrilla wars that were taking place inside Soviet colonies." From this epiphany, he knew his mission. "I had heard about the contras and Afghanistan, of course, and I heard something about Angola . . . And all of a sudden I realized these were not isolated phenomena. I was witnessing a spontaneous worldwide rejection of Soviet imperialism, and nobody knew about it . . . and I realized the only way to actually find out about it was to go there."

For years, Wheeler had been testing his self-reliance and stoicism; he was discovering himself on solitary forays into the wilderness. His ordeals prepared him for the ultimate challenge with "evil," he says. "My background, going to all these remote places, getting to know different and remote people, my philosophy background, gave me whatever skills I have to get to these various [counterrevolutionary] groups, gain their confidence and be with them without much difficulty."

He made arrangements for his expedition by establishing the Freedom Research Foundation; eventually, he secured funds from the right-wing libertarian Reason Foundation. He opened a small office, overlooking the ocean, armed with computers and a wall-sized map to record the progress of the anti-Soviet guerrilla movements.

Ready for his global journey, his khaki fatigues and bulletproof underwear packed in a duffel bag, Wheeler stopped at the White House in June 1983, where Rohrabacher gave him a sendoff. Then he embarked on the Big Safari, his odyssey into "wars of liberation."

The first frontier he crossed was the border separating Honduras and Nicaragua. When he encountered communism, he knew he had arrived at the line between civilization and savagery.

Wheeler's guide was a lean contra named Charley, who led him on a night patrol into Nicaragua, "real Apache country." Suddenly, bullets started shredding the foliage. Charley grabbed Jack by the arm and dragged him out of harm's way. The next morning was the last time Wheeler saw him; Charley turned, raised a clenched fist in salute and shouted: "In Managua!"

Back at the base camp, Wheeler informed Col. Enrique Bermudez, the contras' military strongman, "You are not alone. There are thousands of people like you in Soviet colonies all over the world."

"It was," says Wheeler, "like a revelation to him. I remember just the wonder in Bermudez's eyes when I told him. Nobody had ever said anything like that before. But they certainly wanted it to be the case. Nobody wants to be alone."

The next frontier: Angola. Here Wheeler was the guest of Jonas Savimbi. For 2,500 kilometers, Wheeler traveled on the back of a captured Soviet truck through what he calls "Savimbi's Kingdom." At every village the entourage would stop for a charismatic Savimbi oration, preceded by a big band backed up by a chorus of thirty singers. "It's not like rock 'n' roll," says Wheeler, "but I mean it's some version of it. And they play on the electric guitar and everybody dances and pounds on their drums and has a hell of a time and yells, 'Savimbi!' "

And, again, Wheeler told them they were not alone. For Wheeler's farewell, Savimbi assembled the band, the singers and about two thousand dancers. "Remember, Jack," Wheeler recalls Savimbi saying, "this is a high-stakes game." They embraced, and Wheeler departed for another destination.

"Afghanistan," he says, "just dwarfs everything else. It's just the size of the uprising and the fierceness of it. And we're going after the Soviets. I mean we're not up against the Cubans here. We're up against the Red Army . . . There's nothing like it on the face of the earth."

Wheeler slipped into Afghanistan with a small band of *mujaheddin*. He gained the trust of one by comparing him to Wild Bill Hickok. Even in barren and blasted Asia, Wheeler found the Wild West. There were good guys and bad guys and it was High Noon every day.

Wheeler and his *mujaheddin* staged a lightning raid. "Well, we had a great time," he says. "I mean it was night—all activities happen at night—and the Soviets started firing these rockets and recoilless rifles, and finally they hit the power station, and it was just like a movie, a war movie, the tracer bullets and explosions and bombs . . . But they were missing and we were racing around, all down these alleys, and mortars were exploding, and we're all laughing and doubled over laughing and tears were pouring down our faces. We were embracing each other and laughing so hard we could hardly run because they were missing. And it was quite a time, quite a time."

He has returned three times since. "Afghanistan is like a magnet," he said. "I don't know how to describe it. . . . You dress like them and they make you part of them. It compels you to go back. And so I'll be back."

Afghanistan, however, did not complete his *tour d'horizon*. He recalls speeding through the thick jungles of Cambodia on a Yamaha DT-125 motorbike; witnessing the execution by decapitation of a "spy" in the camp of guerrillas in Mozambique; and trekking with the resistance in Ethiopia. And everywhere he went he said, "You are not alone."

When he stopped at the White House in November 1983, equipped with slides, the president's speechwriting staff—the most concentrated collection of ideologically correct people in the administration—gathered in a darkened room. Wheeler's message leaped beyond intractable budgets and congressional deadlocks, "the humdrum of government," according to a White House source. This was not some mundane realignment of the Republican Party; it was, rather, a cosmic realignment of the planet. Now, conservative ideology began at the barrel of a gun.

"Jack," says a White House source, "was the one who brought it all together. He took random struggles and crystallized the concept that they were part of the same historical movement." After hearing Wheeler, several of Reagan's speech writers say they filled the president's speeches with references to "freedom fighters." By 1985, the president himself was expounding the Reagan Doctrine in his State of the Union Address: "we must not break faith with those who are risking their lives on every continent, from Afghanistan to Nicaragua, to defy Soviet-supported aggression."

To the friends of Jack Wheeler, Secretary of State George Shultz was also sounding a lot like Jack Wheeler. "You recognize some stuff in there," Wheeler says a National Security Council official told him. "You like that, don't you?" Yes, Wheeler did like it.

Wheeler started exhibiting his sound-and-light show to conservative groups, galvanizing a movement beginning to splinter in the penultimate phase of the Reagan presidency. "Wheeler, with his adventurous activity and his slides, which are gripping, really captured the imagination of a lot of people," says new right leader Paul Weyrich. "The conservative movement is sometimes fractured by other kinds of issues. But the Reagan Doctrine unites it across the board."

Wheeler became a popular speaker at right-wing events, where he invariably exclaims, "We got rhythm, we got soul, we got freedom and rock 'n' roll!"

In 1985, he got the notion that all the guerrilla leaders he had met should convene "in liberated territory"—a media event of the first magnitude. So he persuaded Lew Lehrman, the drugstore tycoon, former New York gubernatorial candidate and president of Citizens for America, to sponsor a happening.

Wheeler circled the world, assembling rebels. In June 1985, in Jamba, the provisional capital of "Savimbi's Kingdom," the leaders of four guerrilla movements awakened, literally, to a lion's roar and issued this declaration: "Our struggles are one struggle." A "Dear Lew" letter to Lehrman from Reagan was read: "Their goals are our goals." And Lehrman vouchsafed to each rebel a framed copy of the Declaration of Independence.

The organizer of this extraordinary conference remained in the background. But Wheeler surfaced at a 1985 Senate subcommittee hearing as a witness on anti-Soviet insurgencies, which he asserted were "the only hope for genuine and lasting peace."

Now, in April, 1986, as military aid to the contras again comes to a vote, Wheeler is nowhere to be found. Perhaps he is leading another safari, which after all is his livelihood. His travel company (now called Wheeler-Blanchard Adventures) has advertised an "Expedition to Liberated Angola . . . plus a Halley's Comet Safari in Botswana (cost: $6,920, without airfare)." Those who signed up were promised "a parade of over a thousand guerrillas in their honor" and the chance to "personally meet Jonas Savimbi." The date of departure was declared "confidential."

His friends refused to reveal his whereabouts. "As we speak," said Rohrabacher, "he is in an unnamed foreign country, doing freedom's work."

It is expected, however, that he will return soon—his wedding is scheduled for May. "Do you want to see her picture?" he asked recently. She is a beauty consultant with red hair, pearly teeth and ruddy cheeks. Her name—her real name—is Rebel Holiday.

(April 1986)

Michael Ledeen's
High and Low Adventures

One by one the mourners file past the stricken *Partisan Review,* once the most influential and prestigious journal of the New York intellectuals.

P.R.—the very letters still evoke awe in certain circles. It had for years been living a kind of posthumous existence, mainly as the subject of nostalgic memoirs. And yet it still had its importance, if only because it stood as a monument to the achievements of the New York intellectuals, a family scattered and shattered by death and politics.

On the eve of the Iran-contra scandal, the journal that had featured Jean-Paul Sartre and T. S. Eliot, Lionel Trilling and Edmund Wilson, Delmore Schwartz and Saul Bellow—and Dwight Macdonald, Andre Malraux, Mary McCarthy, George Orwell, Arthur Koestler, Ignazio Silone, Arthur M. Schlesinger Jr., Hannah Arendt, Norman Mailer, Susan Sontag, and virtually the entire pageant of midcentury intellectuals—turned to a new writer. It had been drifting rightward for a while, slowly fitting itself to the fashions of the neoconservatives, from Star Wars to the Reagan Doctrine. Now, William Phillips, one of *P.R.*'s founders and its editor, wanted an article on the meaning of "the national interest" to serve as the basis for one of *P.R.*'s famous forums. The writer he selected in the fall of 1986 was Michael Ledeen, a mysterious ideological adventurer, even then engaged in an adventure that would bring calamity to the Reagan presidency, playing "a key role in the initial contacts between the United States and Israel vis-à-vis Iran," according to the report of the Senate Intelligence Committee.

When Ledeen's contribution was sent out for comment, letters of resignation from contributing editors came back in return. Ledeen, as far as they were concerned, was one step beyond the pale. His reputation—he had been denounced on the floor of the Italian Parliament as an "intriguer" by the head of military intelligence—preceded his piece. Many of the *P.R.* illuminati sought to cast him into outer darkness.

Daniel Bell, a Harvard professor and contributing editor, is an *éminence grise* among the New York intellectuals, present at every tortuous twist of their decades-long journey, author of such seminal books as *The End of Ideology* and *The Coming of Post-Industrial Society*. He cofounded *The Public Interest*, which has since become one of the salient neoconservative journals, but was established to offer anti-ideological, pragmatic analysis. When Bell chose to drop his name from the masthead of *The Public Interest* and to break with the neoconservatives, many of them old friends, he published his declaration of independence in the fiftieth anniversary issue of *P.R.*, explaining himself to those most important to him in that venue. He refuses to comment publicly on Ledeen's article and its commissioning, but his withdrawal of his name from the *PR* masthead was like the withdrawal of the mandate of heaven.

"People like Dan Bell and I didn't want to be involved in such a discussion," says Diana Trilling, a distinguished critic, the widow of Lionel Trilling, who was the preeminent literary critic of his generation and the moral center of the *PR* universe. She is more than the keeper of the flame, though she is that, too. When Bell declined to participate in the Ledeen symposium Diana Trilling initially urged him to reconsider, saying that he had an obligation to respond. He protested, however, that the piece had no merit. Upon reading it herself, she too decided that "I didn't want to have any discourse on this level, an unworthy level, unworthy of the intellectual enterprise as I define it. This was a practical action program . . . Ledeen's no intellectual . . . There's been a debasement. The neoconservatives, they really have debased the intellectual process, my chief argument against them. Sometimes some of them say that they descended from my husband. He'd be appalled at the way they have factionalized and polarized the intellectual life. I'm sure he would loathe it."

"It's not just that Ledeen is a neocon, it's that he's a con," says Leon Wieseltier, the literary editor of the *New Republic* and contributing editor to *P.R.*, who quit. His connection to the world of the New York intellectual fathers is not tangential: He is Trilling's last graduate student. In his letter of resignation, Wieseltier called Ledeen "an intriguer and an operator and an opportunist," an opinion based "upon personal acquaintance with the man in his milieu . . . If *P.R.* is embarrassed now by the revelation that Ledeen took part in the disgraceful Iran affair, it deserves to be: his predilection for such activity is well-known. You could have been warned."

"It is completely innocent," protests Edith Kurzweil, *P.R.*'s managing editor. "We hope to get to the issues. That's what William was thinking of."

"I think William's very disingenuous about it," says Dennis Wrong, a professor at New York University and contributing editor to *P.R.* "William is not well, he's an old man, it's possible his judgment might have been defective on all this. It's hard to believe, though. I alternate between feeling sorry and annoyed with Edith and William about their disingenuousness."

William Phillips himself, a frail eighty years old who endured more than a half-century of intellectual controversies, last week was placed in a hospital's intensive care unit, stricken with pneumonia. "He was in terrible shape," says Kurzweil. "Terrible."

Ledeen, for his part, says, "I'm not talking to the [*Washington*] *Post* anymore"—at least not directly. All inquiries are handled by his lawyer, R. James Woolsey, who processes Ledeen's written responses. In them, Ledeen still nurtures the belief that his article will see the light of day: "According to my conversations with him [Phillips], it has not been rejected but is still under consideration. Since the piece was originally written long before the Iran-Contra story broke, there was nothing in it about Iran. Mr. Phillips felt that *Partisan Review* could not publish the piece without my including something about Iran. The piece has recently been revised and resubmitted."

Ledeen was unaware of Bell's resignation and had been led to believe by Edith Kurzweil that Leon Wieseltier "resigned for reasons unrelated to my article." ("So bizarre," says Wieseltier.) Ledeen added, "I hope that the piece, once published, attracts as much attention as it has prior to publication." "I don't know how to handle it yet," says Kurzweil. "I don't think we can print the piece. I don't think we will. I really don't know . . . Ledeen hasn't been informed."

"If it's published," says Wrong, "who's going to be left to publish the magazine?" The brush of the venerable *P.R.* with a veiled character from the Iran-contra scandal is a tale of two cities and two different types of intellectual. "It reveals something about the New York intellectuals and their politics, alas, that they are New York intellectuals, often quite parochial about Washington," says Wrong.

P.R. was launched in 1934, with the backing of the Communist Party, to wage the ideological struggle in the field of culture. But the young restless radicals who edited the journal broke with the party line, reforming *P.R.* as an independent entity. The New York they inhabited was "like the other side of the moon," Phillips wrote in his memoir. It was a life of youthful outsiders, first and second generation immigrants, mostly Jewish, completely removed from practical politics. They were an incestuous, squabbling family like no other, at the same time incredibly provincial and cosmic in outlook, consumed with world-historical events and ideologies.

The twin obsessions of the New York intellectuals were modernism in art and literature and Marxism in politics. They defined much of the anticommunist liberalism that dominated the postwar era. And in time the critical sensibility of the magazine was absorbed by much of the larger American intellectual community. *P.R.*'s positions became almost an orthodoxy, the avant-garde co-opted by its own success.

By the 1960s the generation of the 1930s had become middle-aged and tenured. These aging radicals were dismayed and often bewildered by the new generation that dismissed their wisdom. The rejection of the new generation was so total, among a few, that even the Beatles were condemned as "anti-thought," according to one eminent figure. In this generational schism can be found one of the roots of neoconservatism, an offshoot of the New York intellectuals. *P.R.*, however, did not join the united front against the new. Phillips viewed the fresh currents of the 1960s as a hopeful revival of the earlier radical spirit he himself had experienced in the 1930s. And *P.R.* began to publish sympathetic pieces. But Phillips's move was belated, occurring in the 1970s, when what he was allying himself with was already fading.

In his 1983 memoir, *A Partisan View,* Phillips dissociated himself from the "extreme positions" of the neoconservatives. The reviews by neoconservatives, in return, were ferocious. And, according to a friend of Phillips, he was shaken. It was then that he began the trek to the right. Finally, at the instant before the scandal began to throw neoconservatism into a tailspin, he arrived at Ledeen.

Michael Ledeen came to conquer Washington. He was part of a small wave of immigration to the capital of neoconservative intellectuals, numbering a few dozen at most, who arrived at National Airport in the late 1970s to undermine the Carter administration. The elders of this group were disgruntled New York intellectuals who were trying to extend their reach into Washington. They no longer saw themselves as alienated critics, but as players in the game of power. At every station where ideology and policy crossed in the 1980s, the neoconservatives could be found close to the switch—

supply-side economics, the contra war, and the scandal. Ledeen appeared to the neoconservatives as enigmatic and yet knowing. They provided him with an informal network. They got him jobs at think tanks, grants, introductions, published his articles, invited him to parties, and arranged for him to speak at conferences.

His career began as a student of fascism. In 1977, he published an admiring biography, *The First Duce*, about Gabriele D'Annunzio, an Italian ideological adventurer, "a poet-warrior," as Ledeen put it, who was a precursor of Mussolini. D'Annunzio held parliaments in contempt, considered politics a form of theater, and believed in the rule of a charismatic leader at the crest of masses mobilized by myth and symbols. D'Annunzio, Ledeen wrote, "possessed the key to modern politics," providing a "common point of departure" for "radicals of both Right and Left." Ledeen's academic work, however, did not earn him tenure. He left Washington University at St. Louis, where he taught, amid accusations of plagiarism, a charge he has denied. His research into Italian politics led not to more research, but to practice.

The details of his Italian career—or charges about it—have been elaborated by an indictment issued by the Criminal Court of Rome against Francesco Pazienza, a political intriguer who was convicted of many crimes; interviews given by Pazienza; and a 171-page report of an investigation conducted by the Italian Parliament. Pazienza was a deputy to the chief of Italian military intelligence and a leading member of a clandestine organization called P-2, a parallel hierarchy of right-wing generals, colonels, and politicians that attempted to stage what the Italian press has called "a silent coup" through "a strategy of tension." When the pervasive influence of P-2 was exposed in 1981, the Christian Democratic government fell. Indictments were handed down charging P-2's members with many crimes, including "subversive association with the aim of terrorism" and its cover-up.

After Pazienza was convicted of a long list of crimes, he told Jonathan Kwitny of the *Wall Street Journal* that Italian military intelligence, then under the control of P-2, had paid Ledeen at least $120,000, at least some of it into a Bermuda bank account, and that Ledeen operated under a code name—Z-3—charges Ledeen has denied.

The indictment against the convicted Pazienza notes that "in collaboration" with Ledeen, Pazienza "succeeded in extorting, also using fraudulent means, information—then published . . . in the international press—on the Libyan business of Billy Carter, the brother of the then president of the United States." According to

Pazienza, the Italian military intelligence, under P-2, gathered information by clandestine means about Billy Carter and gave it to Ledeen, who co-authored a piece in *The New Republic* with Arnaud de
Borchgrave, now editor of the *Washington Times*, breaking the damaging "Billygate" story.

In Italy, during the transition between the Carter and Reagan
presidencies, Ledeen and Pazienza appointed themselves a liaison
team between the Italian government and the incoming administration, according to then U.S. Ambassador Richard N. Gardner—a
charge Ledeen has denied. But almost as soon as the new team was
in Washington, the secretary of state, Alexander Haig, named Ledeen a consultant on international terrorism. He was now widely
acknowledged as an expert of the school that believed that a "terror
network," run by the Soviets, was the fount of international terrorism. Since terrorism is apparently a problem without any apparent
solution, the "terror network" became an ideological device for promoting a certain version of anticommunism. Every hijacking and car
bombing became an illustration of global geopolitics, rather than of
intractable regional strife.

Ledeen's position within Washington partly depended upon playing a sensitive game, establishing his prominence in two realms. To
the foreign policy specialists, he presented himself as an intellectual,
a "big-picture" man. In the meantime, he appeared before the intellectuals as a foreign-policy expert who had a hall pass to the White
House situation room.

Ledeen's résumé, a wonderful sociological document for future
historians of the Reagan epoch, lists his voluminous publications and
concludes with details of his television appearances, from "Nightline" to the "McNeil-Lehrer News Hour," where he frequently appeared as the expert. He wore his articles the way Oliver North wore
his medals; they constituted his credibility, which made all else possible, including a televised appearance on "This Week with David
Brinkley." His public persona, in the meantime, helped sustain his
secret activities as consultant to the National Security Council. He
was appointed to this position in 1983 by NSC adviser Robert C.
McFarlane, who aspired to a towering Kissingerian reputation but
possessed inadequate intellectual gifts.

The administration apparently considered Ledeen an expert on
the international left. After the invasion of Grenada in 1983, he was
asked to assess the internal documents of the deposed Marxist New
Jewel Movement. And he was appointed the administration's ob-

server to the Socialist International, the worldwide gathering of socialist leaders.

In April 1985, his book, *Grave New World*, was in the stores. What
makes it a document of lasting historical interest is not its neoconservative clichés on foreign affairs, but its elaborate acknowledg-
ments to those eminences of the moment whom a courtier might
most wish to flatter: "to the Honorable David Abshire, currently
American ambassador to NATO, who directed the Center for Strategic and International Studies so well and permitted me to work
there . . . to the Honorable Robert C. McFarlane, who through
friendship and the force of his example showed me the meaning of
intellectual courage and discipline . . . to the Honorable Jeane Kirkpatrick, whose clarity of thought and political courage are so well
blended with her personal warmth and breadth of human understanding . . . to Norman Podhoretz, whose amazing intuitive understanding of American culture goes hand in hand with his excep-
tional stylistic and logical rigor; to Midge Decter, who has
somehow combined the talents of an extraordinary leader with
those of the selfless colleague . . ."

In May 1985, Ledeen traveled to Israel to discuss Iran with Israeli
officials, another step on the road to what would become the deal.
From that would flourish the diversion of funds to the contras, the
solution to the problem North had been contemplating since the
passage a year earlier of the toughest version of the Boland Amendment restricting aid to them. (McFarlane is quoted in the Senate
Intelligence Committee's report of February 1987 as saying that Ledeen "had been acting on his own hook"—a charge Ledeen has denied.) A few months later, in August 1985 after the deal with Iran and
the diversion to the contras were set in motion, Ledeen assailed the
"prejudice against secrecy" in an article in *Commentary* magazine:
"One is left with the suspicion that the moralistic complaints against
secrecy, or against the unpleasant necessities of counter-terrorism
and of the war against Soviet-sponsored proxies in Central America,
are nothing more than excuses for abandoning any serious attempt
by the United States to fight back."

In that article, Iran appeared in his list of "radical Arab states"
against which the United States needed to "fight back." And: "Our
Central American policy of bringing the fight to the Sandinistas,
although it has achieved a largely unacknowledged degree of success,
is now treading water, and continues mainly because of private-
sector funding of the contras rather than because of any significant
American governmental action." By then Ledeen sat astride the con-

nections that led to both ends of the scandal: the arms-for-hostages part and the arms-for-contras part.

One measure of the intellectual standards of certain segments of the intellectual right in this period was the respect and stature accorded Ledeen. And while they were promoting his career, he was promoting Manucher Ghorbanifar, an Iranian arms merchant, to the CIA and the National Security Council (NSC). On December 22 and 23, 1985, Ledeen introduced Ghorbanifar to the chief of the CIA's Iran desk. His internal report of the meeting, according to the Tower Commission's report, was sarcastic: "Ledeen is a fan of Subject and describes him as a 'wonderful man. . . . [sic] almost too good to be true.'" Later, Ghorbanifar, whom CIA officials believed to be a "crook," liar, and possibly a paid Israeli agent, acted as a go-between in the arms sales to Iran. Interestingly, the notes between Oliver North and John Poindexter, then his superior, recorded on the NSC computer and revealed in the Tower Commission's report, express North's suspicions that Ledeen was skimming money from the operation, a charge Ledeen subsequently denied. In the first note, on January 16, 1986, North wrote:

> You [Poindexter] should be aware, however, that it is my opinion, based on my meeting w/ Gorba [Ghorbanifar] on Monday night [January 13], that Gorba tells Ledeen everything. Ami [Amiram Nir, counter-terrorism adviser to Israeli Prime Minister Peres] suspects that there is probably a secret business arrangement among [Adolph] Schwimmer [Israeli arms merchant], Ledeen and Gorba that is being conducted w/o the knowledge of any of the three respective governments [the United States, Israel, Iran] and that this will result in at least some cross-fertilization of information. This may not be altogether bad if we can keep in touch w/ Ledeen enough to get a feel for what is really going on. I have no problem w/ someone making an honest profit on honest business. I do have a problem if it means the compromise of sensitive political or operational details. We might consider making Mike a contract employee of the CIA and requiring him to take a periodic polygraph. Yes? No?

In another note, on January 24, 1986, North wrote:

> [CIA Director William] Casey shares our concerns. More recent information tends to indicate that there is even further grounds for concern given what may well be/have been a financial arrangement among Schwimmer, [Yaacov] Nimrodi [Israeli arms merchant], Gorba and our friend.

The Tower Commission suggested: "Perhaps because of these doubts, Ledeen ceased to be an official American contact with Ghorbanifar." But the Tower Commission and the congressional committees investigating the Iran-contra affair also concluded that there was a paucity of evidence to substantiate North's conjecture. The commission also added that it had "seen no evidence" to prove the charge of skimming.

At the same time, Ledeen had set himself up as a corporate consultant, using his connection to the NSC to justify his fees. In 1986, he implored North's secretary, Fawn Hall, to arrange a meeting with two agents from the Drug Enforcement Agency (DEA). According to the Report of the Congressional Committees investigating the Iran-contra affair:

> They met at Ledeen's office. Ledeen told them he was a very good friend of North's. Ledeen said he had a $30,000 contract with Continental Airlines and he wanted to know how he could stop DEA from seizing their airplanes if cocaine was discovered on board. The agents arranged for Ledeen to meet the DEA regional director in Miami regarding the problem.

Even then, Ledeen was advancing his reputation as a scholar. When the chance of appearing in *P.R.* loomed, he jumped. By publishing his article, *P.R.* would be granting him a legitimacy among intellectuals that only it could grant. The magazine was no longer what it was, but *P.R.* still carried the freight of an honored past.

His eight-thousand-word piece is an excellent summary of Ledeen's position. It may be the best summary of the position of many neoconservatives, who have echoed its arguments as the Reagan administration's foreign policy has unraveled.

In it, Ledeen blames foreign policy "chaos" on the press; the Congress ("One cannot conduct foreign policy with more than 500 secretaries of state"); and lawyers and judges ("they give opinions on the legality of proposed policies, and therefore they can often eliminate certain policy options before they even enter the broad debate"). He also blames "a pernicious pseudo-democratic theory according to which everyone is entitled to a say in policy, regardless of his or her qualifications." These forces and this idea inhibit "those few persons who are seeking to advance the national interests of the United States." (Who are these "few persons"? Ledeen does not say. But he implies that they are an élite with opinions like his.) And, after citing a French conservative about the necessity of "breaking of law from time to time," Ledeen proposes a change in two laws that "forbid us" to conduct a minimal "counter-terrorism policy": "One is a law that prohibits American officials from working with murderers; the other is an executive order, dating to 1975, prohibiting any official of the American government to conduct, order, encourage or facilitate assassination." *Partisan Review*'s editors sent the piece out to contributors in anticipation of a lively symposium. "You may agree or disagree," says Kurzweil. "It's a viable position." Shortly afterward, the controversy exploded.

"We reacted with horror to running Ledeen in the magazine," says Dennis Wrong. "This is like sending 'The Protocols of the Elders of Zion' [a classic anti-Semitic tract] to get some thought on Jewish culture . . . I still may very well resign myself. I can't bring myself to say to William to pack it in, which may well be the very best thing after this long and brilliant history. William doesn't know how sad this is."

"It's very sad that a magazine that was in some sense the school in which people like me learned should have come to this pass," says Irving Howe, the critic, author, editor of *Dissent,* and contributor of many significant pieces to *P.R.* "Why did it have to come to this? I felt it was like finding out a cousin was involved in public malfeasance. It's still a cousin. You feel embarrassment and shame, which goes beyond political differences. It's a pathetic ending." Paradoxically, the incident restored *P.R.* for a moment to its old role: shaping the temper of the intellectuals in an uncertain period. But it has done so by sheer inadvertence.

In a sense, *P.R.* has been a casualty of Reagan's Washington. The Iran-contra scandal differs from the Watergate scandal partly because of the appearance of new Washington types, including the ideological adventurer. Ledeen used the glamour of intellect to impress the powerful and the glamour of power to impress the intellectual. But when he played power politics with the truly powerful, as in the Iran-contra affair, and when he entered into intellectual combat with the genuinely intellectual, as in the *P.R.* affair, he was undone.

(February 1987)

The Rise and Fall
of Richard Perle

When Richard Perle stepped down as assistant secretary of defense on June 1, 1987, he believed he could have it all.

Critics called him the "Prince of Darkness," but he saw himself vindicated as a true champion of western security. And he would have the benefits that have accrued since leaving government, including $300,000 from Random House for a forthcoming novel; "at least" $50,000 from *U.S. News & World Report* for a monthly column; consulting retainers; lecture fees; and an office at the American Enterprise Institute.

Perle had thrived in the power vacuum in national security policy that opened up during the collapse of the Nixon presidency, and for the rest of the decade he had attempted to block every effort at arms control by Republican and Democratic administrations alike.

When Ronald Reagan came to power, so did he, and throughout the 1980s he continued to confound rivals and their schemes for arms control. By the time Perle left the Pentagon, he had done more to shape the administration's nuclear arms policy than perhaps any individual except Reagan himself.

In fact, the intermediate nuclear force (INF) agreement, which was signed during a summit meeting between Reagan and Mikhail Gorbachev in 1987, had its origin in a proposal advanced by Perle in 1981—a proposal his critics say was a public relations ploy to gloss over Reagan's initial opposition to arms control.

Out of office, Perle never intended to be without influence. The familiar short, spherical figure, often topped by a Greek fisherman's cap, frequently visited the Pentagon as a consultant to Secretary of Defense Caspar Weinberger, or showed up at Foggy Bottom, as the State Department is called, where he signed on as a consultant to Secretary of State George Shultz. And, twice after leaving office, he could have been found at the White House, where he had been summoned by President Reagan to advise on the INF treaty with the Soviet Union.

But the appearance of Perle's on-site power has been belied by a new reality. When Soviet Foreign Minister Eduard Shevardnadze was in Washington in September to confer with Shultz, Perle's former top deputy and acting successor, Frank Gaffney, was pointedly kept out of the important meetings, though representatives of the State Department and the National Security Council (NSC) were present.

With the retirement of Weinberger, Perle's ultimate link to the top was severed. Virtually the instant Weinberger departed and Frank Carlucci arrived, Gaffney was forced out. By midnight Friday, Gaffney's belongings were boxed and he was gone. On the spot, Gaffney called a press conference to express his "worries" about the Reagan administration's eagerness for an arms control agreement.

Almost immediately, rumors circulated that this was the beginning of a purge of the Perle network at the Pentagon, but Perle himself suggested that the ousting of his allies would run counter to the interests of the new defense secretary. "Frank Carlucci strikes me as too shrewd a bureaucrat to conduct a purge," he said. Soon, however, another of Perle's allies, Fred Iklé, the under secretary of defense for policy, quit. The Weinberger-Perle axis had been toppled.

In the crucial weeks leading into the summit, Perle's reaction to it was visible on the TV news program "Nightline," but unseen at the negotiating table. His fame may have been building just as his influence was waning. Perle must contemplate his arms legacy from his Chevy Chase home.

His recent wealth can be measured by the enormous hole gouged in his backyard, where his new study will be. But even as Reagan and Gorbachev prepared to sign an arms agreement, Perle, who held the key Pentagon arms control post in the Reagan administration, negotiated with contractors and inspectors.

But his hours are his own, as he likes it. He has more time to be with his wife Leslie and eight-year-old son Jonathan.

The icons once featured on Perle's Pentagon walls are in storage, awaiting display in the study. There is, of course, the picture of his late mentor, the Democratic hawk of hawks, Senator Henry (Scoop) Jackson, for whom he worked throughout the 1970s. There is the testimonial letter from twenty conservative Republican senators, sent Perle on his leaving the Pentagon, expressing "our profound hope that we will not be without your guiding hand in these last two years of the Reagan administration." And there is the framed Winston Churchill quote, which succinctly summarizes his approach:

Never give in,
never give in
never, never, never, never
in nothing great or small,
large or petty—
never give in.

Now Perle has the leisure, if he wishes, to sit at home in the afternoon, sip his espresso, play Bach's Goldberg Variations on his new compact disk player and pet his mutt, Rembrandt. "He bit Rick Burt," says Perle, referring to the U.S. ambassador to West Germany who, as an assistant secretary of state for politico-military affairs, was among Perle's chief rivals. "He's basically a good dog."

Slouched in a wicker chair, feet up, peering over his expansive waistline, Perle recites his favorite bit of doggerel, by Hilaire Belloc: "Pale Ebenezer thought it wrong to fight, but Roaring Bill who killed him thought it right."

"It's a comment of moral judgment on international affairs," he says. "More espresso?"

Thus in a single sweep he reveals two Perles: the overlord and the sybarite. Together they have been an effective team, advancing a pugnacious policy by means of personal charm.

Perle, at forty-six, is the self-indulgent prisoner of luxe, a man for all desserts, beluga caviar, Monte Cristo cigars, Gauloise cigarettes ("Don't tell my wife"), and bread imported from a favorite Parisian bakery. In the late 1970s, he contemplated franchising a chain of soufflé restaurants: the gourmet's mushroom cloud. In office, he was the Robin Leach of NATO, using its meetings to explore the great attractions of Europe.

To his enemies he may be the Prince of Darkness, but to those who know him well he is Richard the shopper. "I never shop in the United States," he says. "You learn a lot when you shop abroad. I don't think there's anyplace where I can't find something."

His friends consider him, as one put it, "one of the most wonderful people in Washington." They know him as a gracious and generous host, a delightful companion and, above all, a loyal ally in the greater cause.

Even in a mood of self-satisfaction, he expresses concern for two friends tainted by the Iran-contra scandal—Assistant Secretary of State Elliott Abrams, whom he recruited to come to Washington and work for Jackson, and Michael Ledeen, who, at key moments, carried messages among the National Security Council staff, the Israeli government, and Israeli and Iran arms merchants. Perle wonders if Abrams will be "all right" and why journalists have written terrible things about Ledeen. "At least," he says, "Elliott's not going to satisfy critics of the Central American policy."

History, Perle asserts, has absolved him. With the INF agreement pending, he claims he has blocked "bad" arms control in favor of "good" arms control.

"It's a very important agreement as a precedent establishing the principle I've been arguing for for twenty years," he says, "which is that you have to have the patience of Job to get good agreements out of the Soviet Union."

When Perle became assistant secretary of defense, his power, in a normally third-rank job, became almost total because of the vacuum above him. Reagan, who had strong ideological intuitions, was unengaged with the detail of a subject that is nothing if not detail. And Weinberger, who had the greatest mandate for military spending since the end of World War II, had scant knowledge of nuclear strategy.

Weinberger was a lawyer in search of a brief, and Perle was a walking brief. "To a substantial degree, Weinberger relied upon Richard to present him with options and strategies," says a high-ranking Department of Defense official. "Senators and congressmen have no desire to stress how day-to-day activity within those institutions is influenced by the staff," says Perle, the former Senate staffer. The same applies to cabinet officers.

Perle has viewed all previous arms control treaties in the light of the appeasement of Hitler at Munich. Russia, in his use of the analogy, is Nazi Germany. "I don't see any point in denying the analogy because it touches Soviet sensitivities," he says. And he has long taken to flinging quotations from Samuel Hoare, a prominent British appeaser, at his opponents, as if they were hell-bent for a nuclear Munich.

"What I've extracted," he says, "is the dynamics in which one gets caught up in desiring negotiations to succeed. As a result, one's objectives get transformed so that in the end you don't know what you were negotiating in the first place. What becomes paramount is getting an agreement." He adds, "The public, for its part, feels relief and lowers its guard, a psychological price that is quite damaging." To Perle, this popular sentiment for peace negotiations is how democracies perish. We have nothing to fear but the lack of fear itself.

"One reason Perle was effective is that he never said he was op-

posed to an agreement," says a former friend who broke with him
over his tactics. "But deep in his heart the notion of an agreement
is deeply repugnant to him. We discussed this many times. His whole
line of argument about why agreements have to be avoided—once
you start dealing with the Soviet Union you can't control the process,
the political system can't tolerate complexity—this suggests a profound distrust of the American political system."

"I consider his actual views on arms control to be *corpus mysticum*,"
says a conservative congressional source. "On the one hand, he's been
consistent all along in saying a good arms control agreement can be
gotten if we're tough enough. There has to be perfect verification. In
principle, he says such a thing exists. However, Richard has never
met an arms control agreement he's liked. He himself has never,
never, never drafted an arms control agreement, even the 'zero option.' One is left, in understanding Perle, with this *corpus mysticum*.
It has accounted for a lot of his success." (Though he has worked on
the arms control issue with Perle for years, this person does not wish
to be identified. Nor do most of those who have had relations with
Perle.)

As Gorbachev moved point by point to the terms of the "double
zero" treaty—an agreement by both sides to remove medium-range
missiles from Europe—it appeared that Perle might have it both
ways, claiming the credit, proof at last of his good faith, yet remaining the critic. But while he says he approves of the INF agreement,
in the next breath he adds, "The administration, I hope, will exercise
appropriate discipline and not claim that this is the millennium."

For Perle, it is far from the millennium. Even as the Senate is
preparing to consider the agreement, it is moving to reverse his past
efforts to undo arms control. Perle was, after all, the principal architect of the assault on the Anti-Ballistic Missile treaty and the United
States' repudiation of SALT II limits. Thus a culminating achievement of the Reagan presidency is dissolving into a tableau of paradox
and irony. As Reagan puts himself in the now unbroken line
of arms-controlling presidents, the accord may not herald the fulfillment of Perle's arms control strategy but the beginning of its
reversal.

Why is Perle for the treaty? "It is because he invented it, because
it doesn't include strategic weapons and because he despises Euro-
peans," said Henry Kissinger in the *Wall Street Journal* in May 1987.

"Look, there are people who will concoct an infinite number of
theories why I am a dark and malevolent force," Perle says. "And the
1981 theory was that the 'zero option' was a ploy to frustrate any
agreement because the Soviet Union would never agree. The 1987

theory is that I've been hoist by my own petard, that I don't really like this agreement, that it's a bluff, that our bluff was called, and there's nothing we can do about it.

"The 1988 theory will be that I was for this agreement because it will thwart a strategic agreement by saving the administration's appetite for some kind of agreement. It's already beginning to emerge."

Three ideas are advanced to explain Perle's influence. First, that he is brilliant. Second, that he is an uncreative figure, who simply prevents movement toward arms control. And, third, a combination: that he has been clever at stopping things.

A former Reagan administration official and Perle ally, offering a view held across the spectrum, says: "There is nothing easier than stopping something. If you're smart besides, that's a bonus."

Arms control, in fact, is an incredibly laborious process—SALT II took seven years to produce. Progress in negotiations often cuts against the interests of key bureaucracies. Slowing down an already slow machine requires only persistence and manipulative arts.

The culture of the policy community is calm and dry. And when Perle discusses missile throw weights in his plummy voice he can sound like a late-night jazz disc jockey making urbane judgments on the discography of Bix Beiderbecke. He has mastered the art of keeping his head in public. On other occasions, however, he has been less restrained. His charm has its limits. He has relied upon directness, indirection, and misdirection

Those Perle believed were standing in his way were verbally lashed, to their faces and behind their backs. "He gets satisfaction out of being brilliant, and he lets that get in the way of being effective," says Perle's early mentor, Paul Nitze, now arms control adviser to the secretary of state and an architect of the early cold war policy. "He has humiliated people in debate, but he's not persuaded people. He's demonstrating brilliance. People don't like to be humiliated."

"Whenever he saw someone as a political problem," says a Perle associate who worked closely with him for years, "he'd identify a vulnerability. If he disagreed with a person, it was a matter of life and death. There was a willingness to play very rough."

This ally participated in the network of which Perle was the hub; its spokes ran to the Pentagon and Capitol Hill, to the White House, and to Foggy Bottom. "There was a constant discussion of people to be promoted, people to be helped, people to be gotten rid of," he says. "This is a good Bolshevik principle. We have to build our own cadres, people who support our philosophy."

Wherever Perle could exercise influence, balance was not his goal.

For example, as the Defense Department representative to the U.S. Institute of Peace, a nonpartisan federal agency, he "fought the hiring of liberals," says a friend, a former Reagan administration official. "He knows his position and will exploit it to the full. He will never concede." He adds, "His bargaining on the Russians is an extrapolation of his position of operating on personal terms."

Perle's opponents, however, were not easily classifiable by ideology. Conservatives within the Reagan administration who were not following his line were considered especially dangerous because they were competitors for power over the arms control agenda. "He's got his own team of people in the interagency structures," says a high-ranking State Department official about Perle's method when he was in office. "The [arms control] machinery grinds away; nothing gets resolved."

"He was exceedingly smooth, exceedingly articulate, and exceedingly disarming," says a former official who participated in the START arms negotiations early in the Reagan administration. "Sometimes he was quite frank about what he was up to. He'd say, 'The Soviets will never buy this.' And he'd come up with a proposal that was totally outrageous. Then he'd go back and play some bureaucratic games. Papers prepared would be slowed, wouldn't be ready. Very often Perle wouldn't come to meetings."

Perle's influence has been bolstered by his systematic leaking to columnists. Even if he were speaking in his velvet voice, many say they worried that, if they challenged him, what happened in closed meetings would be splashed across the op-ed pages, and they would be depicted as soft on communism. "I've seen the terror he strikes in people," says a former State Department official.

"George Will and I are very old friends," says Perle. "Evans and Novak I know well. They're friends." These three are influential conservative political columnists. And Robert Bartley, the editorial page editor of the *Wall Street Journal,* is also close. For them, according to a conservative journalist who has had a friendly relationship with Perle over the years, he was an extraordinary source, who offered more than information. He provided a map to guide sympathetic writers through the murky shoals of national security policy. His analysis, always against arms control, often wound up guiding their analysis. However, "The notion of leaking information to them—I don't," says Perle. "I'm very careful—It's pure surmise."

"I think it's easy to intimidate liberals," remarks a conservative Senate staffer who has observed Perle do so on numerous occasions.

"It's just putting their names in an Evans and Novak column. That makes them a pariah. And not just liberals."

In 1982, the Commerce Department was rattled by a debate about whether to permit the International Harvester Co., then near collapse, to sell a ten-year-old blueprint for a farm implement factory to Russia. Commerce officials favored the sale. So, too, did the NSC. According to a participant in the crucial meeting on the matter, Perle and a deputy, the only representatives present from the Pentagon, were the lone objectors. In the end, the deal went through, but within days, a startled Commerce Department was strafed by conservative columnists. Will, for example, on January 18, 1982, made detailed references to the proposed deal and concluded: "This administration evidently loves commerce more than it loathes communism."

Another case: In 1978, a CIA analyst, David S. Sullivan, wrote a report arguing that Russia had violated many arms treaties. And he contended that his assessment should be central to an agency intelligence estimate. After Sullivan was overruled, hc leaked his classified report to Perle. Jackson, at that moment, was conducting a holy war against the SALT II treaty and raising the issue of past Soviet violations as a rallying point. Stansfield Turner, the CIA's director, discovered the leak. "Sullivan," he says, "jeopardized important secrets for our country. He quit thirty seconds before I fired him."

Turner then confronted Jackson with Perle's role in the leak. Jackson called his aide into the room. "We had a thorough discussion," says Turner. "And he [Jackson] reprimanded him." Turner urged Perle's dismissal, but Jackson protected him, and the Sullivan-Perle alliance continued over the years. After being pushed out of the CIA, Sullivan joined the Senate staff, and there helped organize right-wing staffers into an ideological network called the Madison Group, named after the Madison Hotel coffee shop, where they met.

When Perle rose in 1981 to his Pentagon post, Sullivan was elevated to counselor of the Arms Control and Disarmament Agency. He was pressured out after a few months and was hired by a group of new right senators. Sullivan was "Richard's enforcer" on the Hill, says a friend of both. Together they pushed for a mandatory annual administration report to Congress on Soviet violations.

Over Perle's opposition, Reagan informally upheld the basic strictures of SALT II, on the advice of the Joint Chiefs of Staff, who warned that the Russians were better positioned to expand their arsenal if the accord were jettisoned. In 1984, the first report on Soviet cheating was provided to Congress, which created an official warrant for abandoning adherence to the SALT II treaty.

In November 1985, on the eve of the first Gorbachev-Reagan summit in Geneva, Weinberger's memo to the president, written by Perle, evoked "German treaty violations" before World War II. Churchill was recalled, and Reagan urged to play the part. This privileged communication was disseminated widely throughout the national security bureaucracies, but it had no classified stamp on it. There was, therefore, no price to pay for leaking it to the press, and portions were promptly published. Finally, on May 27, 1986, the president announced that as far as the United States was concerned SALT II was a dead letter.

The Reagan administration's strategic path through the 1980s has been marked by roads not taken. One such road was Nitze's exploratory effort in 1982 to reach agreement on arms control with the principal Soviet negotiator, Yuli Kvitsinsky—the so-called "walk in the woods." Afterward, Perle furiously undermined any chance of the administration's accepting their tentative understanding. He used the "zero option" as an alternative—unacceptable to the Soviets then, and now the basis of the INF agreement.

"Perle was shaking with anger after the 'walk in the woods,' " says Strobe Talbott, *Time* magazine's Washington bureau chief and arms control chronicler. "He hated every single part of it. He accused Nitze of 'dishonesty.' " The subtext involved more than arms control. Nitze had brought Perle to Washington and given him his first job. Later, Perle attempted to disarm Nitze, expressing regrets. "He told me," says Nitze, "that he had come to the conclusion we'd have been better off if we'd accepted the 'walk in the woods' just as I had negotiated it with Kvitsinsky."

Perle neither confirms nor denies offering Nitze an apology, which would have been tantamount to an apology for the subsequent history of arms control in the Reagan era. Rather, he justifies the course he took. "It was necessary," he says, "to separate the terms of the proposal Paul made from the political implications of putting that proposal forward. On balance, it seemed to me a bad idea to put forward. I think the elimination of these weapons was better—the 'zero option.' " Thus Perle presents himself, not as the foiler of arms control, but as its ultimate practitioner.

Yet Nitze, who wears a red hat in the church of foreign policy and has survived many inquisitions, questions the *corpus mysticum* aspect of the Perle persona.

Did Perle have a strategy for arms control? In his office at the State Department, Nitze leans back in a wing chair and narrows his eyes.

"I'm not sure," he says with great deliberation, "that he had an agenda at all."

It was nightfall in Moscow. On foot and on his own, Richard Perle began exploring the streets.

That year, 1986, was the first time in Russia for the then-assistant secretary of defense, sometimes called the Prince of Darkness for his unremittingly gloomy view of the Soviet menace and his unrelenting efforts over the past two decades to black out arms control.

"You've got to be crazy," he had warned a reporter about to embark for Moscow in 1971. Perle was then the bright young man on the staff of Senator Henry (Scoop) Jackson, the Democrats' chief hawk. "They could throw you in Lubyanka prison."

"I thought he was kidding," says the reporter. "But he wasn't."

But now in Moscow himself, his instincts as the Prince of Darkness gave way to those of the gourmet. He had heard tales of the wonderful richness of Russian ice cream, and his evening wandering turned into an obsessive search for dessert. "I had a hard time finding any," he complained.

Back at the conference, Perle's hard line took precedence over his waistline. Soviet officialdom was consumed with interest in his simultaneous charm and hostility. His rise was something they must have implicitly understood. He had not emerged from campaigns and elections, but from Byzantine bureaucratic struggle. His authority derived from a series of powerful mentors. He propelled his cause through a tightly knit network of like-minded *apparatchiks*. And he believed politics was determined by the "correlation of forces"—a phrase he acknowledges borrowing from the Russians.

Please come back, the Russians implored. And an invitation to a conference the following month in Riga on the Baltic Sea was issued. Alas, at the last moment, Perle could not shake himself free from Washington. His place was filled by Strobe Talbott, *Time* magazine's Washington bureau chief, who had detailed Perle's elaborate efforts at blocking an arms agreement in his book *Deadly Gambits*.

"Where's Mr. Perle?" demanded Gen. Nicholai Chervov, chief of the arms control section of the Soviet military's general staff.

"He decided to stay home," Talbott says he replied.

"That's a great shame," lamented Chervov. "I was looking forward to continuing my discussions with Mr. Perle." The thought was much on his mind. Three times during the conference Chervov mournfully remarked, "It's too bad Perle is not here."

"I think we understand each other," says Perle, who casts himself as a "realist" against the mush-headed "idealists." "I rather like talking to the Soviets. They have adopted the realist view. It's pretty unvarnished."

Out of office since June 1987, Perle finds himself suspended between realist and idealist poles. He is drawn to celebrate the success of the pending treaty on intermediate-range missiles in Europe and the December 7 summit, claiming that his sponsorship of the "zero option" vindicates his method of dealing on arms control. At the same time, he is drawn to criticize the treaty, as he criticizes all arms agreements, for sapping the will for eternal vigilance.

Perle's paradox is also Ronald Reagan's. Together, the gray eminence and the Great Communicator approach the apparent moment of triumph against a backdrop of irony. By Perle's admission, the agreement is "minor," with little strategic meaning, though it has enormous political import. But in terms of sheer policy, it is a cosmetic agreement, the very kind Perle and Reagan campaigned against in the past.

Perle's story is the essence of the controversy over America's nuclear policy since the late 1960s. He has been a key figure in every debate over every major nuclear issue. The current politics of arms control reflect, in great part, the determined and sophisticated work of this one man and his coterie.

From the beginning, Perle's ultimate power base was a father figure. "Richard's effectiveness was really quite easy to explain," says a conservative ally on Capitol Hill. "It's 99.9 percent based on his relationship with [Caspar] Weinberger." And before that, Senator Jackson. And before that, conservative establishmentarian Paul Nitze. And before that, nuclear high priest Albert Wohlstetter. They gave him his hunting license.

The beginning of this story may be traced to the chance meeting beside a Hollywood swimming pool of a teen-age boy and the high priest of nuclear theology.

Richard Perle is the son of a textile manufacturer and a housewife. His father was also a gambler; his brother is retarded. The family ate many of its meals in delicatessens. In his junior year at Hollywood High School, Richard sat next to Joan Wohlstetter, daughter of the author of *The Delicate Balance of Nuclear Terror*. Joan liked Richard and, he says, "she invited me over for a swim." There he met Albert Wohlstetter.

At the Rand Corporation, a think tank of high-powered mental ping-pong sponsored by the air force, Wohlstetter was the theorist of nuclear warfare. Rand's ethos was like that of the Jesuits: members of its order prided themselves on their intellectual superiority and their ability to parse continually more and more rarefied forms of abstraction. The place was detached from politics and yet a crucible of U.S. strategy; from its theories flowed billions of dollars in weapons systems.

Wohlstetter's background was in two powerful methods of logic: higher mathematics and higher Marxism. As an undergraduate at Columbia University, he belonged to a sect of Trotskyists, the Fieldites, who were all young intellectuals, far removed from the proletariat but adroit at conducting world-historical clashes in their heads. By the 1950s, his Marxism had become transmuted into game theory and systems analysis.

Wohlstetter was of a school of nuclear strategists whose teachings included: the idea of a first strike and, it followed, the ability to launch a second strike; the "window of vulnerability" through which may fly numerically superior Russian bombers and missiles; a profound suspicion of arms agreements; and a demand for complete verification of Soviet compliance with treaties, which it was doubted could be satisfied. Wohlstetter's Pentagon briefings, spinning out these notions, were legendary.

After reading Wohlstetter's article on the "balance of terror" in *Foreign Affairs* in 1959, the young Perle and the master strategist "had a long conversation." It marked Perle's induction into the gnostic mysteries of nuclear theory. Richard and Joan went their separate ways. But Richard and Albert "stayed in touch," says Perle. "It was a close personal friendship, as well as an intellectual relationship."

Wohlstetter's ideas became Perle's ideas; his network, Perle's; and, as Perle traveled through the bureaucratic catacombs of Washington, his first mentor remained on call as his intellectual Virgil—always "enormously helpful," says Perle. He himself was never an original strategist. His views were mostly elaborations of Wohlstetter's.

After Perle had been certified at the University of Southern California, Princeton, and the London School of Economics, he got a job with Westinghouse's in-house think tank in Waltham, Massachusetts. But he didn't stay long.

In Washington, in 1969, a newly formed group called the Committee to Maintain a Prudent Defense Policy inquired if the twenty-seven-year-old Perle would be interested in becoming its chief researcher. The recommendation was made by one committee founder, Wohlstetter, to another, Paul Nitze. The torch of Perle's mentorhood had been passed.

The group lobbied to fund an antiballistic missile system (ABM) that, theoretically, could preserve a second-strike capability by knocking enough incoming Soviet rockets out of the sky. "We raised $15,000, of which I put up half," says Nitze. Though the battle was lost, Perle was established in the capital. Nitze recommended him for his next job.

While making the rounds for the ABM, Perle happened upon the office of Senator Jackson, where he discovered like-minded souls. They were similarly taken. "He was the brightest thing around," says Dorothy Fosdick, who was Jackson's chief foreign policy aide. The match was a natural. When Perle first joined the staff, according to a friend, he openly called himself a socialist. "Social democrat would be a more accurate description of how I thought of myself," he explains.

Jackson's nuclear strategy rested on the belief that more was better. International power, as he understood it, flowed from the tip of a warhead: The more warheads a missile could carry, the more power. From the early 1950s, he preached that the Russians were gaining superiority and the United States faced a present danger. The bigger the military budget, the greater the deterrence.

His anticommunism was implacable, but not of the same stripe as that of the Republican right. It was roughly equivalent to the position assumed by many European socialists at the height of the cold war. "Scoop was very labor-oriented," says Fosdick. "He believed the socialist parties in Europe understood the Soviet threat better than some of the liberals and establishment types here."

Perle's parents had died in 1969, the year he joined Jackson's staff, and he came to look upon the senator as a father. "He was paternalistic in every sense, whether it was big budgets for welfare programs or looking after young members of his staff," Perle says. "He was unusually so with me because my father had just died. He felt every young person ought to have a parent. He came naturally to that protective role. I get choked up talking about Scoop even now." If Jackson was the father, Dorothy Fosdick was the mother. Perle and the other staffers referred to her as the *bubbe*, the Yiddish word for grandmother. Her father was Harry Emerson Fosdick, the liberal pastor of New York's Riverside Church. She herself had been deeply involved in the old left, and her hard line was the outcome of her political passage. Communism, the god that failed, was still the pole star by which the Jackson office charted its political direction.

The inhabitants of Jackson's office labeled their quarters "the bunker," which implied a certain spirit that bound the staffers together. "We had a vision of fighting the lonely battle against the forces of darkness, a threat that we were about to be overwhelmed," says a former Jackson aide and Perle friend. Jackson's growing influence was translated, particularly by Perle, into an extensive network. "The network dates from the earliest days," says a fellow occupant of the bunker. In the beginning it included the small band of Wohl-stetter-influenced strategists; congressional aides who followed the lead of Jackson's right-hand man; and conservative columnists, such as Rowland Evans and Robert Novak, who found Perle to be a useful stream of information.

To those dug in in the bunker, Henry Kissinger, who stood astride foreign policy, loomed as the chief villain. They despised détente, which they saw as a warrant for the Soviets to gain nuclear superior-ity. In 1972, Jackson worked against SALT I, dispatching Perle as his agent to stir up opposition. "I collaborated with the staffs of twenty to twenty-five senators, getting speeches written," he says.

His consolation was what is commonly referred to as the "Jackson amendment," which Perle helped write. It stipulated that future agreements must not limit U.S. strategic weapons, according to Jackson's and Perle's particular definitions, at a level inferior to the Russians'.

The Nixon administration argued that SALT I established a strategic balance, in spite of minor numerical differences in the nuclear arsenals. Perle, however, saw in these disparities the opportunity to raise fears about the Russians and arms control. The numbers, he explained to a fellow Senate staffer, were "esthetically displeasing." In the end, unable to defeat the treaty, Jackson voted for it; it was politically untenable for a Democrat with presidential aspirations to do otherwise. But Jackson's hostility to the U.S. delegation was viru-lent and open. "Our people caved in, let's face it," he said. He and Perle were determined to make trouble for future agreements.

Throughout SALT I, Perle had kept careful track of the progress of the U.S. delegation. His most important contact within the ad-ministration was John Lehman, then on the staff of the National Security Council. And, Perle points out, "I had quite a good relation-ship with [then Deputy National Security Adviser Alexander] Haig. He was easy to talk to."

In early 1973, after Nixon's reelection, a bureaucratic guillotine swiftly detached about a dozen key arms controllers from the SALT I–Anti-Ballistic Missile Treaty delegation and the Arms Control and Disarmament Agency (ACDA). The politics were exceedingly com-plex, but what is clear is that Kissinger, under constant bombardment for détente, did not protect those who served him. And Nixon sought to assuage the powerful Jackson by handing over human sacrifices.

"When the purge happened, I asked Perle about it," says an ousted member of the U.S. delegation. "He said, 'Well, it wasn't anything personal.'" Perle reenforces this view: "Whatever was done was done by the people who employed them. The notion that I was responsible for this was ludicrous."

"They were people Scoop had no confidence in," says Fosdick. "They were probably doomed anyway."

But the purge was a stroke for Perle and his network. On the strength of Jackson's recommendation, Lt. Gen. Edward Rowny was appointed as the new representative of the joint chiefs of staff to the arms talks. Also on Jackson's advice, Fred Iklé from Rand was named director of ACDA. Iklé later named Perle's friend Lehman as his deputy.

Rowny, as chief U.S. negotiator to the START talks under Reagan, became a crucial Perle ally—"a vessel," says a source who worked with Rowny. And Iklé, while nominally Perle's superior at the Pentagon, never exercised real power over him, according to various sources.

In 1974, those in the bunker struck a blow against the economic component of détente by linking trade with Russia to restrictions on the emigration of Soviet Jews: the Jackson-Vanik Amendment. (Perle lobbied a member of the staff of Representative Charles Vanik, Democrat of Ohio, to convince him to cosponsor the measure. Later, after its passage, Vanik had second thoughts.)

The argument that the Soviets could not be trusted on human rights was a powerful rhetorical tool used in the opposition to arms control. If they could not be trusted on the one, how could they be trusted on the other? To this day, the Soviets consider Jackson-Vanik an impediment to normal relations with the United States.

During the Watergate scandal, the power vacuum widened. The Ford administration had little time to establish a new coherence in arms control policy. Perle flourished and moved into a new phase of influence.

"Perle would hear from friends in the executive branch that he was losing on some issue in the interagency process," says a former Senate staffer who observed him closely. "It would be leaked to the press that Jackson was threatening a hearing. It was an exercise in intimidation to players opposing their network."

Vice President Nelson Rockefeller was so filled with frustration at the anti-détente campaign conducted from the bunker that at a private meeting in 1976 he pointedly raised the subjects of leaks and loyalty. He claimed "communists" had infiltrated Jackson's staff, and he named two names—Fosdick and Perle. Jackson was infuriated. And Rockefeller eventually apologized. But nothing was resolved. The campaign against détente continued.

In 1976, a presidential election year, the critics of détente raised the decibel level over what they viewed as Russia's growing aggressiveness and potential military superiority. President Ford's new CIA director, George Bush, readily acceded to their demands for an assessment independent of the agency's own experts. Thus was organized the B-team.

Its director was a Harvard professor of nineteenth-century Russian history, Richard Pipes, who had been discovered by talent scout Perle and imported to Washington as a consultant to Jackson. (Nitze was also on the nine-member B-team. And its technical consultant was Albert Wohlstetter.) Unsurprisingly, the B-team produced a grim view of Soviet capabilities and intentions.

When Jimmy Carter became president in 1977, Perle was at first "ambivalent," according to a close associate. "He felt he almost had to be an improvement over Ford and Kissinger. He thought that maybe Carter was a hawk."

A month after Carter's inauguration, Jackson submitted to Carter a twenty-three-page, single-spaced memorandum on arms control, written by Perle. Much of it was polemic against Kissinger and "the burden of past mistakes." In the bunker, the memo was seen as a first and last chance for the new administration. It was, according to one of Perle's allies, a former Pentagon official, an effort to "establish a framework different than one with vomit all over it."

Carter circulated the memo among his senior foreign policy advisers, but none regarded it as a serious basis for proceeding. It was "so irrelevant," says Walter Slocombe, then a high-ranking Defense Department official. "It was simply a list of objectives which there was no way of getting, no chance of negotiating. It had no sense of priorities. And if you couldn't get these things, what would be acceptable to Senator Jackson?"

None of the neoconservatives, who saw Jackson as their champion, received the influential posts they desired. In the bunker, Carter's appointment of Paul Warnke as the director of the ACDA and chief SALT negotiator was greeted as a declaration of ideological war. "It was the last job the Jackson wing of the party might get," says Warnke. "And they had been shut out."

Warnke, a top Pentagon official in the Johnson era and then the law partner of Clark Clifford, former defense secretary, was a member of the Washington peerage, and did not share the assumptions of the hawks about arms control. In *Foreign Policy* magazine, he compared the superpowers' arms race to "apes on a treadmill," a metaphor that enraged the conservatives. Nitze, who had served in the Pentagon with him, had a longstanding antipathy toward Warnke and now regarded him as the epitome of all that was wrongheaded. Nitze issued a call to arms.

The campaign against Warnke's confirmation was more than an effort to pull down an individual. "The real question," says a former Jackson aide who participated in the effort, "was whether you could get thirty-four votes. Then any agreement he produced would be in trouble from the word go." Jackson's office turned into a battle station. "Most of the work," says this former member of Jackson's staff, "was done out of Richard's living room and the bunker." Once again, Perle wrote dozens of senators' speeches. On March 9, 1977, Warnke was approved as SALT negotiator by a vote of 58–40—"a symbolic victory," says the source.

As SALT negotiators slowly crept toward a new treaty in the late 1970s, its opponents rapidly mobilized. In the public arena, their principal vehicle was the Committee on the Present Danger, founded by Nitze and Wohlstetter, among others. Perle, of course, was a charter member. The committee advanced an updated "window of vulnerability" theory, portentously warning that Soviet nuclear superiority was becoming a geopolitical offensive.

The administration tried to placate Jackson and Perle, assigning two plenipotentiaries to Perle—Slocombe of the Defense Department and William Hyland of the National Security Council. "One would have thought we were dealing with a foreign country," says Slocombe. He adds that Perle had "extraordinarily good sources within the government. He knew a lot of what was going on inside."

The president, though, clung to the hope that his enemies would somehow have a change of heart. "President Carter always had the quixotic view that they could be brought around," says Warnke. "The president didn't realize how intractable they were . . . I really don't think President Carter knew what was happening."

When Carter departed for Vienna to sign SALT II in June 1979, Jackson deployed Perle's favorite metaphor, British Prime Minister Neville Chamberlain's trip to Munich in 1938: "It is all ominously reminiscent of Great Britain in the 1930s, when one government pronouncement after another was issued to assure the British public that Hitler's Germany would never achieve military equality—let alone superiority. The failure to face reality today, like the failure to do so then—that is the mark of appeasement." The speech so rattled Carter that he told aides that even if it poured rain in Vienna, he would not unfurl an umbrella, Chamberlain's trademark accessory.

Another humiliating send-off came from Rowny, the joint chiefs' SALT representative, who announced he would not attend the treaty signing. Throughout the negotiations, according to a Perle ally, Rowny had been "a major source" of information to the bunker. "In retrospect, why keep him [Rowny] around?" wonders Slocombe. "People maintained a naïve view that you could get Jackson to support the agreement."

Then the Senate Armed Services Committee produced a report, at Jackson's direction and written by Perle, recommending against ratification of SALT II. "It so poisoned the atmosphere," says a former Pentagon official and Perle ally, still gleeful in the memory.

After the Russians invaded Afghanistan in December 1979, the death knell sounded for Senate passage of the treaty. And Carter, facing a tough reelection campaign, postponed consideration. It was an implicit admission that he had failed to fill the power vacuum.

In the meantime, as the vital signs of the SALT treaty became faint, Perle set himself up as an international arms broker and defense consultant with his old friend John Lehman. But Perle and Lehman, brothers in ideological arms, fell out over money. The rift was so rancorous after their partnership in the Abington Corporation was dissolved that they refused to speak to each other or even occupy the same room. Thus the secretary of the navy and the assistant secretary of defense passed their headiest days of power, which they had labored for years to gain, as personal antagonists.

As the election approached, the occupants and alumni of the bunker prepared en masse to vote for Ronald Reagan. But before committing the heretical act of voting Republican, they asked for Jackson's dispensation. "You're a free woman," Fosdick recalls Jackson telling her.

After Reagan's victory, secretary of state-designate Haig offered Perle a job in Foggy Bottom. But Perle did not leap at a managerial post that would deter him from influencing the arms control agenda. Then Weinberger made his offer. "Marvelous!" says Fosdick, describing Jackson's reaction.

At last, Perle had arrived at the Pentagon station.

Richard Perle's ultimate crusade was launched by what President Reagan called his "dream"—the Strategic Defense Initiative (SDI).

The consequences were immense. Two summits between Ronald Reagan and Mikhail Gorbachev were upset by Reagan's embrace of SDI, and the administration's position was a stumbling block to the third, in Washington.

But in November 1987, the nation seemed to awaken from the "dream." Defense Secretary Caspar Weinberger, perhaps its leading defender, left office, and his chief arms control aide involuntarily followed. Although the president had formerly proclaimed SDI "a cornerstone of our security strategy for the 1990s and beyond," Congress, perhaps foreseeing the end of an era, delicately put the vision beyond Reagan's reach.

The campaign for SDI has been a textbook example of Perle deploying his own strategic weaponry—his network throughout the national security bureaucracies. And it illustrates Perle's commitment to undoing what he considers "bad" arms agreements with the Soviet Union.

Reagan's nuclear legacy remains inextricably bound up with Perle's works over the past twenty years. Still, the president's sudden allegiance to SDI surprised even his closest associates.

In March 1983, Perle and Weinberger were in Portugal for a meeting of NATO defense ministers. Around midnight, as Weinberger was about to go to sleep, a cable arrived containing the final draft of the president's speech on the new defense budget. "I was asked to take a look at it," says Perle. "There, tacked on to the end of the speech, were a dozen paragraphs outlining the Strategic Defense Initiative—and by the way, folks, that's all, folks. I was stunned."

What Reagan was about to propose was nothing less than a revolution in nuclear doctrine. SDI was heralded by the president as a veritable astrodome, able to shield the nation from all incoming missiles. Above all, it denied the logic behind a quarter-century of superpower arms control. That logic was codified in the ABM (anti-Ballistic Missile) treaty, which dictated that neither side would attempt to build a defensive system. Without this treaty, negotiators from both sides agreed, Russia and the United States would be driven to an endlessly spiraling arms race.

Proceeding with SDI required an assault on the treaty. The initiative for SDI came from Reagan; the tactics against the treaty came from Perle. When Perle, in Portugal, first learned about Reagan's "dream," he was disturbed that no advance preparations had been made for this startling change in nuclear doctrine. He banged on Weinberger's door, and got him to leave the matter "in my hands."

Perle managed to delay Reagan's speech for a day. "But," says Perle, "in the end they decided to go forward."

The incident was revealing: Here was the president revolutionizing nuclear strategy, but informing his old friend, the defense secretary, only at the last minute. Weinberger then deferred to his deputy. And Perle quickly mustered his mental and bureaucratic resources in the effort to turn the event to his purposes.

By 1985, Perle's rivals for control of the arms-control agenda within the administration had vanished, including Assistant Secretary of State for Politico-Military Affairs Richard Burt, Perle's generational peer and chief rival, who went into retreat to West Germany as ambassador in 1985. "A marvelous opportunity," says Perle. "My immediate reaction was: Why didn't I think of that?"

With his adversaries gone, Perle's campaign against arms control escalated. To emasculate and, he hoped, to kill the ABM treaty, Perle exploited Reagan's vision of SDI.

It began with a memorandum in the summer of 1985. Fred Iklé, a longtime member of the Perle network and the undersecretary of defense, discovered a young lawyer, a former New York assistant district attorney, a specialist in pornography cases, Philip Kunsberg, working for the CIA. "I asked Kunsberg to go look at the treaty," says Perle.

The resulting nineteen-page report asserted that the treaty did not limit SDI at all; what was wrong, it said, was the earlier interpretation. "I almost fell off my chair," says Perle—a phrase he has repeated many times to many groups. He then unveiled the memo as the official Pentagon position to an interagency group on SDI.

The State Department assigned its legal adviser, Abraham Sofaer, to conduct a formal study. "I'm certain Richard talked to Sofaer about it," says a former Pentagon official close to Perle.

But "I don't recall speaking to Sofaer," says Perle. When told that a close colleague said he had spoken to him, Perle revised his statement: "Maybe I did." (Sofaer denied this.)

Sofaer's report, not surprisingly, favored the reinterpretation. The day after it was produced, on October 4, 1985, high-level officials from the State Department, the Defense Department, the National Security Council, and the Arms Control and Disarmament Agency met. "I proposed," says Perle, "that we accept this interpretation of the treaty as a consensus."

Two days later, on the TV program "Meet the Press," national security adviser Robert McFarlane announced that this radical reinterpretation of the ABM treaty was now administration policy. But what Perle had proposed and McFarlane announced had not yet been approved by the president.

Then, in October 1986, Perle found himself where he had never been before: at a summit, in Reykjavik, seated across the table from Russians, presenting a grandiose plan for the eventual elimination of all ballistic missiles *and* compliance with the ABM treaty for ten years. Gorbachev refused to entertain the idea that the treaty had an expiration date and, moreover, that it allowed testing of SDI components outside of the laboratory.

The summit was over. Perle's brief, ambitious effort at arms control had been dashed by his efforts to undermine arms control.

A month later, the Republicans lost their majority in the Senate. And Senator Sam Nunn, a Georgia Democrat, became chair of the Armed Services Committee, filling a crucial part of what had been a power vacuum.

Perle's network had thought of Nunn as one of its own. As a senator in the 1970s, he had generally followed Henry Jackson's lead, which meant taking Perle's counsel. "Scoop always offered Richard's services to Nunn," says a former Jackson aide. And Nunn had been part of the coalition that kept SALT II from securing support in the Senate.

Unlike the others in the network, however, Nunn's political bloodlines ran back to Georgia, to the pre-Jackson rulers of the Armed Services Committee, Carl Vinson, his great-uncle, and Richard Russell, who stood for loyalty to the Senate above any ideological imperative.

Since Reagan's second inauguration, Nunn and Perle had fought a bitter running battle hidden from view. The source of contention was the obscure Standing Consultative Commission (SCC), which is the embodiment of arms control in practice. Twice a year, this diplomatic body brings together U.S. and Soviet officials in Geneva to resolve disputes about adherence to existing agreements.

Perle has loathed the SCC since its establishment by the ABM treaty. In Weinberger's memo of November 13, 1985, to the president on the eve of the Geneva summit, written by Perle and leaked to the press, the SCC was denounced as "a diplomatic carpet under which Soviet violations have been continuously swept, an Orwellian memory-hole into which our concerns have been dumped like yesterday's trash."

Perle's loathing led him to seek to intimidate and fire its commissioner, Gen. Richard Ellis, a former chief of the Strategic Air Command. But Nunn shielded Ellis. If he had not, says a Senate source close to Nunn, Ellis could have been "run off." As it was, the administration deliberately "underutilized" the forum, according to a House Intelligence Committee report. Contradicting Perle's accusations, it stated that the SCC "has in the past resolved differences . . . and clarified ambiguous situations."

The Nunn-Perle clash had taken a more personal turn in 1986 over Perle's proposal to turn his expert knowledge of bureaucratic infighting into a novel—which evoked a six-figure level of enthusiasm from a publisher. The news evoked outrage from Nunn, who attempted to make Perle appear less a man of principle and more another placeman for profit.

"Perle," Nunn said, "must choose between remaining one of the principal architects of U.S. security policy or undertaking to become a best-selling novelist." Perle, for his part, called Nunn's strike "intemperate and overblown," though he momentarily withdrew the book proposal.

Then Nunn set his sights on Perle's ABM reinterpretation. For three days in March 1986, after a lengthy review of the treaty and Sofaer's study, Nunn held forth on the Senate floor. He called Sofaer's claims "absurd . . . illogical . . . woefully inadequate . . . ideologically driven . . . fundamentally flawed." "Furthermore," said Nunn, the Reagan administration's reinterpretation "constitutes a fundamental constitutional challenge to the Senate as a whole."

Perle explodes at what he considers Nunn's ignorance and ingratitude. "I think," he says, "that my view on this is more authoritative than Sam Nunn's, *who wasn't there.*" It was Perle who was Jackson's strategist—not Nunn. And it was Perle who helped advance Nunn in the Senate. "Scoop [Jackson] made Sam Nunn vice chairman on the Government Operations Committee, *and I was all for it.*" And Nunn's reference to "the rule of law," regarding the ABM treaty, was empty: "It's *rhetoric.*" And Nunn's motive was purely political: "I don't think it's a very *effective* way to run for president." But Nunn was not running for the presidency and he was not alone in his criticism of the ABM treaty's reinterpretation; the treaty's chief negotiator, Gerard C. Smith, called it "disinformation."

On March 26, 1987, the Foreign Relations and Judiciary committees held an unusual joint hearing on the treaty. It was something more: a shadow play of one of the most painful episodes in the history of arms control—the 1973 purge of the ABM treaty delegation. The hearing room was filled with a ghost—Jackson's—and with losers of the purge, who were now witnesses against the reinterpretation. Perle branded their effort "treaty-gate." Perle himself played the role of necromancer, communing with the spirit of the departed Jackson, who had initiated the great purge but had also voted for the ABM treaty.

"I lived through that ratification record and I remember it very well, indeed," Perle testified. "The thing that stands out most clearly is the paucity of discussion on the floor of the United States Senate about the issue that is now under discussion."

"Not Scoop Jackson," growled Senator Edward Kennedy. "Thirteen pages of questions on exotic systems in the record. Thirteen pages."

"Indeed," Perle shot back. "I wrote most of those." Once again, he was staffing Jackson—not the man now, but the icon.

Sofaer, a small, eager man, seemed like a nervous terrier about to be reprimanded. Before his appearance he had conceded that his study "did not provide a complete portrayal of the ratification proceedings" and that he "did not review this material personally." He blamed it all on "young lawyers" on his staff. He told the senators: "Part of what I said there was accurate," about his previous testimony before the Armed Services Committee. He promised he would restudy the treaty.

Perle's circle was unhappy with the hearing, especially with Sofaer's performance. "It's unfortunate Sofaer is as apologetic as he is," complained a former Pentagon official. On April 29, the joint committee called a lawyer who had worked for Sofaer, William J. Sims, who testified that it was Sofaer—not "young lawyers"—who selectively used documents to justify the reinterpretation. But, Sims said, Sofaer was ultimately not in command. "OSD [Office of the Secretary of Defense] seemed to be in the driver's seat," he testified. And he singled out Richard Perle by name.

On September 17, the Senate by a margin of twenty votes voted to prohibit testing of SDI components without its prior approval, thus upholding the ABM treaty. Perle's effort to rewrite history was undone, partly by the record bequeathed by Jackson.

In November, as Weinberger was leaving the Pentagon after seven years, Carlucci, his successor, and White House Chief of Staff Howard Baker reached an accord with Nunn and Congress: In effect, SDI would be restricted by the traditional interpretation of the ABM treaty for one year—that is, until Reagan leaves office.

Whatever anyone proposed on arms control, it had been Perle's tactic to up the ante. He always presented himself as a believer in "good" arms control, stymied alternative initiatives, and forwarded proposals that invariably met with Russian rejection.

The element unaccounted for in Perle's calculations was Gorbachev, who, in March 1985, filled the power vacuum in Russia. He also leaped obstacles to an INF agreement by saying yes to almost every maximalist U.S. position—and then upping the ante himself.

"I don't know," says Perle, considering whether Gorbachev is different from past Soviet leaders and whether his efforts at change are more than public relations ploys. "I can only hypothesize. He recognizes the system is not working well. . . . This is not the first reformist leader in the Soviet Union. Virtually every Soviet leader at the outset has had a reformist quality. I just don't know."

But in his *U.S. News & World Report* column, Perle resolved his nagging doubts, writing that there is "not a shred of evidence" that Gorbachev desires "a respite from the burdens of military spending, a reordering of priorities."

What Perle always feared most about arms control was its effect on American politics. The naïve public, led by naïve politicians, would be deceived into believing a treaty really reduced tensions. Defenses would be lowered, an opening for the first strike created. But the immediate political effect of the treaty for which he bears a major responsibility has been to create a schism within the Republican Party. Senators and presidential candidates challenging the accord, in fact, are basing their opposition on grounds that Perle pioneered.

For decades, Soviet cheating has been an article of faith of those opposed to arms control, and the arguments that verifying Soviet compliance is nearly impossible were finely honed by Perle during the SALT II debate. Because perfect verification is impossible, it is something like proving the existence of God. If the Soviets are successful in keeping their weapons invisible, how can anyone know they are there?

But three presidents—Nixon, Ford, and Carter—rejected the Catch-22 of perfect verification. They believed that potential Soviet cheating could be detected long before U.S. security could be endangered. And so they proceeded on arms control. Still, says Perle, "The Soviet Union will exploit agreements that can't be verified." He adds: "There will always be uncertainty about Soviet behavior, some ambiguity about what they're doing." He explains further, "Verification is very important. The American people distrust the Soviet Union . . . It's important politically."

And Perle has exploited this distrust for years, often citing the appeasement of Hitler at Munich. The application of the Munich analogy to arms control is now employed by Republican presidential hopeful Representative Jack Kemp, who, in a speech on the INF accord, warned of a "nuclear Munich." (Perle still calls himself a "Jackson Democrat," but the candidate he is advising is Kemp's. "I haven't been asked by other campaigns," Perle says.)

Perle always had the suspicion that arms negotiators would become consumed with the process and lose sight of the desired goal. He had hurled this polemical point at the supporters of SALT II. But Reagan's rhetorical abandonment in 1986 of adherence to SALT II, at Perle's prodding, made it apparent that the Russians could be free to deploy as many strategic weapons as they wish. The loophole drains the proposed INF treaty of "military substance," says James P. Rubin, research director of the Arms Control Association. "This is a Perle-sponsored treaty that falls short of the old Perle standards. Maybe Perle himself lost sight of his goals and got caught up in the process." On October 3, partly in recognition of the new "loophole," the Senate voted to require the United States to stay within the SALT II limits—another blow against Perle's legacy.

The approach of the Washington summit accelerated the decline of Perle's influence. Five years have passed since the ill-fated "walk in the woods" of U.S. negotiator Paul Nitze and Soviet negotiator Yuli Kvitsinsky, who informally worked out a plan for reducing intermediate-range missiles in Europe. The Reagan administration is now ready to sign an agreement that is less acceptable to America's NATO allies than the celebrated "walk."

By defending an arms control agreement before the Senate, the administration will be defending the notion that the United States can do business with the Russians. All the abstractions set against this by Perle and his network for nearly two decades was settled when the scratch of Reagan's signature on the treaty was heard.

As if to underline the point, Perle's former deputy, Frank Gaffney—who had followed in Perle's footsteps since their days together in Jackson's bunker—was, on the summit's eve, removed from his Pentagon job. And Perle raised his level of criticism of the treaty he had advocated. "The administration," he said, "has made a serious mistake negotiating against a deadline. The Soviets always exploit this. If the desire for the treaty leads the administration to make foolish concessions, then what they'll get will be unratifiable. It will be rejected."

For the first time in his career, Perle is without a mentor.

" 'Are you for us or the Soviets?' It intimidates some people in the hands of someone who's powerful because he works for people who are powerful," says Paul Warnke, the former chief SALT II negotiator. "But I don't see how Perle without a Jackson or a Weinberger can intimidate anyone."

Perle has privately taken to lavishing praise on Mortimer Zuckerman, the owner of *U.S. News,* who has commissioned his monthly column. But this is a case of an aspiring press lord purchasing a certain Washington byline, not a case of mentor and protégé.

"For most of the 1980s," reflects John Ritch, a top Democratic Senate aide who has known Richard Perle since the 1972 SALT I debate, "Richard had the 'correlation of forces' with him—geriatric Soviet leaders and a president whose ignorance, premises and dreams played into Richard's strength. Once he had the Pentagon nuclear job, dropping spanners into the arms control machinery wasn't even full-time work. Now the advent of Gorbachev changes everything. But Richard had his moment."

Perle's immediate struggle, however, is with his word processor. The initial payment of his $300,000 advance for his novel *Memoranda* has been deposited; the manuscript must be produced.

Some months ago, on his way from the Pentagon to a dinner at the Cosmos Club, yet another tribute upon his leaving office, an anxious Perle pulled his BMW to the curb. His writing habits, he confessed, were terrible. His famous memos were mainly scribbled at the last minute, from midnight to 3 A.M. How could he pace himself? He had chosen to write a novel in the form of memos because memos were something he knew how to write. But how to structure the material? How to develop characters?

Now he belongs to the book reviewers.

(September 1987)

Second Thoughts

It was a curious warp in time. With the Reagan era drawing to a close, former new left activists gathered to both proclaim and condemn the glory days of the '60s as the central experience of their lives.

It was not intended to be a revival. The weekend convocation, in October 1987, at the Grand Hyatt in Washington, dubbed the Second Thoughts Conference, had been elaborately planned to mark the journey from left to right. The ex-radicals would expiate their sins and be blessed by such elders of neoconservatism as Norman Podhoretz and Irving Kristol, who had made the same passage. Thus purified, the newly converted would assume their stations.

"The purpose of the project," said Jim Denton, president of the National Forum Foundation, which sponsored it, "is to mobilize a movement of ex-radicals which sort of exerts its influence, as we say, in the national debate." The aegis under which the event was organized—National Forum—is emblematic of the shift from the left-wing '60s to the right-wing '80s. Its founder is Jeremiah Denton, the defeated new right senator; Jim is his son. The budget is $450,000, provided by flush conservative foundations: Smith-Richardson, Coors, Olin, J.M., Murdoch Trust, Scaife, and Bradley.

But the weekend did not unfold as planned. In the midst of the choreographed conversions, there was a conversion—the wrong way. The apostate was Bruce Cameron, a pro-contra lobbyist and former associate of Lt. Col. Oliver North, who now bore witness to his new beliefs: The contras cannot win and they aren't democratic "freedom fighters."

There was dead silence, quickly broken by boos and hisses, the rending of clothing and fierce accusations. Then the assemblage of elders, in a fit of generational pique, disdained the entire ritual, casting all the *conversos* back into outer darkness for their insufficient self-denunciations. The "second-thoughter" movement was becoming unstuck before it could be glued together.

Appropriately, the leaders of the conversion conference had been leaders of the movement—David Horowitz and Peter Collier, former editors of *Ramparts* magazine, the barometer of the Zeitgeist—when they were the way they were. In their hotel suite hours before the festival of disillusionment was about to begin, Horowitz and Collier psyched themselves into the mood.

"We committed significant treason!" exclaimed Horowitz. Short and stout, with a Trotsky-like goatee and tinted aviator glasses, he was clad in retro-Berkeley style: tight, stone-washed jeans; black lizard-skin boots; and white T-shirt emblazoned, "Nicaragua is Spanish for Afghanistan." Horowitz was such an important figure of the age that "a lot of countries would have killed us!" He went on: "We tried to destroy this country! This country was good to us. It forgave us!"

Collier is Horowitz's Sancho Panza. (The two are more than an ideological team. Together they have written books chronicling the Rockefellers, Kennedys, and Fords.) Collier's dress—button-down shirt unbuttoned at the collar, and cuffed trousers—matched his quiet tone. When Horowitz paused for breath, he filled the gaps: "The '60s was an innocent era. We were murderers in our fantasies. But there was an innocence to it." After getting warmed up, Collier's bitterness began to seep around the edges. His special target was Tom Hayden, the former radical leader, now a California state assemblyman and husband of Jane Fonda. Long ago, he had informed Collier that "fascism was coming." And Collier confesses that he promptly "bought a gun." Now, he resents having listened. He also remembers a wedding in Berkeley where the cake read: "Smash Monogamy." In retrospect, he has decided, this was "dada," not funny.

Horowitz is back: "The '80s left, the Hate America left, is less honest. The '60s left was more honest: Tear the mother down! You have the '80s left posturing as liberalism . . . 'McCarthyism' has become a cudgel to prevent any discussion." Though Horowitz fashions himself in reaction against the new left, his roots are in the old. He grew up in a communist family in New York City. His red-diaper rash turned into the conviction that he was chosen to be the next Karl Marx, whose writings would set millions rushing into the streets. His books on U.S. imperialism poured forth: *Free World Colossus, Empire and Revolution.* He studied in London under Isaac Deutscher, the scholarly ex-Trotskyist and Trotsky biographer. And, having missed much of the '60s, he returned to America in 1967. He moved to Berkeley, ground zero for the movement, and soon became an editor of *Ramparts*.

In the late 1960s and early 1970s, *Ramparts* was the chief promoter of the black-leather-jacketed and gun-toting Black Panther Party. "They disturbed me," said Horowitz. "They were Stalinists." Then, in 1973, by his account, Huey Newton, the party's charismatic leader, persuaded him to raise money and make propaganda. "He was a master seducer." But when the Panther's bookkeeper was murdered, apparently because she knew too much about their shakedown operations, Horowitz began to lose his faith.

When Horowitz abandoned radicalism, he also left his wife and children, escaping into conservatism and Beverly Hills. "When I was a Marxist, I was puritanical," he said. "Then I got loose." Now, however, he says he's sympathetic to Tipper Gore's crusade against salacious rock 'n' roll lyrics. "I feel," said Horowitz, as he prepared to chair the conference, "like I'm the first Horowitz to step foot on the country."

The weekend's purge trial began on Saturday, with the victims also serving as judges. After convicting themselves, they urged the assembled to trust their political judgment.

Jeff Herf, a former member of Students for a Democratic Society and now professor of strategy at the Naval War College, said: "This was really embarrassing; the communists were really as bad as supporters of the war said they would be." His failure was one of theory: "I viewed the war through Marcusean and Adornoesque prisms"—a reference to two abstruse theoreticians popular with the new left. Herf said the '60s were not "wasted years," and his statement was not "a repudiation." In the back of the room, a staunch right-winger who apparently had never had a second thought muttered about the "chummy celebration of how bad they were."

After luncheon speeches by contras, it was time for Nicaragua. Robert Leiken, an ex-Maoist turned pro-contra lobbyist who now teaches at Harvard, reviewed the reviews of his articles: "There are penalties for opposing the left. Watch out for your job or reputation."

Then Bruce Cameron arose, visibly shaking, constantly sweeping his hand back across his gray hair. His commitment to Third World revolution in the 1960s had, in the 1980s, found the contras as its object. He had been a crucial player in getting them aid. Now, he declared, he had "third thoughts": The contras are "an army without a vision of a future society . . . the contras cannot win . . . I have great

doubts whether there can be a democratic counterrevolution . . .
There is no wing of the Democratic Party soft on communism . . .
Liberals are not procommunist and anti-American." And, he an-
nounced, he was now a lobbyist for "the Peoples' Republic of
Mozambique."

"Boo!" shouted Reed Irvine, the conservative press critic. "Boo!"
hollered Arnold Beichman, the anti-Soviet specialist at the Hoover
Institution. Norman Podhoretz, the neoconservative editor of *Commentary*, could not stop shaking his head.

A break was called. Seated in his chair, Cameron trembled uncon-
trollably. "I want to cry," he said. Arturo Cruz Jr., the Social Democratic contra leader and ex-boyfriend of North's secretary, Fawn
Hall, embraced Cameron. Cruz felt a bond of personal emotion that
transcended the opinion of the moment.

Cameron had been a China scholar, radicalized by the Vietnam
War, who worked with Fonda and Hayden in the Indochina Peace
Campaign in the early 1970s. During the Carter administration, as a
lobbyist for the liberal Americans for Democratic Action, he worked
on human rights issues. That led him to an interest in the Nicaraguan
revolution. He traveled there and eventually became disillusioned
with the Sandinistas. When he became convinced that the Reagan
administration wanted a negotiated settlement, he supported aid to
the contras on that basis. One of those who convinced him was Oliver
North. "I liked him," said Cameron. "His energy was infectious. He
was absolutely seductive." Through the conservative network
around the contra issue, Cameron met Carl (Spitz) Channell, a right-
wing fund-raiser who has since pleaded guilty to violating tax laws.
Channell raised money for Cameron's lobbying. North's "courier,"
Robert Owen, set up an organization that Cameron called the Center
for Democracy in the Americas. By the end of 1986, after successfully
lobbying for $100 million for aid to the contras just months before,
Cameron had had a change of heart. The talk of reforming the contras, he decided, was a sham. "They were behaving like thugs. There
just was no change." The Iran-contra scandal stunned him. "I was
shocked," he said. "I had a couple of clues, but not enough." Not only
were the contras "undemocratic," but the Reagan administration
was "antidemocratic in its relations with Congress." The idea of the
contras as "freedom fighters who could win" struck him as "a fantasy."

Cruz Jr. tried to halt the harsh criticism. "I will always love him,"
he said, gesticulating with a cigar. "He has the right . . . My father
[former contra leader Arturo Cruz] is no longer in the resistance
because of what Bruce said." But Cruz could not hold back the flood.

"Stale, specious arguments," said Leiken, who had been Cameron's comrade in the contra cause. "I could go on at length about the progress of the contras . . . You are an American who works on the Hill . . . another form of imperialism, another form of isolationism." "He's the one who's going to get all the press attention," chimed in Irvine, demonstrating his expertise. Leiken started attacking the press. "The coverage of the *New York Times* is very depressing."

"There is a line for this conference!" shouted Horowitz, now at the microphone. "If someone has not come to the conclusion that communism is a threat, then they haven't had second thoughts." Referring to Cameron's antiwar lobbying of Congress, he said, "I might have done what Bruce did, pull the plug on the people of Vietnam. The effect of pulling the plug was the death of three million people . . . I'm never, never going to pull the plug on an anticommunist struggle again!" The session was over, and walking toward the door Horowitz denounced Cameron for another crime: "He dominated the whole afternoon! It'll probably be the lead!"

Cameron sat at his seat, running his hand through his hair, a portrait of anguish: "I tried hard to work in good faith with the administration, and they didn't work in good faith . . . I didn't know it was going to come out like this."

Dinner was served. At the head table sat what Horowitz called the "panel of elders," collected to deliver a benediction and pass the torch. They were not in the mood for generosity.

The first speaker, Hilton Kramer, former art critic for the *New York Times* and editor of the neoconservative journal the *New Criterion,* wasted no time denouncing the conference: "morally catastrophic . . . not a single mention of the counterculture . . . Well, you were all immoralists. And we are all paying the price for the agenda let loose."

The wraithlike William Phillips, founding editor of *Partisan Review,* the ur-journal of the New York intellectuals, then reminisced. "Let me remind you, [in] the 1930s . . . we were called reactionaries . . . we were called Trotskyites." (Nothing the "second-thoughters" could do would ever match that lost glory of factionalism.)

Irving Kristol, godfather of the neoconservatives, with influence over many right-wing foundations, was next. "I have rejected at least fifty articles on 'second thoughts,' " he said. In his opinion, the important statements had already been made. The 1930s were real, the 1960s unreal.

Norman Podhoretz came forward now to reject the self-purges of the morning: "a desperate effort to cling to . . . lesser values." The confessors, in his mind, remained members of the counterculture. America faced "threats from within and without . . . ideas flowing from the counterculture . . . the corrupted and poisoned culture, which is our major problem."

This sheer generational resentment was beyond ideology. And for all the raging about the "anti-Americans," what the elders seemed to fear most were the aspects of American culture they didn't understand, such as rock 'n' roll. Only Nathan Glazer of Harvard, in his closing seconds, referred to current realities: the change in Soviet leadership, for example.

It was an evening of nostalgia.

But the second thoughts project is not played out. There is still a considerable sum left over for Horowitz and Collier, with which to pursue its goals. The duo is trying to market a syndicated political column. They are rustling up speaking engagements. They are thinking about restarting *Ramparts* to reflect their new concerns. They are taking trips to Nicaragua. And they are writing a book on the generation that came of age in the 1960s. Its title: *Destructive Generation.*

"About the money," said Horowitz. "I made only $60,000 this year. The previous year I made $250,000. I did this for the cause, for love."

(October 1987)

PART V

Between a Rock and a Hard Place

Robert Dole's
Republican Undead

A specter is haunting Reagan—the specter of Republicanism.

All the wizards of the new conservatism have entered into an alliance to exorcise this specter: Meese and Kirkpatrick, Gilder and Gingrich, the Heritage Foundation and political action committees. In 1984, Ronald Reagan disdained to conceal his aims. That ancient member of Americans for Democratic Action never evoked the glorious past of the Grand Old Party. He ran for reelection as the true heir of Roosevelt. Reagan—not Walter Mondale—was the ultimate "real" Democrat. "It's morning in America again," proclaimed his television ads, echoing the Rooseveltian optimism. Reagan, declining to detail his future policies, declared: "You ain't seen nothin' yet." But after his victory he offered no conservative version of F.D.R.'s second New Deal.

"Yet" arrived before Christmas, and, as promised, the American people were vouchsafed a vision of nothin'. The Tuesday team gave way to the doomsday team. David Stockman's budget cutters and calls for austerity replaced denunciations of Mondale's "gloom and doom." Reagan's landslide triumph had made the Democrats disappear, but not the deficit. The administration's thematic vital signs started to go flat. It's nightfall in America again.

The regular Republicans, supposedly consigned to the dustbin of history by the conservative "revolution," struggled to their feet. Unsteadily at first, then with a loud, firm tread, they began marching toward the cameras. One after another they came—Robert Dole of Kansas, Richard Lugar of Indiana, Robert Packwood of Oregon, John Chafee of Rhode Island. They had stayed the course. In the Senate, the regulars elected Dole majority leader, suppressing a conservative insurgency, and took control of every open post within the Republican caucus.

This is their moment, partly because for fifty years the federal deficit has been their issue, despite the fact that whenever they strenuously campaigned on the question, they lost. It's an issue whose time has come and gone and come again, brought back from the shadows by a Republican president who has fostered the biggest debt ever. By dispensing with traditional GOP nostrums, Reagan promised, among other things, to produce a budget surplus. Having failed at this feat, he is stuck with a "second New Deal" that is taking on the coloration of the "real" Republicanism. It would be an exaggeration to say that the regular Republicans have come back to life, because their reemergence in the Senate has been caused by the peculiarities of that body, not by any change in the political balance of the country. But if they are not exactly alive, neither are they as dead as they had seemed to be as recently as the 1984 Republican convention. They are something in between: the politically undead.

Conservatives, meanwhile, are experiencing rage. They believe that they won the election and the traditionalists have usurped power. "What happened to 'morning'?" wonders Vin Weber of Minnesota, a young activist in the House. To the conservatives, who insist that economic growth will shrink the deficit, it seems that Mondale is the victor, with his name changed to Dole. "I never thought growth would deal with the deficit," says Dole. "Mondale's view of it was all right. He was the wrong salesman."

The fissure between conservatives and regulars has several fault lines. It is a split between the ascendant Senate majority and a House caucus, the Conservative Opportunity Society, a minority within a minority. In the Senate, the party controls the strategic levers, whereas in the House the movement group is stymied by a Democratic majority. The split is also a difference between political generations, between older men who have felt the fear of political extinction and younger men whose careers have paralleled the Reagan rise. Finally, the split is doctrinal. Eliminating the deficit is at the center of the traditionalist's world view. They seek a fiscal stringency that attempts at least the appearance of equal sacrifice. The conservatives, however, want to cut only social programs. For them, the deficit is both an opportunity and a danger. Ironically, Reagan's policies have created an impasse that makes possible his goal of negative government. The deficit has become an instrument of conservative social policy, just as it was once a mechanism for liberal social policy. But its enormous size calls into doubt the credibility of supply-side economics, the conservative claim to the mantle of growth and optimism. If tax cuts don't increase revenues or investment, as advertised, but do increase deficits, supply-side economics may turn out to be mainly a stimulus for the traditionalist position. Unlike the conservatives, the regulars are not opposed to government in principle. "There are people in the new right who feel the government should defend the shores and deliver the mail and that's it. That's it. You won't find anyone like that in the Republican Senate leadership," says Senator John Heinz, newly elected chair of the Republican Senate Campaign Committee. The traditionalists want to make government run more efficiently, like a well-organized business. Their conservatism is the impulse to reform and conserve yesterday's liberalism. Their stance is based less on an explicit creed than on an implicit disposition. A movement located beyond the bounds of the party is foreign to them.

This burst of Republicanism may be the rise before the fall. In 1986, twenty-two GOP senators face reelection. A net loss of only four seats turns the Senate over to the Democrats. In this century there have been six mid-second-term elections. In no instance did the party holding the White House lose fewer than four Senate seats. Moreover, after 1986, the approaching Republican convention will assume greater force. If the regulars can't translate their strength from the Senate caucus to the convention, they will be reinterred once again. Their reign may be a short-lived phenomenon—the wave of the past. For the moment, though, they hold sway.

The Republican assertion in the Senate is quite traditional. Dole's rise and the capture of the committee chairmanships by the regulars was hardly a break with the past. Dole is the latest of a line that stretches back to Robert Taft, the conservative midwestern Senate baron, who could never transfer his strength from the congressional caucus to the GOP convention. He was beaten time and again by Thomas Dewey's political network, which ran from governor's mansions to clubhouses. While the Taftites ruled the Senate, the Deweyites won the presidential nominations. Even the 1964 "draft [Barry] Goldwater" movement was rooted among former young Republicans trained in the Dewey operation. When Reagan became president, there were few true Reaganites in the Senate. The two senators who ran against him in the 1980 primaries, Howard Baker and Dole, had gone nowhere; like Taft, they prospered in the institutional setting, not among the broad electorate. The Senate regulars are a fusion of latter-day Taftites and Deweyites, whose differences have been muted in the face of the newer brand of conservatism, regionally based in the Sunbelt, where Republicans have a shallow history. In the states of greatest conservative strength, the GOP is a novel party for volatile voters.

The "moderate" wing of the Republican Party depends upon the logic of the old two-party system for its sustenance. The moderates represent states with big cities, smokestack industries, and diverse ethnic groups; the parties are fixed elements. "The Democratic Party in Pennsylvania is the party of political bosses," says Senator Heinz. "That creates great opportunity for any Republican." With a machine Democrat as an opponent, the Republican can pose efficiency against patronage. "Good government" Republicans like Heinz must temper their partisan appeals in order to attract Democrats; their "moderation," moreover, is mostly a matter of positioning, making a virtue out of lack of intense ideological conviction.

The moderate has thus rendered himself almost completely unsuitable for Republican presidential politics. He has crafted his appeal too generously; he can't survive among the decidedly conservative GOP primary electorate, where a vibrant constituency can be animated by ideology. In the Senate, this species of moderate becomes the natural ally of the neo-Taftite. They share a common Republican patrimony that separates them from the Sunbelt conservatives. In the cockpit of the Senate, the party dominates the movement. And Bob Dole presides.

According to the conventional wisdom there are two distinct Doles—the good Dole and the bad Dole. The bad one was a Republican hatchet man who assailed "Democrat wars" and snarled at Nixon's detractors. The good Dole sponsored the food stamp program and voted for civil rights bills. While Dole's savage sense of humor may have been slightly toned down in recent years—the savagery doesn't usually overwhelm the humor now—he is fundamentally unchanged. He hasn't moved much; the planets have. "I don't know that I've changed that much," he says. "I consider myself a traditional conservative." He is what conservatives were like before Goldwater. And he is a particular variety. His support for food stamps and civil rights isn't a drift away from his roots. They are Republican and progressive positions. Alf Landon of Kansas, after all, was a progressive Republican. Dole is unyielding in substance, but as times change he is viewed from a new angle.

He offers the masterful practice of political brokerage, lightened by black humor. His economics are an unspoken moral code, puritanism on the plains. "I've grown up in the Republican Party," he says. "I've heard time after time, heard it from business people and farmers, about deficits. And we've run it up bigger than all the administrations in history. Deficits are *bad*. It ought to be a top priority. You can't live on a credit card forever."

Traditional Republican thinking about the federal deficit has its source in the yeoman economy, where farmers and artisans lived in constant terror of debt, which portended foreclosure and ruin. More-over, debt undermined moral character. What kind of weird doctrine would teach that a penny saved is not a penny earned, but instead the cause of the Depression? How could one get something (i.e., prosperity) for nothing (i.e., debt), as the Keynesians suggested?

Dole repeatedly says that things aren't "easy." During World War II he suffered wounds that hospitalized him for a year and left him without full use of his right arm. He believes in success achieved by hard work, in reward as compensation for effort. It's not surprising that he's offended by Reagan's economics.

With Reagan, we're not in Kansas any more. The shift from small-town society to mass consumer culture has been accompanied by a shift in political types. In the conservative cosmology, the shift has been from the undramatic Taft to the prickly Goldwater to the smooth Reagan. Reagan knows that good luck can last a lifetime. His wife has even named their new dog "Lucky." He stresses pleas-ure; Dole emphasizes pain. Reagan offers self-indulgence; Dole, self-discipline. *His* new dog is named "Leader."

Reagan remains the inveterate New Dealer by not being taken in by the metaphysics of deficit fear. Although he decries it, deficit spending sustained the recovery guaranteeing his reelection. Keyne-sianism and Reaganism are similar in that they undermine the old puritan sense of guilt. The difference is that Reagan denies what the liberals used to acknowledge: that there are times when deficits are actually good.

Reagan's innovation allowed the Republicans to overcome the stigma of stagnation attached to them since Hoover. The effort to escape this crippling label led Nixon, who attacked Kennedy's "growthmanship" in 1960, to proclaim himself a Keynesian a decade later. Reagan was led to enact a perverse Keynesian program, which conservatives insist on calling the death of Keynesianism. But Bob Dole is not confused. Supply-siders, he believes, "don't face reality. They've always got another base to cover. Everyone believes we have to reduce spending. I'm not sure they want to make these choices. It's crazy."

From the start, Dole was wary of supply-side economics. But as chair of the Senate Finance Committee, he played the good soldier, supporting his president's tax cut measure. In August 1981, when the bill was signed, the administration projected a budget surplus for 1984. Recession and deficits followed instead. Dole wanted to raise taxes. In March 1982, he proposed $105 billion in increases. No dice. Then, in August 1982, he helped shepherd a $98.9 billion increase through the Senate, a bill hailed by liberal tax reformers for its fearless closing of loopholes. Dole wanted the pain to be shared by even the undeserving rich. The measure was the largest tax hike in history, a direct repudiation of the Reagan program passed just the year before. Then Dole proposed another increase. But the recovery appeared and pain had limited appeal.

Except to Walter Mondale, who campaigned on a promise to raise taxes. Reagan announced that taxes would be raised "over my dead body." And he pledged not to cut Medicare and Social Security and defense. The public, massaged by his feel-good campaign, was in no mood for sacrifice.

Shortly after Reagan's reelection, the Treasury Department released a remarkably equitable tax reform program, which Reagan did not embrace. The proposal, and Stockman's draconian budget-cutting plan, had the effect of inspiring virtually all the lobbyists in Washington to mobilize their resources against each specific change. In 1981, Reagan was able to enact his complete economic program only with a unified coalition of businesses, arrayed behind his unwavering leadership. This time, the tax and budget bills appeared destined to be handled separately, almost ensuring that the contentious interests could focus their energy on their immediate and narrow concerns. How could the president generate political momentum amidst legislative chaos? "I see the business people chewing up the tax bill and spitting it out," says Dole. "They're so busy on that they don't have time on budget restraint. In 1981, giving it away was easy. Now, we're taking it away. It's much more difficult." To Dole, the deficits make budget cutting and tax reform a necessary but Sisyphean task. "I don't know how we'll do it. It may be a stalemate."

The netherworld that Reagan described as Mondale's inferno may be the fate of the traditional Republicans as they are engulfed in the political economy of stagnation. While the moderates try conscientiously to grapple with the fiscal dilemmas created by enthusiasm for the Laffer curve, the supply-siders are already happily hunting the next snark—the gold standard. The moderates are about to be impressed into the conservative inopportunity society. Their Republicanism dooms them to respond in the traditional manner: they will continue to seek the ever-elusive balanced budget. Even as the economy mutates into new post-industrial forms, their conception of it remains unchanged.

In 1986, the Republicans must again confront the consequences of Reagan's economics, with results that historical precedent suggests may differ from the experience of 1984. Paradoxically, the regulars' continuing control of the Senate depends upon the conservatives' success. Swept into office on Reagan's coattails in 1980, many conservatives are extremely vulnerable. But by losing, they would destroy the regulars' power base. Without the Senate, the traditional Republicans would have to fall back on national political networks if they wish to influence the convention. *Bob Dole for president?* Influence in Washington would not count for much, especially among primary voters who regard "big government" as the fount of the country's troubles. The traditionalists, however, think almost exclusively in institutional terms. Their strength, after all, comes from their links to permanent structures—constitutional and corporate. This establishment is in place, but not in motion; the regulars have no movement to carry them against the conservatives in 1988. "Where's the base outside of Washington?" inquires Robert Teeter, a Republican pollster with close ties to the White House. "When you get to the convention, the Washington strength doesn't hold. Dole doesn't have a natural base. With these guys there's nothing at the end of the string." If the regulars lose the Senate in 1986 and fail to sustain a presidential candidacy in 1988, they must return to the limbo they occupied for decades.

What frustrates the conservatives now, however, may benefit them later. If the Republicans lose control of the Senate, the conservatives will blame the regulars, even if conservative losses are the proximate cause and conservative policies the underlying cause. "The arithmetic is against the Senate moderates," says Representative Vin Weber, the conservative Republican of Minnesota. "And history is against them. Their response is exactly wrong. Rather than making the themes that worked in 1984 those of 1986, they are ensuring they won't have those positive themes. Look at the Reagan ads. Find the one that says: Vote Republican and make hard, nasty decisions. It's a deadly game they're playing. It's heading us toward disaster in 1986. The bad news is that we'll lose the Senate in 1986. The good news is that it won't make any difference."

Six weeks after the president's reelection, his leadership is absent or at least incredibly subtle. Some believe there's a guiding intelligence in this vacuum, that chaos is a deliberate strategy, a classic Reagan gambit. But a fierce factionalism has been triggered, a preview of the Republican fragmentation that appears inevitable when Reagan departs. The party and the movement are already at war.

(January 1983)

The Old Republic
and Edward P. Boland

Edward P. Boland seems an improbable man at the storm center.

Seated behind his nameplate in the front row of the select committee on the Iran-contra scandal, the seventy-five-year-old congressman from Springfield, Massachusetts, has peered through his clear-frame glasses, almost clinically inexpressive during the first phase of the congressional hearings. In his spare opening statement about the clash between "policy and constitutional principle," it was typical of the self-effacing Boland that he never mentioned the amendment that is at the heart of the clash and bears his name.

The Boland Amendment is actually a changing series of measures governing aid to the contras, reflecting the shifting sentiment of Congress on Central American policy. Outrage at the secret mining of Nicaragua's harbors led to the framing of the amendment's most ironclad version. From October 1984 to September 1985, it prohibited funds "available to the CIA, DOD or any other agency or entity of the United States involved in intelligence activities" from "supporting, directly or indirectly, military or paramilitary operations in Nicaragua." But far from halting a subterranean foreign policy, Reagan's men, directed by Lt. Col. Oliver North of the National Security Council, began to construct what Richard V. Secord, one of North's "contractors," has called "the enterprise"—a clandestine apparatus to provide for the contras until the White House could again persuade Congress to resume the funding.

Partly as a consequence of the Boland Amendment, the scandal may be gathering into a crisis. What is at issue is beyond partisan divisions, beyond the combat of contras and Sandinistas. The question now, Boland believes, is whether the president and the National Security Council staff are above the rule of this law. If they are, the old republic, as Boland understands it, will have been replaced by a new imperium.

Reagan, in fact, signed the Boland Amendment and has said he was adhering to its strictures, but his ultimate defense is that he is exempt: "It so happens that it does not apply to me," Reagan told *U.S. News & World Report* on May 25, 1987, while denying that he had violated it. "And there is nothing that has ever been in the Boland Amendment that could keep me from asking other people to help the rebels." "Swiss cheese," said retired Major General Secord, referring to the amendment, not to his numbered Swiss bank accounts.

In a concerted display of op-ed strength, conservatives have contended that the Boland Amendment was the real crime, usurping the president's rightful prerogative in foreign policy and breaching the separation of powers. "Unconstitutional in intent," opined George F. Will, the columnist.

As slings and arrows are hurled at Boland, he remains taciturn. "The attack is building all the time," he says. "Maybe that's the only way out for them." But Boland dismisses the view that the passage of his amendment was a symbolic indulgence or an unconstitutional doctrine. "It's not even a law? Swiss cheese full of holes? The first amendment that was offered passed in 1982. That passed [the House] by 411 to nothing—to nothing. That was the first one. . . . Does the National Security Council come in under it? I think so. Obviously, there was no question raised by the administration at the time it was passed. You know, they've got the whole Department of Justice to ask for legal opinions. If they thought it was unconstitutional that would have been a good time to question it."

In the meantime, the Boland Amendment is scourged. "George Will does it," says Boland. "Oh, he's a smart, intelligent guy. Who's the other columnist? Charles Krauthammer. He's a good writer, incidentally. He's smart. So you get him. You get James Kilpatrick. You get the *Wall Street Journal* and the *Washington Times.* That's about the size of it."

For all that, says Boland: "It is the law . . . No technicalities there. No confusion there . . . It is as clear as a bell—clear as a bell." And if it is the law, he continues, "It would be a very significant question, given the way the hearings are going, if the law was broken by this administration. That question will be answered in time, and it may well be answered by the court."

The Boland Amendment is more famous than Boland. He has no interest in fifteen minutes of fame, preferring thirty-four years so far of national political influence. A conspicuous display of importance,

to him, would be gratuitous and imprudent. "I don't like the lime-
light in this situation," he says. "I think you have the responsibility
of staying out of it." His biographical entry in the *Congressional Direc-
tory,* inserted by him, is three terse lines: name, party, district, and
congresses to which he was elected. It is the shortest entry in the
book. No one remembers Boland ever having called a press conference. And he never gave an interview about his role as the first chair
of the House Intelligence Committee.

But Boland's modesty does not reflect his standing where he is best
known—the House of Representatives. "When you get done writing
all the history, the reason this whole strategy of the administration
unraveled is that they decided to lie to Eddie Boland rather than to
tell the truth," says Representative George Miller, a California Democrat. "This is not a guy who's a flash in the pan. What you had were
all his years of credibility." And when he proposed the Boland
Amendment, says Miller, "people had to take a step back and say,
'Whoa, this is Eddie Boland.'"

"If the Boland Amendment had been anyone else's it wouldn't
have passed. It would not have had the institutional significance,"
says former Representative James Shannon, the Massachusetts attorney general, who has been close to Boland. "It wouldn't have happened if you didn't have someone from the background Eddie comes
from." "I'm not a fan of the Boland Amendment, but I am a big fan
of Eddie Boland," says Representative Richard Cheney of Wyoming,
chair of the House Republican Conference. "You won't find as many
members of the House as respected as he is. He took the Intelligence
Committee when it was brand new and made it into something
significant. On our side of the aisle you won't find anyone to say
anything bad about him."

Boland's devotion to his office has been almost priestly. He married
at sixty-two, after having roomed for twenty-four years with Tip
O'Neill, whose family remained in Cambridge. "Frankly," says the
former speaker of the House, "his life was politics. He studied every
night."

Many mornings Boland eats breakfast with a couple of members
of the Massachusetts congressional delegation. He is of an older Irish
American political strain that is not breezy or casual. He is given to
long silences, especially among those with whom he shares implicit
assumptions such as the old political virtues of loyalty and friendship. "He honors the New England code: Only talk when it improves
the silence," says Christopher Matthews, O'Neill's former press secretary.

Boland has lived his political life within hierarchies as complex as the Vatican, and slowly risen. He appears to be the opposite of a true believer, but is governed by so deep a belief in how the American government is supposed to function that it is inseparable from who he is. Only after this belief was profoundly offended did he begin to formulate his amendment. His intent was to restore, not obliterate, the separation of powers. "He is one of those quiet men of the House who, in fact, make it work," says Senator Daniel Patrick Moynihan of New York who, as former vice chair of the Senate Intelligence Committee, worked closely with Boland. "He has absolute integrity and no personal interest, only the interest of his district and his country . . . The office is his vocation. There is none other." "A lifetime," says Boland of what he has contributed to politics. "I've been here a long period of time—hell, eighteenth term."

Boland's parents were immigrants from County Kerry, Ireland. And his father was a railroad worker. He grew up in the Irish ethnic neighborhood of Hungry Hill, where politics was as natural as breathing. In Springfield, Boland came to know other young politicos: Lawrence O'Brien, who became John F. Kennedy's crackerjack campaign operative and Democratic National Committee chair, and Joseph Napolitan, who became a founder of modern political consulting and an international strategist.

But Springfield politics, unlike Boston's, was not noted for its colorful chicanery and clamor. "The elections are very civilized compared to Boston, less vitriolic," says Napolitan. Within Massachusetts, Springfield has been a crucible of first-rate political figures who have played secondary roles to Boston politicians. In this light, Boland has been the exemplary Springfield politician.

In 1934, when the midterm election results resoundingly reaffirmed support for the New Deal, the twenty-three-year-old Boland, just graduated from the Boston College Law School, was elected to the Massachusetts legislature, a body dominated by Republicans. Two years later, he was joined by young Tip O'Neill. While O'Neill stayed on, becoming the first Democratic speaker of the Massachusetts House of Representatives, Boland returned home to become the Hampden County register of deeds. He was so popular in this minor post that he wound up securing both the Democratic and Republican nominations for reelection.

In 1952, the year of Eisenhower's ascendancy, Boland was elected to Congress, arriving in Washington with his old friend O'Neill. Together they rented an apartment and became known as the capital's odd couple. O'Neill, tall and stout, was the sloppy one; Boland, short and thin, was the neat one. "Eddie was the alarm clock," says one who knows them. The refrigerator was stocked with beer and cigars. "I don't think we ever had a meal in the place," says Boland. At every station of O'Neill's progress, Boland was there. "I nominated him for the position of majority leader twice, and for the office of speaker five times. He won each time," he said in a warm tribute delivered on the occasion of O'Neill's retirement.

O'Neill always believed that their Bay State experience gave them a head start in Washington. "They play a hard cruel game," says O'Neill about the Massachusetts legislature. "If you come to Washington, you have a five or six-year advantage on your freshmen congressmen."

Boland soon became friendly with another young Massachusetts representative, John F. Kennedy, five years his junior. According to O'Neill, "They were very close." Both of them broke with most of the delegation to vote for the St. Lawrence Seaway, thought to threaten the local economy, as a sign that they could transcend parochial limitations. Kennedy's 1960 presidential campaign was a crusade to Irish Americans of the Democratic faith, and Boland was a knight. His assigned duchy for the general election was Ohio (which finally voted for Richard Nixon). Boland's office is a veritable shrine to Kennedy, containing a small bust of him and three framed pictures, one showing Boland shaking J.F.K.'s hand as Lyndon Johnson looks on.

Over the years, Boland quietly accumulated seniority, quietly promoted O'Neill within the leadership, and quietly helped transform ailing Springfield into a thriving post-industrial center through the adroit use of federal programs. In 1973, he quietly married thirty-five-year-old Mary Egan, a bright lawyer who had been president of the Springfield City Council. "A surprise," says O'Neill. It was whimsically remarked in Springfield that Egan was the only serious potential rival for Boland's seat. Every weekend, he quietly commuted home. And within six years he had four children.

His political vulnerability reached the vanishing point. He had not faced a serious challenger in decades. In 1982, he spent $47 on his reelection campaign. An infinitesimal four percent of the voters in his district regard him negatively, according to a 1987 poll conducted by Joseph Napolitan. "He doesn't make a lot of noise," says Napolitan. "And he does extraordinarily well."

O'Neill, in the meantime, had become speaker. Every Wednesday, at 6:30 A.M., he was briefed by the CIA. "It was so confidential," says O'Neill, "I couldn't tell my wife. So after about three months I said to myself that this is crazy. There ought to be an intelligence committee." In short order, the House created one; and so did the Senate. "Everyone I put on that committee I trusted," says O'Neill. "I knew of nobody more trustworthy than Eddie—of the greatest sincerity, dedicated to the country, and dedicated to keeping his mouth shut." When the Reagan team moved into Washington, Boland had been chair for four years.

By the end of 1981, the administration had secretly organized the contras. In December, in a closed session of the House Intelligence Committee, officials explained that these contras existed only to halt arms flowing from the Nicaraguan regime to the rebels in El Salvador. Boland's skepticism, according to a source, was aroused. And he expressed it in a confidential letter to CIA Director William Casey. But he did not rush to controversy. Every step he took was carefully measured. Thus began the tortuous history of the Boland Amendment. Throughout 1982, Tom Harkin, then a Democratic representative and now a senator from Iowa, advanced a bill that would cut off all funds to the contras. He was a Vietnam veteran, and he feared another quagmire.

"I wanted to believe the administration in what it wanted done: interdict the flow of arms into El Salvador," says Boland. With old-fashioned bipartisan spirit, Boland crafted what may be considered the first of several incarnations of the Boland Amendment—which continued to finance the contras but prohibited them from using the money "for the purpose of overthrowing the government of Nicaragua or provoking a military exchange between Nicaragua and Honduras." The administration gave the signal, and the Republicans in Congress unanimously supported the measure.

"That doesn't prohibit anything," muttered Casey, after this Boland Amendment passed in December 1982, according to a former staff member of the Intelligence Committee. And within the House Democratic Caucus, the younger and liberal members argued that the administration's policy was deceitful. Boland, however, kept them at a distance. "He thought we were young, irascible, pretty far to the left," says George Miller. "He essentially didn't believe me for a long period of time." Says James Shannon, "He is instinctively cautious, has great respect for the institution of the presidency, and believes the president should have real authority over foreign policy. He didn't have the built-in questioning that the younger Democrats have. He would never have moved if the administration had been honest. But they lied."

In the spring of 1983, Boland was traveling in China with O'Neill. Every day, the U.S. Embassy provided him with press clippings. Says Boland: "Christopher Dickey [of *The Washington Post*] was traveling with a contra group. The clear evidence he got from those who were contras and leaders was that they were interested in overthrowing the government of Nicaragua, more interested than in the interdiction of arms . . . There was deception there." Then more news stories appeared, featuring the contras boasting about the road to Managua. And Boland began to move.

His personal emissary, Representative Wyche Fowler Jr. of Georgia, then a member of the House Intelligence Committee and now a senator, was dispatched to Central America to investigate. He reported to Boland that his amendment was being violated. Reagan, for his part, claimed on April 14, 1983, that he was "complying fully" with the Boland Amendment: "We are not doing anything to try and overthrow the Nicaraguan government."

In an unusual secret session of the House on July 19, Boland led the debate. "He was so determined and so deliberative in his presentation," says Miller. "You felt this is an institutional inside player; his best friend is the Speaker; you felt this guy was standing on ten feet of concrete in his argument. He came in that determined voice to send the signal to members of Congress that this whole policy was a subterfuge. He wasn't going to misrepresent to his colleagues what was going on. It was his pride, his sense of the institution. That's why the issue turned. He started to occupy center stage. He started getting larger and larger." A week later, Boland spoke out again on the House floor.

"This secret war is bad U.S. policy," he declared, "because it does not work, because it is in fact counterproductive to U.S. interests, because it is illegal."

The House promptly cut off all aid to the contras. The Republican-dominated Senate appropriated $50 million. And a compromise—$24 million—was eventually granted. Then, Boland learned that the CIA had mined Nicaragua's harbors months previously without informing either the House or Senate intelligence committees. He took the floor on April 14, 1984: "The first announcement—the first announcement—of the mining was made by the contras—the contras—not by the Intelligence Committee, not by the CIA, not from the briefings that we heard, but made by the contras on January 8 . . . Acts of war by the United States against Nicaragua are wrong, absolutely wrong."

"The instinct to deceive overwhelmed them," says Moynihan about the administration. "I think the whole committee was distressed," says Boland. The atmosphere was one of "shocked disillusion," says Moynihan. Senator Barry Goldwater, then chair of the

Senate Intelligence Committee, sent Casey a letter expressing the collective dismay. Boland himself was prompted to introduce the toughest version of the Boland Amendment. Its intent, as understood by the committee, was never in doubt.

"The notion that it might be ambiguous was never broached in any conversation in the Intelligence Committee," says Moynihan. "The matter was thought settled, a policy was thought reversed." "You could make a technical argument that it was not specific enough, but one has to strain to reach that conclusion," says Senator William Cohen, a Maine Republican and vice chair of the Senate Intelligence Committee.

The loophole that Reagan claimed, that the NSC was not included in the amendment and therefore not subject to its fiat, was never thought to be a loophole by Congress. By law and history, the NSC served the president solely as an advisory body, and thus lay beyond congressional oversight. Nobody imagined that the NSC would be transformed into "the enterprise." The administration, according to Cohen, has created "a Catch-22 problem": It insisted that the NSC was not operational and argued that the Boland Amendment did not apply because it failed to mention the NSC. "Sophistic," says Cohen of this logic. "They transfer the activities to the NSC and say they are not covered by the Boland Amendment."

"The amendment," says Boland, "is crystal clear."

But the administration refused to consider the issue settled. It followed a two-track policy. In public, it sought congressional approval of military and "humanitarian" aid to the contras. In the aftermath of Reagan's landslide reelection, a decisive bloc of House Democrats quivered and, in 1986, voted $100 million for the contras, which passed. "No, $100 million does not buy a contra victory," said Boland during the debate. "It buys continued fighting to no apparent conclusion." Meanwhile, in private, the administration constructed "the enterprise" to transgress the Boland Amendment and covertly finance the contra war. Soon, Reagan's men were found on the doorstep of the Ayatollah Khomeini, offering arms for alms.

In the end, the improbable man turns out to have been the inevitable man. When confronted with what he came to regard as a reign of deception, Boland could not turn away. On the opening day of the select committee's hearings, Arthur Liman, the Senate committee's chief counsel, watched Boland quietly assume his seat. "The first witness who sees Boland will have a heart attack," he said offhandedly.

The administration has disputed the amendment's relevance. Wit-

nesses like North's former aide, Robert Owen—"the courier"—trace
the origin of the entire affair to Congress, which acted "wrongly in
stopping funds for the effort." Conservative opinion makers offer
similar jibes. Yet the official who was supposed to "monitor Ollie,"
Assistant Secretary of State Elliott Abrams—"Mr. Kenilworth"—
told the panel that the amendment applied to everyone in the administration. On June 8 another witness, Bretton Sciaroni, the counsel to the President's Intelligence Oversight Board, confessed that his
classified opinion of September 1985, that the amendment did not
apply to the NSC, was based on superficial and incomplete evidence.
Still, he clung to his opinion. Sciaroni explained that he had flunked
the bar exam four times, that this was his debut at analyzing legislation, and that his was the only legal analysis of the amendment made
by the administration. "Very useful," said Boland, of Sciaroni's testimony. "Very enlightening."

   As the crisis builds, so does the heated ideological contention
around the Boland Amendment. To which Edward P. Boland simply
replies: "It is the law."

(June 1987)

Left at Sea: The Institute

for Policy Studies

The Institute for Policy Studies (IPS) is the Pluto of think tanks, the one farthest from the Reagan sun. In the cold, left-wing reaches of the Washington solar system, off Dupont Circle, a small band huddles together, planning to gain mastery of the political "Force." "What we're playing for," said Marcus Raskin, a senior fellow at the institute, "is the spirit of the times."

In the 1960s, they seemed to possess the power to divine that spirit. Even President Nixon saw fit to recognize Raskin and Richard Barnet, the IPS's founders, by inscribing their names on his "enemies list." "They have not caused developments so much as anticipated them," wrote Garry Wills in an article in *Esquire* on the institute in 1971.

But after six years of Reagan, the IPS appears to be the think tank that time forgot. "We've spent twenty years with Republican presidents," said Robert Borosage, its director. "And Carter was an enigma. The posture we've been in for a generation has been defensive. And we're in middle age now." The IPS was not created, however, to be completely estranged from power. The institute began in 1963 as the left wing of the Kennedy administration, with access to the White House and State Department. By speaking "truth to power," as Raskin put it, power would gradually cede ground; the strength of the argument would carry the day.

Since 1964, when Lyndon Johnson won a landslide victory and the postwar Democratic consensus seemed secure, the left and right have gradually traded places. Conservatives turned what was widely regarded as a far-fetched ideology into the conventional wisdom; left and liberal ideas that were once considered mainstream were relegated to the fringe. Part of the credit for this dramatic role-reversal belongs to the conservatives themselves, who have expended enormous energy stigmatizing their opponents as subversive. By making them seem illegitimate, the right-wingers attempted to narrow the debate. This tactic also allowed them to explain events by reference to the concerted actions of a liberal establishment, at the very center of which, according to various right-wing accounts, stood the IPS.

But by 1976, when another Democratic president assumed office, the IPS was already well on the road to irrelevance. Its internal chaos was symptomatic of the broader intellectual confusion that was befalling the Democrats and the Carter administration. Just as the turmoil at the IPS rendered it incapable of helping anyone, including itself, the general Democratic failure sealed its isolation. Nevertheless, as the IPS declined in actual influence, its stature grew in conservative demonology; it passed from influence to fable. During the conservative ascendancy, the institute has been a major right-wing obsession and convenient target.

In 1980, after the appearance over the years of many denunciatory articles in right-wing publications, *Midstream* magazine published the most lavish tribute, "IPS: Empire on the Left." Its author, Rael Jean Isaac, wrote about the IPS as "an unprecedented success story: the achievement of the New Left, after its supposed demise, in shaping United States policy." The institute, she charged, spun a spidery "network of interlocking directorates" in the interest of "the Soviet line." This view of the IPS reached an apotheosis in fiction. In 1981, a novel entitled *The Spike* was published, written by Arnaud de Borchgrave (now the editor of the Moonie-owned *Washington Times*) and Robert Moss. The story's action revolved around a think tank called the Institute for Progressive Reform, a thinly disguised version of the IPS, depicted as "a classic communist front operation" that gains control over the Congress and the National Security Council.

Apparently inspired by *The Spike*, Senator Jeremiah Denton, Republican of Alabama, held hearings in 1981 before the Senate Subcommittee on Security and Terrorism that focused on the IPS. In his opening statement, Denton said he intended to investigate the communist "power to transmit ideas. I believe it needs exploring, that whole biology." De Borchgrave, in his capacity as fiction writer, was called as an expert witness. That year the conservative Heritage Foundation issued several cautionary reports on the IPS "network." Another Heritage report on "terrorist cadres" also mentioned the IPS.

In 1983, when the IPS staged a conference on disarmament with

U.S. experts and Soviet officials, twelve new right senators and seventy representatives wrote a letter to Secretary of State George Shultz, asserting that the IPS "has for 20 years supported foreign policy objectives that serve the interests of the Soviet Union." The neoconservative polemicist Joshua Muravchik, writing in the Winter 1984–85 issue of *World Affairs,* attempted to provide a more theoretical view, entitled: " 'Communophilism' and the Institute for Policy Studies." The political species that Muravchik labels "Communophiles" are not, strictly speaking, communists; rather, they are sympathizers with "communist movements." Muravchik, however, still entertains the "possibility" that "one or more members [of the IPS] are in fact covert disciplined communists." In 1985, the right-wing Council for Inter-American Security distributed a pamphlet called *The Revolution Lobby,* with a special section devoted to the IPS. This "lobby" on Central America, according to the authors, tries to turn senators and representatives into "saboteurs of American foreign policy, if not out and out advocates of Communist revolution."

"I think the purpose of the attacks," said Barnet, "was to attack Jimmy Carter and to encourage the Democratic Party not to listen to our ideas. They wanted to make us pariahs. One effect has been cutting back the limits of acceptable discourse. We underestimated public relations, the steady barrage of right-wing talk. You read what they say about us and you wouldn't believe the debate has shifted to the right."

The conservatives have been so riveted by the IPS partly because they appreciate the potential power of a politics of ideas, borne out by their own rise from irrelevance. As confusion enveloped the liberals and Democrats, the right steadily grew more coherent, bound together by belief in an ideology whose propagation has been invested in a ministry of think tanks. To a great degree, these think tanks are the Washington right wing. Ironically, this politics came to them from close observation of the left. In fact, the Heritage Foundation was founded in direct emulation of the IPS. Said Paul Weyrich, the new-right leader who was the first president of Heritage, "The thought occurred to me that if an operation as overtly left as the IPS could get by with having an impact on the Hill, then a respectable conservative institution could have an even greater impact. Most of what we did, we did in absolute imitation of what we saw the left doing. There's no doubt they greatly influenced our understanding of how things happened."

What happens at the margin can alter the course of the mainstream, as the conservatives have demonstrated. The right has achieved what the left only dreamed. "One of the most valuable lessons that history has to teach us," said President Reagan at a Heritage Foundation dinner on April 22, 1986, "is that after the most terrible frustration and discouragement sometimes change can come so quickly and so unexpectedly, it surprises even those who have made it happen. This is particularly true in Washington."

To explain their present marginality, the IPS's thinkers frequently invoke objective conditions, particularly the rise of the right. According to Barnet, some Democrats, disoriented by the conservative din in Washington, "accept the simplest premises of the right-wing attack." But the distance of the IPS from influence has been due to certain self-defeating impulses as well. Their work, flowing from their opposition to the Vietnam War, has indeed been far more concerned with Third World nations than with the United States. "It's critical to be critical," said Barnet. "There's always a danger of appearing to be an apologist of something you're trying to explain in a hostile political environment." Especially when some associated with the institute express a romantic "solidarity" with Third World movements whose Leninism invariably leads to disillusionment. Barnet added, "There's a perception that we're overly concerned with the Third World. I think it's a fair criticism. Our biggest weakness is in domestic policy."

In spite of the persistent right-wing accusations that the IPS is a conspiratorial nest of Marxist-Leninists or the central committee of world "Communophilism," the place more nearly resembles the stateroom scene in the Marx Brothers' movie, *A Night At the Opera*, in which the purposeful, the oddball, and the merely curious crowd themselves into a small cubicle. Senior fellows are often unavailable for interviews because they are taking a stint as the switchboard operator. The paint is peeling, the posters are unframed, the elevator doesn't work. In the dingy warren, hundreds of students come and go, attending courses at the institute's Washington School. The déclassé style that meant political commitment in the 1960s remains in fashion here. Flannel-shirted assistants dash from floor to floor (no elevator), clutching the latest pamphlets.

The twenty resident scholars of the IPS include former Democratic presidential candidate George McGovern; Roger Wilkins, the civil rights thinker; Barbara Ehrenreich, the feminist author and co-chair of the Democratic Socialists of America; and Isabel Letelier, widow of the assassinated Chilean exile leader. Another two hundred illuminati—the associate fellows—who may receive small grants, drop in from time to time. They are generally like-minded on the issues, but there is no IPS "line." "There isn't a political agenda per se," said Raskin. If anything, there is a feeling among many of the institute's fellows and friends that it is too woolly and undisciplined. Earlier this year, before he joined IPS's board, McGovern remarked: "At IPS you have highly intelligent, marvelously motivated scholars who are not well structured, a kind of conglomerate of bright minds going off in various directions without any serious effort to influence public policy. I say this with affection. I wish it weren't true."

"On the left, what passes for the left, when things are bad, connections break down," said Irving Howe, author of *Socialism and America* and editor of *Dissent* magazine. "I make an analogy to the period between World War I and the early 1930s. You went through a right-wing period. Nevertheless, there was very important preparatory work being done that contributed to the New Deal, work done by socialists, liberals, labor people. While the left didn't create a socialist America, it made a contribution toward creating a welfare state. The task of the moment is something like that. While we don't have a totally coherent set of proposals, there are people preparing the ground. We don't see that clearly yet. And it may not happen. . . . There isn't even a halfway equivalent of what's being done on the other side. A programmatic ideological preparation takes years. . . . In the end, you have to turn to people with ideas. Insofar as IPS contributes to this work, fine."

The ideological hegemony that conservatives currently exercise, especially over the Washington political community, according to Barnet, may be because "people on the right had a much more perceptive view of the importance of ideas than the liberals. They were selling an ideology. The Democratic ideology was that there was no ideology. That was wrong. The problem is that there's no ready-made ideology, no single issue, that can be trotted in from the wings. The difficulty and the opportunity is that there is a crisis of all ideologies. They've all had severe failures in their own terms." Says Raskin, "This is a period of shifting sands. People are looking for first principles to hang onto or ideas to serve as guideposts."

With the air ringing with calls from all sides for new ideas, Barnet hears echoes of the past, another period analogous to the late 1950s, when another aging but popular Republican president was in the White House and liberals groped for alternatives. "In a way," he said, striking a hopeful note, "it's like the beginning."

The Institute for Policy Studies was set in John F. Kennedy's

Washington to serve as a respectable left-wing intellectual center that would create new ideas and criticize the old—a U.S. version of the British Fabian Society. The transition from Kennedy to Reagan, from liberalism to conservatism, is encapsulated in the IPS's story—a story of liberal decline, squandered opportunities, and dashed hopes. The decline was not simply a progression of lost debates; there were also murders, ideological inquisitions, and espionage.

In 1959, the seventh year of the Eisenhower presidency, a small group of youthful Democrats in the House of Representatives began to articulate an impatience with both the exhausted administration and the old New Deal. They wanted to transcend both. Eleven of them, almost all a decade younger than their colleagues, launched what became known as the Liberal Project, which brought them together with scholars to define new policies. These policies "must be much broader than the kind of economic liberalism promulgated in the 1930s," wrote Marcus Raskin, the legislative counsel to an obscure Iowa representative.

Raskin, the catalyst of the Liberal Project, was a graduate of the University of Chicago and its Law School, and a wearer of the thin ties and oval, tortoise-shell glasses that were emblems of the intense intellectual of this strange interim period—post–Adlai Stevenson and pre–John Kennedy. Raskin had been a pianistic child prodigy but gave up a promising career because he felt he could never attain the other-worldly heights of a Rubinstein. He chose to become a virtuoso of public policy instead. His mind is in a constant storm, simultaneously raging with swirling clouds of abstraction and the most precise proposals.

The year after Kennedy was elected, Raskin was appointed deputy to McGeorge Bundy, the national security adviser. On April 14, 1961, Raskin sat at a long table with the generals and wise men—Secretary of State Dean Rusk, Walt Rostow, Paul Nitze, John J. McCloy—to plan disarmament policy. "If this group cannot bring about disarmament, then no one can," confidently announced McCloy, who was in charge of the administration's disarmament policy. Raskin rolled his eyes, catching the eye of another eye-roller—Richard Barnet, McCloy's aide at the State Department. The next day the Bay of Pigs fiasco was launched.

In the age of the best and the brightest, Barnet's résumé was impeccable. He had graduated from Harvard summa cum laude and then attended Harvard Law School, Harvard's Russian Research Center, and Princeton's Center for International Studies. Then he wrote a book on disarmament. He seemed built to specification for the world of Foggy Bottom, as the State Department is known. Yet he was already somewhat disillusioned. "I was quite struck by the relationship between academics and the government," he said. "They were essentially servicing the bureaucracies, not challenging the assumptions. It was a narrow group. Kissinger was very much around."

He and Raskin decided to leave the government in order to find a better vantage place from which to influence it. Washington was then in the Stone Age of think tanks; there were not more than a handful. Following the dominant model of the Brookings Institution, the few that existed aspired to the appearance of utter neutrality and "value-free" research. Barnet and Raskin, intent on creating a different kind of institute, ventured to Brookings itself, to meet with the director of studies. (They were accompanied by Steven Muller, now the president of Johns Hopkins University, who was a founding trustee of the IPS.) The suggestion was made that they join Brookings, which they politely rejected.

Barnet and Raskin founded the IPS in 1963 with another premise in mind. "We would ask the value questions in policy," explained Barnet. "We would have a dialogue with people in power, but also with the public. We thought about whom we served. We had great confidence in ideas." Their self-image was as "public scholars"— intellectuals as activists and activists as intellectuals, a seamless fusion of roles. Still, the founding of the IPS struck a lot of the people they knew as a bizarre innovation. "They were amazed we were doing such a thing, such a crazy undertaking," said Barnet. Still, he added, "the relationship to the administration wasn't bad." The White House and the State Department, their former places of employment, remained open. And certain liberal circles, which then had a good measure of influence, benevolently encouraged a critical center that would challenge the natural tendency of established power toward drift and inertia.

Initial funding came from James Warburg, the investment banker and F.D.R.'s former adviser, and Philip Stern, the Sears' heir. The first chair of IPS's board of trustees, appropriately, was the old New Dealer, Thurman Arnold, senior partner at Arnold, Fortas and Porter, the formidable Washington law firm, and author of the classic debunking of conservative ideology, *The Folklore of Capitalism*.

Some ideas emanating from the IPS might have seemed eccentric; others might be immediately applicable. The point was to generate and test them. When Kennedy's New Frontier was transmuted into Lyndon Johnson's Great Society, a few notions incubated at the IPS, such as the Model Cities program and the Teachers Corps, became policy. And the IPS, where officials and scholars mingled daily, became a regular part of the policy-making culture. (Assistant Secretary of Labor Daniel Patrick Moynihan, for example, was an active participant in the education seminar.) With Lyndon Johnson acting as social reformer, the IPS seemed to embody the title of Raskin's book, *Being and Doing*. "We believed," said Raskin, "there was a set of problems that could be solved easily." Then reform gave way to foreign war: Next stop, Vietnam.

Vietnam was the liberals' war, and it provoked a civil war among the liberals. The president and his supporters believed that the war extended the goodwill of the Great Society to the Third World: TVA on the Mekong. Guns and butter—we could have it all.

In the early days of the war, in 1961, Benjamin Cohen, the quintessential Rooseveltian brain truster, who had crafted much of the second New Deal, sought out Raskin, then working in the White House. "This could be an endless military enterprise. The possibilities of domestic reform would probably disappear," Cohen warned, according to Raskin's recollection. That summer, Raskin helped Christopher Jencks, then an editor at the *New Republic* and later an IPS fellow, to put out a special issue of the magazine critical of the war. By the mid-1960s, most of the intellectuals had deserted President Lyndon Baines Johnson, and his administration lost the ability to justify itself. The IPS scholars, who had partly contributed to the aura of progress surrounding his Great Society, now mustered their skills against the war.

In 1965, the year the United States first bombed North Vietnam, Raskin and Bernard Fall, an associate fellow at the IPS, edited *A Viet-Nam Reader*, which became an essential text for the teach-in movement that swept the campuses. Fall was a French journalist who had witnessed the French defeat in Indochina and whose view of the war's futility, buttressed by firsthand experience, became the general view at the IPS. In 1967, Fall returned to Vietnam and was killed when he stepped on a mine.

The IPS itself became the site of a perpetual teach-in, with congressmen and their aides bustling in and out of countless seminars. In the House of Representatives, the antiwar caucus organized, informally known as "the group," its roots traceable to the Liberal Project. At every twist and turn in the legislative battle, the group, assisted by the IPS, forwarded resolutions, designed amendments, and monitored appropriations. In the meantime, Barnet and Raskin maintained a friendly, personal relationship with William Fulbright, chair of the Senate Foreign Relations Committee, which he employed as an instrument against the war. Senators Eugene McCarthy and George McGovern, among others, were also friends.

The administration, however, responded to the transformation of the IPS from critical helper into unhelpful critic by infiltrating FBI informers into the institute and wiretapping its telephones. In 1968, the velocity of events accelerated. In Boston, the first great antiwar trial was staged. The defendants, accused of conspiracy to encourage young men to resist the draft, included Dr. Benjamin Spock, the nation's foremost pediatrician, the Rev. William Sloan Coffin, the Yale chaplain—and Marcus Raskin. Each represented a distinct dissident element within the liberal coalition. "The trial," Raskin said, "was an attempt by a liberal administration to say that the institutions we were part of had to go along or there would be trouble." In the end, all were acquitted. But by then, said Raskin, "liberalism was engulfed."

After the convulsive Democratic convention in Chicago, he tried to organize something called the New Party and to convince Eugene McCarthy to run for president as its candidate. He declined; the New Party came to naught; and Richard Nixon became president. As liberalism imploded, the IPS's scholars attempted to comprehend why. Barnet suggested that liberalism of the classic cold war variety had become beholden to the "national security state," a leviathan that demanded a permanent war economy, a constant and ideal enemy, and unending manipulation of public opinion. In his 1968 book, *Intervention and Revolution,* he described the hot locus of the cold war moving to the Third World, pitting the "national security manager" against the revolutionary. In the name of rationalism, the manager attempted to contain liberation movements and prevent "undesirable governments." Vietnam was the obvious case in point.

Barnet's critics have accused him of "isolationism" and worse. "The issue," he wrote in 1968, "is not isolationism versus interventionism, for the developed world and the underdeveloped world are fated by geography and economics to be involved with one another. The question is rather the legitimacy of the forms and the purposes of intervention. . . . it has never been satisfactorily explained why a . . . counterrevolutionary posture advances American national interests or democratic ideals." For two decades, Barnet has elaborated these themes. In an essay written in 1986, he wrote that "the ideology of the national security state distorts the meaning of security by defining it in primarily military terms." The true "comparative advantage of the United States" is its "economic potential and the promise of liberty." Yet by stressing the military side, "the nation offered competition in the one field of combat in which it was easiest to match it. . . . Thus the implied promise of the national security state has never been fulfilled."

Liberalism itself, according to Barnet, has been distorted into an image of big government run amuck. "Part of the anti–big-government feeling, democracy not being served by government, stemmed from IPS," said Raskin. Paradoxically, the immediate beneficiary of the left critique was the right wing, which appropriated the anti-big-government feeling for its own ends.

In 1972, the Democrats' candidate for president was George McGovern, who had been an original member of the Liberal Project. (Raskin had been the first person to propose to McGovern that he run for president—in 1967.) "I would have tried to use Barnet's and Raskin's expertise," McGovern said. "They would have had easy access to me." But Nixon remained in power: Next stop, Watergate.

"Watergate" was more than a series of events, from break-in to cover-up. It was also a paradigm for the Nixon administration's application of paramilitary means to domestic politics. The clandestine operations against the IPS that had begun under Lyndon Johnson reached absurd heights under Richard Nixon, with FBI agents trying to decipher the institute's work from typewriter ribbons retrieved from the garbage. The IPS seemed to be at the center of the universe. When Nixon left office, vertigo set in. The post-Watergate, post-Vietnam period of the mid-1970s was a peculiar interregnum when little new appeared to be happening. "It was a time of exhaustion," said Raskin.

Much of the intellectual work at IPS had been built upon metaphors drawn from the Vietnam War. Extrapolating from the Selective Service's statement on the "channeling" of young men, Raskin suggested that Americans, like the Vietnamese, were being "colonized." He described hierarchies—the "violence colony" (the military), the "plantation colony" (the economy), the "channeling colony" (education), and the "dream colony" (the mass media). Yet these metaphors fell flat before the flat figure of Gerald Ford, chair of the demobilization committee, who aroused no enthusiasm and no enmity, capturing the spirit of the time. "The left or the liberals did not know how to struggle for the center," said Raskin. "There was this open space, which moved no place. What happened was that the right took legitimacy. Liberals were never able to recover."

In Washington, the history of the left played itself out in miniature within the IPS. It became the cockpit in the capital of an eclectic new left, which was a revolt against the old—the old left, the old right, and the old liberalism. But the new had its roots in the old.

Sam Rubin was an American success story, an immigrant who became a millionaire, the first mass marketer of perfume, peddling it at drugstore counters. The name he adopted for his line of products: Fabergé. The shrewd entrepreneur also happened to be a committed leftist. In 1948, he was among the chief financial supporters of the Progressive Party, a left-wing split from the Democrats, heavily influenced by the Communist Party, that nominated former Vice President Henry Wallace for president. Two decades later, Rubin became the major financial backer of the IPS.

Cora Rubin, Sam's daughter, attended the University of Wisconsin, one of the birthplaces of the new left in the late 1950s. She was acquainted with those students involved in the movement, but she was "older and aloof," recalled one of them, Ronald Radosh, now a professor at the City University of New York and co-author of *The Rosenberg File*.

The Labor Youth League (LYL) was the Communist Party's youth group. Radosh was an officer, and Saul Landau, later a senior fellow at the IPS, was a member. LYL members were not card-carrying party members, but "it was the equivalent," said Landau. In 1956, Soviet leader Khrushchev exposed Joseph Stalin at the Twentieth Party Congress as a mass murderer. Then the Soviet Union crushed the Hungarian revolt. "It was devastating," said Landau. "The whole thing dissolved. All the assumptions were destroyed, especially for young people like me. I was twenty. After that I took nothing about the Soviet Union on faith and became very skeptical."

At Wisconsin, a group of graduate students gathered around the historian William Appleman Williams, who taught that the United States was as responsible as the Soviet Union for the cold war. (Williams later became the president of the Organization of American Historians.) In the fall of 1959, these students started a theoretical magazine called *Studies on the Left*, the first new left publication. Landau was a founding editor. "The intention," he said, "was to break with party dogma and doctrine, but without falling into the cold war. We would be free of the domination of Moscow via the U.S. Communist Party. And we'd be free of anti-communism."

In 1960, according to James Weinstein, the editor of *In These Times*, an independent socialist weekly, who was part of this group, "Landau was looking around for something to do. We talked him into going to Cuba." A year earlier, Fidel Castro had victoriously marched into Havana. He was the graduate student as revolutionary, the guerrilla intellectual. "I can remember Landau giving a speech," said Radosh, "about how Castro was great because he made the revolution against the communists—an independent, humanist, noncommunist revolution." In Cuba, the revolutionary frontier, Landau met Castro and made a film—*Fidel.* Landau viewed Third World revolutionary movements as essentially nationalist, and he tended to see Castro in this mold. Yet, Radosh, who was turning in a neoconservative direction, charged that Landau was "the leading apologist of Castro." Landau himself said, "For me, Cuba is not a terribly attractive model. It's not the kind of society I want to live in. The stuff that seemed exciting to me twenty-five years ago—revolution—doesn't seem exciting now." When Sam Rubin began contributing to the IPS, Cora and Landau became reacquainted. She had married Peter Weiss, a lawyer who became chair of IPS's board. During the Vietnam War, she traveled to North Vietnam, met with the leadership there and helped set up the Committee of Liaison with Families of Servicemen detained in North Vietnam, the only conduit between the prisoners of war and their families.

In *The New Radicals,* a 1966 book on the new left, Landau and Paul Jacobs (later an IPS fellow) wrote that the young radicals "have confused their anti-war principles and clear understanding of America with apologies for the Viet Cong. Their need to link themselves with the revolutions in Asia, Africa, and Latin America often leads them to romanticize guerrilla movements." The accusation of Third World romanticism, a failure to come to grips with the often grim results of liberation movements, particularly those organized along Leninist lines, was precisely the charge leveled against the IPS by some of its critics.

When Landau taught as a visiting professor at the University of California at Davis in 1985, he was the first target of the right-wing Accuracy in Academia, formed to purge classrooms of un-American ideas. "They put a spy in my class," said Landau. "I told him he could stay." The campus was blanketed with leaflets denouncing Landau as a "Castro agent." "My classes swelled," he observed.

"I don't think anyone has an uncritical attitude toward Leninist revolution," said Raskin. "There's nobody who's uncritical. What people are concerned about is the use of the communist label to stop thought. I just think the charge is nonsense. The idea that the people at the institute are not aware of what happens to societies split apart by revolutions is nonsense." In fact, perhaps the most searing and penetrating critique of Third World revolution gone mad, a 1986 book by Elizabeth Becker, *When the War Was Over*, about the Cambodian Khmer Rouge, was written while she was a fellow at the IPS. This was not an illustration of a new turn in the IPS line, because there has never really been an IPS line. Maddeningly, the place's idiosyncrasy confounds both its detractors and defenders. "I don't know anyone at IPS during the Vietnam War who ever made the argument that the Vietnamese were saints," said Barnet. "I don't think that's why people are attacking us. We have been most crushed by the failure of those revolutions which showed the greatest signs of democracy—Chile and Jamaica."

For the IPS, the tragic Chilean revolution was not an abstract, distant event. After Salvador Allende, the elected socialist president, was overthrown in a military coup d'état, Orlando Letelier, the former foreign minister and ambassador to the United States, became the director of the Transnational Institute, an affiliate of the IPS, to study North-South global relations. In September 1976, while he was driving through Sheridan Circle in Washington, D.C., a remote control device detonated a bomb in his car, killing him. Also dead was Ronni Karpen Moffit, Raskin's young assistant, who had just been married. The moment of martyrdom confirmed the worst fears of repression. Many at the institute anticipated even more acts of violence.

A federal investigation disclosed that the assassination was an act of state terrorism, ordered by high Chilean officials. In 1978, a federal grand jury handed down three indictments for conspiracy to murder against three senior members of the armed forces, but the Chilean government refused to extradite them. Letelier's widow, Isabel, came to work at the IPS as a senior fellow.

In 1986, another Third World revolution that aroused great interest at the IPS erupted. And Peter Weiss stepped down from his position as chair of IPS's board to serve as the attorney for the newest revolutionary leader—Corazon Aquino of the Philippines.

The fascination of the new left with revolutions abroad was partly a consequence of their rejection of the old left. Having discarded the schematic blueprint in which the industrial proletariat would bring about a new order, the new leftists went on a quest for other agents of change. Third World revolutionaries, from China to Cuba to Algeria, argued that their struggles had supplanted the working class. The countryside of the Third World would surround the cities of the

West, according to Lin Piao. "Two, three, many Vietnams," suggested Che Guevara.

As the war dragged on, the hunt for surrogate proletariats became more desperate. Perhaps blacks fit the pattern. Then feminists proposed women as the oppressed majority. And then some argued that the true oppressed vanguard consisted of homosexuals. This proliferation of vanguards led, in short order, to a politics of factional purity.

At the same time, "participatory democracy" remained the watchword. And the harshest anti-authoritarian demands were placed by many of the new leftists on the often fragile institutions they had helped create, a moral stringency that frequently caused messy crack-ups. The IPS felt the stress of the political currents it had encouraged. The disability that overcame the IPS in an extreme form—fragmenting pressures from a multitude of grasping constituencies—was a refracted foreshadowing of the strains that would beset the Democratic Party.

In December 1976, within months of Letelier's assassination, the institute's financial crisis came to a head. Many of the foundations and individual donors were no longer willing to fund much of the research. Sam Rubin was particularly horrified at the lack of internal discipline at the place, and he funneled most of his money to the Transnational Institute. Representative scholarship of the period included such articles as "Lesbians in Revolt" and "The Seven Days of Creation from a Buberian-Feminist Perspective." "The problem," said Barnet, "was the infinite expansion of claims on the place. Every subject was valid. There was a kind of pseudo-democracy, an ethos of participation, that excluded establishing priorities." In the name of participation, "an alienation occurred, of the people who were most senior, who had built the institute and raised the money," according to Raskin. Some of the most distinguished thinkers, friends of Barnet and Raskin, who had agreed to come to the IPS as fellows, were rejected: Hannah Arendt, Hans Morgenthau, Herbert Marcuse, Erving Goffman.

Forced to cope with the shortfall of cash, Barnet and Raskin offered a plan of general cutbacks. The response by eleven of the fellows was to form a union and demand salary increases and absolute democracy in the workplace. Some claimed that they were discriminated against because they had written no articles or books. And some of the women felt a special sense of grievance. "A lot of women who came into contact with IPS were feminists who felt angry that IPS didn't get 'IT,' a feeling that feminism was not really internalized there," said one of them. "You know, the founders were men, the senior fellows were men. Isabel Letelier didn't represent domestic feminism. The feminist movement was always being trivialized. That was a very basic split on the left. It's a major reason why organizations fell apart."

Moreover, "within the left, forming a union had a certain cachet," said James Weinstein, who closely observed the events. "It was a question of protecting their situation, a power play. They [those in the union] were an impediment to the institute playing a serious policy role." Said Raskin, "People got more and more into constituency organizing without ever figuring out what could be done together. At the institute people were no longer talking the same language. It was a kind of freak-out. It was very hurtful." In the settlement, Barnet and Raskin gave the dissidents $470,000, a third of the IPS's endowment, to build their own institute as they wished. Unable to raise more money or even to work together, they soon dispersed.

As this self-destructive episode unfolded, a new Democratic president, Jimmy Carter, assumed office. The IPS, which existed to provide intellectual energy on just such an occasion, was prostrate. In any case, its scholars "paid very little attention to the Carter administration, a big mistake," said Raskin. "I think the door was open. We didn't even walk through it. Carter appeared to us to be more of the same. We made an error. We were moral snobs."

Carter sought a national consensus without a clear policy. "The administration didn't know what to do and it stopped generating enthusiasm," said Paul Warnke, who was Carter's chair of the Arms Control and Disarmament Agency and later a member of the IPS's board. "Carter and his group didn't understand Washington. It didn't surprise me that the IPS didn't have much influence. Almost nobody had influence."

In 1980, Ronald Reagan triumphantly entered a capital where the liberals and the left had already been defeated. The last period of social reform had occurred fifteen years earlier, during the truncated Great Society.

"Ideas have always counted in Washington," said I. F. Stone, the journalist and author who has lectured at IPS forums. "What has really changed is that right-wing ideologists have suddenly flowered. Suddenly, the atmosphere has grown very ideological. They have a lot of money behind them. Intellectuals are a commodity like other commodities . . . The town is lousy with conservatives. IPS is about the only think tank on the left."

What it feels like to be left-wing in a conservative age can be broken down into distinct stages, something akin to grief: First comes shock—disbelief that a conservative is actually president and that he actually has a program. Then comes fear and trembling—fright that the program is a new inquisition. Rage and protest follow, succeeded by a recognition of the need for new thinking.

The IPS has always attempted to operate on two levels: its "public scholars" are ideally supposed to be activists and intellectuals. But Reagan's siege of liberalism has forced the IPS to invest much of its activist energy in constructing defensive fortifications. "They're fighting a rearguard action, as the liberals are generally," said Stone. "They're fighting for what's good in the past, not breaking new ground." This activism has placed the institute's fellows near the center of some of the most dramatic issues, from South Africa to Central America, and in the midst of tumultuous movements, from Jesse Jackson's presidential campaigns to the nuclear freeze campaign. "The urgent thing was to limit the damage," said Barnet. "It was not a political environment congenial to new ideas."

The intellectual work of IPS's scholars is more tentatively descriptive of new realities than prescriptive, more an initial critique than a full-blown program. Barnet, for his part, has focused on Reagan's foreign policy. "More and more," he said, "policy isn't defined in terms of interests but in terms of perceptions. It is conceived and defended as theater . . . The problem with Grenada, a humanitarian intervention, was the theatrical framing. It was the use of Grenada, more than Grenada itself, Grenada as 'rollback'—presenting a view of the world that 'sells' allows you to do what you want." This is the essence of Reagan's "neonationalism."

During the 1984 presidential primary campaign, Raskin and Barnet advised candidates George McGovern and Alan Cranston. Saul Landau, who has won an "Emmy" for one of his films, shot some of McGovern's TV ads. In 1988, Raskin advised Paul Simon. In both campaigns, Robert Borosage, the IPS's director, offered advice to Jesse Jackson. Borosage had been brought into Jackson's campaign by a new IPS fellow, Roger Wilkins—the former assistant attorney general, Ford Foundation executive, editorial writer for the *New York Times* and *The Washington Post*, and nephew of the late president of the National Association for the Advancement of Colored People, Roy Wilkins.

Wilkins came to the institute because he felt it was the only place where he could be a "public scholar," an activist and a writer. From his IPS office, appointed, like all the fellows' offices, with an old battered desk and peeling paint, he helped organize the waves of demonstrations before the South African embassy. To Jackson, he has been a senior adviser. "The relationship between Jesse and IPS is built on me," said Wilkins. "To me, he listens very well, but he's not known for listening. He listens better to people he knows can take him or leave him. Jesse and I have known each other for a very long time, more than twenty years, since he was working for Martin [Luther King Jr.] and I was in the Department of Justice. As an older fellow, I have not always approved of everything Jesse has done; nor have I always approved of his style. Having said that, my sense is that his run in 1984 was historic and constructive. It seemed to me the most important initiative to come out of black America since Martin's death." Wilkins added that Jackson's 1984 campaign, while "very positive," did have "significant negatives, negatives everyone knows, the 'Hymietown' business and Farrakhan, terrible and a disaster. That was my position in the campaign, and it's my position now. I say quite harsh and ugly things to Jesse. There are a lot of people who won't stand up to him. But that long preceded my coming here . . . In 1988, I think a lot more people are going to be able to hear him because it's not the first time they've looked at him."

For Wilkins, Jackson's campaign was one way to cope with the Reagan years. "Looking in horror" is how Wilkins describes the period. The defensiveness that the other IPS fellows experience is magnified from a black perspective. "Things have happened in these last five years that I wouldn't have believed could happen," said Wilkins. "Initially, that takes away a lot of your creativity. It's not time to experiment."

The scholars at the IPS do not have any absolute answers. They do not have a new ideology, a new new left, or a new New Deal. But they do have the conviction that we are passing through a fundamental transition that has not yet assumed a fixed form. And they believe that the conventional categories of left, right, and center are becoming obsolete. "I'm glad to be called left because I don't want to be called right," said Barnet. "But it doesn't make sense because those terms suggest that there are three programs, coherent ideas, that are contending with each other. The steam has gone out of all the major ideologies, whether it's Marxism, or pure capitalism, or even the standard mix that goes by the name of social democracy. They are all basically nineteenth-century ideologies; they are all in crisis. At the same time, I think there is an awareness by citizens generally that ideas and values are important. Almost all politicians understand now that values, and not purely economic issues, have a hold on people. This is an age that is waiting for new ideas that can explain what is happening and provide some kind of structure. It is one of the reasons there is an impatience with the institute. People want answers."

"Politicians are retailers of ideas," said I. F. Stone. "It's an important function. But we haven't gotten the formulations yet. We really don't know what to do. You can't put on the same clothes and march to the same music. I'm not sure IPS has answers on that score. It's very hard to understand what's happening in your own time." And Raskin says, "The problem of the prevailing ideologies is that they start with the assumption of the progress of science and technology that does not take account of the effects of this knowledge. The Challenger, the Chernobyl meltdown, and the Bhopal disaster are examples of the unintended consequences of knowledge. The old ideologies must be transcended. These ideologies impair our understanding. We have to continue searching."

In 1962, National Security Adviser McGeorge Bundy asked Raskin, his deputy, to contribute material to a speech that President Kennedy would deliver at the Yale commencement. "I said that the major problems we faced were not technical or administrative, but moral and political," Raskin recalled. Kennedy's speech was a critique of conservative economic "myths" about government and spending—"myths" that might now be summarized as Reaganism. "There is a danger," said Kennedy, "that illusion may prevent effective action." He concluded by saying that "technical answers, not political answers, must be provided." It was a conclusion diametrically opposite from what Raskin had suggested.

"The question of the relevance of that speech goes to the right wing," Raskin said. "They have asked the categorical, value questions, realizing that facts don't answer everything."

(March 1988)

PART VI

The Abuse of History

The Munich Analogy

To solve his Bitburg problem, President Reagan urged forgetfulness. In memorializing the end of World War II, he said we should refrain from "reawakening the memories and so forth."

His problem was the "and so forth." Reagan forgot that in forgetting he would also erase the basic premise of his own ideology: that totalitarian regimes like the Nazis must never be appeased. Then, to solve the problem of amnesia, he offered a revised history. Once we put "the memories" to sleep, we could talk about another World War II, where Nazis were "victims just as surely as the victims in the concentration camps." But in remembering, he remembered the war in a way that removed the foundation of his worldview.

Memories of World War II lie at the center of Reagan's foreign policy perspective. As if to prove the point, at the same time that he was saying, "I don't think we ought to focus on the past," his conservative supporters were frantically evoking the Munich Pact of 1938 as a warning against what they see as appeasement of totalitarianism in Nicaragua. Which were we supposed to do, forget or remember?

By saying that Germans have "a guilt feeling that's been imposed upon them" and that the SS soldiers buried at Bitburg "were victims," Reagan was suggesting that World War II was a war like other wars and that the Germans who fought were soldiers like other soldiers. He trivialized the war's moral and historical significance. The purest expression of evil in modern times, the gravest threat to western civilization, was transformed into simply an unfortunate occurrence. In doing so, Reagan reduced the justification of his foreign policy to the vanishing point.

He forgot how the mythic structure of World War II evolved into the mythic structure of the cold war—that the linchpin was Munich, a symbol of appeasement of aggressors. The aggressors were not ordinary bullies, but a unique species: totalitarians. Yet by interring World War II, Reagan was interring Munich with it. His appearance at Bitburg turned into a political nightmare, which became an ideological catastrophe, the worst kind of problem for an ideological president.

"Munich" does not refer just to an obscure episode long ago, but describes an entire attitude that has governed much of U.S. foreign policy in the postwar era. The traumatic events leading to World War II were epitomized by the Munich Pact, in which the British and French gave Hitler a bite of Czechoslovakia—the German-speaking Sudetenland—to appease his appetite. "Peace in our time," declared British Prime Minister Neville Chamberlain, waving the treaty. Yet appeasement only encouraged Hitler, who grabbed the rest of the country and most of Europe shortly afterward.

"Appeasement" first entered our political vocabulary during the 1940 presidential campaign. On one side were those who wished to aid the besieged Britons—the interventionists—while on the other side stood those who wanted to preserve U.S. neutrality—the isolationists. Franklin D. Roosevelt introduced the theme in a speech to Congress, castigating "apologists for despotism and those who aid them by whispering defeatism or appeasement." The Democratic Party platform denounced "the spirit of appeasement," capturing it, for the moment, as a partisan phrase. And Democratic stump speakers railed against the Republicans as the "party of appeasement."

After the war, the communists were assigned the role previously played in U.S. rhetoric by the Nazis. The 1949 communist takeover in Czechoslovakia was the most conclusive confirmation of the equation, eerily reawakening memories of Munich. But even earlier, in Western Europe and Greece—with the Marshall Plan and the Truman Doctrine—the "interventionists" attempted to check Soviet expansionism; there could be no appeasement. Initiation to membership in the bipartisan postwar consensus required obeisance to the lesson of Munich.

The isolationists, led by a minority of Senate Republicans, fought a rear-guard action but became isolated themselves. Most Republicans, however, joined in the consensus. Their leader in the Senate, Arthur Vandenberg, justified their new position with a new slogan: "No more Munichs!" The embittered isolationist faction attempted to gain vengeance by turning Munich against the Democrats. They charged that the Yalta agreement, negotiated by President Roosevelt, had delivered not only Eastern Europe but China to the communists. Yalta, in their view, was Munich all over again, a case of betrayal. Their rallying cry became: "Who lost China?" Secretary of State Dean Acheson called this the beginning of a "revolt of the primitives," culminating in McCarthyism. The reference to Yalta added a new variation on the Munich theme: the enemy within.

In 1951, the most subtle version of the Munich analogy appeared with the publication of Hannah Arendt's book, *The Origins of Totalitarianism*. In it, she argued that communism and Nazism constituted "a novel form of government"—totalitarianism. Although superficially opposites, these two systems were at base the same, sharing a reliance upon total ideologies and total terror. Once one understood totalitarianism, it was clear why appeasement could never work. "It is," wrote Arendt, "in the nature of totalitarian regimes to demand unlimited power." How could the unappeasable be appeased? Arendt's magisterial argument attempted to be all-encompassing, but her theory neglected other crucial reasons that nation-states behave as they do, including nationalism and geopolitics. In highlighting the similarities between particular dictatorial régimes, she muted the differences. Still, the concept of totalitarianism made a profound impression, becoming an accepted tenet of the Munich metaphor.

Vietnam subjected the metaphor to the acids of reality. If we did not intervene, it was argued, we would be appeasing, which would be an incentive to aggression. Embellishments were added: If we withdrew, the countries of Asia would fall to communism like dominoes; and because communism was totalitarian it was also monolithic. "We shall find a Red China much more voracious and much more dangerous, if they should discover that this technique is successful," said Secretary of State Dean Rusk in 1966. Yet no matter how diligently the teachings of Munich were applied in Vietnam, they perversely achieved the opposite effect of what was expected.

The Munich metaphor was further shaken by détente. More than anyone else, Richard Nixon upset the equation of the communists with the Nazis and, therefore, the metaphor. His policy was motivated above all by realpolitik, not the idea of totalitarianism. This outlook permitted him to engage in an unprecedented economic relationship with the Soviet Union. Then, he found China, which hadn't been "lost" after all, but only misplaced. Both Nixon and Kissinger operated beyond the boundaries of the Munich metaphor without substituting another in its place, leaving a legacy of ideological turmoil.

In the 1970s, the neoconservatives suddenly emerged as a political force in the opposition to Nixon's revisionism. They were liberals moved right, yet insistent that their position was merely the preservation of the old "interventionism." Détente, they argued, was a form of appeasement. In an essential neoconservative text, *How Democracies Perish*, Jean-Francois Revel labeled the architects of the Munich Pact as "pioneers of détente." To conservatives steeped in the Munich precepts, détente appeared to be history repeating itself. Just as at Munich, an unholy exchange occurred in which the democracies gave and the totalitarians took. The most sinful departure from ideological orthodoxy committed by Nixon and Kissinger, according to the neoconservatives, was their implicit assumption that the Soviet Union is moved by the traditional concerns of great powers more than by ideology. If that were true, the conservative article of faith— the Munich metaphor, and especially its corollary about totalitarianism—would make no sense.

The neoconservatives view Third World revolutions as a prospect for two, three, many Munichs. They believed the country was suffering from a "Vietnam syndrome"—a fear of quagmire—paralyzing our will to intervene. The syndrome itself was a reflection of what the neoconservative editor of *Commentary*, Norman Podhoretz, called "the culture of appeasement," a mélange of pacifism, homosexuality, and American self-hatred.

The alternative, contended neoconservative Jeane Kirkpatrick in a famous article in *Commentary* in 1980 praised by Reagan, was to make a distinction between "authoritarian" and "totalitarian" regimes. We must recognize that "violent insurgency headed by Marxist revolutionaries is unlikely to lead to anything but totalitarian tyranny." As proof, she cited the example of Nicaragua. Her reduction of Arendt's theory to a political formula gave it a contemporary angle.

The Munich metaphor already had great appeal to Ronald Reagan, and he revived its rhetoric in his attack on President Carter. "We're seeing the same kind of atmosphere we saw when Mr. Chamberlain was tapping his cane on the cobblestones of Munich," he said. Soon, Kirkpatrick was ambassador to the United Nations, and the doctrines of Munich were restored as the cornerstone of U.S. foreign policy.

But at Bitburg, Reagan tipped over an ideological domino. The affair was so shocking because it was so unexpected. Reagan ruled the kingdom of symbolism for five years; and after his second landslide, nearly everyone conceded his mastery of it. The Bitburg affair unfolded in the heart of this realm, the world of images. Yet Bitburg is more than a case of fumbled symbols, for Reagan's confused image-making precipitated an ideological disaster. Bitburg played out like one of Carter's crises, a seemingly endless series of daily humiliations. Fearful of being depicted like Carter, the White House refused to give in to those pleading that the president go to "another place" instead. His staff worried about the Carter who changed his mind, not about the Carter who, by gestures like toasting the Shah of Iran, contradicted his own rationale and undermined his moral authority. They were preoccupied with the wrong Carter.

Although Reagan misstated the facts—"very few [Germans are] alive that remember even the war"—it is not the facts that are undermining him. Reagan uses facts to illustrate his ideology; if one fact won't serve, another will. Refuting his facts can't upset him because the refutations don't upset his assumptions. What makes Bitburg so devastating is that it is a symbolic miscue, an error on Reagan's own terms. So often in the past, his geniality has softened the hard edge of his ideology, enabling him to promote his agenda. And he has campaigned successfully for a lifetime against "gloom and doom," night and fog. But now this instinct betrayed him. His geniality led him to avoid the unpleasantness of visiting Dachau and to assuage the hurt feelings of Chancellor Helmut Kohl, who was excluded from last year's celebration of the Allies' landing in Normandy in World War II. Thus as Bitburg unwound, it became an exercise in the evil of banality.

At the very moment the president was blurring the meaning of Nazism, his supporters were desperately attempting to wield the Munich metaphor on another front. The battle over the military funding for the contras in Nicaragua was seen by the neoconservatives as a battle between those who view the world through the lens of Munich and those who view it through the lens of Vietnam. The clash of metaphors is ultimately a clash of generations. "It's not Vietnam that's the appropriate analogy—it's Munich," said Kirkpatrick. According to this reasoning, the Sandinistas are insatiable totalitarians who can never be appeased—like the North Vietnamese, like the communists, like the Nazis. But the logic was insufficient to pass the funding. For a brief moment, the Vietnam metaphor—the march of folly—conquered the Munich metaphor; the experience of the young overrode that of their elders.

The White House staff discerned no connection between Bitburg and Nicaragua. And they resorted to treating the Holocaust as a special-interest question, like low farm prices. "Obviously," said Chief of Staff Donald Regan, "the Jewish people in the United States, as well as a lot of veterans, are very upset at the president's going there, but I think this has been explained time and time again." And Communications Director Patrick Buchanan, according to NBC News, scribbled over and over on a pad, "succumbing to pressure of the Jews." Appeasement was out.

But the neoconservatives, unlike the White House staff and Reagan himself, understand that nothing less than the fate of the ideology is at stake. In a column in *The Washington Post*, Podhoretz argued that the president's Bitburg trip "undermines the very foundation on which Mr. Reagan's foreign policy in the present has heretofore stood" and undermines the "conceptual basis for resisting communism in Central America." But the neoconservatives' jeremiads went unheeded, and Reagan went to Bitburg. They were Reaganites without Reagan. Like the Trotskyists, they have been left in the position of defending the purity of a doctrine that they say has been betrayed.

On April 25, the day after new funding for the contras was defeated, Secretary of State George Shultz delivered a speech about the "Vietnam analogy," attempting to resolve the gathering ideological crisis. "We were not thinking about Munich as such, but it's the same debate as the 1930s," said a State Department source close to Shultz. "Dean Rusk used to cite it." In the Shultz version the "folly of isolationism was again revealed" in Vietnam. He reiterated the Vietnam syndrome in which we became infected with "introspection, self-doubt and hesitancy." Today, "our goals in Central America are like those we had in Vietnam." Nicaragua is Vietnam is Munich. "How many times," he asked, "must we learn the same lesson?"

There was, however, only one Munich metaphor. That there are competing Vietnam metaphors expresses the breakdown of consensus, a fissure between generations that has riven even the foreign policy elite. The logic and timing of Shultz's speech leads to a familiar, if sectarian, framing of the Munich metaphor: Who lost Nicaragua? But the original metaphor itself was most dramatically expunged by Reagan at Bitburg.

(May 1988)

gan gets stuck he starts over. Time and again
·ican revolutionary, Tom Paine: "We have it
e world over again." In this spirit Reagan
"new beginning."

·er, did not begin auspiciously. He moved
 farm crisis to defeat over military aid to
ns disaster over the Holocaust. At Bit-
·ed wood. And after his experience with
·r, at a graveyard impervious to his
lim. His respectful appearance at the
vhere SS soldiers are buried, did not
·y, but from the point of view of the
the incident rendered his themes
·rating was at stake: If his second
·ew Republican majority fade?
 Disney World, where he de-
·n" organized around tax re-
 inauguration, Reagan had
·ition. Now, he attempted to
·efore he dropped 10 points
 missed marching in the
·her marched. Time was
·an instinctively placed
·natural understanding
·ity. His own career as
·ation for his unparal-

to his roots. He had,
·y ceremonies at Dis-

neyland in 1955. Laying rhetorical wreaths at the shrine of Micke
Mouse was a familiar rite for him. Here was a utopian grassroot
America, a monument to the founding father, Walt Disney, who said
"If you can dream it, you can do it." And it all began, the presider
explained, when a "farm boy" discovered that "he could enterta
people by telling stories about a little creature with a high voice, r
trousers and yellow shoes and white gloves." In Reagan's versi
Disney's life was a populist parable of one of the "heroes of progre
against "government." The Disney story was a preview of Reag
coming attractions.

Once again, Reagan was transforming history into fable. I
fense of his tax plan, he summoned from the past emotion
images of populism, which he redirected to fit his political
Reagan's populism, however, is more than a desire for popu

Tax reform has been on everyone's mind in Washington—
ing Reagan's—for months. As early as mid-1984, the admini
was quietly committed to making tax reform an issue. Some
sional Democrats were also committed. But Walter Mondale
stress the deficit and Reagan chose not to complicate his d
The distractions of the early days of his second term de
introduction of tax reform. But those problems also gav
greater political immediacy.

The White House staff conceived of a new improved
Without an instant remedy, Reagan might no longer def
lic discourse and, anticipating the 1988 struggle to succ
conservative movement might disintegrate into hostile
the short run, the president's staff hoped that tax r
overcome the immediate damage to his popularity. In
they wanted to use the issue to help forge a conservativ
would last beyond Reagan's tenure.

To attain the desired realignment, the Republic
swell with voters who see the GOP as the party of "
the country-club set. The "revolution," in short, m
Tax reform is a means to an end, in the service of
if sustained, may lead to a momentous political shif
spherics are not *beside* the point; they are *to* the poi
perceptions of his economic program determines t
the Republican Party. The play's the thing.

Whatever the administration is doing to the ta
is the word being employed to justify it. On

The Uses of Populism

Whenever Ronald Reagan gets stuck he starts over. Time and again he has quoted the American revolutionary, Tom Paine: "We have it in our power to start the world over again." In this spirit Reagan labeled his first term the "new beginning."

His second term, however, did not begin auspiciously. He moved from intransigence over the farm crisis to defeat over military aid to the contras to public relations disaster over the Holocaust. At Bitburg he seemed lost in a haunted wood. And after his experience with the ultimate Old World horror, at a graveyard impervious to his magic, his powers appeared to dim. His respectful appearance at the cemetery at Bitburg, Germany, where SS soldiers are buried, did not fatally damage Reagan's popularity, but from the point of view of the new White House political team, the incident rendered his themes incoherent. More than his approval rating was at stake: If his second term failed, would the dream of a new Republican majority fade?

Recently, the president traveled to Disney World, where he declared a "second American Revolution" organized around tax reform. Just four months earlier, at his inauguration, Reagan had announced this very same populist revolution. Now, he attempted to recapture those sunny days of January, before he dropped 10 points in the polls. The high school bands that missed marching in the inaugural because of the inhospitable weather marched. Time was starting over again. At Disney World, Reagan instinctively placed himself in the stream of popular culture; his natural understanding of it is one of the main sources of his popularity. His own career as a pop-cult figure has been indispensable preparation for his unparalleled political rise.

Going to Disney World was a kind of return to his roots. He had, after all, been the television host for opening-day ceremonies at Dis-neyland in 1955. Laying rhetorical wreaths at the shrine of Mickey Mouse was a familiar rite for him. Here was a utopian grassroots America, a monument to the founding father, Walt Disney, who said: "If you can dream it, you can do it." And it all began, the president explained, when a "farm boy" discovered that "he could entertain people by telling stories about a little creature with a high voice, red trousers and yellow shoes and white gloves." In Reagan's version, Disney's life was a populist parable of one of the "heroes of progress" against "government." The Disney story was a preview of Reagan's coming attractions.

Once again, Reagan was transforming history into fable. In defense of his tax plan, he summoned from the past emotions and images of populism, which he redirected to fit his political needs. Reagan's populism, however, is more than a desire for popularity.

Tax reform has been on everyone's mind in Washington—including Reagan's—for months. As early as mid-1984, the administration was quietly committed to making tax reform an issue. Some congressional Democrats were also committed. But Walter Mondale chose to stress the deficit and Reagan chose not to complicate his campaign. The distractions of the early days of his second term delayed the introduction of tax reform. But those problems also gave the issue greater political immediacy.

The White House staff conceived of a new improved beginning. Without an instant remedy, Reagan might no longer define the public discourse and, anticipating the 1988 struggle to succeed him, the conservative movement might disintegrate into hostile factions. In the short run, the president's staff hoped that tax reform would overcome the immediate damage to his popularity. In the long run, they wanted to use the issue to help forge a conservative majority that would last beyond Reagan's tenure.

To attain the desired realignment, the Republican ranks must swell with voters who see the GOP as the party of "the people," not the country-club set. The "revolution," in short, must be populist. Tax reform is a means to an end, in the service of an attitude that, if sustained, may lead to a momentous political shift. Reagan's atmospherics are not *beside* the point; they are *to* the point. How he shapes perceptions of his economic program determines political reality for the Republican Party. The play's the thing.

Whatever the administration is doing to the tax code, "populism" is the word being employed to justify it. On May 14, 1985, then Treasury Secretary James Baker told the Houston Chamber of Commerce that "frustration with the tax system is deeply rooted in populism, and populism has been an enormously influential force in America's development." According to Baker, the new populism directly traces its political lineage to the "huge populist movement around the turn of the century."

Yet that movement advocated increased governmental regulation of the marketplace, even the nationalization of key industries, in the name of a society of opportunity. The movement was subsumed within the Democratic Party and found a champion in William Jennings Bryan, the "Great Commoner." In the climactic presidential election of 1896, the populists were decisively defeated by the Republican Party. And the outcome made the GOP the normal majority party until the Depression of the 1930s. It is among the more curious historical ironies that the future of the modern Republican Party should be determined by its embrace of "populism."

But are the Republicans really populists like the old-time populists? Is the Great Communicator the reincarnation of the Great Commoner? The program of the putative Republican populists is, in fact, a reversal of the original populist program. (Among the planks of the populist People's Party platform of 1892: "We demand a graduated income tax." The United States had no federal income tax then, much less a progressive one.) If a link exists between those populists and these populists, it cannot be a continuity of demands; it must be something more abstract, a continuity of themes.

Populism, then and now, is built upon a series of simplifications· There was a golden age, which can be restored. The countryside, where authentic values are cultivated, is posed against the city, where false sophistication is bred. Conspiring against "the people" is a small élite, a faceless monopoly. Finally, the people's dreams are thwarted because of the illegitimate, perhaps foreign, source of the élite's power.

In classical populism, the "people" were independent farmers, and the monopoly was a conspiracy of Wall Street tycoons, personified by bankers who manipulated the money supply and railroad rates. They were transforming America into a foreign place, destroying the Jeffersonian vision of agrarian democracy.

Throughout his career, Reagan has rearranged the folklore of populism for his own particular ends. The golden age existed before the New Deal, which created the monopoly of big government. Individuals, who live on Main Street, are victimized by an élite lodged in Washington. Issues have no value on merit alone; they are ways to highlight the morality play. Tax simplification has meaning only as populist revival.

Reagan has sought a new animating principle to avoid the pitfalls of the second term, just as Franklin D. Roosevelt discovered economic regulation—creating institutions and practices Reagan now opposes—to give life to the second New Deal. Unlike his hero, whose philosophy was constant improvisation, Reagan's program is drawn from a fixed ideology. Tax reform is simply its latest form. The new principle is the old principle; the second term is based on the same idea as the first term. That idea, of course, is economic individualism: If we are liberated from government constraints, we will find our fortunes in the free market.

Although there is perennial public sentiment for a more equitable tax system, no mass movement is stalking the land as in the late 1970s when a tax revolt, beginning with Proposition 13 in California, helped lift Reagan into the presidency. If a populist revolution occurs, it must be organized by the White House, where the notion of a second American Revolution originated. The theoretical constituency of the plain people motivated by anger and resentment, which current polls are not detecting, has to be called into being. This is a daunting challenge since the main beneficiaries of the revolution are the wealthy. According to an analysis by the Center on Budget and Policy Priorities, for example, in the administration's plan, someone with a taxable income of $200,000 will get a $9,000-plus tax cut; someone with a taxable income of $20,000 will get a cut well under $200.

When the Great Communicator delivered a populist address in defense of his plan, his formulations were familiar, but his logic carried him past any of his previous rhetorical destinations. On one side are "the people," composed of "individuals" and "families." This category is all-inclusive, except for the "special interests," an unspecified force that Reagan refers to as "they." "They" have controlled "our tax system," making it resemble the corrupting Big City, "Washington itself: complicated, unfair, cluttered with gobbledygook and loopholes."

Then Reagan declared that "in both spirit and substance, our tax system has come to be un-American." According to his syllogism, if the tax system is "like Washington," it must follow that the nation's capital is "un-American." Reagan has called Washington many names before, but this is the first time he ever suggested it was foreign soil.

He explained that it was essential to construct a new dramatic scene. "We have made one great dramatic step together," he said, referring to his triumphant first-term tax cut. "We owe it to ourselves to take another." The golden age he was evoking was not simply the pre-New Deal idyll. He added to it "1981," a golden age of optimism. Thus he attempted to re-create his own past.

In his closing sentences, Reagan spoke of "dreams" four times— "dreams" that we must make "real," but are endangered by "special interest raids of the few." Yet more than special interests, albeit real, can impede making populist dreams into populist reality. For there are inherent tensions within Reagan's proposal, Reagan himself and the nature of populism.

Can the president repeat his 1981 policy victory? The problem with invoking the glory of the recent past is its present consequences. Reagan's tax reform is presented as the salvation from loopholes, many of which were put in place by his 1981 tax bill. The main difference between 1981 and 1985 is the deficit; yet Reagan's ideology demands that his reform be "revenue neutral" in order to prevent government, the agent of unhappiness, from getting bigger.

The White House's concessions to the special interests during the crafting of the administration's proposal took it far from the Treasury Department's earlier and more pristine offering. When these concessions are toted up, the bill may actually be "revenue negative," adding billions to the deficit.

The tax reform, therefore, could lock the deficit in place, driving the budget process; assaults on government programs would continue to be the order of the day. Thus, Reagan's tax plan fulfills his ultimate aim—dismantling big government.

To be revenue neutral, the cost of Reagan's lower tax rates must be made up by eliminating the state and local tax deduction. In addition, the bill favors services over manufacturing of durable goods. When these provisions are laid over each other, a political map is discernible. The states that would lose the most from this measure are mainly in the Northeast and Midwest, essential to any Democratic presidential strategy. Thus, Reagan's tax reform might also have the effect of redistributing resources to the Republican's political base, stimulating its future growth.

Reagan himself embodies the tension of his program. He is a self-made man, yet his rise was financed by millionaire friends. Reagan is the Everyman who has become rich and wants to preserve the comforts of the millionaires. His image remains that of a man of the people; at the same time, his instinct, as Lou Cannon, White House correspondent of *The Washington Post*, has reported, is privately to wish for the end of all corporate taxation. For Reagan's plan to work, no matter how inconsistent with classical populism, his image must remain consistent.

Tax reform is an effort to provoke political change by means of populist appeals, but the history of populism is double-edged. It expresses not only the aspirations but the venom that follows when hopes are dashed. The original movement drifted from economic to moral crusades. William Jennings Bryan's career charts this trajectory, from the Cross of Gold speech against the plutocrats to the prosecution of the Scopes trial against the Darwinists. In the South, populism was sidetracked when the movement was turned from economic equality to racial division.

Populism emerges from a suspicion of power and an obsession with the purportedly exotic vices of a cosmopolitan élite. When the promised golden age is not restored by economic nostrums, populist movements have become embittered and xenophobic. Populism has sought to destroy the élite's cultural corruption and replace its cosmopolitanism with a native purity.

The tenuous balance within populism is reflected in the contrast between James Baker's Treasury Department and Edwin Meese's Justice Department, between tax reform and the pornography commission. If any tax bill is passed, Reagan will naturally claim victory. But if the results do not satisfy the populist resentments he has raised, what happens to the constituency he has aroused? Some may demand that the economic dream be made real, while others may turn to inflammatory cultural issues. Should that happen, hopes for the great realignment would evaporate.

For the moment, though, Reagan is in command of the debate. He has found his way back to the position he enjoyed last year, when his television ads declared, "It's morning again in America." The past, it seems, can be re-created. Now, it's morning again, again.

(June 1985)

The Crisis of
Sympathetic Magic

The Iran-contra scandal is about more than international arms dealing, Swiss bank accounts, and political skulduggery. It is a crisis of "sympathetic magic"—the phrase used by anthropologist Sir James Frazer in his classic *The Golden Bough*, to explain how the strength and well-being of a ruler translates into the strength and well-being of society.

"You can see the present situation in classical terms," says Stanley Tambiah, a Harvard anthropologist. "The waning of the power of the divine king is related to the health or prosperity of the kingdom. As the country's problems have been mounting, this president's waning powers have become very evident."

The Tower Commission report, apart from its hard-boiled narrative, was a finding on Ronald Reagan's magic. The public assigned him almost supernatural gifts, temporal and spiritual. More than a figure who proposed policies, Reagan was the personification of dreams. The revelations about his presidency, therefore, add up to much more than political embarrassment. With disbelief no longer suspended, the dreams themselves are disturbed.

"It reminds me very much of notions of divine kingship, a conception of earlier societies that applies today," says Tambiah. Clifford Geertz, an anthropologist at the Institute for Advanced Studies at Princeton, says, "Reagan's view of history was mythological from day one."

Reagan talked openly about how an idealized past—an idyllic small-town America—could be restored. Soon it would be "morning again," his 1984 campaign commercials promised. In his second inaugural address, Reagan spoke of a world that "transcends time." There would be a "Great American Comeback," he insisted in his 1986 State of the Union message—in which he added: "As they said in the film

Back to the Future: 'Where we are going, we don't need roads.'"
Exactly where that led has been spelled out by the Tower Commission.

Reagan's magic depended on the perception of his strength. "He had managed to create a distance between himself and his fellow human beings which was on the model of chieftains and kings," says Marvin Harris, an anthropologist at the University of Florida. "He was said to have a Teflon suit on; he was immune to the slings and arrows of ordinary circumstances. It's absolutely a miracle that Reagan was able to keep that aura of secular sanctity." Reagan's survival of an assassination attempt early in his presidency helped armor him. "That episode," says Harris, "was extremely important in making him appear invulnerable." In a way, he had risen above mortality. His strength would become the strength of the body politic. But the circumstances that had conspired to build the image of his strength also conspired to undo it.

"Reagan alleged that he had control," says Marshall Sahlins, an anthropologist at the University of Chicago. "That was the glaring contradiction: between what he actually delivered and the control he claimed to have had over the presidency, the country and the world. If the sacred is above the wear and tear of worldly, empirical events, then he was at least like the sacred."

After his unsuccessful challenge to Gerald Ford in the presidential primary of 1976, his campaign managers worried about his persona: the defeated and aging contender, his ideas stale, his rhetoric rigid. In 1980, however, he came to be identified with a resurgent American neonationalism, which combusted at the Winter Olympics, when the U.S. hockey team upset the Russians and the crowd spontaneously chanted "USA! USA!" The frustration over the hostages held by Iran provided a tableau against which Reagan's old-fashioned patriotic rhetoric suddenly seemed contemporary. By giving voice to the general outrage, he made his election a national catharsis. And the release of the hostages on inauguration day could be interpreted as "sympathetic magic."

Reagan's fortune has been a hostage to hostages. The Tower Commission's report asserts that Reagan was obsessed with the hostages held in the Middle East, but does not chronicle the role of hostages in recent American political history.

America, as Reagan's most fervent supporters saw it, was psychologically held hostage by a malady called the "Vietnam syndrome"— a fear of repeating the Vietnam experience through the exercise of our strength. "The world was felt to be out of control since Vietnam," says Sahlins. "So everybody was elevating him. If he could be stable, the country would be stable." "He promised to make us stand tall in the saddle," says Harris. "We would no longer be ashamed of our power. The way to do that was to engage in another Vietnam-like adventure." Nicaragua was where the syndrome would be exorcised. By staging a counter-Vietnam, Reagan would become stronger than ever.

But the two adventures that were meant to add glory to the Reagan legend crossed and went haywire: The arms deal to release hostages was joined with the covert funding of the contras. Reagan fell swiftly, no longer able to deflect the facts with themes and parables. The president who disdained detail was trapped by the detail he had ignored. "The more the kingship becomes ceremonial and ritualized, the more the king is removed from the turmoil of everyday happenings," says Tambiah. "This goes back to the kingdom of Bali; there are many analogies. The king becomes a prisoner in his own kingdom. He is put in a gilded cage. This reminds me of what [former chief of staff Donald] Regan is said to have done to this president."

The characteristics that previously gave Reagan a mythic quality were suddenly seen in a different light. "The man who is distanced from turmoil is derelict in his duties," says Tambiah. "The man who has this magical way, this personal charisma, becomes not good at running things." Reagan could not retreat into the mythological past that he had pledged to restore. The past, suddenly, had become his own past, and he could not shape it in his own terms.

For Republicans, especially the right wingers, he was supposed to be like Franklin D. Roosevelt, a personality who provided the identity for a party. Reagan's success would make everyone forget the profane Richard Nixon, his Republican predecessor. Instead, like a recurring nightmare, the scandal came upon the magical president—Watergate redux.

Reagan had always claimed that evil was a conglomerate of external forces, including the Kremlin and Washington, D.C. The inner fiber of America, by contrast, was pure. But now the decay was within the administration. "Reagan's whole career was to simplify government and he sits atop of something hydra-headed," says Harris. When the president appeared at the press conference that unveiled the Tower Commission's report, he promised to "study" its report. He hoped to learn how his own administration has been conducted. But blaming Washington for his woes will be awkward. "All presidents create some sort of illusion of who they are," says Geertz. "Once that's lost, and it isn't always lost—F.D.R. maintained it until the end—there's not another role to play. It's like watching a play and the character starts forgetting all the lines. It dissolves. All of a sudden there's a little man back there."

But what happens to the magical ruler whose powers fail him? "In classical terms," says Tambiah, "a king whose power waned was put to death, either literally or metaphorically. He was ritually killed or ceremonially removed."

The day after the release of the Tower Commission's report, Reagan's tainted chief of staff Donald Regan was finally pushed out—a ceremonial beheading. In his place emerged Howard Baker, in effect the regent of what was left of the Reagan presidency. The former Senate majority leader is a master of the mundane art of compromise—what Reagan frequently has derided as "politics as usual." When Baker makes things happen, it is not because he possesses magic. The administration is now in the receivership of the Republican establishment Reagan has fought against his entire political life. In appointing Baker, his kingship ended.

Our long national daydream is over.

(March 1987)

The Conservative Crackup

As long as historians study the presidency of Ronald Reagan they will debate the effect of conservative ideology on his policies. In the Iran-contra scandal, the goals of an extreme anticommunism were placed above the rule of law. Ironically, this subversion violated the fundamental tenets of classical conservatism. What were these people—these conservatives—thinking?

The right wing of the Reagan era cannot truly be understood without understanding the old left. Contemporary American conservatism is not encrusted with tradition. As a gathering political force, it dates from the 1940s and early 1950s. Conservative thinking on foreign policy was established largely by former communists. Many of them were Trotskyists who, unlike the Stalinists, were almost all intense intellectuals, defined primarily through their penetrating analyses of Stalinism. This world of endless polemics and sectarianism was the formative experience for many of today's neoconservatives. For them, the battle against Nicaragua's governing Sandinistas is the central issue of our time because it directly carries on their consuming struggle on the left against the Stalinists. Other right wingers tend to see communism as satanic—as Reagan's "evil empire." But when they descend from moral absolutism into the realm of policy, they usually adopt the specific approaches of the neoconservatives. Ignazio Silone, the Italian novelist, wrote in the classic volume of essays on disillusionment with communism, *The God That Failed,* "The final struggle will be between the Communists and the ex-Communists." In the Reagan presidency, this war has been waged by proxy through the contras.

The obsessions that animated the Iran-contra scandal cannot be found by searching the writings of Edmund Burke, the great English political theorist of the eighteenth century. Nor can they be located in the legacies of conservative figures of the American past such as the Ohio Republican Senator Robert Taft. They can be traced, however, to controversies surrounding the "war communism" of the early Soviet state. This sensibility of permanent life-or-death struggle against encircling foes was ripped from its context and implanted in the modern right by one of its founding fathers, the former Trotskyist James Burnham.

In the age of Reagan, this paranoid vision of a nation "at risk," as former National Security Council (NSC) aide Lt. Col. Oliver North breathlessly put it in congressional testimony, became the idea underlying national security policy. A concept at the fringe of American thought thus was enshrined in Washington; the extreme became the center.

The archaeologist of the Iran-contra scandal may find as yet undiscovered riches in the political culture of conservatism. Consider, first, Burnham's contribution. The ideas and language with which conservatives discuss foreign policy were almost all defined by Burnham. His vision was of America in the final conflict. He switched from the left wing to the right, yet retained the metaphor of *der tag*, the final day of victory. At the heart of the Burnham doctrine was Leon Trotsky's theory of permanent revolution reborn as an imperative of permanent counterrevolution.

In the 1930s, Burnham was the editor of the *New International*, a journal affiliated with Trotsky's quixotic Fourth International. In 1940, when the Soviet Union invaded Finland, the Trotskyists offered tortuous logic in its support. Russia may have been a "degenerated workers' state," but, Trotsky argued, it was still a "workers' state." Burnham put the stress on "degenerated," not on "workers." After he and Trotsky debated, Burnham split from the party.

Burnham then produced two highly original works on the nature of managerialism and ideology: *The Managerial Revolution* (1941) and *The Machiavellians* (1943). Some of his most acute writing of this period appeared in the *Partisan Review*, the central journal of the New York intellectuals, many of them Trotskyists turned into liberal anticommunists. During World War II, Burnham joined the Office of Strategic Services, the forerunner of the CIA. At the onset of the cold war he began issuing manifestoes that evoked an intense and instant response from the right. *The Struggle for the World* appeared fortuitously the week of the announcement of the Truman Doctrine in 1947, the policy of containing communism in Europe. "The Third World War began in April 1944," Burnham wrote, citing an obscure incident involving communist-inspired Greek sailors. The only way to "get along with Russia" was to rid it of its communist masters.

Burnham was not an advocate of containment. In his 1952 book *Containment or Liberation?* he argued that the United States faced a stark choice between "appeasement" and "liberation." Among those he classified as "appeasers" was Dean Acheson, then secretary of state. In addition, he derided George Kennan, the diplomat who originated the containment policy, for lacking "a powerful emotion concerning communism, a hatred of communism." Containment, Burnham wrote, had the vice of being "essentially and unavoidably defensive." By contrast, the "policy of liberation is by its essence offensive" and is "the only defense against a Soviet world victory." The key to the struggle, he said, was Eastern Europe, where the United States should organize an armed "Resistance." While the resistance gathered strength, the United States should "prepare for general war."

The Trotskyist influence still could be sensed in Burnham's thought. Just as Trotsky believed that the Russian Revolution had been betrayed by Joseph Stalin, Burnham believed that the inevitable counterrevolution was betrayed by President Franklin Roosevelt. At the Yalta Conference of 1945, Burnham suggested, Roosevelt handed over Eastern Europe to the U.S.S.R.—an act of appeasement echoing then-British Prime Minister Neville Chamberlain's and then-French Premier Edouard Daladier's 1938 capitulation to Adolf Hitler in Munich.

The Yalta betrayal—the liberal stab in the back—became a key corollary to the conservative approach to foreign policy, applied to more than Eastern Europe. Hence the question, Who lost China? The belief in betrayals explained global change, offered domestic political advantage, and expressed the resentment accumulated from years of conservative political defeats. After Roosevelt's death, questioning the loyalty of those with whom conservatives disagreed became a crucial political instrument of their revenge.

The Republican Party's platform of 1952 was Burnham distilled to his essence. The "defensive policy of 'containment' " was denounced, the Truman administration accused of appeasement, and the promise made to "repudiate all commitments contained in secret understandings such as those of Yalta which aid Communist enslavements." For good measure the platform stated, "There are no Communists in the Republican Party." The implication about the Democrats was obvious. On the dais, speaking to the cheering delegates, was the newest conservative hero—Senator Joseph McCarthy.

That convention marked an ideological turning point for conservatism. After the defeat of the standard-bearer, Robert Taft, who was wary of cold war interventionism, the conservatives furled their old isolationism and marched into the cold war by affixing Burnham's phrases to its banners. But the Taftites-turned-Burnhamites had no true standard-bearer, and they awaited one. For the moment they supported then Vice President Richard Nixon, who earlier had been the nemesis of the accused Soviet spy Alger Hiss. But Nixon's inclination to advance his ambitions by compromising with the eastern establishment wing of the Republican Party worried them.

The moment of truth for the Burnham doctrine came in 1956, when the Hungarians rose in revolt against the U.S.S.R.—precisely what Burnham called for. President Dwight Eisenhower felt that the only realistic policy was to stand back. "Liberation was a sham," wrote Stephen Ambrose in *Eisenhower: The President* (1984). Eisenhower "had known it all along, which made all the four years of Republican talk about 'liberation' so essentially hypocritical." Burnham's disciples used the moment to denounce Eisenhower. Surprisingly, Burnham leaped to his defense, arguing that his inaction must be accepted as "part of the reality of our time." Soon, however, Burnham reverted to his old formula, which he tapped out in his *National Review* column, "The Third World War."

By the time of Reagan's election, Burnham had become a "cult hero for many conservatives," noted John Judis in his perceptive essay in the August 31, 1987, issue of the *New Republic* shortly after Burnham's death. His influence "profoundly affected the way America views itself and the world," according to the citation on the Medal of Freedom, the country's highest civilian award, bestowed upon him by the president in 1983. "And I owe him a personal debt," said Reagan, "because throughout the years traveling the mash-potato circuit I have quoted you widely."

Reagan was not the only member of his administration acquainted with Burnham's thought. In 1955, a new conservative magazine called *National Review* was incorporated. The lawyer who drew up the papers was William Casey. *National Review*'s editor, William Buckley Jr., had met him the previous year. Casey happened to be a director of the Henry Regnery Company, then the only devotedly conservative publishing house in the country, which had published young Buckley's first two books. In the early days of *National Review*, Casey attended about a half-dozen editorial meetings where Burnham was present, according to Buckley. "I don't think they were close socially," he said. "But they knew each other well. The chances are 99 out of 100 that Casey read his books. And he definitely read the magazine. He would have read Burnham there. He definitely would have been familiar with Burnham's thought."

In light of Burnham's influence, take into account the political climate of Washington in April 1985 as the United States was about to step into the shrouded process that became the Iran-contra scandal. The capital was then filled with ideological energy, like the upper atmosphere before an electrical storm. Before 1980, conservatives had prided themselves on their estrangement from the capital. By 1985, they inhabited a semiexclusive Washington ghetto of their own making. The thousands of conservatives gathered in Washington felt two intense emotions. The first was triumph—an immense gratification in Reagan's 1984 reelection. This glorious victory was taken as a vindication of the long-held conservative assumption that the country indeed believed as conservatives believed. And yet, only months after a sweeping victory, something had gone seriously wrong.

Thus followed the second emotion—overwhelming frustration at the Democratic-controlled House of Representatives for denying aid to the contras, the "moral equal of our founding fathers," according to Reagan. The conservative president had just won forty-nine states, but was being perversely thwarted. Those on the right assumed that, having captured the countryside, the capital was rightfully theirs. But it was not.

In fact, their broad program never enjoyed a majority base. Aid to the contras, for example, never received major public support. If anything, the 1984 vote for Reagan, according to the polls, was a mandate for him to pursue an arms-control agreement. The military buildup of the first term had ameliorated much of the popular fear of Soviet superiority.

Like the liberals, the conservatives were perplexed by Reagan's popularity. They could not fathom why, if he was so well-liked, his policies were not quickly enacted. (Liberals, in the meantime, wondered why, if so many of his policies were unpopular, he was so well-liked—hence the term "Teflon president," to whom nothing sticks.) Conservatives mistook public acceptance of Reagan's persona for general acceptance of his ideology. But public-opinion polls throughout his presidency had revealed the disconnection. His reelection campaign was relentlessly devoid of issues and just as relentlessly filled with personalized images. Right-wing frustration was an almost inevitable by-product of a politics of appearances.

As the Iran-contra deal was being nurtured in private that April, the public debate in Washington was turning into an ideological din. The enemy threatened from without, chaos from within. The patriotism of the president's critics was cast into doubt. A sneering contempt for international law was taken as a sign of restored vigor in foreign affairs. And America's fiery end was seen in congressional deliberations on aid to the contras. Between the positive pole of exultation and the negative pole of bitterness crackled bolts of rhetorical lightning. "We're going to be committing U.S. forces . . . to clear out these Soviet bases . . . or we're going to be fighting along the Rio Grande," said retired army General John Singlaub, a fund-raiser for the contras who turned up in Washington that month after one of his forays to Central America. (Two years later, he was called to testify about his activities before the congressional Iran-contra investigative committees.)

April 1985 was the tenth anniversary of the Vietnam War's end, and there was much talk of learning from Vietnam and shaking off the fear of war. "The record is clear for all to see: A Communist peace kills more than an anti-Communist war," wrote Nixon in the opening part of a five-part series, "No More Vietnams," published in the conservative *Washington Times.* Nixon's series concluded with a stern warning: "Our cause must be peace. But we must recognize that greater evils exist than war." His article stressed a frequent theme in the conservative media. The lesson of Vietnam, as taught by Nixon and the others, was to be applied directly to Nicaragua. As the House considered $14 million in aid to the contras, an SOS was sent out. "Urgent Message. Today President Ronald Reagan Needs Your Help. Your Call Today Can Save Freedom in Nicaragua. . . . This time, America herself is at stake. Call Your Congressman Today," read a full-page advertisement in the *Washington Times.*

The group responsible was the American Conservative Trust, one of several letterhead organizations operated by Carl ("Spitz") Channell, who later pleaded guilty to criminal charges brought by the Iran-contra special prosecutor. Lieutenant Colonel North and Elliott Abrams, the assistant secretary of state for inter-American affairs, helped him raise the funds for his enterprise, primarily from elderly and wealthy right wingers. Much of the money intended for the weapons account ended up supporting Channell's homosexual friends, according to a report on National Public Radio on April 9, 1987.

On the contra issue, the president portentously implied in a radio address on April 20, 1985, that the opposition to his program might have alien influences: "The Sandinista communists are lobbying your senators and representatives. Together with the misguided sympathizers in this country, they've been running a sophisticated disinformation campaign of distortion and lies." How did the disinformation effort work? The *Washington Times* ran a five-part series on what it called "The Network"—"a massive but almost invisible spiderweb of hundreds of left-wing groups and organizations, linked together by sinewy threads of personnel, ideology and politics." The failure to realize the president's program was blamed on a conspiracy, centered in Washington, that used the Nicaraguan civil war as an issue to extend its shadowy influence.

Most conservative publications, biweeklies like *National Review* or monthlies like *Commentary*, are removed from the capital by time and space. Perhaps the one that captures the right-wing state of mind in Washington in its most immediate form is the *Washington Times*. Although some of the reporters on its staff are not believers in the cause, most are. After the administration and conservative members of Congress, the publishing conglomerate consisting of the *Washington Times* and *Insight* and the *World and I* magazines is the capital's principal employer of conservative activists.

The *Washington Times*, owned by the Korean founder and prophet of the Unification Church, the Reverend Sun Myung Moon, has been a special part of the political culture of Reagan's Washington that sets it apart not only from the Washington of the past but from the rest of the country as well. Its editor is Arnaud de Borchgrave, a former foreign correspondent for *Newsweek* whose major contribution to current thought has been as co-author of a 1980 novel, *The Spike*, which spun a tale of a left-wing Washington think tank, controlled by the KGB, that oils the liberal establishment. The *Washington Times* is closely and mainly read by conservatives, including the president.

Also that April, aid to the contras loomed larger than ever as a conservative imperative and was cast as an element in the world historical march of a new doctrine: the Reagan Doctrine. This doctrine was never proclaimed by the president but was discovered by a number of columnists. One of them, Charles Krauthammer, wrote in the April 1 issue of *Time*: "Ronald Reagan is the master of the new idea. . . . He has produced the Reagan Doctrine." Krauthammer added that Reagan's decision to make his doctrine a "footnote" to the 1985 State of the Union address was "as much a tribute to Mr. Reagan's prudence as to his modesty." Krauthammer concluded by calling for scrapping U.S. adherence to international law: "The West, of late, has taken to hiding behind parchment barriers as an excuse for inaction."

Krauthammer is a former speech writer for Vice President Walter Mondale, who turned neoconservative after Reagan's election. He became a close friend of Elliott Abrams, an assistant secretary of state, and the protégé of the conservative columnist George Will, and was invited by the White House to dine with Reagan. His columns have appeared in *The Washington Post,* the *New Republic* (of which he is also an editor), and *Time,* and he won a Pulitzer Prize in early 1987. He believed that in the Reagan Doctrine he had coined a "new idea," but he actually landed on territory that had been settled decades earlier by Burnham. Krauthammer, however, seemed unaware of the intellectual antecedent. He asserted in the February 17, 1986, issue of the *New Republic* that the Reagan Doctrine "deserves the honorific 'doctrine' because it is a successor to the Truman, Nixon and Carter doctrines, which variously attempted forms of containment." He also claimed that the Reagan Doctrine meant "rolling back Soviet acquisitions." It therefore was both containment and liberation with a global reach, an approach that went beyond Burnham's Eurocentric formula. Containment or liberation? asked Burnham. Yes, answered Krauthammer. The Soviet Union would be contained in Europe as its advances were rolled back in the Third World.

Krauthammer's semantics were extracted not from a historical analysis but from out-of-date labels. The "dominant view of the Democratic Party," he wrote in the *New Republic* article, was "a new and ill-disguised form of isolationism." By contrast, Reagan Doctrine advocates were "neo-internationalist." The subtext of these easy abstractions was the foreign-policy conflict of the 1930s and 1940s, when the conservatives tended to be isolationist and the liberals tended to be internationalist. By reversing these reference points, Krauthammer attempted to tar contemporary liberals as false. His work was an amplification of the famous line of former U.S. permanent representative to the United Nations, Jeane Kirkpatrick, delivered at the 1984 Republican National Convention, that the Democrats were the "blame America first" party—a play on the America First Committee, the leading isolationist group prior to World War II. The Reagan Doctrine was in part a polemic device used by neoconservatives to cast the Democrats as betrayers.

Kirkpatrick, in April 1985, was the person most lionized by the Washington right. The former ambassador to the U.N. and former Democrat just then had formally announced her conversion to the Republican Party. Many dinners were held in her honor. On April 16, about seven hundred conservatives gathered at the Capital Hilton hotel to salute her. Adolfo Calero, the contra chieftain, delivered the toast. Two women, he explained, were considered sainted by the contras: "One is the Virgin Mary whom we call 'Our Lady.' The other is Mrs. Kirkpatrick, who is known as 'The Lady.' " Kirkpatrick then spoke about the opposition to aiding the contras in light of "appeasement" and "Hitler's rise." The lesson of Munich was the lesson of Nicaragua, she said. Historical memory was on the side of the contras.

That May, Michael Deaver, the White House deputy chief of staff and master scenarist, left his post, having arranged as his departing gesture the wreath-laying ceremony in which, during a trip to West Germany, President Reagan honored German victims of World War II by visiting a cemetery in Bitburg where members of Hitler's SS were also buried. Patrick Buchanan, the conservative columnist, had just entered. Before he began work as communications director, he reread one of his favorite books, Burnham's *The Suicide of the West.*

Buchanan gave up more than his syndicated column for his White House office. He also gave up a chair on the latest talk-show entry, "The McLaughlin Group"—a distinct sacrifice in a city where even the most torpid program about current events is viewed as avidly as the latest movie in Los Angeles. On the show, a panel of mainly conservative pundits offer clownish exaggerations of themselves. Their performances expose a certain slice of contemporary Washington in its sharply rightward tilt and reward for glib belligerence. But that month, the usually voluble Buchanan was off the air and refusing to speak to the press. On every issue, from Bitburg to the contras, his main contribution to the White House was the sensibility of the bunker—"us versus them."

A sociologically intriguing sign of the period was a pro-contra lobby called PRODEMCA. This operation showed the curious effect of the old left on Reagan's Washington. Most of the PRODEMCA leaders were registered Democrats with old left backgrounds. Its chief operative, Penn Kemble, still belonged to the Social Democrats USA (SDUSA), a group whose history is a tangled web of Trotskyist sectarianism and Socialist party factionalism. Max Shachtman, one of the SDUSA's founders, had been Burnham's comrade in the Socialist Workers' party. Together they opposed Trotsky on the Finland question and left the party. Shachtman offered Marxist arguments on behalf of Nixon's 1972 reelection campaign.

The PRODEMCA neoconservatives prided themselves on the private briefings they received from Lt. Col. North, and they disseminated tidbits of the information he dispensed through the newsletters and journals at their disposal. The usefulness, to the Republican administration, of Democrats acting as a pro-contra lobby gave PRODEMCA its leverage in Washington. In 1986 it played an active role in persuading a swing group of mainly southern Democrats in the House to provide $100 million in aid to the contras. Other Democratic leaders, notably Representative Les Aspin of Wisconsin, chair of the House Armed Services Committee, were also influenced to support contra aid by PRODEMCA activists.

In 1987, however, it was revealed that PRODEMCA had accepted tens of thousands of dollars from the right-wing fund-raiser and confessed criminal conspirator Carl Channell. After news of the scandal broke, PRODEMCA hastily attempted to return the money. It succeeded in moving the money, but the transaction still was uncovered by the press.

Neoconservatives were especially traumatized by the fall from grace of Elliott Abrams (the son-in-law of Norman Podhoretz, editor of *Commentary*, and of Midge Decter, a noted neoconservative), who ran the contras' war from the State Department and confessed he had misled Senate and House committees. The neoconservatives understood what happened only in the narrow context of sectarian ideological politics. Decter used the July–August 1987 issue of *Contentions*, the newsletter published by the Committee for the Free World, to defend Abrams, comparing the behavior of the "investigators" of the Iran-contra committees to the "performance of the late Senator Joseph McCarthy." The erstwhile role of communists as victims, in other words, was now occupied by conservatives. Up was down and down was up; but the neoconservatives' frame of reference remained the vanished world of the old left from which many of them had initially emerged.

At best, conservatives expressed a utopian idealism far removed from the squalid facts. The actual meaning of the Reagan Doctrine was not to be found in an abstract formula. Instead, it was located in the Swiss bank accounts that were to serve as the funding mechanism for CIA Director William Casey's free-floating, supercovert action agency. The diversion was a mere foreshadowing of what was to come. Congressional oversight was not part of the plan; nor, necessarily, was approval by the chief executive, particularly if the president were not Reagan. "Director Casey had in mind, as I understood it, an overseas entity that was capable of conducting operations or activities of assistance to the U.S. foreign policy goals that was a 'stand alone,' it was [to be] self-financing, independent of appropriated monies and capable of conducting activities similar to the ones we had conducted here." North testified on July 10.

In this light, the worthy rhetoric about "democratic revolution" was less a description of empirical reality than a rationalization of what was hidden from view. At worst, conservative rhetoric was sheer disinformation: conservatism as the cover-up. However, conservatives failed to come to terms with the uses and abuses of ideology in the Iran-contra affair. The conclusion of the hearings provoked little remorse or introspection on the right. Rather, conservative anguish about "paradise lost" deepened.

Consider now Reagan's contribution. For years he regaled audiences with apocryphal stories: Welfare queens drove Cadillacs, trees caused pollution, and missiles launched from submarines could be recalled. No press conference he held as president was complete without an error of fact. His fables and mistakes were endless, and collected together composed a seamless worldview. Reagan was a cheerful mythomaniac who never allowed unsettling facts to complicate the picture. His errors did not appear deliberate or malicious, but were in the service of his sunny and innocent vision of "morning again in America," which was central to his appeal. His irrepressible optimism was his greatest contribution to conservatism, a movement that before his messianic appearance was characterized by fits of resentment—the "paranoid style," as described by the historian Richard Hofstadter. Reagan commanded public trust in great part because of his personality. And conservatism was no longer viewed by most political writers as Hofstadter had described it. Then came the Iran-contra scandal.

Reagan's presidency, in the end, has not had the miraculous effect of fostering an optimism and confidence among conservatives that will last beyond his term. This would have been his greatest contribution to the future of the right. After the scandal, the old trouper still might be able to sustain optimism on occasion, but others on the right cannot. Their infatuation with North was a sign of their collapsed faith in Reagan. With the Reagan romance waning even before he leaves the White House, many conservatives instinctively have returned to a primal state.

The themes reverberating at the height of Reagan's ascendancy in the Washington of spring 1985 were not quelled by the scandal. What endured was the conservatives' frustration that events had failed to cooperate with their theories.

Consider, then, Lt. Col. North's contribution. Since its ancient infatuation with General Douglas MacArthur, the right has reserved a hallowed place for the hero worship of a would-be military strong man. Until the Iran-contra scandal, Reagan appeared to conservatives as the ideal image of strength. With his frequent saluting in his comings and goings, the World War II veteran who served in Culver City, California, by making motivational movies, constantly reminded the audience that he was commander in chief. But disillusion set in after the dealings with Iran's Ayatollah Ruhollah Khomeini's régime were exposed. The image of strength began to evaporate.

The lieutenant colonel, bedecked with medals, personified the conservative veneration of a mystical American state but contempt for the actual national government. While most conservatives merely wished they could transform the government in Washington into their instrument, North actually did something about it. Their romantic vision of the state consisted of a mélange of patriotic symbols, among which were uniforms, heroes, and real weapons. The scandal was so damaging to the mythmaker Reagan—and to conservatism— because it was more than a deal. It was a transference of sacred symbols representing American power—missiles—to a demonic enemy who was offering further humiliation, not peace. After the scandal's revelation, many on the right found it difficult to muster their support for Reagan. After North's testimony, which was filled with lengthy right-wing declamations, a new cult of personality gathered about him.

North had become a favorite speaker even earlier at meetings of the right-wing Council for National Policy (CNP), a group modeled on a vulgar Marxist understanding of the Council on Foreign Relations, which was assumed to be the central committee of the liberal establishment. The CNP's gatherings included the most prominent leaders and financiers of the right, from the former television evangelist and Republican presidential candidate Pat Robertson to the beer magnate Joseph Coors; from the Heritage Foundation's president, Edwin Feulner, to the retired General Singlaub. One condition of membership is a pledge not to reveal the identity of the other members or the workings of the group. Its view of world politics is premillennial and fatalistic, combining elements of evangelism and Burnhamism. The CNP, where conservative activists mingled with conservative donors, was a prefiguration of Channell's fund-raising operation. It took a brilliant performance by North—more brilliant than Reagan's—to keep this constituency captivated, in view of the arms sales to Iran. The fervor he inspired also demonstrated the conservatives' undying will to believe. Their rallying around North was a rallying around their mystical notion of the state, which Reagan had offended.

North's political philosophy, if it can be called that, was a peculiar strain of authoritarian populism. When he spoke of a world "at risk," he was providing a simplified version of Michael Ledeen's *Grave New World* and a dozen other turgid tracts. North's genius was alchemical, distilling heavy ideology into a compelling tale. In this he was the sorcerer's apprentice, following in the tracks of his commander in chief.

As North stressed, he was willing to do anything, even stand on his head in a corner, to carry out the orders of a charismatic president. To justify his position that the president is a de facto monarch, North turned constitutional scholar, citing the 1936 Supreme Court decision *United States* v. *Curtiss-Wright Export Corporation*. In that case, the Court considered a criminal conspiracy by the company to sell arms to Bolivia in violation of a joint congressional resolution and presidential proclamation. North argued that its decision in favor of the United States upheld the president's prerogative to act with a broad mandate in conducting foreign affairs. A president needed only to declare a "covert action" to do what he desired. North quoted Justice George Sunderland: "The president alone has the power to speak or listen as a representative of the nation." And North quoted a statement of George Washington's that was cited in the decision: "Caution and secrecy was one cogent reason for vesting the power of making treaties . . . with the President." North's scholarship, however, was as faulty as his diplomacy. The Court did not rule that the president had unlimited powers in foreign policy. On the contrary, it stipulated that full and plenary power rested with the president and Congress together. North's quote from Washington also was egregiously tendentious, for he cut it off before its finish, in which Washington said that the president may make treaties only with "the advice and consent of the Senate."

The next witness before the Iran-contra committee, John Poindexter and his superior at the National Security Council, continued North's reasoning. He argued that executive orders need not be approved directly by the president himself. Subordinates need only to apply the president's ideology and carry out the appropriate response, as in the diversion of money to the contras. Such was the leadership principle of the Reagan presidency.

What made this authoritarianism inflammatory was its mixture with populism. Congress, especially, was the object of loathing. Its failure to take up the leader's mission with lock-step enthusiasm was not seen by North as a proper constitutional exercise or as a reflection of popular sentiment. Rather, its passage of various Boland amendments restricting aid to the contras was regarded as symptomatic of its inner rot.

The Vietnam War figured prominently in North's Manichaean vision. The former combat marine perceived it just as the vengeful Freikorps storm troopers of Germany perceived World War I. It was a war lost at home by conniving politicians who had stabbed the country in the back; the peace was nothing less than a betrayal. "We won all the battles and then lost the war," North testified on July 9. "We didn't lose the war in Vietnam. We lost the war right here in this city." Once again, in Nicaragua, the craven politicians were perpetrating another double cross. "I came back from a war that we fought in Vietnam to a public that did not understand; in my humble opinion, they had been lied to," said North. "The American public did not know what we suffered, what we endured, or what we tried to achieve. And I think the same thing prevails for the Nicaraguan resistance today." If North's effort to apply the lesson of Vietnam to Nicaragua failed, a larger conflict loomed: "apocalypse now."

But even at the moment of his greatest appeal, he was not widely embraced as a national hero in spite of all the hyperbole. According to a July 9 CBS News–*New York Times* poll of public opinion taken by telephone as he completed his testimony, only 18 percent of those questioned thought of North as a hero. In a poll by ABC News on July 11–12, 64 percent viewed him as a victim. One month after he finished his testimony, his status as media-appointed "folk hero" dimmed. North's lasting impact has been less on the public than on the conservatives. He left a tincture of authoritarian populism on conservatism that might yet spread in a troubled future.

Yet, few conservatives felt remorseful about the Iran-contra scandal. They believed that it was, as Buchanan put it, a "coup d'état" staged by the liberal establishment in revenge for Reagan's two electoral victories, just as Watergate was a coup by the liberals that overthrew Nixon. Their postscandal thinking on foreign policy consists of reiterations of past positions with an even harder edge of bitterness against those they feel are responsible for thwarting their goals. Routine attacks on "the imperial Congress" have echoed from *Commentary* and the *Wall Street Journal*'s editorial page. George Will, the conservative columnist, assailed the Boland Amendment as a pseudolaw, "designed as a license for accusations and recriminations from a Congress more comfortable arguing about the legality than the wisdom of politics." The press was also a target, especially for the *American Spectator*'s press columnist—Michael Ledeen.

Even as President Reagan moved to sign an agreement with Moscow to scrap intermediate-range nuclear forces (INF), the conservative opposition to arms control heightened. Many became increasingly disillusioned with Reagan because of the INF accord. Virtually all supported the radical reinterpretation of the 1972 Antiballistic Missile (ABM) treaty instigated within the administration by Richard Perle, then the neoconservative assistant secretary of defense. The assault on the ABM treaty, the concrete basis of nuclear deterrence, was a fundamental assault on arms control itself.

The chief defender of the treaty as it was approved by the Senate in 1972 was Sam Nunn, Democrat of Georgia and chair of the Senate Armed Services Committee. On October 6, 1987, Krauthammer laid down the neoconservative line in a column in *The Washington Post* entitled "Sam Nunn and the Imperial Senate." It was exemplary of the best intellectual work the neoconservatives offered after the scandal. On the one hand, Krauthammer argued, Nunn has his opinion; on the other hand, the State Department's legal adviser, Abraham Sofaer, has his. Meanwhile, as the administration negotiates, "one of the Soviet demands is American acceptance of a narrow interpretation of the ABM treaty. But Nunn wants to give it away for nothing." Nunn's position on the treaty, Krauthammer continued, is really "the Soviet position." And whether it is "legally correct is not just unclear, it is irrelevant."

Unmentioned in the column was the report of the Senate Foreign Relations Committee of September 22, 1987, on the interpretation of the ABM treaty, which described Sofaer's deliberate and selective use of documentation to make his case. "The Administration," the report concluded, "was proceeding not on the basis of genuine legal analysis but from a policy compulsion that sought no more than a legal veneer." In a stinging rebuke, it stated that Sofaer had "done a disservice to the Office of Legal Adviser." Nunn's position, after all, is not "the Soviet position." It is also the American position, as upheld by three presidents and supported in a letter of March 1987 by six former secretaries of defense. Moreover, it is the law, passed by the Senate and signed by the president. In a rule-of-law society, it is not "irrelevant." But Krauthammer took none of this into account.

In the meantime, there was no new neoconservative thinking about a solution to wars in Central America. Reagan's initial endorsement of the Arias peace plan, named for Costa Rican President Oscar

Arias Sánchez, was generally considered a sellout of the contras. Delegations of angry conservative leaders pressured Reagan to abandon it. Finally, in early October, he caved in to his own instincts and advanced his own plan, which was a transparent attempt to override Arias's effort. James Wright, speaker of the House, called Reagan's plan "ridiculous" and the outcome of lobbying by the "extreme right wing." After the scandal, a strong strain of infantile rightism emerged, an admixture of crude assertion and wish fulfillment. It perhaps was expressed most succinctly by Irving Kristol, the publisher of the *National Interest*, the leading neoconservative foreign-policy journal. In its inaugural issue in 1985, Kristol had called for a "war of ideology." The *Washington Times* reported on its front page, on October 2, 1987, that Kristol, in a meeting with his magazine's editorial board, had suggested that the Sandinistas transform themselves into the kind of régime he desired or "we'll invade." Kristol's statement was presented as that of a serious intellectual.

As the post-Reagan succession approaches, the right wing has become increasingly excited and anxious. Its state of mind is incorrigible, and the movement is far more than a nuisance.

If a Republican succeeds Reagan, he would immediately confront a crisis of governance. Right wingers would demand important cabinet and subcabinet positions, particularly in foreign policy, where they feel they have been denied by Reagan. They would be able to present conservatives with better credentials to the new Republican administration than they could to Reagan in 1981. This will be one of the fruits of Reagan's presidency.

The next Republican president could attempt to meet them part of the way, which would both give them some power and keep them from complete power. The conservative cadres' ideology would take precedence over their concern for the fate of the administration as a whole or of goals they did not share. If sufficiently contained, they would carry their struggle into the Republican primaries of 1992. In that arena, the influence of the conservative movement should not be discounted. Another conservative figure may have emerged by then. And the right would be encouraged by its own history, from its takeover of the party in 1964 with then Arizona Senator Barry Goldwater through its near dislodging in 1976 of an incumbent president, Gerald Ford, by Reagan. A future Republican president's knowledge of this past may inspire fear in him, and concessions to the insatiable conservatives. But no moderate Republican can govern coherently if he grants significant footholds within his administration to the right wing. And perhaps no Republican president can survive politically if he does not.

If a Democrat is elected president, the right-wing assault on his foreign policy will quickly reach a fever pitch. His election will be seen as somehow illegitimate, gained by means of the "coup d'état" of the Iran-contra scandal. The Reagan administration's conservatives will then be distinguished "formers," whose credentials will lend public credibility to their harsh criticisms. The conservative columnists and polemicists will grind away. If the Democratic president does not have a clear sense of his own policy, the confusion will be highlighted and exploited to the fullest. Carter's presidency remains a relevant cautionary example. His lack of clarity in policy led to internal divisions that in turn were aggravated by an ideological assault mounted by the right. A future technocratic president who, like Carter, fails to appreciate the political importance of ideology will be vulnerable to its thrusts. Without a sense of ideology, a Democrat will ultimately fail to control the intellectual and political atmosphere.

The problem of the next administration, whether Republican or Democratic, is in large part the problem of Washington. The capital is the location of the strongest concentration of conservative activists in the country outside of Orange County, California. Reagan spent his political career campaigning against Washington as the embodiment of all that is wrong. Yet one of his enduring political legacies will be the conservative encampment in Washington, seeking to make good on the unfulfilled promises of his presidency.

(Winter 1987–88)